Harvard Economic Studies

VOLUME CVIII

The studies in this series are published by the Department of Economics of Harvard University. The Department does not assume responsibility for the views expressed.

CANADA in the
WORLD ECONOMY

By

JOHN A. STOVEL

HARVARD UNIVERSITY PRESS

Cambridge, Massachusetts

1959

TO CADDY LAKE, AND TO THOSE WHO HAVE

SHARED ITS PLEASURES

Preface

This book is a considerably revised, extended, and reorganized version of a doctoral dissertation accepted at Harvard University in 1949. It was originally initiated as a study of the Canadian economy in the interwar period, following a suggestion made by Professor Seymour Harris. Investigation of the historical background led immediately to the well-known study by Professor Viner of the Canadian balance of payments during the period 1900–1913. My reaction to this isolated "empirical verification" of the "classical" capital transfer theory was that it owed its success mainly to a fortuitous set of circumstances that could be given another rationale. I outlined the bases for my skepticism to Professor A. H. Hansen, who encouraged me to reintroduce a reexamination of the Viner period into my study.

The text as it finally emerged encompasses the period from pre-Confederation to 1957, with its major emphasis being upon changes in the Canadian balance of trade and balance of payments during the years 1900–1913 and the interwar period. Virtually all the basic research had been completed by 1951, when I was fortunate to have the manuscript accepted for publication in the Harvard Economic Series. Ill health and a transfer from the academic environment into business delayed further work, most of which has taken the form of a thoroughgoing reorganization.

I would like to tender thanks to the many typists who have assisted me through the years, and in particular I would mention the assistance made available to me at the School of Business Administration of the University of Minnesota. And to my wife

Dorn I am grateful for many dull hours of proofreading and chart preparation.

I wish to express my indebtedness to Professors G. Haberler and A. H. Hansen of Harvard University for kind advice, guidance, and encouragement, and also to Professor D. H. Robertson of Trinity College, Cambridge, where I spent the year 1946–47 on an I.O.D.E. Postgraduate Overseas Fellowship for the Province of Manitoba. To Mr. G. S. Watts of the Bank of Canada and to Mr. C. D. Blyth, Chief, International Payments Section, Dominion Bureau of Statistics, I am very grateful for reading and commenting on an earlier draft of my manuscript. In addition, Mr. Blyth has always been most generous in making available to me published and unpublished data on the Canadian balance of payments. In revising Part III I was fortunate to have the keen criticisms and useful commentary of Professor Viner of Princeton University. The final draft and its reorganization owes much to the editorial advice of Professor J. K. Galbraith of Harvard University. Mrs. John Korbel of the Harvard University Press has also given able editorial assistance, at a time when her difficulties were increased as a result of a world study tour leaving me with no fixed address. Finally, I am very obligated to my friend Professor Theodore Morgan of the University of Wisconsin for his careful reading and criticism of almost the entire manuscript, to which it owes improvement in many matters both of presentation and substance. Needless to say, I alone am responsible for any errors of fact or of judgment.

John A. Stovel

Caddy Lake, Manitoba,
Santa Barbara, California,
and Delhi, India.

Contents

Contents

Tables

Charts

Canada in the World Economy

I

Introduction

Canada is one of those fortunate countries which has benefited most in the economic development of the western world. Today, with the neighboring United States, it shares the fruits of the most advanced economic development the world has seen and of the world's highest standard of living. With one of the largest areas under one national sovereignity, Canada has remained relatively small in population; after decades of substantial population increase she recently attained the level of some 17 million. Like other countries with small populations but with relatively high standards of living, the specialization and foreign investment essential in attaining high incomes have entailed relatively large volumes of transactions across her frontiers. Exports, visible and invisible, have at times exceeded one third of the net national income.

Historically, an important aspect of world trade has been its high degree of variability, and Canada has been very vulnerable to the impact of such changes in view of her great dependence upon foreign trade. The cyclical price flexibility of agricultural and forest products, minerals, and other basic and raw materials has multiplied the volume changes, when these are translated into value terms. While Canadian net national income declined to 55 per cent of its 1929 value by 1933, merchandise exports sank to 37 per cent of the 1929 level. Not only have Canadian exports and imports fluctuated widely along with national income (a general cyclical experience for most countries), but they have fluctuated very widely in their relation to one another. This variability of the balance of trade is associated with wide variations in flows of capital and has been an important element in the Canadian balance-of-payments disequilibrium. The accompanying table illustrates the variability of the merchandise trade balances, and demonstrates that this variability tends to be more extreme for the raw-material or agricultural exporting country. In Table 1, the differences between the most "favorable" and the

Table 1. *Variability in balances of trade*

Country	Percentage
(1925–1929)	
United Kingdom	10
United States	15
Australia	28
Germany	30
New Zealand	34
Canada	52
Netherlands East Indies	65

Source. League of Nations, *International Currency Experience* (Princeton, 1944), p. 91.

least "favorable" yearly trade balance (i.e., between the highest export or lowest import surplus, and the lowest export or highest import surplus) have been estimated for the five-year period 1925–1929. These differences are then expressed as a percentage of the average annual imports during that period to arrive at the following indications of the relative range of variation in the balance of trade. Such variability as this may lead to considerable pressure on the balance of payments, as well as on other facets of economic life.

NATURE OF THE CANADIAN ECONOMY

Canadian economic history until recent decades has been in large measure the story of a development based on one or a few staple commodities. With such a development the motif is inevitably great change and flux. Any innovation affecting the production of or demand for these staples will have profound and far-reaching effects for the economy based upon them.

Canadian geography[1] serves in large measure to explain this economic specialization. Canada's most industrialized and populated area is the so-called St. Lawrence Region, a lowland belt bordering the St. Lawrence River. Here are located the two major cities of Toronto and Montreal as well as the prosperous and populous southern peninsula of Ontario, which lies wholly south of the rest of Canada, its tip extending south of northernmost California. Since the days of the sailing ship, this area has been offered decreasing — and today relatively insignificant — economic competition by that other region of early settlement, the Maritime Provinces. These areas of early settlement have been relatively more economically self-sufficient than other regions of Canada.

Other areas of economic significance have become so as a result mainly of large scale farm agriculture (the Interior Plains), and mining and forest industries (the Canadian Shield and the Cordilleran region of the West Coast). Here relatively scarce natural resources, the development of which do not require intensive settlement, are the key to the economic history. The nature of the economy of these regions has been relatively specialized, with marked dependence upon exports and imports. Long associated mainly with the production of staple cereal grains, the Interior Plains also have become notable recently for their petroleum resources. Other Canadian staples have derived mainly from the Canadian Shield, that vast V-shaped area of ancient rocks surrounding Hudson's Bay, and from the Cordilleran region, examples being fur, lumber, pulpwood, copper, nickel, gold, and iron.

In transportation, Canada has been fortunate compared, for example, with most countries of Latin America. The Rocky Mountains are the only difficult height of land that East-West Canadian transport has had to overcome. However, one thousand miles of the sparsely settled Canadian Shield (sometimes referred to as the Great Bridge) separate Eastern Canada from the prairie West. On the asset side, however, there is the St. Lawrence River and Great Lakes waterway system, the largest inland chain of lakes in the world, which extends two thousand miles into the heart of the continent from the Gulf of St. Lawrence. This natural

[1] *Canada Year Book* (Ottawa, 1945), p. 1ff.

transport system, with later additions of man-made canals, has played a central role in Canadian natural resources from the earliest days to the present time. The two-fold Canadian policy of promoting the trans-Canadian railway system and of a protectionist tariff has been an additional factor in promoting East-West transport flows. This policy has of course inhibited the frequently more natural North-South flow of goods between the various Canadian economic regions and the United States.

INTERNATIONAL TRADE

The basic "classical" assumption for international trade analysis was international immobility of labor and capital as distinct from their mobility in domestic and interregional trade. The other factor of production in the "classical" triad, land, is immobile both internally and internationally. These immobilities gave rise to the differing relative scarcities and hence differing relative prices which served as the basis for exchange. It is recognized today, and this is particularly relevant to the Canadian experience, that there may be considerable mobility internationally of labor and capital, and considerable immobility domestically.

Other factors may frequently assume more importance in distinguishing international from domestic economics. Differing currencies are involved in exchange between countries, and the monetary and fiscal policies pursued by national governments become significant. In addition to the natural barriers affecting the flow of commodities, which are reflected in transport costs, there are the artificial restrictions imposed by governments through tariffs, quotas, and exchange control. Canada has relied more heavily on the first, and relatively less heavily on the latter two, than most developing countries. This is partly explained by the fact that her initial bursts of economic development occurred in the period prior to World War II when quotas and exchange control were less in favor.

Another set of influential factors (which might be considered under the heading of monopolistic competition[2]) are generally applied in the international trade field less than realism would require. Preferences for national goods and services serve to differentiate these goods and services. There are reasons, related

[2] E. H. Chamberlin, *The Theory of Monopolistic Competition* (Cambridge, Mass., 1933).

to similarity in language, in culture, and to the rules of the business game as embodied in law and commercial practices, for preferring to deal with fellow nationals. Less protection and less favorable treatment are likely to be accorded foreigners in business dealings and in the labor market. The analysis of noncompeting groups has its applications on the international plane. However, it is obvious that nationality is coextensive in greatly varying degrees with factors of consequence here, such as language, race, color, membership in a certain club or union, or graduation from certain socially valued schools or universities. This lack of coextensiveness is particularly apparent in the Canadian situation. Cultural and language factors restricting competition on an equal basis between French and English Canadians loom larger than those appearing in the relations between English Canadians, the British, and Americans. Analogously in the United States, but stemming from the factors of race and color rather than of language and culture, a somewhat similar situation affects the economic integration of the Negro. In conclusion, it is clear that while the factors considered above provide a basis for the special attention given to international trade, there is an arbitrariness in assessing the degree of their significance, and many of these factors are also significant in other sorts of exchange, for example, in interregional trade. The fact that statistics for trade between nations are much more readily available than for trade between regions, communities, and other social or economic categories has, of course, been one important reason for the attention they have received.

Canada, like any country, has its unique features. We find that features more or less peculiar to her situation and historical development have tended to enhance her integration with the leaders in western economic development: first, the pioneer England, and, increasingly the present leader, the United States. Factors inhibiting the movement of goods, services, people, and ideas have not been so weighty as in most other cases of international trade and economic development. The distinctiveness of the Canadian social and economic environment and relations must not be forgotten when an effort is made to draw analogies with other countries in connection with their problems of economic development.

In Part I an eclectic theory of balance-of-payments equilibrium is developed. This contrasts in two important respects with the "classical" Mill-Taussig theory which Professor Viner attempted to verify empirically in his well-known Canadian study. First, capital imports are regarded not only as the initiating disturbance in the balance of payments — one possibility — but also as an induced effect of changes in the current balance, and as a common effect, along with the current deficit, of innovations and profitable investment opportunities. The changes taking place are related to the historical uniqueness of the particular stage of Canadian economic development and to the fluctuations of the business cycle. Second, emphasis is placed on the international shifts in purchasing power and their propagation, whereas in the Mill-Taussig theory these are not explicitly recognized, attention being immediately directed to the relative price changes presumed to be associated with the gold flows, an extension to the international sphere of the quantity theory of money. Partly as a result of this emphasis, the similarity rather than the dissimilarity of the adjustment under gold standard conditions and paper standard arrangements becomes apparent.

In Part II the Canadian balance of trade and payments is studied in its relationship to economic development preceding World War I, secular and cyclical, the latter with particular reference to the booms of 1849–1855, 1871–1875, and 1896–1913. The basis for Canadian specialization in certain staple products is indicated, and emphasis is laid upon the interrelation between these staples and the governmental schemes for transportation developments with their financial and political implications. In Chapter 9 special attention is devoted to the tremendous changes that took place in Canada during the era of rapid expansion from 1896 to 1913. Large-scale immigration and capital imports accompanied the settlement of the prairie West and the emergence of wheat as the new Canadian staple export. Development was not solely agricultural by any means, however, and at the end of the period Canada was further removed from being a relatively primitive, agricultural, raw-material producing type of country.

Industrialization and urbanization proceeded apace. The end of the first decade of the century saw Canada relatively self-sufficient with respect to basic iron and steel products, for example. This aspect of the situation is reflected in the international accounts, which are examined in detail, capital imports from Great Britain being associated in large measure not with imports of capital goods from that country but with imports of consumer goods and raw materials from the United States. Both technically and with respect to a greater margin for the self-financing of further capital formation, the basis for further substantial economic development had been provided.

In Part III a critique is advanced of Professor Viner's analysis of the Canadian balance of payments during the years 1900–1913. The theoretical, historical, and statistical analysis of Parts I and II provide the major basis for this critique. With regard to Viner's empirical verification, objections are raised to the inadequacy of his price indices, particularly those for domestic prices in Canada and the United States, which are singularly erratic due to the idiosyncrasies of certain components of the indices. With respect to the balance-of-payments statistics one must be satisfied with much less than perfection, but there is unjustified inconsistency in the use of the direct estimates for some years and the indirect estimates for others. On certain occasions Viner uses an even less adequate measure of capital imports, the net deficit on current account, which excludes the large untransferred borrowings that were left abroad as external short-term assets of the Canadian banks. In addition to these short-term capital movements, there are significant transfers of funds for the payments of interest and dividends and for immigrants' remittances which offset long-term capital movements and which Viner neglects when considering the effects of the latter. During the period 1900–1913, little more than one half of the offsets to capital imports consisted of goods and services which conceivably might be responsive to the relative price changes postulated in the Mill-Taussig theory which Viner was attempting to verify.

The significance of capital imports in causing relative price changes in the manner assumed by Viner is questioned. Reference is made to a number of alternative causal factors, including domestically financed investment, innovations effecting cost changes in certain industries, increased transport facilities, immigration and population increases, urbanization, and an enhanced demand for Canadian exports.

The question is then raised as to the importance of the relative price changes, no matter how caused, in effecting the transfer of capital through their influence on the commodity export-import ratios — an essential link in the Mill-Taussig sequence. Actually, little more than one half the transfer was effected by an increased import surplus. Viner himself notes that the restrictive influence of the relative price changes on Canadian exports was unimportant, but he does not assess this influence with regard to the increases in the volume of imports. There is much reason for contending that the price effects were relatively minor in a period when Canadian national income actually doubled. It is significant, too, that the buoyant prices associated in the Viner analysis with capital imports were in evidence as early as 1896, while capital imports did not take place on a very large scale until almost ten years later.

Finally, my approach contrasts with Viner's in stressing the cyclical conjuncture in which capital imports came to play an important role only at the later stages, the cyclical propagation of purchasing power being emphasized in a process in which capital imports were only one of many interrelated factors that gained prominence as the result of profitable investment opportunities and rapid economic development.

In Part IV there is an investigation of the interwar period and of the postwar boom and the severe depression of the thirties. In view of the tremendous disturbances of these years the rapid adjustment of the balance of payments with generally small short-term capital and gold flows and with comparative stability of exchange rates calls for an explanation, which is attempted. The most significant economic developments of the period are traced, and the rise of two new export areas in Central Canada and British Columbia noted. Prairie wheat found its way almost wholly to Britain and Europe, while the greater part of the mineral and forest products from the two areas mentioned moved south to markets in the United States. The new exports were distinctly less unifying in their economic and political influence than wheat had been.

Chapters 19 and 20 are devoted to an analysis of structural changes in the balance of payments, attention being concentrated upon the years 1913, 1928, and 1937. Important facts are the relative decline of capital and current transactions with the United Kingdom from 1913–1928, while the United States, "Other Commonwealth," and all other countries gained. The year 1937 indicated the reversal of the trend toward increased proportional current payments to the United States, the result partly of Imperial Preference, but more importantly of decreased Canadian investment activity and of consequentially reduced requirements for imports which derived very largely from the United States. Contrary to a commonly held opinion, the United Kingdom did not regularly furnish Canada with a means of financing her current deficit with the United States, which was effected, for example, during 1927–1932, by capital imports from the United States and current credits with other countries.

Chapter 21 represents an attempt to analyze the adjustments in the balance of payments of the interwar period insofar as they might be revealed by the calendar year statistics. The behavior of the varied capital and current account items is scrutinized. Generalization is difficult for these years in which, for example, there are frequent shifts from net capital imports to net capital exports, the latter having been made possible by Canada's increased industrial and financial maturity. Varying behavior is seen to be related to excess capacity in the depression of the thirties. The shocks to the Canadian economy seem to have originated largely in variations in exports, equilibrium being effected primarily through alterations in investment and incomes leading to similar variations in imports. Concurrent fluctuations in United States and Canadian investment would have been possible without the intermediation of exports if Canadian business men had taken their cue from expectations to the south.

That these Canadian expectations were sustained, however, presumes a dominant role for the United States in the world economy, and an eventual effect upon Canadian exports. The United States business cycle, directly and indirectly, appears to be the primary propagator of the Canadian fluctuations. Where adjustments within the current account are incomplete and capital movements participate, their role would seem to be one of effect rather than cause. Tariffs, exchange rates, and relative price changes assume relatively little independent significance as far as can be judged from the statistical evidence, which is dominated by the cyclical variations in investment and incomes. The conclusion stands out that the propagation of the business cycle internationally as reflected in the Canadian international accounts is often not very different from what would be revealed by the examination of payments between two areas enclosed within one national boundary. A further conclusion may be reached with respect to Canadian government policy during the depression of the thirties. While not perverse, it can be described as passive rather than positive. In that respect, it did not differ from that of many other countries of the time, whether these countries were major or peripheral.

The concluding chapter deals with the period following World War II and the lessons that may be learned respecting economic development in the Canadian experience. Improvements in government policy are observed, especially with respect to the exchange rates. The period has been one of prosperity relatively somewhat greater than that enjoyed by the United States. Large deficits on current account have been financed largely by huge capital imports from that country. A brief final section stresses great dissimilarities in the Canadian situation of the last century and that of those economically underdeveloped countries of the world which pose such grave problems in the international economy of today.

CONCLUSION

My approach to the subject matter is historical, theoretical, and statistical.[3] It is historical in that I have striven to treat each episode in the context of historical development over a considerable period of time. The approach is also theoretical, not in building models of the closed system variety, but in using theory

[3] For a similar approach see R. A. Gordon, "Business Cycles in the Interwar Period: The 'Quantitative-Historical' Approach," *American Economic Review*, May 1949, p. 47f.

as a guide in order to suggest the many types of possible relationships that may have been operative. In Part III the critique of the Viner study is launched from the standpoint of a theory of balance-of-payments equilibrium alternative to the "classical" Mill-Taussig theory which Viner was attempting to verify. The elaboration of this eclectic theory in Part I is basic not only to the analysis of the 1900–1913 and preceding periods, but also to the interpretation of the interwar and postwar periods in the chapters that follow. Finally, the approach is statistical in that an attempt was made to quantify wherever possible and to present ample statistical evidence upon which interpretation could be based. Typical behavior in the various statistical time series was sought, but an attempt was made to avoid the overgeneralization characteristic of the usual multiple correlation analyses, and to this end historical uniqueness has been emphasized. Among the advantages of the approach adopted have been the avoidance of confinement to particular short periods of time for which requisite time series were available, the resultant ability to make intercomparisons over greater periods of time than are generally feasible in more refined statistical analysis, and the relative ease in taking due cognizance of qualitative data. However, despite these advantages in my approach, and despite the technical defects of multiple correlation analysis applied to a short period of time series data, I have not hesitated to employ its results, on the principle that any quantifying, no matter how risky, is frequently better than none. Finally, many approaches, alternative to the one I have taken, could of course be ably defended. Inquiry would obviously be handicapped if it were possible to select only one path.

PART I
THEORY OF THE INTERNATIONAL BALANCE OF PAYMENTS

I I

Discussion of Terms

The theory to be developed is meant to be eclectic in its origin.[1]
The Keynesian influence has been tremendous in most areas of
economics and is pervasive in the pages which follow. The significance of Keynesian thinking in the field of international economics has been neatly summarized by Nurkse:

> The income approach to international trade was not by any means
> entirely new. For over a century, writers on international trade had
> referred occasionally to shifts of purchasing power or changes in rela-
> tive demand. The Keynesian approach, however, seemed to yield a
> more comprehensive and consistent account of international monetary
> relations than had ever been given before. It furnished at one and the
> same time an explanation of two related matters: (a) the adjustment
> process of the balance of payments and (b) the international trans-
> mission of fluctuations in economic activity and employment. The
> result has been a fruitful marriage of two subjects that previously led
> quite separate existences under the conventional names of interna-
> tional trade theory and business cycle theory.[2]

The income approach to the study of foreign trade movements, as
exemplified in the multiplier technique, is useful mainly in explaining
fluctuations in the *volume* of trade. The classical doctrine of comparative costs in its various formulations was primarily concerned with
the *composition* of a given volume of trade.[3]

[1] A. E. Kahn, *Great Britain in the World Economy* (New York, 1946),
Chapter 2, has elaborated a rather similar eclectic theory.
[2] R. Nurkse, "Domestic and International Equilibrium," *The New Economics*, ed. S. Harris (New York, 1947), p. 264.
[3] Nurkse, p. 268.

The theory is also marked by the influence of Schumpeter, in particular his analysis of the role of innovation in relation to economic development and business cycles.[4] This analysis of a fundamental feature of the capitalist process provides a much needed complement to much of the Keynesian reasoning, which has suffered as a result of its neglect of economic growth.

There is no intention in the chapters to follow of attempting a broad criticism of classical international trade theory. Interest is directed particularly to a criticism of the "classical" Mill-Taussig theory in its application to an analysis of the transfer mechanism. Most of the much criticized basic assumptions of the classical theory, such as perfect competition, constant costs, constant proportions of the factors of production, international immobility of the factors of production, and internal mobility of the factors of production, are usually considerably modified by the numerous proponents of the "classical" approach, in their use of the theory to interpret reality. The original assumptions, however, despite their modification, may have an unfortunate influence on the approach to and interpretation of the facts. This is notable in the case of the price-specie-flow analysis of the Mill-Taussig theory which suffers from the presumptions of the quantity theory of money although an attempt may be made to avoid any rigid interpretation of it.[5] It might also be observed that the "classical" theory tended to neglect economic growth and the cyclical processes, and in its emphasis upon immobility of labor and capital internationally tended to underestimate the similarity between interregional and international trade, particularly in the century preceding World War I.

Like the Mill-Taussig theory of capital transfer for which it is designed to substitute, the following eclectic theory is mainly directed toward the solution of problems of relatively short-run adjustments in the balance of payments, but unlike the former theory it does not abstract from cyclical and secular movements. Little attention is to be given the question as to whether such

[4] Kahn, *Great Britain in the World Economy*, also has a debt to Schumpeter, under whose guidance he undertook his study. See especially his preface and page 34.
[5] Nurkse in *The New Economics*, p. 265.

adjustments tend towards long-run equilibrium with an optimum resource utilization.[6]

Unlike the "classical" Mill-Taussig theory, the theory proposed does not lend itself to concise formulation, with the lines of causal relationship being clearly set forth. The aim is to investigate the many possible interrelationships. In practice, unfortunately, it may be impossible to demonstrate conclusively which of these is significant and in what degree. One is forced to emphasize the individuality of each historical concatenation, no matter how intellectually unsatisfactory this may be.

Metzler[7] sums up the problem when he points out that there is no manageable general equilibrium theory of capital transfer which is both (1) sufficiently simple so that the properties of the system may be examined and (2) sufficiently complex so that the relevant factors of adjustment may be included. The following theory will certainly be lacking in the first respect, since it will be developed with a view to indicating as many significant lines of causal relationship as possible. In any particular situation, not only parameters but the degree of importance of the various functional relations must be assessed, so that it may be impossible to arrive at definitive conclusions. This is, of course, a great disadvantage, but there is a corresponding advantage in that we are not so likely to become attached to any particular theoretical relationship. I hope to show that such an attachment had an unfortunate effect upon Viner in his analysis of the Canadian situation.

An attempt will be made to make the theoretical generalizations as all-inclusive as possible. They must not be adapted solely to specific types of disturbances. The Mill-Taussig theory is generally explained in terms of a loan or an obligatory remittance from one country to another. The disturbance to international

---

[6] See J. Viner, *Canada's Balance of International Indebtedness, 1900–1913* (Cambridge, 1924), pp. 302–306 — hereafter referred to as *Canada's Balance*. Note that this question is merely incidental to Viner's main analysis and testing of the "classical" theory, being discussed only briefly in his conclusion. Also, he does not consider situations of less than full employment.

[7] L. Metzler, "The Transfer Problem Reconsidered," *Journal of Political Economy*, June 1942, p. 397.

equilibrium was traditionally viewed as occurring on capital rather than on current account, and as being an unusual transfer. But, as pointed out by Professor Haberler,[8] the capital transfer problem is concerned with merely one instance of the operation of the mechanism which keeps the balance of payments in equilibrium.

Professor Viner is an outstanding expositor and defender of the "classical" theory among contemporary economists. His own position respecting the primary origin of disequilibrium has become guarded since the appearance of his Canadian study. He has observed that "there is no apparent *a priori* reason why the dependence [between capital movements and trade balances] should not be as much in one direction as the other." [9] In historical experience "the initial disturbances may come in various combinations, or may originate at home or abroad, or simultaneously in both." [10] Viner notes that some writers have attempted to generalize on the basis of empirical evidence. "Thus Keynes, for instance, has maintained that historically the international movement of long-term capital had adjusted itself to the trade balance rather than the trade balance to capital movements, whereas Taussig has supported the opposite, and traditional, view." [11] Explicit consideration was not given this question in Viner's *Canada's Balance*, nor does it appear to my knowledge in the older writers. The traditional model defended by Viner in *Canada's Balance* arbitrarily emphasized one disturbing factor and gave the impression of a particular view of the historical process (see Chapter 10).

Viner's most recent statement of his position lends qualified support to the Taussig viewpoint.

It seems clear to me, for instance, that in the case of Canada before the war [World War I] the fluctuations in the trade balance were much more the effect than the cause of the fluctuations in the long-term borrowings abroad, whereas in the case of New Zealand the

[8] G. Haberler, *The Theory of International Trade* (London, 1936), p. 63.
[9] J. Viner, *Studies in the Theory of International Trade* (New York and London, 1937), p. 364 — hereafter referred to as *Studies . . . International Trade*.
[10] *Studies . . . International Trade*, p. 364.
[11] *Studies . . . International Trade*, p. 364.

fluctuations in her balance of indebtedness since the war seem to be clearly the result rather than the cause of the fluctuations in her trade balance. . . . Examination of such data as are readily available confirms, however, the orthodox doctrine that . . . major long-term capital movements have, as Taussig maintains, mainly been "disturbing" rather than "equilibrating" in nature.[12]

From a consideration of the question as to whether the principal disturbing factor is the current account or the capital account it is a very short step to the posing of a third alternative, that of mutual interdependence between the current balances and capital movements. This is one alternative that will be favored in the theory I am proposing. The final possibility is to consider whether there may be secular or cyclical factors operating on both the trade balance and capital movements. This is the "common cause" approach that in my view throws much additional light upon the process of balance-of-payment equilibration.[13] If in typical historical developments there are common influences acting on both the capital and trade balances, and if these common influences tend to produce offsetting changes in the capital and current accounts, then the problem of equilibration to a disturbing force arising on capital or current account is much diminished in significance.

DEFINITIONS

The international balance of payments (see Table 27 and the Statistical Appendix) is defined as a list of claims and counterclaims to payment in gold, bank balances, or legal tender of any currency arising with reference to the residents of a given nation during a given accounting period, such as a year.[14] The claims to payment are conventionally referred to in international accounting as receipts or credits, and are given a numerical positive sign in the balance-of-payments statement. The counterclaims to payment (or claims to payment due residents of other countries) are referred to as payments or debits, and are given

[12] *Studies . . . International Trade*, pp. 364–365.
[13] See Chapter 7.
[14] For a further discussion of the definition and terminology, see S. Enke, "Some Balance of Payments Pit-falls," *American Economic Review*, March 1951, pp. 161–164; and Chapter 9, under "Viner's Statistics."

a numerical negative sign in the balance-of-payments statement. To identify claims to payment as "payments" and the counter-claims as "receipts" is misleading, so that the terms credits and debits would be preferable.

The international balance of payments is, then, an accounting statement of debit and credit items which, including the residual (or net error and items unaccounted for), are equal and offsetting. The technical equality is not of particular interest from the theoretical point of view, and it is to the changes in the various items that attention must be directed. The technical equality is, of course, not an indication of equilibrium, and definitions of equilibrium in the balance of payments have customarily selected one or more items[15] whose net flows were said to tend towards zero under equilibrium conditions.[16] Generally, in "classical" theory and in the Viner statement of it in particular, equilibrium conditions were so stated as to exclude net capital and net gold flows.[17] More recent definitions of balance-of-payments equilibrium have generally treated long-term capital movements as compatible with equilibrium. Further, at least some types of short-term capital movements were treated as analogous to gold movements, it being admitted that the development of deposit banking had made these a notable addition to the supply of international money. Viner had stressed this analogy between gold and short-term capital, but his treatment was rather equivocal, and it did not result in a redefinition of equilibrium which

[15] A. I. Bloomfield, *Capital Imports and the American Balance of Payments* (Chicago, 1950), p. 223, maintains that all induced movements of gold, short-term and long-term capital would ideally be selected. But he observes: "Conceptually, however, the distinction between 'induced' (or 'balancing') and 'autonomous' items is very imprecise; statistically it is even more so." He quotes R. Frisch, "On the Need for Forecasting a Multilateral Balance of Payments," *American Economic Review*, September 1947, p. 536, to the effect that the items selected should be those with the highest degree of liquidity.

[16] See Haberler, *The Theory of International Trade*, p. 18.

[17] Viner, *Canada's Balance*, pp. 145–146. This implies a timeless model of the stationary state variety with zero net investment. See J. Robinson, "The Foreign Exchanges" in *Essays in the Theory of Employment* (London, 1937), where she outlines conditions for a short-run equilibrium with no gold and short-term capital movements, and a long-run equilibrium of the circular flow variety in which net investment and savings are zero and exports are equal to imports.

would take specific account of short-term capital movements. Of the earlier classical economists, J. S. Mill was only one of several who noted the various roles of short-term capital in the balance of payments. Mill emphasized the view that its adjusting function was confined to very temporary disturbances.[18]

With the several reservations to follow, equilibrium in the international balance of payments will signify[19] a set of conditions in which, over a period of time sufficiently long to exclude seasonal and minor fluctuations,[20] there is equality between the total demand and supply of foreign exchange, without a continuing positive or negative algebraic sum of short-term capital plus gold movements, or substantial depreciation or appreciation of the currency, or default, or intergovernmental aid, or measures of trade or exchange control designed to bring about the balance.[21] If any of these characteristics are features of a country's international situation, they may be taken as prima facie evidence of disequilibrium in that country's balance of payments. The gold and short-term capital movements and the exchange rate variations are in general associated with factors operating to reestablish equilibrium, while the other criteria are indicative of the inadequacy of these equilibrating tendencies or of interference with the operation of the balancing forces. An alternative way of defining the condition respecting gold and short-term capital movements would be that disequilibrium exists if the current

---

[18] J. S. Mill, *Principles of Political Economy* (London, 1920), p. 618. Viner in his *Studies . . . International Trade*, pp. 408–409, has shown the error of C. Iverson, *Aspects of the Theory of International Capital Movements* (London, 1935), p. 99, in thinking Mill was the first to deal with short-term capital movements.

[19] For a similar definition see Kahn, *Great Britain in the World Economy*, p. 9.

[20] This is therefore a definition of cyclical rather than long-run balance of payments equilibrium, so that cyclical fluctuations are not excluded.

[21] If any of the criteria cited are autonomous rather than equilibrating or induced by the balance-of-payments situation, they need not be taken as evidence of disequilibrium. However, attempts to distinguish autonomous and induced elements forsake the obvious advantage of clear-cut conceptual and statistical discrimination. The International Monetary Fund, *Balance of Payments Manual* (Washington, 1950), p. 108f, for example, distinguishes "special" official financing and compensatory official financing, the latter being defined as "undertaken broadly to balance international transactions during the reporting period."

account deficit or surplus is not offset by long-term capital movements.[22]

The foregoing definition of equilibrium in the balance of payments is drawn up from the point of view of the foreign exchange
market. It does not attempt what is considerably more difficult
and controversial, namely, going behind the foreign exchange
market to indicate those relations of costs, prices, and incomes
that are necessary conditions of equilibrium.[23] Such discussion
usually pertains to a longer run type of equilibrium with which I
will not be so intimately concerned in my balance-of-payments
analysis. The criteria of the above formulation of equilibrium conditions differ from those of Nurkse[24] and of Triffin[25] (to the latter
of which Haberler[26] gives his assent) in that the maintenance
of satisfactory levels of income and employment is not included.
Equilibrium in the narrow sense of my definition is therefore
quite compatible with large-scale unemployment. The definition
is not normative and leaves unanswered the thorny question of
establishing satisfactory criteria for an equilibrium exchange rate
facilitating both an international balance and satisfactory levels
of employment.[27] However, despite the possible compatibility of

[22] There are those who might argue that this should read " — not offset
by stable, nonspeculative long-term capital movements which from the point
of view of the motive of the investor could not be considered as short-term
capital." Unstable, speculative, quasi short-term long-term capital movements
would then be included among the criteria of balance-of-payments disequilibrium.

[23] A. H. Hansen, *America's Role in the World Economy* (New York,
1945), appendix B, "A Note on 'Fundamental Disequilibrium' "; S. Harris,
G. Haberler, A. H. Hansen et al., "A Symposium," *Review of Economic
Statistics*, November 1944. These articles by Haberler and Hansen are reprinted in revised form in *Foreign Economic Policy for the United States*,
ed. S. Harris (Cambridge, 1948), pp. 379–397. C. P. Kindleberger, *International Short-Term Capital Movements* (New York, 1937), Chapter VII.

[24] Nurkse, "Conditions of Monetary Equilibrium," *Essays in International
Finance*, No. 4 (Princeton, 1945).

[25] R. Triffin, "National Central Banking and the International Economy,"
International Monetary Policies (Federal Reserve System Post-War Economic Studies No. 7, Washington, 1947), pp. 77–78.

[26] Haberler, "Comments," *International Monetary Policies*, p. 99.

[27] The definition is similar to that of Kindleberger, *International . . .
Movements*, p. 115, but differs notably from Keynes' definitions, in which
the criterion of equilibrium neglected short-term capital movements. See A.
I. Bloomfield, "Foreign Exchange Rate Theory and Policy," in *The New
Economics*, p. 297, where J. M. Keynes, *A Treatise on Money* (New York,
1930), I, 161–163, is cited.

my version of equilibrium with underemployment equilibrium and even with rapid changes in the level of incomes, one or more of the various criteria of balance-of-payments disequilibrium which were listed would in general probably appear.[28] My definition, I believe, furnishes a concept which is highly useful in approaching the historical material with which I will have to deal.[29]

SHORT-TERM CAPITAL MOVEMENTS

Short-term capital movements figure significantly in the preceding definition of balance-of-payments equilibrium. Further, some of the controversy relating to the definition of equilibrium involves short-term capital movements. There is justification, therefore, in undertaking a rather detailed treatment of them.

The conventional criterion of short-term capital is based upon the form which the loan operation takes. The term of short-term capital is usually considered as being less than a year. Thus it would generally include open-book credits, bank deposits held abroad, bills of exchange, etc., while long-term capital would include bonds, mortgages, titles to property, corporate shares, etc.[30] This criterion is one on which the statistician must lean heavily even though it may not be entirely to his taste. The economic theorist has found this definition to be inadequate for many purposes, particularly with the growth of ready markets which facilitated the short-term holding of nominally long-term investments. The trade in outstanding securities internationally has at times been exceedingly large.[31] Kindleberger therefore

[28] See, however, Triffin, *International Monetary Policies*, p. 76: "One of the clearest cases of a fundamental disequilibrium owing to currency devaluation is the experience of Belgium following the devaluation of the British pound in September 1931. And yet, both the balance of trade and the balance of payments improved rather than deteriorated during most of the overvaluation period." There is an analogy in the Canadian experience of the thirties. The balance-of-payments disequilibrium will not necessarily ensue if the country concerned permits a relatively greater deflation at home than abroad.

[29] The application of the definition is by no means limited to this particular purpose. See, for example, note 41 and the concluding paragraph of this chapter.

[30] Kindleberger, *International . . . Movements*, p. 3.

[31] A. I. Bloomfield, "The Significance of Outstanding Securities in the International Movement of Capital," *Canadian Journal of Economics and Political Science*, November 1940.

defines short-term capital with regard to the motive of the investor.[32] This criterion is of little assistance to those attempting to measure statistically the international short-term capital flows. Furthermore, it is subject to the criticism that the individual's intentions at the time of investment may not give a clue as to whether the capital is long or short term, an important reason being that the subsequent date of sale of an asset may be determined by later developments in the security markets.[33] No simple criterion can be wholly satisfactory, and the various factors to be kept in mind must be related to the specific problem under consideration.

Kindleberger adopts a classification of short-term capital, useful for expository purposes, which I will detail briefly:[34]

(1) *"Equilibrating"* short-term capital movements result directly in a compensatory way from changes in other items of the balance of payments. It is unfortunate that this new usage of the term "equilibrating" must add to the already considerable confusion resulting from the great variety of ways in which it is employed. We are later informed by Kindleberger that this particular type of short-term capital movement is always equilibrating in the normal sense in which the word is employed in association with short-term capital, i.e., it postpones or eliminates the necessity for gold movements or exchange rate changes. But other classes of short-term capital may also be equilibrating in this sense as well.

(2) *Speculative* movements of short-term capital are inspired by actual or prospective alterations in the foreign exchange rate, being effected by professional speculators who plan to reconvert and who do not cover the exchange risk. Such movements are equilibrating in the normal sense of the term when the exchange rate variation is expected to be temporary, as in the case of a movement to one of the gold points under gold standard conditions. If the unidirectional exchange rate movement is expected to continue, such speculation will be disequilibrating in its influence on merchandise account.

[32] Kindleberger, *International . . . Movements*, p. 3.

[33] F. A. Hayek, *Monetary Nationalism and International Stability* (London, 1939), p. 56.

[34] Kindleberger, *International . . . Movements*, pp. 7–13.

(3) *Income* movements of short-term capital take place in response to the attraction of a higher interest rate or of the discount of the forward rate of exchange of a currency. The shifts of outstanding securities where the motivation is the prospect of capital appreciation have also been included by Kindleberger in this category. Bank discount policy may result in the income movements being equilibrating, but if the discount rate is adjusted beyond a certain point, gold movements in one direction may not only be eliminated by the offsetting short-term capital flows, but these may be so large as to induce gold flows in the opposite direction. For example, a high short-term interest rate may attract both short-term capital and gold, as appears to have been frequently the case in England prior to World War I.[35] Kindleberger does not give an example for the case of outstanding security movements. An instance of an equilibrating movement here might be that of an autonomous increase in exports leading to increased incomes, which together with increased liquidity and a decreased interest rate, stimulate a flow of funds to foreign security markets, thus reducing a possible gold inflow.[36] An instance of a disequilibrating movement could be found in an outflow of funds induced by rapid capital appreciation in foreign security markets which, assuming no change in other categories of the balance of payments, would have to be countered by an outflow of gold.

(4) *Autonomous* movements of short-term capital take place in response to fears for the principal. The transfer is usually conducted with the capital of the owner and not with borrowed funds, as may be the case with regard to speculative movements. Autonomous movements tend to be disequilibrating.[37]

[35] Kindleberger, *International . . . Movements*, p. 151.

[36] See Robinson, *Essays in the Theory of Employment*, pp. 201–202. This instance and others supplied for illustration are possibilities and cannot be generalized upon. For example, in the instance just given the business expansion associated with the increase in exports might well be accompanied by increased profits and prospects of capital gains which could induce a disequilibrating inflow of capital.

[37] These movements of flight capital are therefore frequently accompanied by gold movements that bear an opposite numerical sign in the balance of payments statement. For an excellent study of abnormal capital transfers see A. I. Bloomfield, *Capital Imports and the American Balance of Payments, 1934–39* (Chicago, 1950).

With this brief analysis of the nature of the various types of short-term capital flows completed I turn again to a discussion of equilibrium in the balance of payments.

APPLICATION AND LIMITATIONS OF DEFINITIONS

Many authorities would question the adequacy of my definition of balance-of-payments equilibrium on the grounds that the criterion of equilibrium should be absence of net gold and *equilibrating* (or induced) short-term capital movements.[38] They would, therefore, consider the inflow of disequilibrating capital which was offset by an outflow of gold (or in other words the acquisition of external short-term assets in exchange for gold) as evidence of disequilibrium in the balance of payments. My view is that such an exchange of liquid assets need not give rise to any problems nor be considered as evidence of disequilibrium if it does not reach large proportions, or if it is effected as a result of the policy of the banking authorities. Even the problem of large gold losses due to a private short-term capital exodus may be on a different plane to the problems of fundamental disequilibrium associated, for example, with relative price or cost differentials. This is more clearly the case, under conditions of foreign exchange control, when, as Nurkse observes, disequilibrating short-term capital movements should certainly be controlled.[39] Nonetheless here is a possible limitation of my definition which should be kept in mind. The advantages of having a statistically measurable criterion is in any event clear enough.

The definition I have given would not hold for a growing gold-standard country without gold mines which would be acquiring gold and foreign short-term assets in the normal course of events as its money supply and foreign trade expanded. Nor would it apply to the situation of a country producing gold for export. The gold movements in the foregoing instances are analogous to

[38] For example, Haberler in "A Symposium," *Review of Economic Statistics*, p. 178; and Bloomfield in *The New Economics*, p. 297, and in *Capital Imports and the American Balance of Payments, 1934–1939*, pp. 223, 224. Nurkse, *Essays in International Finance*, No. 4, pp. 4–5, takes the opposing point of view, including, as in the definition I have given, disequilibrating as well as equilibrating short-term capital movements.

[39] Nurkse, pp. 4–5.

normal commodity exports and imports. They could not be taken as evidence of disequilibrium.[40]

The possibility of an underemployment equilibrium, while no balance-of-payments disequilibrium is evidenced by my particular criteria, has already been pointed out. Yet a further possibility which indicates the limitations of the definition and its application is to be found where one category of the balance of payments is influencing another category simultaneously or with a very short lag. If such movements are offsetting, disequilibrium and rapid equilibrating action may be present without being reflected in movements of gold or of short-term funds. Another possibility is that cyclical and secular changes may effect offsetting movements in different categories of the balance of payments, so that in a dynamic and unstable situation, with, for example, large capital movements, there may be negligible strain on any mechanism of equilibration to which such cyclical and secular changes are external. To generalize, it might be stated that the particular definition adopted focuses too much attention on the gold and short-term capital movements as evidence of disequilibrium. However, no definition could be wholly satisfactory under all circumstances, and there is much to be said for the reserved and qualified use of the definition which I have proposed.

Some discussion of the applicability of the definition to recent and current international economic problems might help to clarify further its significance. Note that the definition is not one that applies only to the relatively *laissez-faire* world of the nineteenth century. The degree of controls in effect that are designed to maintain a balance in the international accounts is specifically taken account of as one of the criteria of disequilibrium in the balance of payments. A relaxation of such controls would be taken as prima facie evidence of a movement toward equilibrium.

In a world of controls, the various tendencies toward equilibrium may be inhibited or even entirely suppressed. Complete

[40] These qualifications are very important for the case of Canada. An attempt has therefore been made to separate in the statistics monetary gold movements that reflect the Canadian demand for monetary gold reserves and nonmonetary gold movements as they would occur in the absence of this Canadian monetary demand. See The Statistical Appendix.

suppression, however, would be characteristic only of an extreme authoritarian country such as Russia, where the operations of the economy are almost completely subservient to government directive. In less extreme cases the tendencies toward equilibrium should still be taken into account in realistic analysis. Since the tendencies are controlled, we have what is sometimes termed a controlled disequilibrium situation. The concept of equilibrium may prove useful in appraising such situations, analogous to the instance where we compare the controlled price of a rationed commodity with an estimated free market price in hypothetical circumstances of uncontrolled supply and demand.

Now let us apply the definition to the much discussed concept of an alleged world dollar shortage.[41] I would maintain that we have here a dramatic expression well suited to popular usage, which can be given fairly clear meaning, and which applies very well to an experienced set of circumstances. I define dollar shortage as a strong disequilibrium in the United States balance of

[41] Much debate has been centered on the question as to whether the dollar shortage is a chronic one. The term chronic is to my mind too strong and implies undue optimism with respect to the predictive qualities of economic analysis. However, many reasons could be cited for expecting the dollar shortage to continue beyond a postwar transitional period during which the objectives of European reconstruction were accomplished. These reasons include the disequilibrating effects of a number of factors that could not be offset by feasible income, price, and exchange rate adjustments, adjustments that are frequently limited by attempts to maintain political equilibrium. These factors include (1) discontinuous changes in innovation that weaken foreign competitive positions; (2) the high propensities to consume, to invest, and to import from the United States that are to be found in many foreign countries, particularly the underdeveloped regions of the world; (3) the difficulty of providing long-term private capital exports from the United States; (4) elements of imperfect competition that impede inroads by foreigners in the United States domestic market, e.g., those deriving from the comparatively greater efficiency of American merchandising techniques in home markets; (5) the political and economic factors inhibiting many effective tariff decreases where they would markedly assist the foreign exporter but would harm domestic sectional interests; (6) the potency of many American customs administration restrictions on imports; (7) the increasing proportion of American incomes being devoted to manufactured articles and services where the domestic producers are more favored than, e.g., in the case of standardized raw materials. There are many other factors to weigh in the balance, such as the relative level of defense expenditures in the United States and other countries, and the closely associated question as to how relative national price levels will be affected. The probable outcome is certainly not conclusive.

payments vis-a-vis other countries, as evidenced — for example, in the recent postwar period by an inflow of gold in the first postwar years — by substantial depreciation of foreign currencies, especially in 1949, by United States governmental aid to other countries, and by controls maintained with a view to protecting foreign balances of payments. Despite the substantial loss of gold by the United States in 1950 and the withdrawal of foreign short-term capital (both positive algebraic items in the international accounts), I would argue that the even greater United States foreign aid plus the fact of continued foreign restrictions upon imports indicated a continuing, though lessening, dollar shortage as defined.

I I I

The "Classical" Theory and Its Critics

The "classical" theory of the balance of payments and its equilibration has been developed mainly through the discussion of the mechanism of capital transfer following the granting of an international loan.

This theory, which emphasizes the importance of price changes in the equilibrating action, was first developed by Hume and Thornton, and, although opposed by Ricardo and other nineteenth century economists, who denied the necessity for price changes, it has misleadingly been entitled the classical Ricardian theory of capital transfer.[1] This theory has been ascendant until recent years, although on different occasions it has been the subject of heated controversy. In the *Quarterly Journal of Economics* of 1918 it was defended by Taussig and attacked by Wicksell,[2] who held that the shifts of purchasing power could effect the transfer of capital without the necessity for relative price changes. In the debate on German reparations Keynes, taking a most un-Keynesian view of the problem, appeared to accept the theory, while it was opposed by Ohlin.

Among the "classical" economists who defended the theory and

[1] Viner, *Canada's Balance*, pp. 191ff; and Viner, *Studies . . . International Trade*, pp. 290ff.

[2] Viner, *Studies . . . International Trade*, pp. 304ff; F. W. Taussig, "International Trade Under Depreciated Paper," *Quarterly Journal of Economics*, 31:374ff; and K. Wicksell, "International Freights and Prices," *Quarterly Journal of Economics*, 32:404ff.

gave it a definite exposition was J. S. Mill, while in later years it was elaborated by F. W. Taussig, who emphasized differential behavior of sectional prices within the broad national price levels and assigned them a role in the equilibrating mechanism. I will direct my attention mainly to this more refined form of the "classical" exposition and, following Viner's example, will refer to it as the Mill-Taussig theory.

THE "CLASSICAL" MILL–TAUSSIG THEORY

The "classical" theory after Mill as understood by Viner comprises the following causal time sequence:[3]

(1) An increase in the price of bills on the borrowing country following the granting of a loan.

(2) A flow of gold from the lending to the borrowing country, when the exchange of the lending country reaches the gold export point.

(3) Relative price changes, an increase in the borrowing country, and a decrease in the lending country.

(4) A change in exports and imports effected by these price changes, the borrowing country acquiring an unfavorable balance of trade and the lending country acquiring a favorable balance.

(5) After the unfavorable trade balance of the borrowing country had become exactly equal to the rate of borrowing, the return of the exchanges to parity, the cessation of gold movements, and the stabilization of relative prices in the two countries at their new levels.

Taussig[4] in his analysis of relative prices stressed that, as a corollary of this reasoning, import prices in the borrowing country would tend to rise least, while prices of its produce little subject to international exchange would tend to rise most. The latter were termed "domestic commodities." Intermediate price rises would be encountered by the export commodities. These relative price changes would stimulate imports and depress exports, thus generating an import surplus in the borrowing country in a manner compatible with the "classical" approach to the problem.

[3] Viner, *Canada's Balance,* p. 146.
[4] See *Canada's Balance,* p. 209ff., for an exposition and history of this improvement on the original "classical" statement, which he traces back to Cairnes.

IMPORTANT CRITICISMS

The main opposition to the "classical" theory of capital transfer originally came from the school of thought that has emphasized the international transfers of purchasing power, the main argument running in terms of shifts in demand schedules rather than in terms of movements along the demand curve. Viner has honestly admitted to having "sinned" in not according recognition to the "fairly obvious proposition" that the shift in demand of itself contributed to the adjustment of the balance of payments, but he argues that the shift of purchasing power "must be regarded as implicit even in the Hume-Thornton-Taussig type of formulation, since otherwise the changes in prices which they postulate would have no immediate explanation." [5] It was certainly not generally explicit in this formulation, or in Mill or in the earlier writings of Keynes, and consequences of the demand shift other than the relative price movements were largely neglected. As Kahn remarks, "one scans the writings of Keynes or Taussig absolutely in vain for the slightest recognition that the shift of purchasing power directly influences demand curves." [6] The same criticism cannot be made, however, of all writers in the classical vein, as has been demonstrated by Viner. [7] Several of these, including Ricardo and Bastable, actually went so far as to deny or question the need for any relative price changes whatsoever in the equilibration mechanism. [8] Mill explicitly recognizes the purchasing power shift in an isolated instance, but it was not incorporated into his theory of the transfer mechanism. [9]

Among contemporary economists, Ohlin has been a strong adherent of the purchasing power shift approach. [10] Iverson, another contemporary, has entitled this approach the "modern" theory,

[5] Viner, *Studies . . . International Trade*, p. 294.

[6] Kahn, *Great Britain in the World Economy*, p. 23n.

[7] Viner, *Studies . . . International Trade*, pp. 295–304.

[8] Professor G. A. Elliott of the University of Toronto has pointed out in discussion with me that this position of Bastable was taken in his *Quarterly Journal of Economics* article of 1889 but was no more incorporated into his *Theory of International Trade* than was Mill's isolated recognition in his general theory.

[9] Viner, *Studies . . . International Trade*, pp. 300–301.

[10] For example, B. Ohlin, "Transfer Difficulties, Real and Imagined," *Economic Journal*, June 1929.

developing a position similar to Ohlin's, which he contrasts in an extreme, uncompromising manner with the Mill-Taussig theory. Iverson[11] is unable to comprehend what strikes him as being a curious apostasy on the part of Ohlin,[12] who claims that his (Ohlin's) theory of capital movements is a modification of that of the Harvard School led by Taussig, which in turn is based upon the Thornton-Mill theory. Ohlin is vague and possibly overly compromising in making this claim. He adds, "In certain important respects it [Ohlin's theory] differs from Taussig's theory. I am not certain whether there is any important difference in principle between the analysis below and that presented by Professor Viner." But Ohlin is unequivocal on one point, stating definitely, "Taussig's and Viner's theories are different." Ohlin's interpretation of Viner's standpoint seems to be based, not upon Viner's *Canada's Balance,* but upon personal unpublished correspondence and conversations with him, in which Viner doubtless incorporated more explicit recognition of his earlier neglect of the purchasing power shifts, as he has in his 1937 publication, *Studies in the Theory of International Trade.*

The analysis pursued by Ohlin[13] appears to be in line with the harmonizing view taken by Professor Haberler of the role played by the price movements in the transfer mechanism. Haberler states; "The truth lies in this case midway between the two conflicting theories, both of which are one-sided and give an oversimplified picture of the facts. For in reality one can conceive both cases in which transfer involves changes in the general price level and cases in which it does not involve them." [14] Haberler subsequently notes his agreement with Ohlin that "the analysis must be in terms not of general but of sectional price levels." [15] The type of relative price changes emphasized in Ohlin's argument is not general price changes or changes in the terms of trade, which he holds fulfill a negligible function in the transfer process, but sectional price changes, especially prices of domestic as com-

[11] C. Iverson, *Aspects of the Theory of International Capital Movements* (London, 1935), p. 296.
[12] Ohlin, *Interregional and International Trade* (Cambridge, 1933), p. 410n.
[13] *Interregional and International Trade,* pp. 421–427.
[14] Haberler, *Theory of International Trade,* pp. 72–73.
[15] Haberler, p. 76.

pared to prices of internationally traded goods and services, which are a function of the direction taken by the newly acquired purchasing power and the relevant demand and supply elasticities. These sectional price changes were accorded full recognition in Viner's Canadian study, and, as he acknowledged in his analysis, he was following the example set by Taussig. Viner[16] is not wholly unfair to Iverson[17] when he remarks: "The inclusion in the 'classical' doctrine of special treatment of the prices of domestic commodities he [Iverson] seems to regard as a peculiar aberration, accidentally in the right direction, of the 'classical' writer."

Kahn has also attempted to minimize the difference between the "modern" treatment of Ohlin and Iverson and the "classical gold-flow terms of trade analysis." He points out that "the major stress in the 'modern' treatment is on the shift of factors of production within the countries as a result of differential movements of sectional domestic demands. . . . If the factors are actually to be shifted from one line to another, there must be relatively full employment. Under these conditions, how such a shift may be induced other than by changes in sectional prices and hence in relative rates of remuneration is not clear."[18] This statement appears to exaggerate the degree of mobility of labor in response to wage differentials. Also, it neglects the fact that as a result of imperfections of competition in the factor and product markets there may be an approximation to infinitely elastic supply conditions. A shift to the right in the demand curve for labor under such conditions may result in an inflow of labor into the industry from areas of "disguised unemployment" where the marginal product of labor was exceedingly low. There is no necessity for relative price and wage rate changes under such circumstances. The shift of resources may be said to be due to shifts of purchasing power and not to relative price changes, which, if they do occur, are generally more appropriately regarded as a by-product or symptom of the purchasing power shifts, and not as a significant force leading to a change in resource allocation.

Kahn does indicate in his statement a weakness found in both

[16] Viner, *Studies . . . International Trade*, p. 327n.
[17] Iverson, *Aspects . . . International Movements*, pp. 398; 472–488.
[18] Kahn, *Great Britain in the World Economy*, pp. 23–24.

Ohlin's and the earlier "classical" treatment, namely, the usual assumption in both analyses of full employment conditions. Such an assumption does of course exaggerate the degree of price and factor movement. Parenthetically it might be noted that Ohlin does commence an analysis of the secondary rounds of expenditure stemming from the initial primary shift in purchasing power.[19] These, of course, are the content of the foreign trade multiplier which has since been paraded onto the theoretical stage. Had Ohlin seen the potentialities in this brand of analysis he might not have been so ready to assimilate himself into the Taussig School, which incorporated in its particular brand of analysis exaggerated emphasis on relative price changes.

In an expanding economy as well as in an economy of unemployed resources, much of the price movement and more of the internal movement of the factors of production may be avoided. Ohlin[20] has not ignored the lead given by Professor J. H. Williams[21] in stressing the part played by international movements of capital and labor and the notable easing of the adjustment in a progressive economy which was receiving additions to its productive factors. Indeed, Ohlin's analysis is so thorough that it is rarely possible to accuse him of sins of complete omission. But as Ohlin himself has frankly noted, "On the whole . . . the aspects of international trade which are concerned with the business cycle are left out of account." [22] Much of the inadequacy of his analysis appears to derive from this fact.

Certainly much of the controversy between the proponents of the "classical" approach and the proponents of the approach emphasizing shifts of purchasing power rather than relative price changes has been rather sterile. The major gains in the controversy appear to be (1) the explicit admission that, whether relative price changes play a role or not, the purchasing power shifts

---

[19] Ohlin, *Interregional and International Trade*, pp. 411–413. Professor P. T. Ellsworth in his book *The International Economy* (New York, 1950), p. 334n, has also observed this passage. Ohlin's analysis appears, it is interesting to see, in his section entitled "The Monetary Mechanism," which accords more weight to monetary factors and to monetary policy than would much recent economic analysis.

[20] *Interregional and International Trade*, p. 428; chap. xvii.

[21] J. H. Williams, "The Theory of International Trade Reconsidered," *Economic Journal*, June 1929.

[22] Ohlin, *Interregional and International Trade*, p. 331n.

are essential to the process; (2) the price changes are subsidiary in the sense that it is the shift in demand which brings them about;[23] (3) with analysis of the primary shift of demand and its impact, there appears at least the start of the multiplier process, which, as will be demonstrated later, makes balance-of-payments equilibration feasible without reliance on relative price changes; (4) attention is directed in the more realistic analysis to the relative importance of price changes and demand shifts, a difficult question to handle. The task in the ensuing chapter will be to take the analysis of the shifts of demand beyond the level reached in these earlier controversies.

[23] Where prices change in anticipation of shifts of demand, they are still subsidiary in the logical sense.

I V

International Shifts of Demand

The transfer of purchasing power is now universally recognized as providing a major basis for whatever price changes may take place, even though the latter has been designated by some schools of thought as being the most significant equilibrating factor. Therefore, it seems at the very least expedient to commence discussion of the theory with an explicit analysis of these shifts in demand. Normally, the analysis has commenced with the gold standard assumptions. I have avoided this practice for two reasons: (a) shifts of purchasing power may occur under gold standard conditions and yet be unaccompanied by flows of specie, for which, as we have seen, movements of short-term capital may substitute; (b) I wish to avoid the usual dichotomy in the treatments of the gold and paper standards, and, by introducing gold flows into the analysis only as a subsequent step, their significance is less likely to be exaggerated.

THE PRIMARY SHIFTS

Every international payment on either capital or current account, being a two-sided transaction, involves a shift of purchasing power from the nationals of one country to the nationals of another. Such a payment is tantamount to a flow of short-term capital where it is effected, as in the usual circumstances, by the transfer of a bank deposit to the recipient of the payment. Either individuals or banks in the receiving country acquire deposits abroad; that is, they acquire a form of short-term capital. In the case where the banks acquire the deposits abroad the operation is normally that of the individual payees exchanging their foreign deposits, directly or indirectly through the banks, and receiving the domestic deposits they require in return.

The influence upon effective purchasing power of these flows of short-term funds is dependent on many and on complex circumstances, the cyclical conjuncture being particularly important. They do not normally constitute as direct a potential demand as do domestically owned deposits, since they frequently operate only through the money markets. However, they might at times provide an immediate basis for inflationary investment expenditures while, on the other hand, domestically owned deposits may at times be held idle.[1]

The initial acquisition of the bank deposits abroad would be classified by Kindleberger as an "equilibrating" short-term capital movement (see Chapter 2), while if the holder of these funds allowed them to remain abroad as a result of policy, the classification would be a speculative, an income, or an autonomous short-term capital movement according to the motive of the holder.

The question now to be answered is: Assuming an increase in payments disturbing to the balance of payments equilibrium, what is the contribution of the primary purchasing power shift to the adjustment? At the outset I will present an oversimplified description, which in fact is indicative only of tendencies that in certain circumstances may be negligible. First, the transfers of short-term capital act as stopgaps compensating in a rather passive manner for the discrepancies between other receipts and expenditures in the balance of payments.[2] Secondly, a portion of the

---

[1] For more detailed discussion see Kahn, *Great Britain in the World Economy*, pp. 11–15; and Ellsworth, *The International Economy*, pp. 293f and 308f, where it is argued, not altogether convincingly to my mind, that there is no reason to expect domestically owned deposits to be more active. In any event, in a peripheral country like Canada, as distinct from a clearing center such as Great Britain, an excess of receipts over payments to foreigners will result in an increase of bank deposits and the money supply, and not merely a shift within a given total of deposits from foreign to domestic ownership. Thus, in a peripheral country the tendencies to adjustment as a result of the purchasing power shift are likely to be stronger than in a clearing country.

[2] Nurkse in *The New Economics*, p. 271. This is referred to by Professor Ellsworth, *The International Economy*, p. 317f., as a short-run adjustment as distinct from what he terms long-run adjustments due to income and price changes.

purchasing power transferred to the receiving country will be expended on imports of commodities and services and to this extent there is an immediate real transfer serving to equilibrate the balance of payments. The residual portion of the purchasing power transferred is devoted to goods and services domestically produced, thus increasing incomes and purchasing power further. This constitutes what is to be referred to as the secondary increase in purchasing power — the multiplier effect. The paying country, on the other hand, suffers a primary and secondary reduction of purchasing power and consequently of imports, thus making her contribution to the adjustment of the balance of payments.

Both the "classical" and purchasing-power-shift analyses have tended too freely to assume this deflation in the remitting country and inflation in the receiving country. As initially observed, this is an oversimplified case. It is more probable in the case of a peripheral than of a clearing country. On capital account it is more likely to be found in the instance of direct investment or of the flotation of new securities on foreign markets where the disturbance arises. Even in this instance there may be no net contraction of purchasing power in the remitting country if the funds involved derive from idle balances or from credit creation. In the case of autonomous short-term capital movements or in the case of capital repatriation, there may be no net direct primary or secondary purchasing power changes, since shifts of idle funds and the liquidation or creation of bank loans are likely to be involved in both countries. In some disturbances arising on current account, such as an autonomous shift in demand from domestic to foreign commodities, the likelihood is that there will be a close approach to the simplified description above. Apart from these essentially velocity-of-money problems, there will be factors causing the flows of potential purchasing power and the flows of goods to differ in their relation to one another. The time element is important here, e.g., the initial purchasing power transfer may be inflationary in the capital-importing country only to be offset in time by a net inflow of goods and services and there may be a consequential deflationary effect.[3] This is a limited quantity theory of money approach to the problem, though it

[3] Viner, *Studies . . . International Trade*, pp. 434–435.

may be of some explanatory value. The questions of whether the
goods imported are investment or consumption goods, competitive or complementary with the domestic production,[4] and
whether they are exported from the lending country, are all more
important. The importance of the time element, in turn, may not
be assessed without investigating the nature of the innovation
and investment activity with which the capital flows are associated. The possibilities here are complex and infinitely numerous.
Each historical case must be examined in order to determine the
degree to which the tendencies of the orthodox, simple variety
appear to be present.

SECONDARY SHIFTS — THE MULTIPLIER

It is the secondary shift of purchasing power which, after
earlier neglect, has come into prominence in the adjustment
mechanism as a result largely of the Keynesian approach. Unless
the primary shift is effective in reducing imports and increasing
exports in the lending country while increasing imports and
decreasing exports in the borrowing country, in both instances to
an extent sufficient to accomplish a transfer of goods and services
equivalent to the purchasing power shift, secondary purchasing
power shifts will follow. White[5] has expressed the opinion that
the primary demand shift (his analysis also neglects explicit consideration of the influence of the secondary shifts upon the trade
balance) may well approach the accomplishment of the transfer,
but this would appear greatly to exaggerate its importance.

[4] H. Feis, "The Mechanism of Adjustment of International Trade Balances," *American Economic Review*, December 1926, p. 603.

[5] White, *The French International Accounts, 1880–1913*, p. 28. White
(pp. 24–25) goes further than Viner in *Canada's Balance* and further than
other analyses of his period, by introducing and considering fluctuations in
incomes and employment. "If the supply of domestic goods (and services)
cannot be increased, then additional domestic purchases can come only from
goods that would normally be exported, or . . . from the diversion of some
of the factors of production from export goods." He reasons that an expansion of domestic activity will necessitate a lesser contraction of exports and
that there will be, as a result, a lesser contribution through export changes
to the transfer of the loan. Like others writing before the advent of
Keynesian economics, White neglected the influence toward reduced exports
and expanded imports deriving from the subsequent rounds of purchasing
power which stem from the domestic purchases resulting from the primary
purchasing power shift.

The secondary purchasing power shifts will be recognized as the subject matter of the multiplier analysis, which deals with income generation through successive spending flows.[6] This analysis, originally designed to deal with the expansionary effects of domestic investment, may be generalized to deal with any income-generating expenditure not determined by the past level of income.[7] A decline in such income-generating expenditure would, of course, cause the multiplier to operate in a reverse, contracting direction. The multiplier may be expressed as a function of the marginal propensity to consume (or to save) and the marginal propensity to import. I leave aside for the moment the acceleration principle and induced increases of investment, only noting that some writers have chosen to express the multiplier as a function of the marginal propensity to import and the marginal propensity to spend on both consumption and investment.[8]

The multiplier has been applied in the foreign trade sphere to income-generating expenditures originating on current account, in exports[9] or in an export surplus. There is no reason for my particular purposes thus to confine the analysis. Analogous income-generating expenditures arise on capital account, in imports of capital, or, in words which better stress the analogy with current account transactions, in the export of long-term securities.[10]

Professor Machlup[11] has explored the equilibrating possibilities of the secondary demand shifts in his excellent study of the

[6] Nurkse in *The New Economics,* pp. 266ff; and R. Goodwin, "The Multiplier," also in *The New Economics,* ed. S. Harris, pp. 482ff.

[7] This income approach has become dominant in recent years, but mention should be made of A. W. Marget, *The Theory of Prices,* 2 vols (New York, 1938–1942), who has convincingly argued that there is no essential conflict between the quantity of money and income approaches. The latter, however, I regard as more serviceable, and more instructive, in its emphasis. See H. H. Villard, "Monetary Theory," pp. 316ff., in *A Survey of Contemporary Economics,* ed. H. S. Ellis (Philadelphia, 1948); and A. H. Hansen, *Monetary Theory and Fiscal Policy* (New York, 1949), pp. 83ff.

[8] For example, L. Metzler, "The Transfer Problem Reconsidered," *Journal of Political Economy,* June 1942.

[9] Exports may be taken as representing current account credits.

[10] See Chapter 19, "Pre-World War I period compared."

[11] F. Machlup, *International Trade and the National Income Multiplier* (Philadelphia, 1943). See also the path-breaking articles by F. W. Paish and W. A. Salant in American Economic Association, *Readings in the Theory of International Trade* (Philadelphia, 1949).

foreign trade multiplier. On the basis of the Machlup assumptions the balance-of-payments adjustment, contrary to "classical" reasoning, is shown to be normally incomplete. These assumptions exclude the possibilities of induced alterations in price levels, bank policy, interest rates, and investment activity which would be consequent upon the continued flow of gold and short-term funds. The final adjustment is brought about by changes in the level of incomes inducing changes in consumption and savings alone, for investment is treated as autonomous.

For the purposes of illustration take a simple case where the exports of a given country increase from a position of import-export equality in response to an increase in the world demand for them. The export surplus with the accompanying evidence of balance-of-payments disequilibrium, the gold and short-term capital flows, will not be wholly eliminated in the process of adjustment, given Machlup's assumptions. Incomes increase, and consequentially imports increase; but savings also increase. The fundamental income identity for an open economy equates savings to net domestic investment plus the balance of payments on current account. In terms of Robertsonian process analysis utilized by Machlup, we would say that income increases to a level at which the export surplus (reduced by induced import increases) exactly offsets the increase in the level of savings. The adjustment is then complete as far as the Machlup model is concerned, but we are left with a condition of balance-of-payments disequilibrium. The theory indicates a *determinate* level of disequilibrium, thus contrasting with the earlier purchasing power arguments in indicating the extent of the income changes and how far the adjusting process would go.[12]

The fact that equilibration remains incomplete on the basis of the Machlup assumptions does not mean that relative price changes must therefore play an important role. The theory that I am engaged in developing places even more stress on the other Machlup *ceteris paribus* restrictions. In the short-run process of equilibration, induced changes of investment, which will substitute for the balance of payments on current account in providing offsets to savings, are likely to prove very important. Induced

[12] See, for example, L. A. Metzler, "The Theory of International Trade," *Survey of Contemporary Economics* (Philadelphia, 1948), pp. 218–220.

changes in interest rates and in banking policy will operate to influence investment further in an equilibrating direction (these matters will be given more attention in Chapter 5).

Although it may be impossible to determine the multiplier statistically, and although the dangers of assuming constant marginal propensities must not be disregarded,[13] the multiplier may be a most helpful pedagogical device as it is utilized by Machlup and Metzler in illustrating tendencies to equilibrium in the balance of payments. The theoretical analysis usually runs in terms of fluctuating employment or output, price effects being assumed away. If it runs in money terms, price changes — essentially a by-product — may be supplementing the income effects and may be relegated to a subsidiary role in the analysis. The importance of output relative to price variations will be indicated by the relevant elasticities of supply and demand. As an obvious example, where wage cuts are accepted, equilibrium may be possible with a lesser increase in unemployment.

Statistically, the multiplier is most frequently applied to merchandise exports, but it should logically apply to the other payments on income or current account as well. Professor Haberler[14] in making this point quotes Clark to the effect that "a decrease in annual amounts payable overseas has exactly the same effect as an increase in export income, and should be included with it." Professor Haberler points out how this overstates the case in not taking account of differing propensities to consume, so that decreases in interest payments may not lead to an expansionary effect equivalent to a similar increase in exports. Indeed, it would be foolish to expect it. Further, the decline in interest payments — for example, from Canada to Britain — might also serve to reduce the Canadian export market and produce relatively long-run maladjustments. However, this difficulty of varying propensi-

[13] For example, James S. Duesenberry, *Income, Saving, and the Theory of Consumer Behavior* (Cambridge, Mass., 1949), reasons cogently that in the short-run saving depends on the relation of current income to past income, and is not in linear relation to current income. The long-run consumption function, on the other hand, is held to be a linear relationship. As Duesenberry points out, Professors Hansen and Samuelson have maintained for some time that there is a cyclical variation in the consumption functions. See especially pp. 76ff and 114–116.

[14] G. Haberler, *Prosperity and Depression* (Geneva, 1941), p. 463. He cites C. Clark, *The National Income of Australia* (London, 1938), p. 93.

ties does not apply solely to nonmerchandise as compared with merchandise items in the balance of payments. It also applies between different types of commodity exports. The propensities may also be so disturbing to our analysis as to vary cyclically or secularly. Some of these problems, with particular reference to the Canadian economy, will be discussed in Chapter 19. These difficulties are only handicapping if we desire to set determinate values on the propensities, and they do not eliminate the tendencies towards equilibrium with which we have been concerned.

There has been considerable discussion as to whether it is the export surplus or total exports to which the multiplier should be applied. It has been shown by Professor Robertson[15] that the various formulas may be reduced to one another by changing the multiplier whenever different multiplicands, e.g., export or export surplus, are employed. Mathematical identity does not mean, of course, that one formula is as convenient or as useful as the other. This question has been debated at some length by Haberler and Polak.[16] They conclude that, as in the long, drawn-out savings-investment controversy, there has been considerable confusion due to an inadequate distinction being made between the static, instantaneous relations and the dynamic, lagged, or serial relations. Agreement is reached that the dynamic analysis is preferable, and that for such analysis conditions seem likely to favor the use in the multiplicand of a change in the level of exports rather than of the export surplus.[17] The major difficulties in the way of analysis are pointed out as being a considerable instability of the marginal propensity to import, and the likelihood of autonomous changes in imports. This might be more exactly expressed if it were said that the major difficulties were to be found in the import-income function because of the likelihood of its shifting and because of the possibility of the marginal propensity to import changing other than as the result of a movement *along* a curvilinear function. Reasoning by way of analogy with the serial interpretation of the investment multiplier, ex-

[15] D. H. Robertson, "Mr. Clark and the Foreign Trade Multiplier," *Economic Journal*, June 1939, p. 354.

[16] G. Haberler and J. J. Polak, "The Foreign Trade Multiplier," *American Economic Review*, December 1947.

[17] See Haberler, *Prosperity and Depression*, p. 468, where an earlier defense of the use of the export surplus is to be found.

ports may be seen to be a selection more appropriate than the export surplus. The increase in income would be a multiple (the multiplier) of the increase in exports (analogous to investment), and the stimulus to an increase in income would continue until the induced increase in imports (analogous to savings) equalled the initial increase in exports. The export surplus, reasoning by analogy, would be no more appropriate in the multiplicand than the investment-savings differential.

Haberler and Polak also conclude that if there were a simultaneous increase in exports and in autonomous imports, nothing in general could be said; or, in other words, parallel upward shifts in imports and exports must be considered neutral by the multiplier analysis. There has been much controversy over this proposition. Harrod [18] has based his preference for the use of total exports in the multiplicand partly upon the fact that in the international propagation of prosperity and depression the rise and fall of exports taken as a whole are much more significant in the cumulative process than the export-import differential.

Let us first dispose of the case where the increases in imports are induced by changes in the level of income. The following argument in favor of Harrod's position can be adduced. In a cumulative upward process, imports may increase in anticipation of increased incomes that have derived in foreign trade multiplier fashion from autonomous export expansion. The time lag between the increase of exports and the induced increase of imports might thereby be reduced to zero, so that no export surplus would appear. Nonetheless, the causal sequence of the multiplier analysis would not be altered, in the sense that the increase of exports would still be the primary determinant of the increase of incomes and imports. In an extreme case there might occur a prior increase of imports in view of anticipated export and income increases, which would mean a reverse or negative lag for imports in the sequence. Haberler and Polak concur that the serial interpretation of the multiplier, using the export surplus, is inconvenient when there is a marginal propensity to import other than zero, and when induced imports ensue that alter the magnitude of the export surplus through the period of adjustment.

In the case where the changes in the level of imports are

---

[18] R. F. Harrod, *International Economics* (Cambridge, 1939), p. 144.

autonomous, the interpretation of Harrod given by Stolper[19] appears relevant. Stolper suggests that Harrod may have been thinking in terms of variations in the "average propensity to spend" on consumption plus investment, i.e., in terms of shifts in the consumption and investment schedules. If such changes, however, are not only independent of changes in the level of income but are also independent of changes in the level of imports or exports, equal changes in exports and imports do not provide us with an explanation for the variation in incomes. The explanation is the subject matter of business cycle theory and must be sought in the reasons for the autonomous shifts in the consumption and investment functions.[20] Stolper, however, argues that imports will not necessarily substitute for domestically produced goods but, because of complementary relations, may actually stimulate further domestic production of both consumption and investment goods.[21] This argument may then read that the increase in imports will induce increases in the consumption and investment functions; it is not to be confused with the situation where the country may be "unstable in isolation," the slope of the combined consumption plus investment functions being greater than unity, so that an increase of exports is overcompensated by an even greater increase in imports.[22] The Stolper case, like the overcompensation situation, has its special assumptions and indicates a possibility rather than a general case.[23] We are left with the conclusion drawn by Haberler and Polak that, in general, autonomous parallel changes in imports and exports must be regarded as being neutral in their effect

[19] W. Stolper, "Volume of Foreign Trade and the Level of Income," *Quarterly Journal of Economics,* February 1947, p. 309.

[20] I am using the terms consumption and investment functions in the sense that L. Klein, *The Keynesian Revolution* (New York, 1947), used the terms investment and consumption schedules. For one graphical example by Klein see page 115.

[21] Stopler, "Volume of Foreign Trade and the Level of Income," *Quarterly Journal of Economics,* February 1947, p. 293.

[22] L. Metzler, "The Transfer Problem Reconsidered," in American Economic Association, *Readings in the Theory of International Trade* (Philadelphia, 1949), especially pp. 193ff.

[23] Haberler and Polak, "The Foreign Trade Multiplier," *American Economic Review,* December 1947, pp. 904–906; and A. I. Bloomfield, "Induced Investment, Overcomplete International Adjustment and Chronic Dollar Shortage," *American Economic Review,* September 1949, p. 972n.

upon incomes,[24] although in special circumstances, it seems to me, there may be a strong case for the Stolper possibility.[25]

One final matter concerns the application of the multiplier analysis to situations where there was relatively full employment of the labor force. Such was the situation in Canada during the period 1900–1913. It might be argued that the multiplier mechanism, with its emphasis on income rather than on price effects, would in these circumstances be relatively inoperative. This view is not, in my opinion, correct. Professor Hansen,[26] for example, has maintained that income inflation and deflation in the industrialized countries took the form mainly of cycles of employment and unemployment, whereas, in the period prior to World War I in the primary producing countries, it took the form mainly of price inflation and deflation. It is true that price changes were generally greater in the newer regions, but there were also tremendous changes in real national incomes, as was clearly the case with Canada,[27] where, in my view, they were more important than the price changes, not only in relative size but in relative effectiveness.

Where we are dealing with a country whose population and national income is small relative to the world's population and income, there is a basis for a high elasticity of supply of commodities, labor, and capital to the country concerned. This tends to prevent large price increases, and immigration and capital imports facilitate substantial increases in output. Further, ex-

[24] A distinction should be made between the possible expansionary effects of autonomous parallel increases in imports and exports and the enlargement of national income attributable to an increase in tax-financed government expenditure. In the latter case, an increase in income may take place with no accompanying increase in private consumption and investment functions as a result of the government injecting into the income stream a part of private income that otherwise would not have been spent for consumption or for capital formation. In the case of the parallel autonomous increases of imports and exports, as was argued above, the expansion of incomes, if it took place, would be reflected in an upward shift of the private consumption and/or investment functions.

[25] For a good argument for the Stolper position relating to experience following World War II in which, however, the automatic equilibrating forces have been suppressed, see G. W. Stolper, "Notes on the Dollar Shortage," *American Economic Review*, June 1950, pp. 285–300.

[26] A. H. Hansen, *Monetary Theory and Fiscal Policy* (New York, 1949), p. 200.

[27] Chapter 8, "Early Growth."

perience has shown that output in the region of full employment is capable of further expansion in the relatively short run, even where we have a close approach to a closed economy, as in the case of the United States. Longer hours may be worked, non-workers may be drawn into the labor force, and shifts of labor and other resources to a higher-productivity occupation are likely to occur. The latter shift may be even more important in a less developed economy, and is sometimes referred to as a reduction in concealed unemployment, when the shift is one of labor from an exceedingly low-productivity occupation.

For these reasons I would assert that income changes and the foreign trade multiplier mechanism have a high degree of explanatory value even in the circumstances of full employment where price changes are more in evidence. This contention is strengthened where we are dealing with a region or country relatively accessible, but relatively small in comparison with the remainder of the world economy. I would therefore maintain that economic adjustments and reallocation of resources both between and within countries were more dependent on income effects in circumstances of full employment than has been generally recognized. The "classical" analysis does not come into its own with conditions of full employment.

V

Capital Formation and the Credit Supply

The multiplier theory discussed in the foregoing section has generally included only imports and consumption expenditures in the successive spending rounds. There is good reason for treating investment (in the sense of capital formation) separately. The behavior of investment activity is sufficiently distinctive to warrant this. The development of a more adequate theory of investment is probably the prime need of improved business cycle analysis. In the following section we are on even shakier ground than in the treatment of income-consumption and income-import relations.

FLUCTUATIONS IN INVESTMENT

At the outset we must distinguish between autonomous and induced investment. It is the latter to which most attention will be directed in the discussion to follow. By induced investment I mean changes in investment which are related directly to changes in income or which have an indirect relation to income through the intermediation of variables that are related to both income and investment.[1] Autonomous investment is here defined as that investment which is not a function of past, current, or future income. It may be explained (e.g., in Schumpeterian cycle theory, where it is attributed to innovations) or it may be unexplained.

[1] Duesenberry, *Income, Saving, and the Theory of Consumer Behavior,* pp. 73–75.

Traditionally the acceleration principle has been the most important concept utilized in attempting to account for induced investment. The elementary statement of the acceleration principle or, as it is sometimes called, the theory of derived demand, is that when current demand for consumer goods expands, a multiple expansion of investment in plant and equipment and in housing will result.[2] The multiple expansion is due to the fact that an increase in the services from durable goods requires an increment to the stock of the durable goods in addition to the normal replacement of the existing stock. The effect is short run as far as investment net of replacement is concerned, for once the stock of durable goods has been adjusted upward to the new, higher level of demand, only continued replacement will be necessary. The acceleration principle is essentially a dynamic one, in which the increase of investment is a function of the rate of change of consumption through time.[3]

For a number of reasons the operation of the acceleration principle is not dependable.[4] (1) Cyclical expansions begin from a position of unused capacity, when the ratio of output to capital is abnormally high. This ratio will probably decline as output expands and excess capacity is drawn on in lieu of adding to plant and equipment in order to satisfy the increased demand, as the acceleration principle assumes. The operation of the generally employed acceleration principle requires that the capital-to-output ratio remains fixed. (2) The capital-output ratio may alter significantly for another reason. The addition of more efficient plant and equipment will result in a decline. This would

[2] The acceleration principle may also be shown to apply to investment in inventories. For an excellent survey of the literature on the acceleration principle see Haberler, *Prosperity and Depression*, pp. 85–105.

[3] Not only may investment expand with a view to meeting expanded consumption; it may also increase in order to make an expansion in the production of capital goods possible. Professor W. Fellner has used the phrase "investment for further investment" in *Monetary Policies and Full Employment* (Berkeley and Los Angeles, 1946), p. 24, to describe capital formation in the capital goods' industries. Professor R. A. Gordon, *The Dynamics of Economic Activity* (selected chapters, mimeographed, Berkeley, 1948), chap. 6, pp. 57–58, concludes that it is best to relate the induced investment to changes in both consumption and investment or changes in total incomes, rather than relating the induced investment to consumption alone.

[4] Hansen, *Fiscal Policy and Business Cycles*, pp. 282–284; and Gordon, *The Dynamics of Economic Activity*, chap. vi, pp. 54–62.

reduce the requirements for an expansion of investment. (3) A further objection to the acceleration principle as stated lies in the fact that the increases in plant capacity and additions to inventory which are undertaken are dependent more on anticipations than on changes in current incomes. This provides one explanation for the fact that net investment does not appear to decline with a decline in the rate of increase of current consumption or income, as the acceleration principle would imply — rather both tend to decline together.

An adequate theory of investment requires more knowledge of the determination of entrepreneurial anticipations and the influence of the state of certainty or uncertainty with respect to these expectations than we possess at present.[5] There are, however, certain plausible hypotheses which have been posited that provide us with theories of induced investment alternative or supplementary to the acceleration principle. Among these let me mention several that appear to be of considerable importance. These hypotheses all recognize that the primary motivation for undertaking investment activity is the expectation of profits, and therefore give prime consideration to the influences working upon profit anticipations. Among the possible influences upon profit expectations, Tinbergen considers the current and recent past levels of total profits, the price of capital goods, and the rate of interest. Using the multiple correlation technique, he concludes that the predominant influence is the level of profits which affects the rate of investment activity with an average six-month lag.[6] Kalecki[7] expresses the change in investment as a function of the change in profits and of the level of investment of a previous period. Since Kalecki holds the level of investment to be a primary determinant of income with a lag, it would follow that there would be a close relation between changes in current incomes and current rates of investment, since the two sets of changes are held to be induced by past levels of investment. Yet

[5] For example, A. G. Hart, "Keynes' Analysis of Expectations and Uncertainty," in *The New Economics*, ed. S. Harris, pp. 415–424.

[6] J. Tinbergen, *Statistical Testing of Business Cycle Theories* (Geneva, 1939), I, 56–57; and also his *Dynamics of Business Cycles*, trans. and modified by J. J. Polak (Chicago, 1950), pp. 166–172.

[7] M. Kalecki, *Essays in the Theory of Economic Fluctuations* (London, 1939), chap. vi.

another thesis is maintained by Angell,[8] namely, that investment
is functionally related through anticipations to the changes in
income three to six months previous. Fellner[9] argues in favor of
yet another relationship, in which profit expectations are held to
be influenced by the investment-income ratio, since uncertainty
might be expected to increase as this ratio increased. We are
obviously not treading on too firm ground in this field of analysis,
but it seems reasonable to conclude that profit expectations are
more influential on the rate of investment than the rate of interest, and that expectations to a large extent are likely to be based
on extrapolations of current or recent levels or changes in levels
of profits, investment, and/or incomes. Different performances
from country to country, from cycle to cycle, and from one phase
of the cycle to another may, however, markedly limit the possibility of generalization.

At this point I wish to discuss briefly the relation of capital
imports from abroad to the level of capital formation and the
level of incomes. This discussion not only is connected with the
matters related to fluctuations in domestic investment dealt with
in this chapter, but also bears upon the analysis of the foreign
trade multiplier in the preceding chapter. Two extreme cases
might be distinguished at the outset.

In the first case, capital imports are assumed to be the initiating factor in the expansion.[10] Let it further be assumed at the
outset of the examination of this case that the rate of capital
formation is equivalent to the rate of borrowing from abroad.
Unless the marginal propensity to consume is unity or greater,
there will be positive domestic savings induced that will operate
as partial offsets to the foreign financed capital formation. In
addition, of course, the induced import surplus would be providing the other portion of the total offset.[11] The borrowing country
would then be acquiring gold or passively providing net short-
term capital exports. It is probable, however, that the expansion

[8] J. W. Angell, *Investment and Business Cycles* (New York, 1941), pp.
71–72, 79.
[9] Fellner, *Monetary Policies and Full Employment*, p. 46.
[10] Capital imports, investment, incomes, etc., are all thought of in the
succeeding analysis as increases over an initially prevailing level.
[11] See in Machlup, *International Trade and the National Income Multiplier*, pp. 29, 37, the situations with and without induced savings.

of investment and incomes will serve to stimulate the expansion
of still further investment activity, financed from domestic rather
than from foreign sources. This will induce further import increases and will diminish the rate of acquisition of foreign exchange reserves. On the assumption of a marginal propensity to
consume of about three fourths and a marginal propensity to
import of about one fourth, it has been estimated that a level of
investment of about one and one half to two times the level of
capital inflow could be maintained without experiencing balance
of payments disequilibrium.[12] If this "expansion ratio" should be
exceeded due to excessively high marginal propensities to consume and invest, the effect of capital imports would be to produce a deteriorating balance of payments.

In the second extreme case, domestically financed investment
is assumed to initiate the expansion. An import surplus will be
induced by the expansion of investment and incomes. There
would be an added attraction for capital to flow from abroad in
response to improved profit expectations associated with the
expansion. The awareness of interest rate differentials and of
better prospects for profits might find its way abroad only with
a lag. Borrowers confronted by a shortage of domestic investable
funds might take the initiative in stimulating the interest of
foreign lenders. If a sufficiency of foreign funds were not induced,
the drain on foreign exchange reserves would tend to inhibit the
expansion, the depressive influence being particularly strong for
a gold standard country. The capital imports could here be regarded as playing an essential permissive role.

The usual circumstances would be a compound of these two
extreme cases. It will be argued (in Chapter 7) that mutual
determination rather than unidirectional causation is a typical
relationship, and further that alterations in the current and capital
accounts are frequently best depicted as the result of common
influences. At this stage of the discussion, however, it is important only to note that capital imports may at times be a factor,

---

[12] J. J. Polak, "Balance of Payments Problems of Countries Reconstructing
With the Help of Foreign Loans," *Quarterly Journal of Economics,* February
1943, pp. 214–215. It is interesting to observe that for Canada, 1900–1913,
the ratio of investment to the net capital balance averaged 1.83. In the
early years of the period the ratio was 3 to 4, rather high in the light of
Polak's analysis, so it appears to me. See Table 10.

although not necessarily the sole factor or the dominant one, inducing or permitting increases in capital formation. For an open economy such as the Canadian one it is a factor that may not be left unaccounted for in a discussion of the fluctuations in investment.

THE SUPPLY OF CREDIT

Domestic deposits are likely to expand immediately with the primary shift of purchasing power to the receiving country.[13] The banks simultaneously acquire an equivalent amount of short-term assets abroad which they may normally exchange for gold.[14] This acquisition will permit multiple credit expansion to take place. The secondary shifts of purchasing power in the receiving country plus added investment activity will promote increased credit demands partially or wholly offsetting to the augmented supply of credit. (In the remitting country, the tendency to parallel contractions in the demand and supply of credit is likely to be much less strong.) Multiplier analysis frequently assumes infinite elasticity of bank credit at the going rate of interest, and with a shift in purchasing power from abroad the increasing liquidity will in fact tend to produce this elasticity.

The shifts in purchasing power will tend further to affect equilibrating changes in interest rates. Since each international transaction "alters the supply of means of payment and banking reserves, it involves a relative upward pressure on interest rates in the remitting and/or a relative downward pressure in the receiving country. Such pressure becomes fully reciprocal . . . only when short-term credits cease to ease the transfer and payments are effected by gold flows."[15] This follows if the banks of the respective countries observe the rules of the gold standard game. Thus where one country has developed an export surplus, increasing liquidity will result and, with the downward pressure

[13] In a clearing country as distinct from a peripheral type of country like Canada, total deposits may remain unchanged, with the increase of domestically owned deposits being offset by a decline of liabilities to foreigners rather than by an increase of short-term assets abroad.

[14] Convertibility problems have, of course, become prevalent even in "peacetime" in recent years.

[15] Kahn, *Great Britain in the World Economy*, p. 15.

on interest rates, foreign securities will become relatively more attractive than domestic securities. Here we have a tendency for an equilibrating flow of investment. Nurkse[16] too readily minimizes the possibility of the rate of interest having an effect upon international investment, citing Tinbergen[17] in support of his position. But Tinbergen was considering the influence of the rate of interest (as one among many factors) on the rate of investment in the United States from 1919 to 1932. Even if we accept his finding by multiple correlation analysis that the rate of interest was not important with regard to United States domestic investment in the period studied, we need not accept the thesis that shifts of investable funds internationally will be unaffected by interest rate differentials from one country to another. Certainly, however, such factors as alterations in relative marginal efficiencies of capital and capital appreciation are likely to overshadow the influence of these differentials.

RELATIVE PRICE CHANGES

Induced by the purchasing power shifts and definitely subsidiary to them[18] are the series of price and cost changes of the Mill-Taussig analysis which will tend to implement the primary and secondary shifts of demand where these are inadequate of themselves to secure equilibrium.[19] For example, where the bulk of a foreign loan is spent on domestically produced and consumed commodities, the tendency for their prices to increase will be great, and factors of production will tend to be diverted from exports while imports are encouraged due to their relatively low

[16] Nurkse, writing in League of Nations, *International Currency Experience* (Princeton, 1944), p. 102.

[17] J. Tinbergen, *Statistical Testing of Business Cycle Theory* (Geneva, 1939), pp. 45–49, 128.

[18] For example, League of Nations, *International Currency Experience*, p. 104, where Nurkse refers to the price changes as "merely a by-product of the increase in activity." Also see Harrod, *International Economics*, p. 140.

[19] Some income effects will be induced by the changes in prices, where, for example, a fall in price frees incomes for additional expenditures. Such induced income changes are unlikely to be as significant as those alterations in income that are dealt with in foreign trade multiplier analysis. For a detailed analysis see D. B. Marsh, *World Trade and Investment* (New York, 1951), pp. 211–216.

prices.[20] In the instance where the increase of demand on the part of the borrowing country for the lending countries' exports is very great, and where the terms of trade[21] shift against the borrowing country, the price effects may work to oppose too great a transfer.[22] The price changes must be accounted for in the light of the shifts in demand which take place and in the light of the relevant demand and supply elasticities. Underemployment of the factors of production, and the importance of the two countries' demand and supply relative to total world markets for their exports and imports, are important considerations. Where the elasticity of demand (with respect to loan proceeds and income) of the borrowing country for the lending country's exports is high, the tendency for price changes is reduced. Where the loan proceeds and income elasticity of demand for domestically produced and consumed commodities is high in the borrowing country, but the price elasticity of their supply is low, large price increases will tend to occur.[23] Obviously, the possibilities for variation are numerous and complex, and they will vary not only with countries and commodities concerned, but with the secularly and cyclically shifting demand and supply situations.[24]

[20] The Taussig modification of the "classical" analysis directs attention to sectional prices involving the relationship of prices of internationally traded and domestic commodities.

[21] See Chapter 15 for a discussion of the terms of trade in which the view is expressed that their role has been much exaggerated by many of the "classical" writers.

[22] The effect of the price changes in determining values is likely to be much more important than their effect in inducing changes in the flow of import and export quantities as the classical tradition would emphasize (see Chang, *Cyclical Movements in the Balance of Payments*, p. 12). In the instance referred to in the text the shift of the terms of trade against the borrowing country would actually assist the transfer through its effect in causing import values to rise more than export values, thus contributing to the increase in the current deficit.

[23] The time element is of course very important here. Much of the discussions of balance-of-payments adjustment pertains to relatively short time periods for which computed elasticities, particularly of supply, would be low because the full demand and supply reactions were not complete. It is partly because of the sluggishness of such reactions that income effects rather than price effects assume the major role in balance of payments equilibration.

[24] For a discussion having a particular application to the Canadian situation, see Chapters 13 and 16.

V I

Gold Flows and the Exchange Rates

Gold flows are alternatives to the flows of short-term capital analyzed in Chapter 2. Gold is a universally acceptable type of international money, while foreign reserves in the form of bank deposits held abroad are not. For this reason, and in line with tradition, usually reinforced by legal regulations, banks may tend to react more strongly to gold flows than to net changes in external bank assets. Thus the secondary shifts in demand due to bank credit expansion and contraction are likely to be greater in the case of gold flows. In respect to the primary shifts in purchasing power, the effects in the case of gold flows are two sided. Further, in the case of flows of short-term credits, the purchasing power shifts may be wholly or partially offset in the remitting country by what is tantamount to the *ad hoc* creation of an export in the form of an IOU. While gold flows may be neutralized, gold production is not as facile a process as credit creation.

THE GOLD STANDARD

The significance given to the gold flows in classical theory has been called into question too frequently for elaborate criticism to be necessary here. In the pre-World War I era, the heyday of the gold standard system, its successful functioning has been attributed to the "attainment by London of a central clearing position in the world's financial system, and to the manner in which the responsibilities of that position were carried out." [1] The "high degree of centralization of the world's credit system in London combined with the strong international credit system of Great Britain made the prewar gold standard essentially a sterling exchange system which could not have been restored after the war." [2] Beach[3] arrives at the conclusion that during the years 1881–1913 gold flows to and from the United States and Great Britain are not to be explained on the basis of long-term capital movements, nor on the basis of relative variations in national incomes or price structures, but that differences in short-term interest rates due to cyclical and seasonal monetary stringency are the causal factor. This is how he explains the British imports of gold in prosperity and the exports in depression during the period. Brown[4] holds that even prior to 1914 gold played a minor role as an equilibrating factor in international trade, and instead he stresses its role as a confidence-inspiring factor and as a factor limiting a world-wide overexpansion of bank credit. It does, however, seem safe to say that it was relatively more important than in the interwar period in effecting the primary shifts of purchasing power, although as evidenced by Viner's Canadian study the short-term credits played a significant role in some important capital movements which is not accounted for in the "classical" theory. The volatile shifts of autonomous short-term capital which so attracted attention in the interwar period were, however, notably absent prior to 1914. Sterling balances had been stable and could be characterized as "the world's average balances in the world's active commercial bank." [5] Further, the English banking system was probably more responsive to gold flows, so that the secondary shifts in purchasing power based upon credit expansion and contraction due to the gold movements may have come closer in the prewar than in the interwar

[1] W. A. Brown, *The International Gold Standard Reinterpreted* (New York, 1940), I, x.

[2] Brown, I, xiii.

[3] W. E. Beach, *British International Gold Movements and Banking Policy, 1881–1913* (Cambridge, 1935), pp. 172ff.

[4] *The International Gold Standard Reinterpreted*, II, 775.

[5] Brown, *International Gold Standard Reinterpreted*, II, 782. But see Schumpeter, *Business Cycles*, II, 606, where he notes that any international gold movement patterns of this period were obscured by the speculative movements of short-term capital between central banks.

period to assuming in fact the importance assigned to them in the Mill-Taussig theory.

However, much more significant than these banking and monetary factors in explaining the pre-World War I international balance are the real factors. The most important is the complementary relationship between Britain and the agricultural, raw-material-producing sector of the world economy. Britain was a great importer of foodstuffs and raw materials and a great exporter of manufactured articles.[6] The situation was such as to facilitate the profitable employment of British capital abroad, the real transfer by means of increased British exports, particularly of capital equipment, and the subsequent repayment by means of increased British imports of agricultural products and raw materials, the latter being a natural consequence of the improved supply conditions attributable to the British investments abroad and to the increasing demands of the British market which had initially rendered the investments profitable. This highly integrated and centralized world economy had been disrupted by the end of World War I and indeed the seeds of its disintegration — for example, in the growing economic strength of the United States and Germany and the industrialization of backward areas — were already in evidence in the prewar period.

Nurkse has demonstrated that during the interwar period the orthodox rules of the game for central banking were more often broken than observed.[7] In a period from 1922 to 1938 he has shown that, for 26 countries, domestic assets of central banks moved far more often in the opposite than in the same direction as their international assets of gold and foreign exchange. This was true for both the United Kingdom and the United States as well as for other countries. There was a strong tendency towards automatic (i.e., undesigned) neutralization since an inflow of gold, for instance, would increase commercial bank reserves and

[6] Brown, II, 778. But O. Morgenstern, "The International Spread of Business Cycles," *Journal of Political Economy*, August 1943, p. 303, expresses less interest for his purposes in these complementary relations than in the case of similar countries. "If complementarity exists and the size of the two economies is as widely different as that of Great Britain and Denmark then this case becomes more akin to a regional relationship, with which we are not concerned here."

[7] In League of Nations, *International Currency Experience*, pp. 68–71.

would thus permit the repayment of indebtedness to the central bank. There was, in addition, a frequently pursued policy of designed neutralization on the part of the central banks. At the commerical banking level of the credit structure, still further neutralization was frequent as bank deposits failed to respond to changes in the level of bank reserves. It must be concluded that balance-of-payments adjustment was not generally dependent upon the changes in credit and the money supply called for in the "classical" doctrine since these were so frequently disequilibrating in their effect.[8] Equilibration must have been generally dependent upon income effects which were frequently counterbalancing disequilibrating effects stemming from the change in the money supply.

TRIFFIN'S ANALYSIS

Triffin, in a recent analysis of the pre-1914 British positions, has, I believe, exaggerated the significance of the monetary factors. He strongly emphasizes the role of the short-term capital movements already mentioned, into Britain with the increased discount of the prosperity peaks, and out of Britain with the lower discount rates of a depression and a new recovery. Contrary to "classical" theory, Triffin found the increased discount rates to be associated with improved terms of trade.

To a very large extent, increases in the London discount rates brought about a readjustment in the British balances of payments, not through their effects on the British economy, but through their effects on the outside world and especially on the agricultural and raw material countries. . . .

This shift in international capital movements contributed powerfully to a rapid restoration of equilibrium in the exchange market. However, it tended to relieve rather than accentuate domestic deflationary pressures on the economy, and to that extent to delay or prevent the basic readjustment of fundamental price and cost disparities contemplated by gold standard theorists. It constituted, in a sense, the equivalent of the compensatory monetary policies so strongly condemned by many gold standard theorists. . . .

The effect of such fluctuations in capital movements was to smooth down cyclical monetary and credit fluctuations in the creditor countries, but to accentuate them in the debtor countries. . . .

This improvement in the British terms of trade in periods of rising

[8] Nurkse in *International Currency Experience,* pp. 98–105.

discount rates should not be surprising, in view of the special position of Britain as a financial center for world trade. On purely a priori grounds, it would appear at least as probable as the opposite pattern contemplated by the classicists. What was really discussed by them was the case of price disparities between one country and a large number of other countries equal to the first in importance. Under that assumption, deflation by the first country would force down domestic prices and costs without affecting to any significant extent the level of prices in the rest of the world. . . .

The failure of British discount policy to effect the type of readjustment contemplated in classical theory . . . was due primarily to the *international* character of the London discount market, whose expansion and contraction affected foreign prices as much as or more than British prices. It is also explainable by the fact that producers of agricultural and raw materials are more vulnerable to cyclical and credit fluctuations than is the British economy.[9]

There are several points of criticism which should be directed against the Triffin analysis:

(1) The increase in the discount rate at the height of prosperity in Britain has been attributed primarily to the British need for gold for domestic circulation. It is dubious whether the increased attraction for short-term capital and gold exerted as much pressure on the agricultural raw material exporting countries as Triffin supposes. Other countries, more advanced financially, may well have supplied most of the increased British gold requirements without much restrictive influence spreading to other countries. This is, however, a matter of conjecture and is not the primary criticism to be made against the Triffin analysis.

(2) The basic criticism relates to Triffin's neglect of the nonmonetary factors in the cyclical fluctuations, which he mentions in the last sentence I have quoted from him. The credit fluctuations were only one aspect, probably a minor one, of nineteenth century development, which A. E. Kahn describes as follows:

The development of the world's debtor countries, by means of international and domestic capital, probably fluctuated between greater extremes than did domestic investment in an older country like Great Britain. This was partly because the more exotic foreign ventures were naturally subject to greater vagaries of public psychology, within both debtor and creditor countries. Exuberant optimism and overexpansion and bankruptcy and excessive pessimism followed each other with monotonous regularity. Moreover, the real profitableness of investment

[9] Triffin, *International Monetary Policies,* pp. 59–63.

varied greatly as new geographical areas were opened and settled, new natural resources discovered and exploited, new means of transportation invented and applied, and as, after each initial spurt, short-run diminishing returns inevitably set in. Such fluctuating investment brought wide, continually recurring fluctuations in relative levels of buying power in different regions of the world. This meant, in turn, continual changes in reciprocal trade balances along lines determined by world conditions of supply and demand, which in themselves were unstable.[10]

The greater impact of the cycle upon the less developed areas is surely not so much associated with the discount rate fluctuations as Triffin would have us believe. Railway building, the settlement of vast new areas, and other innovations were certainly not to be associated with monotonically increasing time series.

(3) The decreased discount rate of the depression years was symptomatic of a return to less risky domestic investment in Britain after the fling at foreign investments and their greater profit expectations (see Chapter 8). Note that the reduced discount rate was not sufficient of itself to start the flow of capital exports once again. Profit expectations associated with investment abroad first had to improve. That Britain was able to resort to domestic investment when foreign investment declined certainly reduced the cyclical impact upon her economy. But there was also much benefit to be gained thereby on the part of the agricultural raw-material countries, the economies of which were complementary with that of Britain's. While British incomes were better maintained, as a result, so were British imports.

Imports grew secularly at a much steadier rate than did exports, with the rise of British population, industry, and real incomes and a decline in that proportion of needed food and raw materials which her own productive factors could supply. In times of diminished lending (e.g., 1890–99), this relieved debtor countries of deflationary pressure and hence diminished their need absolutely to cut their purchases from Britain. Thus, Britain suffered no absolute declines in the volume of her exports over any appreciable length of time (i.e., between ten-year cyclical peaks). With the continuous secular expansion of trade, adjustments to these changing capital flows were relatively easy for the British creditor, as well as for the foreign debtor.[11]

[10] Kahn, *Great Britain in the World Economy*, pp. 128–129.
[11] Kahn, *Great Britain in the World Economy*, p. 130. Also see A. H. Hansen, *Fiscal Policy and Business Cycles* (New York, 1941), pp. 347–348.

Canada of course figured in this picture. Reference to Chart I will indicate how well Canadian exports tended to be maintained, even in the slumps, and how the wide fluctuations in Canadian trade occurred in imports.

What I think should be stressed is that the overwhelmingly important reasons for the balance in pre-World War I trading positions are to be found in relationships more basic and fundamental than the financial and monetary arrangements of the gold standard.

EXCHANGE RATE FLUCTUATIONS

Minor fluctuations of the exchanges may occur within the gold points, but the range is normally inadequate toward having any significant equilibrating effects. An exception occurs with regard to short-term funds, when the fluctuations, by increasing the risk of loss, may be sufficient to nullify the inducements for short-term funds to flow in response to international interest rate differentials. But in general only when a country's gold and foreign balances are exhausted, or when it leaves the gold standard and allows its exchanges to fluctuate, will the range of fluctuation be significant in its influence upon the country's balance of payments.

The exchange rate fluctuations tend to produce shifts in the price levels of international goods, and, with the usual reservations which must be made for the disequilibrating influence of expectations of further shifts, the fluctuations tend to be adjusting in their effects.

Exchange variations operate directly on the prices of exports and imports in a manner unlike that of the demand shifts via gold and short-term capital moves, and the equilibrating action is not dependent on a shift of purchasing power. Thus, for example, an appreciation of the exchanges consequent upon capital imports may be reflected almost immediately in an absolute decline in the prices of internationally traded goods, thus assisting the development of an import surplus. Under a fixed exchange system the transfer of purchasing power, if not sufficient in the primary stage to accomplish the transfer, would have tended to a general increase in prices. An absolute decline in export and import prices, would be much less probable than in the case of exchange appreciation, although we would expect export and import price increases to be relatively less than the price increases of commodities produced domestically for home consumption. Variable exchanges do not rule out the purchasing power shifts of short-term funds, although gold movements may be prohibited, and these shifts are likely to play a very significant part in the adjustment. Paradoxical results would follow if the transfers of short-term funds are excluded by assumption. Professor Haberler[12] reasons that the capital importing country would be depressed and the capital exporting country would undergo a price inflation under such circumstances. Assuming that the two countries' relative money supplies are unchanged, and assuming that there is no change in the velocity of money, commodities would increase relative to expenditures in the capital-importing country, while commodities available in the capital-exporting country would decrease relative to domestic expenditures.

The above discussion of the mechanism of international adjustment has excluded the consideration of certain short-run tendencies.[13] There are some very short-run factors that are equilibrating when there is the expectation of a certain continuing norm in the exchange rate, but that become disequilibrating if there arises the expectation of a continuous unidirectional movement of the exchanges. Assuming an exchange depreciation which is expected to be temporary, these factors include the postponing of debt repayment, the decline of banks' foreign balances, the postponing of payments by branch plants to the parent concerns, the speculative purchase of commodities, and the trading in domestic stocks and bonds with sales to foreigners being encouraged by an exchange discount they regard as temporary. Short-term interest rate increases may attract an equilibrating flow of funds if they

[12] Haberler, *Prosperity and Depression*, p. 447.

[13] Indeed I have no more than touched on some of the complex theoretical considerations relevant to the problem of exchange rate fluctuations. For a more elaborate discussion see the articles by F. Machlup and J. Robinson reprinted in the American Economic Association, *Readings in the Theory of International Trade* (Philadelphia, 1949); G. Haberler, "The Market for Foreign Exchange and the Stability of the Balance of Payments," *Kyklos*, vol. III (1949), fasc. III; P. T. Ellsworth, "Some Aspects of Exchange Stability," *The Review of Economics and Statistics*, February 1950; D. B. Marsh, *World Trade and Investment*, pp. 213–216.

are not regarded as a sign of further weakening of the exchanges, but it is important to observe that this is not a continuing flow. A given increase in the short-term interest rate will attract a certain volume of funds, and *ceteris paribus* total short-term funds will remain at the new level until international interest rate differentials are again altered.

VII

The Business Cycle and Economic Growth

I have frequently pointed out that both the theorists supporting the Mill-Taussig analysis and those stressing the purchasing power shift approach have too often neglected cyclical and secular change. In so doing they have exaggerated the explanatory value of an overly abstract theory.

Cyclical and secular changes have been attributed by Professor Schumpeter[1] to innovations, i.e., changes in the production function. Entrepreneurial horizons are expanded, profit expectations increase, and there are new investment opportunities associated with an increased demand for capital and the other factors of production. Alterations in demand functions, which result chiefly from these production function changes but which are external changes from the viewpoint of a particular industry or country, would be associated with these shifts in the production function. Such shifts appear to have been of very considerable importance for Canada in the period studied by Viner, as subsequent investigation will disclose. Both the "classical" theory and the purchasing power shift approach suffer from neglect of this innovational change. If we disagree with Schumpeter in considering cyclical as distinct from innovational change, then we may also say that both these theories suffer from too little consideration of cyclical change as well.[2]

---

[1] J. Schumpeter, *Business Cycles* (New York, 1939), I, 87ff.
[2] See Chapter 5 for a discussion of fluctuations in investment, relatively the most variable cyclical component of national income.

To the extent that these dynamic changes, whether of a cyclical or secular nature, lead to the simultaneous increases of the demand for investable funds in the borrowing country, to an increase in the supply of investable funds from the lending country, to an increase in the demand for the lending country's exports in the borrowing country, and an increase in supply is available in the lending country of the commodities and services the importing country requires, there is a happy coincidence that relieves the stress of the transfer and that may result in the equilibrating tendencies being called into play to a relatively small extent only at the margin. This is the happy coincidence that prevailed in the heyday of British lending. The demand and supply of funds and the need for imports were natural concomitants of profitable opportunities for investment. That the United States played a part in the 1900–1913 Canadian capital transfer led to questions of multilateral adjustments, but that the imports derived from a different source than the loans did not detract from the significance of profitable innovations both as a motive power and as an equalizer in the transfer.

These equilibrating tendencies have been properly stressed by Professor Williams.[3] He pointed out that the economists' foreign trade assumptions ignored the organic elements of the problem, that there was much internal immobility of the factors of production, and also much external mobility as evidenced by "the enormous and increasing drift of capital and labor over the world's surface." [4]

The same profits motivation that moves goods tends to move factors of production, and . . . foreign trade tends to produce an extension of productive factors over the expanding market area. It is true that this applies with special force to the development phase of interna-

[3] J. H. Williams, "The Theory of International Trade Reconsidered," *Economic Journal*, June 1929. Reprinted in J. H. Williams, *Postwar Monetary Plans and Other Essays* (New York, 1947), and in American Economic Association, *Readings in the Theory of International Trade* (Philadelphia, 1949). In this essay, incidentally, Professor Williams expressed the view, unusual at that time, that the facts presented in Viner's *Canada's Balance* seemed to him "less corroborative than the author feels them to be" of "the classical explanations of the trade adjustment mechanism." See "The Theory of International Trade Reconsidered," note 2. Professor Williams did not expand upon this statement.
[4] Williams, p. 209.

tional trade, and particularly to trade between unequally developed areas: but how much of foreign trade, first and last, escapes from these limitations? [5]

Williams' conclusion is

that the relation of international trade to the development of new resources and productive forces is a more significant part of the explanation of the present status of nations, of incomes, prices, wellbeing, than is the cross-section value analysis of the classical economists, with its assumption of given quanta of productive factors, already existent and employed.[6]

"In the older literature there are to be found only scattered and incidental references to the repercussions on the international mechanism of cyclical fluctuations in business activity." [7] The traditional treatment of capital movements was, as in the Mill-Taussig sequence, that of a single factor disturbing pre-existing equilibrium. Not only the classical Mill-Taussig model but also the "modern" Ohlin-Iverson model dealt with cases where autonomous capital flows disturbed internal and external equilibria of prices or incomes.

But in the real world capital movements, especially of the "normal" long-term variety, may commonly be the *result* of internally generated fluctuations in business activity in capital-exporting and/or capital-importing countries and, more particularly, of different patterns of business fluctuations in the two sets of countries.[8]

The common influence which the business cycle has on both capital and current items in the balance of payments provides us with what we may term a "common cause" theory of international equilibration. In this theory both changes on current and capital account may be regarded as induced by internally or externally generated business fluctuations.

Viner, writing for publication in 1937, held that it was too early "to incorporate cycle theory into the theory of international trade, or . . . to apply international trade theory to cycle theory." [9] Keynesian economics prepared the way to a fruitful

[5] Williams, p. 208.
[6] Williams, p. 184.
[7] Viner, *Studies . . . International Trade*, p. 432.
[8] Bloomfield, *Capital Imports and . . . Payments*, p. 264. Also see Kahn, Great Britain in the World Economy, pp. 7–8.
[9] Viner, *Studies . . . International Trade*, p. 432.

marriage of the two subjects,[10] but courtship may certainly be observed before the advent or marked influence of the "new economics." [11]

I have shown that the foreign trade multiplier explains how a change in the level of exports affects the level of incomes and, through the change in incomes, the level of imports. The relationship applies to any increase in the level of effective demand, although the increase in demand may not be generated by an increase in exports. The multiplier mechanism not only accounts for equilibration in the balance of payments, but at the same time accounts for the international propagation of cyclical fluctuations in the level of purchasing power.[12] A cyclical upswing in one country is associated with a higher level of incomes and imports, and the resultant increase in other countries' exports brings about multiplied expansion of their national incomes. The multiplied expansion is the substance of the foreign trade multiplier. The leakage of purchasing power out of the domestic income stream and into imports inhibits the growth of domestic income, while it contributes to the upswing of foreign incomes. The purchase of securities, i.e., capital flows, may serve like purchases on current account to transmit the fluctuations, and likewise may be induced by income changes. This is the basic explanation for the synchronization of business fluctuations between different countries.

The multiplier mechanism, with its stress on the influence of changes in the level of effective demand, is an important element in the "common-cause" explanation of balance-of-payments adjustment. It is, however, not necessarily identical with the common influence affecting the capital and current accounts referred to by Williams, namely, profits motivation. Knapp has criticized supposed empirical verifications of theories that emphasize either relative price changes or relative income changes. Writing in a fashion similar to Williams, he describes the most common cases of capital movements as follows:

Both borrowings and increased imports were but different aspects of a complex underlying situation giving rise to them *both:* namely, the

[10] Nurkse, in *The New Economics*, p. 264.

[11] See Viner, *Studies . . . International Trade*, pp. 435–436.

[12] Nurkse, in *The New Economics*, pp. 260–272; and Nurkse, *International Currency Experience*, pp. 104–105; 199–202.

conditions that made railway-building profitable, the need to import investment-goods and other manufactures from abroad into countries not yet industrialised, and the lack of a capital-market for a long-term development in such places. It is important to emphasize that these underlying conditions satisfactorily and sufficiently explain the *whole modus operandi* of capital importations in such cases, and it is quite redundant to search for special mechanisms of transfer which seem necessary when a sum of money needs to be remitted from one country to another and all other things are assumed equal. If some of the *criteria* postulated by such special theories of transfer (relative price or income movements, for example), are, nevertheless, found by chance to have held in such cases, that cannot be construed to serve as verification of those theories themselves.[13]

In my view, Knapp's version of the common-cause theory does succeed in demonstrating that the margin for which the conventionally viewed equilibrating mechanism is needed *may* be relatively small, but it does not succeed in demonstrating that the multiplier and the various other types of equilibration dealt with in the foregoing pages are irrelevant, even in the supposedly usual case dealt with by Knapp. They are indeed likely to be most important, especially the relative income changes with which Machlup deals, preferably with induced investment changes introduced into the analysis.[14] It would be strange indeed for the economist to minimize the margin in equilibrium analysis.

Nor does Knapp's common cause approach essentially exclude the possibility of the other mechanisms dealt with in preceding sections being significant other than marginally. What it really appears to stress is simultaneity inherent in the interrelated nature of the adjustment process. In such a process there is the difficulty of assigning to any one factor the role of the initiating variable. There are not likely to be the lags assumed in the process analysis of the multiplier income propagation mechanism.[15] Recognition of the role played by expectations and variable time

[13] J. Knapp, "The Theory of International Capital Movements and its Verifications," *The Review of Economic Studies,* Summer 1943, p. 119.

[14] Nurkse, in *The New Economics,* p. 267.

[15] See Chapter 4; and compare C. L. Barber, "The Instantaneous Theory of the Multiplier," *Canadian Journal of Economics and Political Science,* February 1950.

lags may provide us with the key to reconciliation between Knapp's approach and that of conventional multiplier process analysis. Where the expected profitability in both capital and commodity imports is the motivating factor, the expectations must almost certainly imply anticipations of the income changes that play a dominant role in multiplier analysis. Anticipations which precede an actual change may certainly reduce a lag in the process of income propagation without eliminating the explanatory value of the multiplier theory. For these reasons it would appear generally legitimate to handle simultaneous changes on current and capital account induced by profit expectations as if they were identical to changes induced by income fluctuations (or expectations of income fluctuations) along the lines of multiplier analysis. Income changes and profit changes (together with expectations thereof) must be closely correlated.[16] Any contradiction between Knapp's analysis and multiplier theory does not appear fundamental. Indeed it appears that the most generalized form of the common-cause theory should incorporate rather than exclude or contradict the multiplier technique.

The marriage of business cycle and international trade theory in the Keynesian analysis appears to provide common principles of explanation for international economic adjustment.[17] There are, however, a vast number of possible cases of actual adjustment between private long-term capital movements and the balance of payments on current account. There is a tremendous amount of theoretical and empirical work yet to be done in this field.[18] There is nonetheless little doubt regarding the fact of the extreme importance of interdependence between economic growth, cyclical fluctuations, and capital movements. Viner is to be generally criticized for his relative neglect of this vital fact.[19] Though we must fall far short of an ideal, the fact should be given due prominence, especially where empirical work is involved, as in the Canadian case.

[16] Discussed in Chapter 5.

[17] See Bloomfield, *Capital Imports and . . . Payments*, p. 264.

[18] See Chapter 13, as well as the remainder of this chapter.

[19] See the work of Tse Chun Chang, whose *Cyclical Movements in the Balance of Payments* (Cambridge, England, 1951) represents an important step in this area.

Before any a priori description of the relation of business cycles and the process of international adjustment could be accomplished, various possibilities with respect to timing and intensity[20] of the domestic cycle in relation to that of other countries must be distinguished. Other relevant factors listed by Bloomfield include

> the nature of [the country's] economy (including the psychology of its investors and the structure of its capital markets), . . . whether it is typically a net importer or exporter of capital, . . . the importance of capital movements as a stimulant to its domestic activity, and . . . the sources of the capital exported or the uses to which the capital imported is applied. The various individual categories of capital movements, moreover, may behave differently during the cycle, with the result that the cyclical pattern of the total capital flow may also depend upon which of these categories predominates in any given situation.[21]

Let us examine some of the empirical evidence on the subject. My concern is primarily with long-term capital movements on private account, and I exclude from consideration those circumstances where political and noneconomic factors were dominant. Fortunately for my purpose, Great Britain, until World War I by far the most important capital exporter,[22] provides an excellent example of a country whose foreign investments were activated overwhelmingly by the private capitalist's quest for profits. Between the 1840's and World War I, British foreign investments generally exceeded her domestic investment. By 1914 British investments abroad were valued at $20 billion (one quarter of her national wealth), and the foreign investment of France, second

---

[20] Of these two factors unquestionably the relative intensity is generally the more important, especially where annual data are dealt with. Chang, p. 16.

[21] Bloomfield, *Capital Imports and . . . Payments*, p. 304. See also Chapter 7 for other possible considerations.

[22] The typical capital importing country is generally in the earlier stages of its economic development, while the typical capital exporter is generally highly industrialized. A country which remains dependent upon its mineral or agricultural resources and with a very limited industrial development may, of course, become a net capital exporter, especially while heavily engaged in the repayment of principal of earlier foreign loans.

among the capital exporters of that time, was estimated at $8.7 billion (15 per cent of her national wealth).[23]

Canada received almost one quarter of the British capital sent abroad during the period 1900–1913. These years of cyclical upswing correlated with years of increasing borrowing from abroad, and there is evidence to support a similar correlation for earlier years.[24] There appears to be a much firmer basis for generalization in the case of capital-importing countries than in the case of the capital exporters.[25] A number of studies dealing with other countries may be cited to support the proposition that for net capital importers a positive correlation between cyclical fluctuations and capital imports may be expected.[26] The countries dealt with in the studies cited furnish many interesting parallels with the Canadian case. African and Australian capital imports also derived primarily from Great Britain. A large part of the Swedish capital imports came from Germany and France as well as from Great Britain. We can safely assume that in all of these instances profit motivation was the basic factor activating the capital imports. In all cases we find instances where in cyclical downturns pressure was exerted not only by a decline in export values, but also by a decrease in the foreign exchange that had been made available through capital imports. In Sweden we find a marked shift toward the role of a capital exporter coming earlier than in the case of Canada. This could be accounted for by her earlier industrialization which had enhanced her export capacity. In the boom years of 1910–1913 Sweden experienced, not an increase in capital imports as in previous years, but a shift to net capital exports.[27] Forty years of Swedish industrialization had made a substantial export surplus a natural concomitant of world prosperity. Similar experience was encountered by Canada in the

---

[23] See M. Palyi, "Foreign Investment," *Eycyclopaedia of Social Sciences*, VI, 366–369, for the preceding statistical comparisons.

[24] See Chapter 8; and Viner, *Canada's Balance*, pp. 16, 302–303.

[25] Bloomfield, *Capital Imports and . . . Payments*, pp. 304–305. Most of the supporting evidence I am citing has been cited by Bloomfield.

[26] See G. L. Wood, *Borrowing and Business in Australia* (London, 1930), pp. 127, 253; S. H. Frankel, *Capital Investment in Africa* (London and New York, 1938), pp. 191–192; E. Lindahl et al., *The National Income of Sweden* (London, 1939), pt. 1, pp. 288–289.

[27] Lindahl, *The National Income of Sweden*, p. 287.

period 1922 to 1925, and again in the upswing following the depression low of 1932.[28]

A significant parallel in Swedish and Canadian experience during the nineteenth century is the reduction in the import surplus or increase in the export surplus in the early stages of the boom.[29] Canadian data reveal that in the years 1870, 1876, 1880, and 1896 (the latter year represents the beginning of the prosperity period studied by Viner), exports either advanced prior to imports or more rapidly than imports. Only later did imports increase more than exports, the relatively greater increase being made possible by a rise in capital imports. The data suggest that the export increase rather than the capital import increase was the initiating factor in the recovery.

When we come to an explanation of the typical correlation we have viewed, there is certainly room for differences of opinion. The possibilities with regard to both chronological and causal sequence are numerous. I want to emphasize, however, the very limited support to be found for a general explanation based upon the Mill-Taussig model, in which capital movements are depicted as the primary initiating factor (I am not concerned at this time with the exaggerated emphasis in the model upon supposedly potent, relative price changes). The recovery might be initiated through export increases induced by a rise in investment activity and incomes abroad, followed by an upswing in domestic investment and capital imports. Or domestic investment activity and incomes might lead the way, inducing an import surplus that could first be sustained, then increased, through the seal of approval of successful long-term borrowing from abroad. In

[28] See Table 27. On the other hand, the boom years 1920, 1928–1929, 1950–1951, 1955–1957, have paralleled the earlier period 1900–1913 in showing a tendency toward an increased import surplus or decreased export surplus. This is a likely development if the Canadian business cycle becomes relatively intense at a time when there is little excess capacity. It appears to me that Chang, *Cyclical Movements in the Balance of Payments,* for example, p. 206, has displayed inclination toward overgeneralization on the data for a portion of the interwar period, usually the years 1926–1938. He concludes that for Canada, a current account surplus is a normal accompaniment of prosperity.

[29] See Lindahl, *National Income of Sweden,* p. 287, where a characteristic increase in Swedish capital exports during the early part of the upswing is alluded to. See Chart I for the Canadian data.

neither of these sequences is the import of capital initiating in either the chronological or causal sense. The interrelationships are mutual and interacting, and are best handled through a cyclical common-cause approach.

A cyclical change in the marginal efficiency of capital tends to be world wide, not only because of the psychological infection of profits expectations, but because innovations which may be basic to the cyclical change can be imitated in other countries, and because income changes basic to changed profits expectations can be propagated through changes in the levels of imports and exports. The world-wide change in the marginal efficiency of capital causes the demand for funds in the capital-importing country and the supply of funds in the capital-exporting country to shift in the same direction. Thus an increased marginal efficiency of capital will tend toward both an increase of domestic investment and an increase of capital imports, and these increases will prove mutually stimulating. Export increases and expectations thereof will encourage borrowing on the part of the typical capital-importing country in order to finance further increases in export capacity and will simultaneously encourage lending from abroad for the purpose. Increases in domestic investment and incomes will also lead to demands for loans from abroad, if these increases should be the initiating factor. If opportunities for capital expansion appear profitable in the domestic point of view and domestic financing is risked, the likelihood is that foreign capital may likewise be enticed. The expansion of incomes and imports increases the revenues of domestic governments, especially where these are, as in the case of the typical capital-importer in its early stages of development, heavily dependent upon tariffs. These increased governmental revenues would tend to improve the prospects for the flotation and sale of the domestic government's bond issues in foreign markets.

The examination of the cyclical behavior of capital movements from typically capital-exporting countries reveals much more complexity. At least three distinct patterns of behavior appear.[30] Capital exports from Great Britain during the years 1880–1913 were positively correlated with domestic business activity; capital

[30] Bloomfield, *Capital Imports and . . . Payments*, p. 305; H. D. White, *The French International Accounts, 1880–1913*, pp. 214–223.

exports from the United States during the period 1919–1929 were negatively correlated with the domestic cycle; while in the case of France from 1880 to 1913, no significant correlation, either positive or negative, could be discerned.

Bloomfield points out that whereas in capital-importing countries, as we have seen, the movement of capital is both a cause and an effect of business fluctuations, in a relatively self-sufficient capital-exporting country like the United States it is likely to be chiefly an effect. This follows, since exports are not likely to be an important determinant of domestic national income for a major lending country.[31] Much more significant will be the level of domestic capital formation. The most important capital-exporter of the nineteenth century, Great Britain, furnishes, however, an important contrast. The explanation for the positive correlation between business activity in Great Britain and capital exports appears to be the stimulus given by foreign lending to income through its effect upon Britain's exports.[32]

The inverse correlation between capital exports and United States national income during 1919–1929 has been attributed by Bloomfield to the more intense fluctuations in the United States and the attraction of investable funds away from foreign into domestic investment.[33] He concludes that in a world with countries tending to expand and contract together, but with differing leads and lags and with varying cyclical amplitudes, there is no reason for expecting a significant positive or negative correlation.[34] In a cyclical upswing there tends to be a shift to the right of the supply curve of investable funds, but since there is an increase of competing foreign and domestic demand for these funds, it is uncertain whether the outcome will be an increased or a decreased capital outflow. The possibility of generalization is enhanced, however, if capital importers and capital exporters are subclassified.[35] Undeveloped countries whose economies are

---

[31] Bloomfield, *Capital Imports and . . . Payments,* p. 307.

[32] See W. Beveridge, *Full Employment in a Free Society* (London and New York, 1945), pp. 302–305. Also see Viner, *Studies . . . International Trade,* p. 435.

[33] *Capital Imports and . . . Payments,* p. 265.

[34] *Capital Imports and . . . Payments,* p. 308.

[35] See Chang, *Cyclical Movements in the Balance of Payments,* especially chapter I.

strongly based upon agricultural and/or mineral production for export are typically capital importers, and there is a good positive correlation between their borrowings from abroad and national incomes. Well-developed countries like England, well advanced in industrial potential but deficient in raw materials and foodstuffs, have tended, apart from abnormal periods such as the recent post-World War II reconstruction years, toward a significant positive correlation between their capital exports and national incomes. As I have stated, a relationship in which the world economy is dominated by the mutual dependence of these two types of countries is conducive to cyclical equilibrium in the various national balances of payments.

Add two other types of country, and this cyclical equilibrium will be placed in jeopardy, a partial explanation perhaps of the increased instability of the world economy since World War I. The first type is the increasingly important mixed economy, relatively well developed and industrialized, but still heavily depending upon exports of agricultural, mineral, and forest products. Good examples are Canada and Sweden. Here less consistency in the correlation between capital movements and home activity is to be found. The final type is represented by the highly developed, self-sufficient, and volatile economy of the United States, where domestic rather than foreign activity dominates the picture, and which may absorb in times of prosperity some of the capital previously flowing to underdeveloped countries. Apart from political considerations, whether this will happen will depend on relative marginal efficiencies of capital and relative levels of capital formation in the United States and the capital importing countries. Although conclusive generalization does not always appear possible, the same principles of analysis are applicable to the many different cases that may be encountered.[36]

[36] Further investigation might profitably take the line of distinguishing between major cycles and minor (sometimes dominantly inventory) cycles. Related questions are whether the upswing commences from a level of great unemployment and excess capacity, and whether innovations stimulating to capital formation sustain the upswing. For example, the positive correlation between capital exports and Canadian national income during the upswing from 1932 was conditioned by the tremendous excess capacity in many industries, and the resultant diminished requirements for capital formation (see Chapter 19).

MISCELLANEOUS ADJUSTMENTS

There are a variety of adjustments that do not lend themselves to neat categorization, and with which there is not to be associated any fine mechanism which would consistently provide a tendency towards equilibrium. Nonetheless such adjustments may assume an important role in balance-of-payments analysis, and, since it may frequently be shown that they arise from a change in one category of the balance of payments and promote an adjusting change in another category, they must not be ignored, despite the fact that such adjustments could not be depended on to be consistently equilibrating.

Here I will do no more than to indicate certain types of adjustment which I have found of some importance in the Canadian balance of payments and which are not dealt with in the preceding sections. One example is the steady swelling of interest and dividend payments as capital is imported. Professor Angell has observed with reference to Viner's Canadian study that during the period 1900–1913, 42 per cent of the foreign loans was offset by Canadian interest payments on prior loans (plus a small amount of Canadian lending abroad). Angell emphasizes "how rapidly interest charges begin to catch up with even a large volume of new foreign investment, and how transitory any one shift in the balance of trade must be." [37] Until recent years it has not been a frequent practice to arrange for regular amortization payments in the currency of the lending country. Therefore capital repayments have not risen gradually like interest and dividend payments, thus furnishing an adjusting offset to the capital inflow. Instead, retirements have entered the picture many years after the capital inflows, becoming an important factor in the Canadian balance of payments only after World War I.

Capital inflows to developing countries in the typical nineteenth century case were accompanied by substantial immigration. This led to substantial immigrant remittances back to relatives in the homeland and to tourist payments by immigrants

[37] J. W. Angell, *The Theory of International Prices* (Cambridge, 1926), pp. 171–172.

returning abroad for visits. Both items would provide offsets to the capital imports.

Interest and dividend payments, amortization payments and retirements, and immigrant remittances and tourist payments may all provide an adjustment to continuing capital inflows. It should be pointed out, also, that at a later stage in the country's development they may also play a balancing role. Capital imports frequently increase the export capacity of the recipient country.[38] As a consequence the merchandise account position may be very much strengthened to the point where adjustment calls for offsets to a growing merchandise export surplus. The foregoing items could well assist in such an adjustment.

MULTILATERAL ADJUSTMENTS

The discussion so far has given little explicit consideration to the fact that the mechanism of balance-of-payments adjustment must frequently involve third countries as well as operating directly in a bilateral manner. Implicitly I have frequently assumed that only two countries were involved, or that one country was being considered vis-a-vis the rest of the world taken as a single unit. There are of course instances of bilateral arrangements, e.g., the "tied loans" effected by the depression-born American Export-Import Bank. The proceeds of such loans are restricted to payment for exports from the United States. Although British and other foreign lending of the nineteenth century rarely had such conditions attached, adjustments were frequently bilateral in essence, partly because of the essentially complementary relations between Britain and the capital importing countries. Also, although the contractor or manufacturer was usually not closely allied to the institutions involved in exporting the financial capital, long-term credits could nonetheless be arranged for past commitments or for future orders of equipment and raw material. Some form of liaison was evident at times between the exporters and financiers. Bilateral relations like the

[38] For an analysis of the significance of accomplishing such an increase in a borrowing country, see J. J. Polak, "Balance of Payments Problems of Countries Reconstructing with the Help of Foreign Loans," *Quarterly Journal of Economics*, February 1943.

foregoing, where capital export and merchandise export were so closely allied, eliminated any meaningful discussion of the "classical" transfer problem.[39]

These bilateral relations were typical of the most important type of British overseas investment of the nineteenth century, namely, in railways. Hobson has shown that such investments were generally accompanied by increased imports of capital goods, railway equipment, and materials by the capital importer.[40] Viner demonstrated that as a result of Canada's relative self-sufficiency in many capital goods there was only a moderate change in the proportion of capital goods and consumer goods in her merchandise imports during the period of increasing borrowing from abroad.[41] The multilateral nature of the Canadian 1900–1913 adjustment, and the important participation of imports from the United States in the process, will be emphasized.[42] The tendency for borrowing in the later stages of a country's development to increase the predominance of consumption goods in the imports and to facilitate imports from elsewhere than the lending country has also been observed in studies of other capital-importers.[43]

The various types of equilibrating action outlined in my analysis may in general operate indirectly via other countries as well as directly in a bilateral manner. For example, increased purchasing power in the loan-receiving country B may increase demand for country C's exports, and C's income and demand for the lending country A's exports may be consequentially increased. Other countries may enter the chain, and price changes and other equilibrating factors may come in to effect the final adjustment. Machlup[44] elaborates on the equilibration via third countries in his study while maintaining his assumption of no price changes, and thus implicitly denies the contention that where the adjustment is indirect the whole of the Mill-Taussig mechanism of

[39] See Palyi, *Encyclopaedia of Social Sciences*, pp. 365–366. Bilateral relations also assume great importance where direct investments are concerned.

[40] C. K. Hobson, *The Export of Capital* (London 1914), pp. 8ff.

[41] Viner, *Canada's Balance*, p. 277; and Chapter 9.

[42] Viner, *Canada's Balance*, pp. 280ff.; and Chapters 9 and 10.

[43] For example, Wood, *Borrowing and Business in Australia*, p. 199.

[44] Machlup, *International Trade and the National Income Multiplier*, chapter vi, pp. 90ff.

adjustment would necessarily be called into action. Haberler, in referring to Viner's study of the 1900–1913 capital imports into Canada concludes:

The fact that capital imports were balanced by commodity imports not directly but "triangularly" renders possible a verification of the theory [the Mill-Taussig theory] in other particulars. For theory asserts that the intermediate stages (outflow of gold, shift of prices, etc.), while superfluous where equilibrium is reached directly by purchases in the lending country, must necessarily occur where the adjustment is indirect. In the present case one expects therefore the whole mechanism of adjustment to be called into play.[45]

The Machlup analysis has shown that relative price changes are not essential in the adjustment process, and recent analysis that has emphasized the relative income as opposed to relative price changes has tended to view the relative price changes which did occur as by-products of the income changes. It seems likely that where income propagation via third countries was possible that this would facilitate the adjustment process. Relative price changes are partly symptomatic of slow or inadequate equilibration based upon the relative income changes. Therefore the participation of third countries might on this account reduce rather than increase relative price changes. Still more significant, the greater the number of countries involved (assuming that this number is an index of the economic size of an area), the greater the elasticity of supply of the commodities required by the capital-importing country, and the greater the elasticity of demand for its exports. Because of these greater price elasticities, relative price changes postulated in the Mill-Taussig analysis would tend to be less than in a two-country relationship.

There is no implication intended in the foregoing theory that a satisfactory equilibrium will be attained. It may be most unsatisfactory, so much so that steps may be taken to ensure a balance by means other than the equilibrating action. The balance of payments in an accounting sense must balance if all items are included, and unidirectional movements of gold and

---

[45] Haberler, *International Trade*, pp. 98–99. Haberler cites Taussig, *International Trade* (New York, 1927), pp. 124ff., in support of his conclusions.

short-term funds (which indicate disequilibrium in a particular, limited sense) cannot of course continue indefinitely. Where the equilibrating tendencies which I have outlined are inadequate, without, for example, incurring large-scale unemployment, extreme reductions in the standard of living, or considerable dislocation of the established distribution of the productive factors, or conflict with elements in the national plans of controlled or partially controlled economies, either default will occur or the equilibrating tendencies will be inhibited administratively by various forms of interference with the international flow of capital and commodities. What may happen in practice is far too complex for any theory to encompass satisfactorily. Even within the bounds of the theory there are a variety of equilibrating tendencies, and the degree to which each asserts itself is a variant of the historical case in question. Disappointment will be inevitable if too much generality is sought.

PART II
ECONOMIC DEVELOPMENTS PRIOR TO WORLD WAR I

VIII

Early Growth

During the early period of French settlement, fish was the chief Canadian export, but as pioneers pushed in from the east coast and up the St. Lawrence, furs became more important. The fur trade was exploited by the French with the use of lake boat on the upper St. Lawrence route, and by the English with the use of canoe along the Ottawa River; both the lake boat and canoe routes came under English domination after the fall of Quebec in 1760.[1] The view is frequently stated that Canadian development has been controlled because the political factors subordinated the natural geographic and economic pulls to the south. At this particular stage of Canadian history such would not appear to have been the case. An eminent authority[2] holds that Canada remained British *because* of the determining significance of the Laurentian Shield from which fur was derived. The transport of fur to Great Britain, in which the St. Lawrence route figured in an important way, continued because Britain had an advantage over France, and later over the United States, in the production of industrial products that could be traded for fur. This staple provided a temporary basis for the unity of British North America, the geographic entity that produced it.

Two developments led to the rise of a new staple — square

[1] H. A. Innis, *Problems of Staple Production in Canada* (Toronto, 1933), pp. 1ff.

[2] H. A. Innis, *The Fur Trade in Canada* (New Haven, 1930), pp. 396–397.

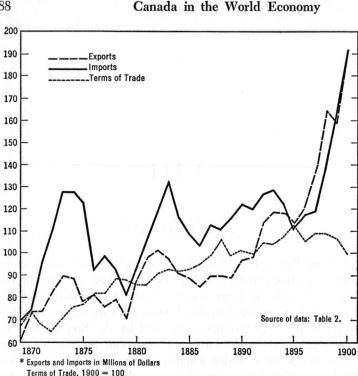

Chart I.   Merchandise exports and imports and the terms of trade, years ending June 30, 1869–1900

timber for use chiefly in shipbuilding — which served as a considerable support to Canada's economy, although the timber trade never became an adequate replacement for the fur trade.[3] The Napoleonic wars shut off from England the normal Baltic supplies and led her to look elsewhere.[4] Secondly, the Eastern Canadian fur trade declined after the English conquest due to its being outcompeted by the Hudson Bay route into the interior. This enhanced the interest of Eastern Canadian commercial interests in forest products.[5] Toward the second half of the nine-

[3] See H. C. Pentland, "The Role of Capital in Canadian Economic Development before 1875," *Canadian Journal of Economics and Political Science,* November 1950, especially p. 460.

[4] V. W. Bladen, *An Introduction to Political Economy* (Toronto, 1941), p. 145.

[5] Innis, *The Fur Trade in Canada*, p. 400.

teenth century another forest product, sawed lumber, took the center of the stage as the domestic and foreign markets for it became more important and the easily accessible supplies of good timber were exhausted. "The lumber industry prospered, first, on the British colonial preference and then on the expanding markets of the United States." [6] The abolition of the preference took place in 1846. Agricultural communities secondary to the lumber industry and dependent on it grew up along the St. Lawrence River. During the Civil War in the United States, Canadian agriculture responded to expanded American requirements, attaining such prominence as to provide exports almost double the value of those of the forest industry. [7] Although the export of agricultural products was to decline immediately after the war, the decline was temporary, and forest products remained relatively less important in the export list until pulp and paper rose to prominence in the third and fourth decades of the twentieth century.

This agricultural development had been too retarded to enable Canada to fill the role British policy designed for her after the American Revolution, namely, that of substituting for the United States as agricultural supplier to the West Indian colonies. Instead, Canada became for decades an important supplier of timber to Britain.

A further important development of the late eighteenth and early nineteenth centuries, encouraging to the growth of Montreal's commercial classes, was the entrepôt trade between the American West and overseas markets. [8] These commercial classes sought three major objectives: the unification of Upper and Lower Canada (today the Provinces of Ontario and Quebec), increased preferences for Canadian goods in Britain, and the development of St. Lawrence commerce. [9] The Act of Union of 1840 which brought the two Canadas together was necessary in order to provide a broader political basis for the financial undertaking involved in improving the St. Lawrence canal system and

[6] Canada, Royal Commission, *Report on Dominion–Provincial Relations* (Ottawa, 1939), I, 26.
[7] Royal Commission, *Report*, I, 26.
[8] O. J. McDiarmid, *Commercial Policy in the Canadian Economy* (Cambridge, 1946), p. 32.
[9] McDiarmid, p. 35.

in building railways. The improvement of the canals commenced in the 1840's and railway construction to supplement the canal system took place in the fifties and early sixties. Both investments failed in their object of attracting the American Middlewest trade, for which trade the Erie Canal continued to outcompete the St. Lawrence. Indeed, the Canadian Grand Trunk Railway did not gain access to Chicago until 1880.[10] By 1866 canal and railway investments amounted to almost sixty per cent of the provincial and municipal debt.[11]

Table 2. *Canadian merchandise exports and imports, 1850–1900*
(millions of dollars)

Years ending June 30	Total exports	Exports to U.S.	Exports to U.K.	Total imports	Imports from U.S.	Imports from U.K.	Merchandise account deficit (−) or surplus (+)
1850	18	6	10	24	9	10	−6
1855	41	20	17	54	29	20	−13
1860	47	22	20	51	24	19	−4
1865	57	29	21	67	27	32	−10
1870	59	30	23	67	22	37	−8
1875	70	28	34	117	49	60	−47
1880	73	30	35	70	28	34	+3
1885	79	36	36	100	46	40	−21
1890	85	36	41	112	51	43	−27
1895	103	36	58	101	50	31	+2
1900	168	58	97	173	102	44	−5

Source. O. J. McDiarmid, *Commercial Policy in the Canadian Economy*, p. 119; for years prior to 1870, McDiarmid does not give the British figures, which are rough residual estimates; *Canada Year Book*, 1940, p. 530, for later years.

The Act of Union had not favored the agricultural interests as it had the commercial. The former were strongly protectionist in sentiment, desiring tariffs against United States produce. It was a disappointment to the farmers when rights to tariff legislation were reserved to the imperial government, which did not favor such protection.[12] Before the decade of the 1840's had run its

[10] W. A. Mackintosh, *Economic Background of Dominion–Provincial Relations* (Ottawa, 1939), p. 16.
[11] Royal Commission, *Report*, I, 25.
[12] McDiarmid, *Commercial Policy in the Canadian Economy*, p. 50.

course, the commercial interests were also voicing their dissatisfaction.[13] The repeal of the Corn Laws in 1846 signalled the adoption by Britain of a liberal commercial policy involving the gradual abolition of the Imperial Preference which Canadian commercial interests had desired to see extended.

Dissatisfaction over the abolition of preference and the delay in obtaining offsetting advantages in reciprocity with the United States were among the chief factors that led in 1849 to a movement for annexation to the United States. This short-lived grouping consisted largely of Montreal traders.[14] The rebellious spirit of the commercial interests and the delay with regard to reciprocity led to the granting by Britain of demands for increased tariffs, for some merchants in their disgruntlement now supported the agriculturalists in their demands. By the 1850's a relatively high tariff policy had taken firm root, and although its motives were chiefly to obtain revenue, the "incidental protection" was certainly not unwelcome to many groups.[15] By 1860 Alexander Galt, the Canadian Minister of Finance, was able to make a declaration of autonomy in the execution of this policy, which, though not approved by the British government, was not opposed by it.[16] The customs tariff produced over 60 per cent of the revenues of the provinces.[17] Galt argued vigorously that Canadian transportation development was dependent upon the customs revenue and that the net result of increasing the tariffs was a cheapening of imports beneficial to Canadian consumer and British manufacturer alike.[18]

A Reciprocity Treaty abolishing tariffs on all important natural products was concluded between Canada and the United States in 1854, being terminated at the instance of the latter in 1866. Its early years were the culmination of a cyclical upswing from 1851 to 1857, a period similar to the years 1900–1913, being characterized by large capital imports from Great Britain, heavy investment in railways, and price rises which outdistanced those

[13] McDiarmid, p. 61.
[14] McDiarmid, p. 69.
[15] McDiarmid, p. 80.
[16] McDiarmid, p. 82.
[17] McDiarmid, p. 135.
[18] McDiarmid, pp. 81–82.

of Britain and the United States.[19] Grain prices were given additional impetus by the Crimean war and reached a peak in 1855, but the general downturn did not come until 1857. Despite the depression, Canadian exports to the United States exceeded the 1855 level in 1860 and with the American Civil War reached up to a new height as war-swollen demand increased.[20] Reciprocity did help to sustain and increase trade, but it was certainly given too much credit for creating prosperity.

McDiarmid concludes that the influence of the lowered tariffs upon Canadian exports was small with the exception of cash crops other than wheat.[21] Elsewhere, however, the same writer concludes on the basis of a one-third increase in trade between the United States and Canada from 1854 to 1855 that "the initial stimulus . . . of reciprocity in 1854 cannot be denied." [22] This is not adequate evidence, for on the same page McDiarmid reveals that during the period 1849–1854 exports and imports between Canada and the United States more than tripled. On the face of it, the upward swing of the business cycle — and not the reciprocity treaty — would appear to have been the significant factor which accounted for the further increases of 1854–1855.

One index of Canadian prices rose from 80 in 1849 to a peak of 155 in 1855, the increases being particularly pronounced in the case of the vegetable foodstuffs index which experienced an increase from 98 to 223 between 1849 and 1855.[23] Dr. A. Shortt, in emphasizing the parallel between this period and 1900–1914, stressed the "rapid rise of values in all lines of domestic produce. . . . The culmination of high prices in Canada was reached during the winter of 1855–56. . . . Prices are in many cases as high in Toronto as in New York to which formerly much Canadian produce was sent. . . . We find the tide flowing in the opposite direction, Canada importing from the United States large quantities of foodstuffs. . . ." [24] Canadian exports increased con-

[19] A. Shortt, "Construction and National Prosperity," *Transactions of the Royal Society of Canada*, December 1914, pp. 295ff.
[20] See Table 3.
[21] McDiarmid, *Commercial Policy in the Canadian Economy*, p. 92.
[22] McDiarmid, p. 84.
[23] K. W. Taylor and H. Mitchell, *Statistical Contribution to Canadian Economic History* (Toronto, 1931), II, 49, 55.
[24] Shortt, *Transactions of the Royal Society of Canada*, pp. 295ff.

siderably along with imports inhibiting the growth of the very substantial import surplus, at a time when Shortt estimates capital imports per capita were as large as the record years 1904–1914.[25] Thus, both increases in exports and in borrowing from abroad were stimulating the expansion of incomes and the associated inflation of prices (see Table 2 for a comparison of the 1850 and 1855 trade statistics).

The chief factors involved in the abrogation of the Treaty were the failure of United States exports to continue this rising trend through the period 1855–1865, the rise of protectionist sentiment in the northern states, and the growth at the same time of anti-British feeling consequent upon various incidents during the Civil War.[26] The United States could rightly complain that reciprocity had not prevented the imposition of higher tariffs in Canada. Although the duties were doubtless not protectionist in aim, but as represented were revenue measures designed to provide financial support for the transport development schemes wherein the government was heavily obligated, "incidental protection" was inevitable in some degree.[27] However, there were other more important reasons for the disappointing behaviour of American exports. As I have noted, 1855 was the peak year of a boom in which price rises were greater in Canada than in the United States, and Canada was importing large quantities of foodstuffs which a few years previous she had been exporting to the United States. The year 1865, in contrast, found the United States in a war boom, with enhanced domestic demands tending to increase imports while simultaneously leaving less available for export. The resultant Canadian export surplus with the United States and the American shortage of specie are held by one Congressional report to have been accompanied by Canadian investments in United States bonds to the extent of $50 millions, probably an exaggerated figure.[28]

[25] My rough estimates suggest that this is probably an exaggeration, and that average annual capital imports per head amounted to perhaps only $10 to $20 in the earlier period, while they approximated $35 in the later years.

[26] D. C. Masters, *The Reciprocity Treaty of 1854* (New York, 1937), p. 204.

[27] Mackintosh, *Economic Background,* p. 13.

[28] McDiarmid, *Commercial Policy in the Canadian Economy,* p. 86. The surplus with the United States was more than offset by the merchandise

CONFEDERATION

The Confederation of 1867 was analogous to the Act of Union in that it was essential to the financial support necessary for transport development, in this case the rounding out of the St. Lawrence system by its extension west and east.[29] Groups in the now united Upper and Lower Canadas took the prime initiative. The policy of a commercial outlet for the American west through a Canadian rail or water system had failed, and an all-United States development stimulated by settlement of the Mississippi Valley was causing net emigration from the British colonies.[30] The Canadas, faced with a closing frontier, seized the opportunity of a consolidation which would provide the political and financial basis for a transcontinental railway system to open up the British Northwest. In such a system they would play the entrepôt commercial role they had envisaged for themselves in their earlier schemes, but the frontier was now to be Canadian rather than American.

Throughout Canadian history close links may be noted between the staple products on which the economy is so largely based, the transportation system, and the financial and political problems of government. Successful large-scale marketing of the staples in a progressive world required continuously diminishing transport costs, and the sparsely settled Canadian spaces could be bridged only with considerable governmental assistance and initiative. The financial pressures and motivations stemming from the heavy financial overheads which national transport development entailed were a primary factor leading to the political consolidations of the nineteenth century.

The first step taken as part of the plan was the acquisition in 1870 of the Hudson Bay Company's territory, which included the great central plain. This purchase "transformed the original

---

deficit with other countries; e.g., in 1865 there was an over-all merchandise account deficit of $10 million, if we can rely upon the statistics. The nonmerchandise current account would doubtless have added to this deficit. However, I do not hazard a guess as to capital exports to Canada from Great Britain, which conceivably may have rendered net investments by Canadians in the United States possible despite the Canadian current deficit.

[29] Innis, *Staple Production,* p. 16.
[30] Royal Commission, *Report,* I, 28.

Dominion from a federation of equal provinces, each . . . vested with its own lands, into a veritable empire in its own right with a domain of public lands, five times the area of the original Dominion, under direct federal administration." [31] This was prerequisite to the Dominion program of railway building and settlement. The older scheme for tapping the Mississippi Valley was not completely abandoned. The Grand Trunk Railway was extended to Chicago by 1880, and continuous improvements were made in the St. Lawrence Canal system. But the latter was primarily allied to the all-Canadian transport strategy which now took first place.

In addition to the land and transport policies, a third policy, that of a tariff-protected industrialization, developed out of Confederation, although it was not explicitly forecast at the time. Protectionist tariff legislation finds less favor in prosperous times, and the new dominion had the good fortune to be born into a period of post-bellum reconstruction and railway-building in the United States. The period 1864–1874 was one of heavy capital imports for the latter country, the railway facilities being doubled in the eight years following the Civil War.[32] Capital imports and railway investment were also buoyant factors in the Canadian economy, particularly during the years 1871–1875 when import surpluses are of the greatest magnitude.[33] With the depression that commenced in 1873, exports to the United States declined,[34] investment programs were curtailed, and the associated imports from the United Kingdom fell off drastically after 1875. The Canadian protectionists added to their arguments the view that the adverse balance of trade with the United States and the accompanying loss of specie were responsible for the general economic difficulties.[35] With the depression, the hope of winning a new reciprocity agreement dimmed and the stage was set for protection.

[31] C. Martin, "Dominion Lands Policy," *Dominion Frontiers of Settlement,* ed. W. A. Mackintosh (Toronto, 1938), II, 223.

[32] C. J. Bullock, J. H. Williams, and R. S. Tucker, "The Balance of Trade of the United States," *Review of Economic Statistics,* July 1919, pp. 222ff; B. Ohlin, *International Trade* (Cambridge, 1933), p. 452.

[33] *Canada Year Book* (Ottawa, 1940), p. 526.

[34] *Canada Year Book,* p. 530.

[35] McDiarmid, *Commercial Policy in the Canadian Economy,* p. 112.

POST-CONFEDERATION COMMERCIAL POLICY[36] AND THE BALANCE
OF TRADE

Sir John A. Macdonald's Conservative government of 1878 had
been elected with a policy of high tariff in its program, a departure from the revenue tariff that had been favored during the
first years of Confederation and during the pre-Confederation
period. A study of the census of 1871 has revealed that although
industrialization had made some advance, there were few of the
important industries of the time that owed their existence to or
were dependent upon the relatively low tariff.[37] Political ma-
neuvering undoubtedly played an important part in the timing of
the policy's adoption, as in larger measure did the "great depression," but certainly, as in the case of all newly settled countries
gaining control over their commercial policy, protectionism
(christened the "National Policy" by the Conservatives) would
have found favor eventually in any case. As it was, although the
protection allied to the earlier revenue tariff was not great, it had
been steadily on the increase, the rising trend being broken only
by the tariff of 1866, and then only as a political concession made
to the Maritime Provinces in order to win them into the Confederation.

To a certain degree it is true that the rising tariff rates acted
as a buffer in a period of decreasing costs of imports, modifying
the rate of adaptation to the decline in natural protection afforded by transport costs. In any case, we can agree with
Mackintosh[38] that with transport costs declining the impact of
the increased duties was lessened. An indication of the importance of the drop in transport costs is found in the fact that the
freight rates from Montreal to Liverpool declined by 85 per cent
during the period 1872–1874 to 1903–1904.[39]

The trend during the period 1871–1896 is one of improving
terms of trade, with import prices falling more than export prices
(see Table 3 and Chart I). One of the important factors tending

[36] McDiarmid, chapters 7–10, for a complete account of commercial policy
in this period.
[37] Mackintosh, *Economic Background,* p. 17.
[38] Mackintosh, p. 20.
[39] Mackintosh, p. 23.

Table 3. *Merchandise exports and imports and the terms of trade*
(years ending June 30, 1869–1900)

Year	Exports (millions of dollars)	Imports (millions of dollars)	Surplus (+) or deficit (−) (millions of dollars)	Export price index (1900 = 100)	Import price index (1900 = 100)	Terms of trade (1900 = 100)
1869	60	70	−10	89.4	133.0	67.2
1870	74	75	−1	88.4	117.6	75.2
1871	74	96	−22	93.4	137.2	68.1
1872	83	111	−28	95.5	145.7	65.6
1873	90	128	−38	99.1	140.1	71.7
1874	89	128	−39	101.0	132.9	76.1
1875	78	123	−45	105.8	135.4	78.2
1876	81	93	−12	109.1	132.9	82.1
1877	76	99	−23	98.1	119.2	82.3
1878	79	93	−14	100.9	113.5	88.9
1879	71	82	−11	91.6	104.4	87.8
1880	88	86	2	93.8	109.4	85.7
1881	98	105	−7	97.5	113.3	86.1
1882	102	119	−17	107.2	117.4	91.3
1883	98	132	−34	109.6	117.8	93.1
1884	91	116	−25	104.8	114.3	91.7
1885	89	109	−20	99.2	107.3	92.5
1886	85	104	−19	96.1	101.5	94.7
1887	90	113	−23	96.3	97.7	98.6
1888	90	111	−21	101.6	95.9	106.0
1889	89	115	−26	101.3	102.1	99.2
1890	97	122	−25	103.5	102.4	101.1
1891	98	120	−22	104.0	104.2	99.8
1892	114	127	−13	103.0	97.8	105.3
1893	119	129	−10	100.7	96.3	104.6
1894	118	123	−5	101.0	93.7	107.8
1895	114	111	+3	96.5	85.3	113.1
1896	121	118	+3	93.1	87.9	105.9
1897	138	119	+19	90.9	83.8	108.5
1898	164	140	+24	97.0	88.8	109.2
1899	159	163	−4	95.4	89.6	106.5
1900	192	190	+2	100.0	100.0	100.0

Source. *Canada Year Book*, 1913, pp. 227, 228, for the export and import statistics. K. Taylor and H. Michell, *Statistical Contributions to Canadian Economic History*, table d, p. 6, for the price indices. The terms of trade are the export price index divided by the import price index.

to produce this trend was the declining transport costs of the period. This factor, together with innovations that speeded cost reductions in Canadian imports, particularly notable in the field of iron and steel products, more than offset any additions to the import price index which may have been attributable to increasing tariffs.

It is interesting to observe that Britain's terms of trade ended a period of decline in 1881 and commenced to improve.[40] That this should be the case for both exporter and importer of raw materials and foodstuffs, the terms of exchange apparently altering in favor of both parties from 1881–1895, is not necessarily attributable to possible errors in the statistics or to the fact that there are other countries party to the exchange. Declines in transport costs would create such favorable changes. If shipping services had been included in British exports, as of course they theoretically should have been, British terms of trade need not have improved.[41] Certainly the example points to one of the innumerable difficulties in arriving at conclusions regarding the gains from trade based on comparisons of the terms of trade as normally calculated.

It would be interesting to be able to investigate for the earlier years of Confederation, as has been done for the years following 1900, the importance of capital imports from abroad in Canadian economic development. There are unfortunately no reliable estimates for capital imports in the years prior to 1900. It seems not unreasonable to assume, however, that the variations in the unadjusted merchandise items (for which there are statistics prior to 1900) represented the greater part of the variations on current account.[42] On the basis of this assumption, import surpluses would be a very rough indicator of the flow of capital from abroad. Gold shipments as recorded by the customs department are included in the merchandise estimates. Of the other current account items it is probable that the deficit due to interest and dividend payments was a dominant and steadily increasing component.[43] This creates the presumption that over the period

[40] W. Beveridge, "Mr. Keynes' Evidence for Overpopulation," *Economica*, 4:7 (1924).

[41] This was pointed out to me by Professor D. H. Robertson.

[42] See Viner, *Canada's Balance*, p. 37.

[43] Compare the first years for which estimates are available, Table 27.

1869–1900, with the possible exception of 1897–1898, there was a constant inflow of capital into Canada. (See Table 3).

The period of most substantial capital imports was 1871–1875, when Canada attracted a share of the huge British capital exports linked to the railway-building schemes which got under way after the Franco-German peace settlement of 1871.[44] Between 1871 and 1875 the Canadian railway mileage doubled.[45]

In these years the building of the Intercolonial Railway was in active progress, the Canadian Pacific Railway was begun, and there was considerable expansion in manufacturing and in large-scale lumbering operations. Most of the capital necessary for these enterprises was borrowed from abroad, especially Great Britain. During these five years the excess for imports over exports totaled $171,000,000.[46]

There were not the great price rises nor the speculation in real estate which attended the boom years of 1849–1855 and 1896–1913, but there were rapid advances in manufacturing, transportation, and commerce.[47]

During the years 1871–1875, 68 per cent of the import surplus arose with Great Britain and 22 per cent with the United States. In the first three years of the period there were rapid increases in imports from Britain. The rise of the import surplus with the United States took place in the last two years of the period, and was attributable to declining exports to that country as well as to increasing imports into Canada.[48] Economic activity had slumped considerably in the United States in 1873, while in Canada it continued until 1875 to be relatively well buoyed up by the investment program. It may be inferred that the major part of the capital imports, which we have seen derived primarily from Great Britain, were transferred via a current account deficit with that country. This is a contrast with the situation of 1900–1913 when, despite the fact that most of the capital imports con-

[44] W. W. Rostow, "Investment and the Great Depression," *Economic History Review*, May 1938, pp. 136ff; C. K. Hobson, *The Export of Capital* (London, 1914), p. 205.

[45] R. M. Breckinridge, *The Canadian Banking System, 1817–1890* (New York, 1895), p. 264.

[46] Viner, *Canada's Balance*, p. 37.

[47] Breckinridge, *The Canadian Banking System, 1817–1890*, p. 266; Taylor and Michell, *Statistical Contributions to Canadian Economic History*, II, 55.

[48] Calculated from the *Canada Year Book*, 1940, p. 530.

tinued to originate in Great Britain, the transfer was effected primarily via current deficits with the United States. The period 1871–1875 is notable as the last in which there existed a substantial merchandise account deficit wth Britain.

Succeeding years were very disappointing to the authors of the Confederation plan for economic expansion. "The Great Depression did not lift until 1896 and it was not until 1897 that the per capita volume of exports reached the level attained in 1873. . . . For thirty years Canada was a land of emigration helping to people the frontier and cities of the United States." [49] The huge wave of British capital exports spent itself and gave way to actual imports during 1876–1878.[50] The downturn of the sixty-year trade cycle that has been characterized as the railroadization Kondratieff[51] was associated in England with a decline in interest rates and equity prices, a decline in prices and profit margins, a decline in risk-taking, and a shift of long-term capital from foreign to domestic investment, but an increase of output and real wages.[52] Of the reduced capital export, larger fractions went to Canada, the Argentine, South Africa, and Australia, while a lesser proportion went to Europe and the United States.[53] A relatively minor upturn of British lending came in 1879, and with it exports of capital to Canada primarily associated with the extension of the Canadian Pacific Railway to the west coast, a piece of construction completed by 1885.[54] There was also an increase in the rate of establishment of American branch plants in the years 1879–1883. This expansion was doubtless stimulated by the protectionist tariff program initiated by the Canadian government in 1879 as well as by the relative prosperity of these years.[55] Railway expansion and the associated capital imports continued into the 1890's but this "did not bring prosperity to Canada in the period under review. The brief trade revival of 1879–1883 faded away and the general world improvement of 1888–1890 was offset

[49] Royal Commission, *Report,* I, 53.

[50] Hobson, *The Export of Capital,* p. 205.

[51] J. A. Schumpeter, *Business Cycles* (New York, 1939), chapter 7, especially pp. 303–304.

[52] Rostow, *Economic History Review,* p. 137.

[53] Mackintosh, *Economic Background,* p. 22.

[54] Breckinridge, *The Canadian Banking System 1817–1890,* p. 287.

[55] H. Marshall et al., *Canadian-American Industry* (New Haven, 1936), p. 13.

in Canada by poor crops and bank failures." [56] The relative economic stagnation did not come to an end until 1896.

Movements in the terms of trade as a factor in the capital transfer mechanism have been given a great deal of attention in economic literature. The question will be taken up at some length in Chapter 15, where considerable space is devoted to the theoretical implications. The reader is referred to that chapter for an analysis of the period 1869–1900, the statistics for the period being portrayed in Chart I without further comment.

One of the significant developments to note in Table 3 is the arrival of the Canadian trade balance at its interwar pattern of a deficit with the United States and a surplus with the United Kingdom.[57] This was the outcome of relatively rapid increases in the last decade of the century in exports to Britain and in imports from the United States, while Canadian exports to the latter rose relatively slowly, and Britain's exports to Canada remained almost stationary. The rapid increase in United States' exports to Canada did not take place until the pressure of her own frontier expansion was eased and then shifted to Canada as the continental frontier reached north across the border.

The greater demands of the American frontier are clearly reflected in the figures for Canadian migration.[58] In each of the three decades of the period 1871–1901 emigration exceeded immigration, the totals for the period being 1,964,000 emigrants, and 1,549,000 immigrants, a net loss of almost half a million. In the subsequent decade of 1901–1911 Canada's gain of 34 per cent in population, from 5.4 to 7.2 million, placed her ahead of all other countries in terms of rate of growth.[59] Large net immigration and huge capital imports in the years preceding World War I indicated the vastly changed circumstances.

The important changes[60] in the composition of Canadian ex-

[56] Royal Commission, *Report*, I, 53.

[57] It should be noted that this was not consistently the pattern of the aggregate current account in the interwar period, there being large net liabilities to Britain on interest and dividend account that outweighed the merchandise export surplus for the years 1927 through 1932. See Tables 18 and 19.

[58] Royal Commission, *Report*, I, 53.

[59] J. B. Brebner, *North Atlantic Triangle* (New Haven, Toronto, and London, 1940), p. 226.

[60] Royal Commission, *Report*, I, 53.

ports in the years following Confederation were partly a reaction from the increased competition of the new American grain-growing frontier and also from increasing United States tariffs after the passing of reciprocity from the commercial scene. Livestock and dairy products, markets for which were expanding in the United Kingdom as population grew and transport costs fell, replaced the grains, vegetables, and fruits as the dominant agricultural export. Forest products in the export list continued their relative decline from the first half of the century as the age of the wooden ship came to a close. An alternative occupation to shipbuilding and shipping was found by many, especially in the Maritime Provinces, in the fishing industry, the exports of which, particularly after 1896, reflect its expansion.

The first decade of National Policy saw many developments in the tariff system which were to remain as permanent features. "These included subsidies to the steel industry, drawbacks and holes in the tariff to encourage domestic manufactures from imported materials, and more highly differentiated tariff schedules." [61] McDiarmid concludes that no important industry owed its inception to commercial policy, and that any credit for expansion must be shared by secular forces operating in that direction. He considers that without protection, however, integration with the emergent large combinations of the United States would have been probable.[62]

The ousting of the Conservatives by the Liberal Party in 1896 did not put an end to National Policy. Steps such as railway subsidies, encouragement to the iron and steel industry, and special consideration for the textile industry were taken, all counter to the Liberal campaign principles as stated.[63] There were significant innovations in the antidumping legislation of 1904, and the selective protection afforded farm machinery and other industrial products through the technique of the drawbacks of 1907.

The first Imperial Preference legislated by the new Dominion had been introduced on salt for the Canadian fishing industry in the year 1870.[64] However, the general preferential tariff was

[61] McDiarmid, *Commercial Policy in the Canadian Economy*, p. 179.

[62] McDiarmid, pp. 201–202.

[63] McDiarmid, p. 203.

[64] T. R. Wilson, "Imperial Preference in the United Kingdom since the War" (unpublished dissertation, Georgetown University, Washington), p. 341.

not introduced until the Liberal Government budget of 1897, the preferential rate being 12½ per cent lower than the general tariff. Some non-British countries were included until 1898, when treaty obligations to them were terminated. The preferential reduction of the general tariff was then increased to 25 per cent, and two years later was raised to 33⅓ per cent.

In 1907, a third column was added to the general and preferential columns in the tariff, it being entitled the intermediate schedule. At the same time the flat preferential rate was abolished, there being introduced specific preferential rates, generally one third the maximum general duty, and with regard to many important classes a 10 per cent *ad valorem* preference.

The intermediate tariff served to provide a basis for negotiating treaties with non-British countries, and where it was applied the preferential margin was thereby reduced.[65] However, it did not apply to United States imports until the treaty of 1935 was negotiated, and the small volume of trade it affected before then was of little consequence. There were, it should be noted, no substantial or important tariff changes in the period 1900–1913, which would raise questions relevant to the analysis in Part III.

---

[65] See D. Annett, "British Imperial Preference in Canadian Commercial Policy" (Harvard University Ph.D. Thesis, 1947), for an intensive study of the preference. This dissertation has since been published under the auspices of the Canadian Institute of International Affairs, Toronto, 1948.

IX

The Wheat Boom, 1896–1913

Wheat was exported in pre-Confederation days and had been the chief farm surplus of Upper Canada.[1] However, it was not the dominant export that fish, furs, and timber had been in their time. Increased and more varied American demands, associated with the Reciprocity Treaty and the American Civil War, resulted in a greater diversity in the export list, and barley, rye, and cattle had become important by the 1860's. Farming was far from being an export industry and was on a very self-sufficient basis. The average income per farm from agricultural products at the time of Confederation was only $60 to $75 per year.[2]

The phenomenal rise of wheat to its dominant position among Canadian exports is recorded in Table 4. Until World War II, when it was displaced by newsprint, wheat remained the leading single export. It is today typical of a group of agricultural, forest, and mineral products of which very substantial proportions are exported. In 1937 Canada produced five times her own wheat consumption (excluding seed requirements for export), ten times her own consumption of newsprint, and twenty times her own consumption of nonferrous metals. She supplied forty per cent of the world export market in wheat, two thirds in newsprint, and forty per cent in nonferrous metals.[3]

[1] Royal Commission, *Report*, I, 27.
[2] Royal Commission, *Report*, I, 27.
[3] Royal Commission, *Report*, I, 179–180.

Table 4. *Wheat exports in relation to wheat production,*
acreage, and total merchandise exports, 1871–1914

Fiscal years	Wheat exports (millions of bushels)	Wheat production (millions of bushels)	Acreage (millions)	Wheat exports (millions of dollars)	Merchandise exports (millions of dollars)
1871	1.7	16.7	1.6	2.0	57.6
1901	9.7	32.3	4.2	6.9	177.4
1911	45.8	132.1	8.8	45.5	274.3
1914	120.4	231.7	11.0	117.7	432.0

Source. *Canada Year Book* (Ottawa, 1945), xivff.
Note. Fiscal years end June 30, with the exception of 1914, the fiscal year having been altered to end on March 31 by 1907. Production and acreage figures are for the census year, i.e., the calendar year immediately preceding. The year 1871 includes the four original Provinces only. Merchandise exports are unadjusted figures for exports of domestic produce and include gold exports as recorded by the customs.

THE SURGING FRONTIER

Wheat became the important nationally unifying commodity giving adequate support to the Confederation railway and settlement plans. The frontier provided the demand eastern industry had been looking for, and the east-west transportation of settlers and goods, plus the return movement of wheat, appeared to justify the costly railway and waterway investment. The settlement and expansion in the West did not depend on the transport developments as a *sine qua non*. The Canadian plains would of course have been exploited as a final frontier of the American West in any case. A vast number of the settlers were Americans, who, bringing their capital and techniques which had been developed on similar soils under not greatly differing conditions, were able to make an immense contribution. The transport developments, however, did magnify the east-west movements and make wheat especially significant for Canada as an economic entity. From 1896 to 1913, one million people moved into the three Prairie Provinces, where the population increased from seven to twenty per cent of the Dominion total. During this time the area of occupied land rose from ten to seventy million acres, and wheat production increased from twenty to over two hundred million bushels per annum.[4]

[4] Royal Commission, *Report,* I, 68.

From the period 1870–1875 to the year 1896 there were certain price and cost shifts encouraging to western expansion based on wheat production.[5] The most important of these was the enormous decline in ocean freights by 47 per cent, the decline in prices of iron and steel products of 34 per cent, and the decline of 23 per cent in interest rates.

Factors additional to transport developments and favorable cost changes which encouraged large scale wheat-growing in the Canadian West include the introduction in 1900 of a new type of early maturing spring wheat called "Red Fife," which, with its shorter growing season, facilitated the push northward. Development of mechanized agriculture, critically important if the most were to be made of the prairie's short growing season, included the reaper and string binder introduced in the 1870's (the tractor and combine did not appear until the end of the period under study). Free, cheap land was provided under the Homestead Act of 1862 and there was an increasing demand for foodstuffs from the growing industrial populations of Europe, which also made the supply of immigrants possible.[6] The circumstances were such that wheat-growing for export became a very profitable industry and its development provided a field for investment with prospectively good returns which was attractive to domestic and foreign investor alike.

The available statistics show an increase in the index of home investment from 100 in 1900 to 509 in 1913, railway construction alone mounting from less than 500 miles per annum in 1900 to almost 2500 miles per annum in 1913.[7] Most of the investment that took place was almost certainly associated with the actual and prospective rise in wheat production. Available statistics indicate that out of a total investment of $4562 million during the period 1900–1913, 25 per cent constituted investment in agricultural buildings, capital, and livestock; 26 per cent was railway investment; and 28 per cent was new building.[8] Certainly the

[5] Royal Commission, *Report*, I, 67, table 13.

[6] V. W. Bladen, *An Introduction to Political Economy* (Toronto, 1941); W. A. Mackintosh, *Economic Problems of the Prairie Provinces* (Toronto, 1935), chap. 1.

[7] W. A. Mackintosh, *Economic Background of Dominion Provincial Relations* (Ottawa, 1939), p. 25, table 3.

[8] See Table 5.

Table 5. *Distribution between industries of investment in Canada, 1900–1913*

Class	Value (millions of dollars)	Percentage
Railways	1180	25.8
Agricultural buildings, capital, and livestock	1120	24.6
Electric railways, and telephones	160	3.5
Industrial working capital	480	10.5
Mines and steamships	80	1.8
New building	1264	27.7
Canals	25	0.5
Public works	167	3.7
Residual	86	1.9
Total	4562	100.0

Note. These estimates are derived from A. Cairncross, "Die Kapital-einfuhr in Kanada 1900–1913, *Weltwirtschaftliches Archiv*, 46 Band (1937 II), pp. 593–633. No deductions are made for depreciation. Values for new building, steam railways, and government expenditure on public works, canals, and other railways have been derived by Cairncross on a calendar-year basis. The initial figures for the other classifications were obtained for the decennial census years 1900 and 1910, the annual data then being interpolated on a population and wage basis. I have extrapolated to obtain estimates not supplied for my particular breakdowns, and have grouped the railway expenditures into one class. More recent estimates have substantially increased the over-all investment figures by more than one half. See K. Buckley, *Capital Formation in Canada 1896–1930* (Toronto, 1955). These estimates have been utilized in A. K. Cairncross, *Home and Foreign Investment 1870–1913* (Cambridge, England, 1953), chapter 3. The proportions given above appear to be compatible with the new estimates, however.

agricultural investment was preponderantly Western. "From 1900–1910 the farming population decreased in every eastern province except Quebec [and the Quebec farms were notably less well to do than the Dominion average]. There was scarcely a family in rural Ontario that had not sent a son and the bay colts and the second-best buggy to Manitoba or Saskatchewan." [9] The railway investment in the West bulked large. "The railway oftentimes pioneered settlement." [10] Housing and community investments of the western settlements, shipping and docking facilities of the Great Lakes, new roads, etc., all go to swell the total. In

[9] O. D. Skelton, "General Economic History, 1867–1912" in *Canada and Its Provinces*, ed. A. Shortt, IX, pt. II, 246.
[10] Skelton, p. 200.

addition, much investment in Eastern Canada would have stemmed from western settlement and increases in wheat production.

The most fundamental single characteristic of the period was a high rate of investment induced by improved expectations of profit from the exploitation of natural resources, which had been newly discovered, newly tapped by the extending railways, subjected to new productive techniques, or converted into profit possibilities by favourable shifts in costs and prices. Overwhelmingly most important were the wheat lands of the Prairie Provinces. Prospective profitableness in the exploiting industries created markets for other industries and for a time investment fed on itself.[11]

This "prospective profitableness" of wheat farming was based on its export markets to an increasing extent as the period proceeded (see Table 4). This in turn showed up in an outstanding lead acquired by wheat over all other exports (as indicated in Table 7). Between fiscal years 1901 and 1914, wheat represented almost all the increase in grain exports, 63 per cent of the increase in exports of agricultural and vegetable products, and 41 per cent of the increase in total merchandise exports.

THE INTERNATIONAL ACCOUNTS

This chapter title, "The Wheat Boom, 1896–1913," follows the example set in an eminent report.[12] There was, however, expansion in the production and export of commodities other than wheat which was of considerable importance, particularly in the earlier years of the period. It was only to be expected that the really notable increases in wheat production and exports should lag behind the western settlement and investment activity. Not until the years 1910 to 1913 did the really outstanding rise in wheat exports take place. From fiscal 1911 to fiscal 1914, wheat flour exports increased $79 million, the increase of total exports being $183 million, while in a period five times as long, namely, from fiscal 1896 to fiscal 1911, wheat and wheat flour exports

[11] Mackintosh, *Economic Background*, p. 24, referring to the period 1895–1920.
[12] Royal Commission, *Report*, I, 66.

increased only $50 million, while total exports increased $176 million.[13]

The increases of total exports that occurred early in the period 1896–1913 were not large relative to the increases which took place in the years immediately preceding World War I, but they were quite significant relative to the export level of 1896, and were all the more important since they marked the end of the doldrums that had retarded Canadian exports since 1873. The change in economic conditions was world-wide, the marked rise of prices, with only brief pauses from 1896–1897 to 1913, being common to the United Kingdom, the United States, Canada, and other countries. These increases raised price indices from what had been their lowest point in over one hundred years.[14] Partly this was the effect of increased gold production beginning in the 1890's.[15] Partly it was an element of the improved conjuncture associated with electrification, a renewed burst of railway construction, and the settlement of new territory. This has been designated as the upward phase of the Kondratieff long cycle.[16] It is notable that the new prosperity got under way while Canadian capital imports were at an ebb,[17] and it was not until 1905, with the commencement of an unprecedented outflow of capital from Great Britain,[18] that Canada's imports of capital became very large in relation to total domestic investment.[19]

In the first years of the period 1896–1913 a few commodities constitute the bulk of the increase in total exports. Between fiscal years 1896 and 1900 the following were responsible for $55 million of a $71 million increment in the total: wheat and wheat flour, $10 million; other grains, $9 million; butter, cheese, bacon, and hams, $19 million; gold, $13 million; and lumber, $4 million. With the exception of gold, in all these instances the increases

---

[13] See the *Canada Year Books* for the export statistics subsequent to 1900, and *Reports of the Department of Trade and Commerce* for the years preceding 1900.

[14] Canada, Department of Labour, *The Rise of Prices and the Cost of Living in Canada 1900–1914* (Ottawa, 1915), II, 21.

[15] Royal Commission, *Report*, I, 66.

[16] Schumpeter, *Business Cycles*, I, 397.

[17] See Table 3.

[18] C. K. Hobson, *The Export of Capital* (London, 1914), p. 205.

[19] Table 23.

were in shipments to the United Kingdom market, the growing importance of which has already been remarked upon.[20] The export increases following 1900 were more broadly shared, the United States markets assuming more importance; and there was increased participation by fisheries products, nonferrous metals with the exception of gold, lumber (particularly in the first half of the decade), newsprint, and wood pulp. There was a notably reduced participation of meat and dairy products, there being an actual decline in the values of bacon, ham, and cheese exports between fiscal years 1901 and 1914.

I will now consider changes not only in merchandise exports, but also in the other categories of payments in the international balance. An investigation will also be made of the importance of price changes on merchandise account, and the geographical distribution of these various types of payments; and attention will be directed to the changes between 1900, the first year for which complete balance-of-payment estimates are available, and 1913, the last prewar year.

The truly enormous increases we find in Table 6 between 1900 and 1913 are centered in merchandise exports and imports, which expanded 2.8 and 3.7 times respectively, in the swelling capital imports related to this greater increase of imports than of exports, and in the interest and dividend payments that flowed in constantly increasing volume to the creditors. Merchandise exports accounted for three quarters of the increase of current credits. The increase of merchandise exports to the United Kingdom in which wheat predominated was almost as great as the increase in exports to the United States, an increase shared by many commodities. Additions to credits gained on nonmerchandise account with the United Kingdom were relatively minor, while the increases due to expenditures of American tourists and to American immigrants' capital (the latter is included in "other credits") were of considerable importance.

[20] The growing relative importance of the British market is significantly related to the fact of an earlier and more intensive participation of the British economy than of the United States economy in the Kondratieff upswing of the later 1890's. Great Britain entered a period defined by Thorp as "prosperity" in 1896, while the United States did not enjoy such a condition until 1898. See W. L. Thorp, *Business Annals* (New York, 1926), chart vi, p. 95.

Table 6. *The distribution by country of the Canadian balance of payments, current account, calendar years 1900 and 1913*
(all figures to nearest million dollars)

Transactions	United Kingdom	Other Common-wealth	United States	Other foreign	All countries
			Exports or Credits		
1900					
Tourists	1	—	5	1	7
Interest and dividends	—	—	2	2	4
Freight and shipping	1	—	3	—	4
Nonmonetary gold	—	—	28	—	28
Other credits	3	—	7	1	11
Total nonmerchandise and gold	5	1	45	3	54
Total merchandise	93	9	44	10	156
Total current credits	98	10	89	13	210
1913					
Tourists	5	1	20	4	30
Interest and dividends	—	—	6	3	9
Freight and shipping	2	—	5	2	9
Nonmonetary gold	—	—	17	—	17
Other credits	12	1	40	3	56
Total nonmerchandise and gold	19	2	88	12	121
Total merchandise	201	25	158	59	443
Total current credits	220	27	246	71	564
			Imports or Debits		
1900					
Tourists	2	—	3	1	6
Interest and dividends	20	2	12	2	36
Freight and shipping	2	—	5	1	9
Nonmonetary gold	—	—	—	—	—
Other debits	3	—	3	1	7
Total nonmerchandise and gold	27	2	23	5	57
Total merchandise	43	4	107	23	177
Total current debits	70	6	130	28	234
1913					
Tourists	18	1	10	8	37
Interest and dividends	99	—	30	8	137
Freight and shipping	6	—	20	3	29
Nonmonetary gold	—	—	—	—	—
Other debits	8	1	33	50	92
Total nonmerchandise and gold	131	2	93	69	295
Total merchandise	143	23	414	75	655
Total current debits	274	25	507	144	950

Table 6. (*Continued*)

Transactions	United Kingdom	Other Common- wealth	United States	Other foreign	All countries
Net current credit (+) or net current debit (−)					
1900	+28	+4	−41	−15	−27
1913	−54	+2	−261	−73	−384

Note. The freight and shipping debit allocations are to be found in Viner, *Canada's Balance*, p. 77, table 16. The geographical allocations for tourist credits and debits are based on *Canada's Balance*, pp. 85 and 86, tables 21 and 22 respectively. The allocations for interest and dividends debits are based on *Canada's Balance*, p. 99, for the year 1900 and on Marshall et al., *Canadian-American Industry*, p. 309, for the year 1913, the proportions given for the year 1914 being used. The merchandise allocations are based on the proportions for the nearest fiscal year as supplied annually in the *Canada Year Book*. Other current items consist primarily of noncommercial remittances and migrants' capital. The proportions for credits in the base of the former are given by Viner, *Canada's Balance*, p. 60, as 74 per cent from the United States and 16 per cent from Great Britain. Immigrants' capital allocations (credits) are based on *Canada's Balance*, pp. 46–47, table 5. Where statistics were unavailable, resort to guesswork was necessary to bridge the gap. This was necessary for other current item debits, freight and shipping credits and interest and dividend credits. The proportions of 1926 were available in the D.B.S., Balance of Payments publication, and served as a rough guide. The allocations made for net current credits or debits for the period 1900–1913 taken as a whole in Viner, *Canada's Balance*, p, 283, were also useful as a guide, especially with regard to noncommercial remittances.

Merchandise imports and interest payments were the two most important items in the increase of total current debits, accounting for 67 per cent and 14 per cent respectively. The increase of merchandise imports from the United States was over three times as great as the increase in imports from Britain. The increase in nonmerchandise debits to the United Kingdom were, however, greater than the rise in similar debits to the United States. This was due to the fact that all but a small portion of the very large additions to interest and dividend payments were received by Great Britain. Increases in "other debits," payable to the United States, are accounted for chiefly by migrants' capital and by noncommercial remittances. Noncommercial remittances are also responsible for the large rise in "other debits" payable to "other foreign countries."

Note that whereas Table 6 refers to the calendar year, Table 7 is on the basis of the fiscal year which in 1901 ended on June 30, and in 1914 ended on March 31. Certain adjustments have been made to the fiscal year statistics to put the two sets of figures on a more nearly comparable basis (see the Statistical Appendix). The calendar year figures for 1913 are considerably higher than

Table 7. *The distribution by country of Canadian merchandise imports
and exports, excluding gold, fiscal years 1901 and 1914*
(millions of dollars)

Group or product	1901			1914		
	United Kingdom	United States	All countries	United Kingdom	United States	All countries
Exports						
Agricultural and vegetable products	18	3	26	121	34	201
Animals and their products	57	10	68	35	32	77
Fibers and textiles	—	1	2	—	1	2
Wood, wood products, and paper	16	12	33	13	45	63
Iron and its products	1	1	4	1	2	15
Nonferrous metals	—	9	9	16	21	40
Nonmetallic minerals	—	6	7	—	7	9
Chemical and allied products	—	—	1	1	3	5
Miscellaneous	1	2	3	1	4	6
Total	93	44	153	189	150	419
Wheat	6	—	7	81	7	118
Total grains	13	—	14	92	15	138
Bacon and ham	12	—	12	4	—	4
Cheese	21	—	21	19	—	19
Fish and fishery products	3	4	11	7	7	21
Lumber	13	8	25	10	20	33
Paper	—	—	—	—	12	13
Pulpwood	—	1	1	—	1	1
Wood pulp	1	1	2	1	5	6
Agricultural machinery and implements	—	—	2	—	—	5
Autos and parts	—	—	—	—	—	4
Copper and products	—	3	3	1	9	10
Nickel and products	—	1	1	1	4	5
Silver	—	2	2	14	5	21
Asbestos	—	—	1	—	2	3
Imports						
Agricultural and vegetable products		38	16	44	98	
Animals and their products		14	6	23	41	
Fibers and textiles		37	61	32	109	
Wood, wood products, and paper		8	4	32	37	
Iron and its products		30	17	121	144	
Nonferrous metals		7	5	13	21	

Table 7. (*Continued*)

Group or product	1901 United Kingdom	1901 United States	1901 All countries	1914 United Kingdom	1914 United States	1914 All countries
			Imports			
Nonmetallic minerals			21	6	74	85
Chemical and allied products			6	4	10	17
Miscellaneous			12	8	23	38
Total	42	104	173	124	372	589
Fruits and nuts			4	—	13	17
Rubber			3			9
Alcoholic beverages			2	3	1	8
Hides and leather			6	3	9	17
Cotton and products	5	2	8	16	17	37
Silk and products	3	—	4	3	1	11
Wool and products	9	1	11	27	2	31
Lumber			3			25
Paper and printed matter			2			9
Agricultural implements			2	—	4	4
Rolling-mill products			8			40
Vehicles and parts			1	1	20	21
Copper and products			1			7
Coal			14	—	47	49
Petroleum and products			1	—	14	14

Note. The export and import classification adopted is that of present official returns of the Dominion Bureau of Statistics. Such classification was not used in the years 1900–1914, but is employed for fiscal years 1901 and 1914 on pp. xx and 507 of the *Canada Year Book*, 1945. There is, however, no indication of how this trade for different groups was distributed between the various countries for fiscal year 1901. Estimates were therefore made on the basis of the known geographical allocations for the export classification then employed, supplemented by known allocations of certain important commodities for which data were given in the *Statistical Year Book of Canada*, 1903. No allocation by classes of imports was available, and no estimates were attempted. Estimates for fiscal 1914 on the classification basis used today were found in the *Canada Year Book*, 1918. The selection of the various commodities and subgroups which are presented in the table was made with a view to (a) their relative importance as a proportion of the group, and/or (b) comparisons between the two years examined or with years of the interwar period, and/or (c) their representative value.

A dash signifies a value of less than $500,000, figures being rounded to the nearest million. A blank signifies that data upon which to base an estimate were not discovered. The merchandise figures are adjusted for gold, and settlers' effects in both years and for wheat in fiscal 1914. See the Statistical Appendix for further information.

the fiscal year figures due in part to a decline in trade which resulted in the first three months of 1914 showing a poorer record than the similar months of 1913. However, the fiscal year statistics, despite the discrepancy, adequately indicate the relative importance of various commodities and subgroups, both within the group for the selected year, and in their changes from one year to another.

Table 8. *The volume, price, and value of export and import groups, fiscal year 1914, expressed as a percentage of fiscal 1900*

Group	Exports			Imports		
	Volume	Price	Value	Volume	Price	Value
Agricultural products	437	122	532	220	119	261
Animals and products	88	122	108	286	104	298
Fibers and textiles	212	87	185	233	129	300
Wood, wood products, paper	140	139	195	446	108	481
Iron and products	665	72	481	398	108	430
Nonferrous metals	282	102	287	581	105	611
Nonmetallic minerals	139	103	143	428	108	460
Chemicals and allied products	866	113	978	269	117	315
Miscellaneous	152	117	177	328	113	371
All groups	213	117	249	317	113	359

Note. This table, compiled from Taylor and Michell, *Statistical Contributions to Canadian Economic History*, pp. 16–19, includes re-exports of foreign produce in the export calculations, but these are relatively small and would not significantly alter the results.

No adjustment for price changes during the period was made. Prices show a generally rising trend from fiscal 1900 to fiscal 1914, those for imports and exports rising 13 and 17 per cent respectively.[21] The greatest price increase for all commodity groupings is one of 39 per cent for exports of wood, wood products, and paper. The only price decreases recorded are for exports of fibers and textiles, and for exports of iron and its products, both relatively insignificant classes. In the import list, price changes are relatively small in comparison with the volume increases, and while they are of greater relative importance in the export list, there is only one group, wood, wood products, and paper, which is characterized by its considerable contribution to the total export increases (in volume terms) and also by a large price rise relative to the increase in volume. In general, the volume changes were a markedly greater contributor to the value increases.

[21] Table 8.

Table 7 indicates important shifts within the export pattern. In fiscal 1901 lumber was the leading commodity in the export list. The agricultural exports came primarily from the mixed, relatively self-sufficient farms of Ontario and Quebec, and not from the "wheat factories" of the prairie west. Cheese exports alone were greater than those of all grains by a long margin, and indeed closely challenged lumber. Exports of bacon and ham exceeded those of wheat. The year 1900, however, had seen relatively poor wheat crops. Thirteen years later there was no question of wheat's lead in the export list. It constituted 28 per cent of the greatly expanded exports as compared with lumber's 16 per cent of total fiscal 1901 exports. Unlike lumber, wheat had no rivals of comparable importance. Another change, of less immediate importance but auguring much for the future, was the rise of paper (primarily newsprint) and wood pulp to more significant proportions of the wood products group. Silver gained a position of dominance amongst the nonferrous metals, but it was to be a transient gain, whereas the similar increases made by copper and nickel exports were to be magnified further in later years.

The altered destinations of Canadian exports point up the diminishing relative importance of the British market despite the large share of wheat and other grains taken by the United Kingdom. In this connection it might be pointed out that the share of wheat going to Britain is exaggerated in the unadjusted export statements (see the Statistical Appendix). There was in the adjusted figures a relative fall in the share of agricultural and vegetable products received by the United Kingdom. The decline in the wood products and animals and products groups exported to Britain was not only relative but absolute. The $14 million of silver exported to Britain made her the largest market pro tempore for Canadian nonferrous metals exports. Gold (for which there are statistics in Table 27) is not included in the nonferrous metals group of Table 7. Nonmonetary gold exports, assumed as destined to the United States,[22] were at a peak at the turn of the century following the Yukon and British Columbia gold rushes and so declined in the period under consideration. Gains in United States markets were otherwise quite general, the most

[22] See Statistical Appendix.

notable being for wheat and other grains, vegetable products, lumber, paper, copper, nickel, and silver. The multiplication of American-owned branch plants producing manufactures that were in part shipped to Empire countries under Imperial Preference are reflected in exports of iron and its products.

Referring to the second section of Table 7, which deals with imports, general increases of threefold or fourfold are observed in almost every category. As Professor Viner has shown, ". . . while the capital borrowings entered Canada to some extent in the form of direct purchases by the borrowers of foreign capital goods, they entered more largely in the form of consumer's goods." [23] This was partly a result of Canada's greater ability to satisfy her own capital-good requirements in the form of heavy machinery, railway rolling stock, rails, etc., than was the case with other less industrially developed capital-importing countries,[24] and also partly the result of the growing activity in nonself-sufficient agriculture and in construction, requiring the maintenance of a large labor force. The increased imports of fruit and nuts and of the textiles illustrate the increased demand for consumer goods, while much of the increase in imports of lumber, rolling-mill products, and coal was devoted to capital goods.[25]

The United States increased the lead over Britain which she had clearly established in Canadian markets toward the end of the nineteenth century, not only absolutely but relatively. In all but the textile group, the United States had a commanding advantage. The participation of other empire and other foreign countries in the Canadian balance of payments remained proportionately small. Their share is considerably reduced by the bias due to transactions being effected via the United States or Britain, with the customs reports failing to acknowledge the country of origin. Gains recorded by other foreign countries in their exports to Canada were greater absolutely but less relatively than those recorded by other Empire countries.

Britain's declining competitive position with regard to her exports had previously been most in evidence in trade depression,

[23] Viner, *Canada's Balance*, p. 279.
[24] Viner, p. 277.
[25] Viner, p. 277.

and it became increasingly obvious in the closing decades of the
nineteenth century.[26] Despite the prosperity of the years 1905
to 1913, which "represented in a sense the last and greatest effort,
when a broad new expansion of younger regions far more than
offset a secularly diminished competitive strength," [27] the British
relative decline continues in Canadian import figures. While this
is due in large measure to Canada's peculiarly intimate geographic and economic relationship to the United States, and to
Canada's increased relative self-sufficiency in iron and steel products which Britain had supplied as a complement to earlier loans,
it is in part due to the generally improving competitive position
of the American Republic, particularly since the last period
(1871–1875) of heavy capital imports.

The situation is well presented by Professor Viner.[28] There was
a divorce of ownership and control with regard to British investments in Canada which was not characteristic of these investments in many other countries. The Canadians and Americans
almost invariably supplied the managerial talent,[29] and any propensity they may have had to purchase in the United States does
not appear to have been inhibited by conditions attached to the
loans. In contrast, approximately 60 per cent of United States
investment was in branch plants and in mining and lumbering
enterprises closely controlled by the investors.[30] Such circumstances were bound to favor imports from the United States. In
many cases the Canadian branches were little more than as-
sembling or finishing or distributing plants, often set up to take
advantage of Imperial Preference. In a few years such plants
could give rise to imports from the United States amounting to
many times the original investment.[31] Manufacturing, assisted by
the tariff, was expanding. This expansion was associated with a
shift in the content of Canadian imports from finished manufactures provided by Great Britain to raw materials such as coal,
petroleum products, and cotton which figured prominently in the
United States export list.

[26] Kahn, *Great Britain in the World Economy*, p. 130.
[27] Kahn, p. 130.
[28] *Canada's Balance*, pp. 284–290.
[29] Viner, p. 286.
[30] Viner, p. 286.
[31] Viner, p. 288.

The styles demanded by the Canadian consumer, the brands and trade-marks to which he had been accustomed by persistent advertising, by similarity of economic conditions and of standards of living, were American rather than British. American sales methods were more effective than the more conservative and old-fashioned British methods. The settlement of the Canadian prairie provinces with their proximity to the important producing regions of the American Middle West, gave American exporters a decided advantage over their British competitors, in freights and in rapidity of communication and delivery, in a rapidly growing portion of the Canadian market. The shift in the character of the imports from relatively light highly-fabricated commodities to bulky raw materials, partially-manufactured products, and machinery and equipment, further handicapped the more distant British exporters, especially in their trade with the interior provinces to which direct water shipment without trans-shipment was either impossible throughout the year or was possible only during the seven months of the year when the St. Lawrence River was open to navigation.[32]

The geographical distribution on capital account — the countries from which loans were received — did not parallel that on current account. As in the nineteenth century, the loans continued to come predominantly from Britain. Of the $2.5 billion of capital exported to Canada during 1900–1913, Great Britain supplied 68.8 per cent, the United States 24.7 per cent, and all other countries only 6.5 per cent.[33] Yet in the early years of the period, British investments in Canada had been even smaller than the American investments that were then taking place. The British investments, in contrast to the American, primarily took the form of fixed-income securities, and their predominant holding of Canadian Dominion, provincial, and municipal securities, plus railroad securities, usually government guaranteed or supported, is worthy of note. Almost one half of the borrowings abroad during 1900–1913 fell into these categories.[34] This type of investment had been encouraged by British Acts of Parliament passed during the years 1889–1900, which had extended the powers of trustees to invest in the securities of the dominions and colonies.[35]

Table 9 shows the contrasting distribution on current and capital accounts. Residual error, and Canadian long-term and short-

---

[32] Viner, *Canada's Balance,* p. 290.
[33] Viner, *Canada's Balance,* estimated from table xliv, p. 139.
[34] Viner, p. 283.
[35] Schumpeter, *Business Cycles,* I, 430.

Table 9. *Surpluses or deficits on current account and capital borrowings, by country, 1900, 1913, and 1900–1913*
(millions of dollars)

	1900			1913			1900–1913		
	United Kingdom	*United States*	*Other countries*	*United Kingdom*	*United States*	*Other countries*	*United Kingdom*	*United States*	*Other countries*
Current surplus (+) or deficit (−)	28	−41	−9	−54	−261	−71	−152	−1707	−506
Capital borrowings	10	18	11	376	135	36	1754	630	163
Capital loans (chiefly short term)	—	—	—	—	—	—	7	133	—

Source. Table 6, and Viner, *Canada's Balance*, pp. 282–283. The current deficit for "other countries," 1900–1913, is a rough estimate based on the figures for the two years 1900 and 1913. All but $50 million of Canadian capital loans represent the acquisition of external bank assets, a short-term rather than a long-term capital movement. Since total Canadian investments abroad are estimated at $137 million (Viner, p. 94), Canadian loans to "other countries" may be regarded as negligible.

term lending, account for the difference between the current deficit and capital borrowings.[36] The data of Table 9 indicate clearly that the capital imports from Great Britain were transferred almost wholly in a multilateral manner by means of current deficits with other countries, the deficit with the United States being overwhelmingly the greatest. With the United Kingdom, Canada had a commodity export surplus of $670 million which offset the bulk of the Canadian deficit on nonmerchandise account of $886 million ($815 million of which represented a net debit due to interest payments). The merchandise import surplus from the United States was slightly greater than the total current deficit, amounting to $1,723 million. The current deficit with all other countries is only partially attributable to the deficit on merchandise account, and appears to stem largely from the current deficits arising from the noncommercial remittances sent from Canada. These would be largely immigrants' remittances. Of a total of $366 million in noncommercial remittances sent from Canada, Viner estimates only $55 million were sent to the United Kingdom and the United States.[37] The transfer of capital from Britain, which was effected so largely by means of a merchandise account deficit with the United States, coupled with a primarily nonmerchandise deficit with countries other than Britain or the United States[38] contrasts with the immediately preceding period of capital imports, likewise from Great Britain, when a merchandise import surplus vis-a-vis Britain seems to have provided the chief means whereby the transfer was effected (see Chapter 8).

The tremendous inflow of capital into Canada, especially following 1905, coincided with a previously unequalled outflow of capital from Great Britain. The latter sent abroad $5,810 million of capital during the years 1901–1912.[39] Of this large sum almost one quarter went to Canada, a country whose population at the

[36] In the estimates for the individual years 1900 and 1913, monetary gold movements (the basis of the calculation of which is indicated in the Statistical Appendix) also account for a small portion of this difference.

[37] *Canada's Balance*, pp. 61, 283.

[38] See *Canada's Balance*, pp. 280ff, where Viner, in emphasizing the triangular nature of the adjustment, neglects this multilateral aspect of the nonmerchandise account.

[39] Estimated on the basis of statistics in Hobson, *The Export of Capital*, p. 205.

beginning of the decade was less than 5½ million. There is no question of the very great importance of these capital imports in this particular period of Canadian economic history. Net borrowings from abroad rose between 1903 and 1913 from 5 per cent to 23 per cent of Canadian national income, and from 30 to 86 per cent of total investment.[40] Capital imports were undoubtedly a most significant factor in the extraordinary rise of investment and national income in this ten-year period when the former multiplied three-and-one-half times and the latter more than doubled.[41]

The import of labor was of such striking dimensions that it deserves to be treated on a par with the migration of capital. The two factors of production displayed an extraordinary international mobility. Between the census years 1901 and 1911, immigrant arrivals of 1.7 million[42] were only partially offset by 1.1 million emigrants,[43] an important factor in the increase of the Canadian population from 5.4 to 7.2 million.[44] In the years immediately following, the rate of immigration rose to a much higher level and in the three years 1911–1913 inclusive immigrant arrivals totalled 1.1 million, a net gain of half a million with emigration of 0.6 million allowed for. The increase in population from 1901 to 1921 was 64 per cent in contrast to an increase of only 24 per cent in the twenty years immediately preceding.[45] Emigration to the United States, which in each of the three decades 1871–1901 had more than offset total immigration into Canada,[46] also increased to record-breaking heights, but emigration to all countries totalled only 1.7 million as compared to total immigration of 2.8 million for the period 1900–1913. It is interesting to note that the immigration during the years 1903–1914 has been estimated as being three times the natural increase, whereas

[40] Table 23. During this period capital imports rose from 23 per cent to 83 per cent of the value of merchandise imports.

[41] Table 23.

[42] Immigration estimated from Table 10 for 1900–1910.

[43] Emigration estimated from Viner, *Canada's Balance*, p. 57.

[44] *Canada Year Book* (1945), xiv. The population census was taken in April 1901 and again in June 1911.

[45] Mackintosh, *Economic Background*, p. 24.

[46] Royal Commission, *Report*, I, 54.

at the peak years of immigration into the United States it had no more than equalled the natural increase.[47]

It would be unfortunate if the reader should be left with the impression that Canada during 1896–1913 was typical of the relatively primitive, agricultural, raw-material producing country to which much capital from relatively advanced industrial countries has flowed in the past. Certainly transportation, agriculture, utilities, and nonindustrial building were much more absorptive of capital than was manufacturing enterprise (Table 5), but the latter made great progress. That the industrialization of the Canadian economy had reached a level during 1900–1913 where dependence upon external sources of supply for many forms of capital equipment was relatively small has already been pointed out. Development was particularly rapid in the period under consideration.

The industrial expansion of Canada after 1896 was remarkable. Between 1896 and 1918, the net value of manufacturing production increased by nearly three times. In spite of an increase of nearly 200,-000 farms in the Prairie Provinces during the period, the proportion of the total gainfully occupied engaged in manufacturing remained about the same. Although a vast agricultural region was added to the economy the ratio of urban to total population increased from 32 to 45 per cent. While the value of agricultural production rose by leaps and bounds — the value of the exports of wheat and flour alone in 1913 was greater than the value of all exports in 1896 — the value of the manufactured goods produced for the home market increased at an even faster rate.

Manufacturing expanded in most of the important categories: the provision of capital equipment, consumers' goods of general consumption and the processing of natural products for export.[48]

From 1900 to 1910 the net value of production of manufactures in establishments with five hands and over rose from $214 million to $564 million. The gains were varied, but the increases in the production of textiles from $33 million to $67 million and of iron

---

[47] B. Ohlin, *Interregional and International Trade* (Cambridge, 1933), p. 326. Note that it is gross immigration to which Ohlin is referring. Statistics for emigration from Canada are much less reliable (see Viner, *Canada's Balance,* pp. 45–57). Doubtless if it were possible to compile similar statistics for certain areas of the United States, they would appear even more striking than those for Canada.

[48] Royal Commission, *Report,* I, 73.

and steel and their products from $35 million to $106 million are deserving of note.[49] The years 1899–1902 were particularly auspicious in the growth of the Canadian steel industry. The consequence was that by the end of the first decade of the century Canada was producing from 90 to 95 per cent of her steel requirements despite a greatly inflated demand. Domestic production, however, was able to satisfy only 55 to 60 per cent of the demands for finished steel products. Following 1900, 90 per cent of the domestic consumption of steel rails was produced in Canada, generally all of the consumption of steel billets, and 80 per cent of domestic pig-iron consumption.[50] The preceding survey, historical and statistical in emphasis, clearly shows what extraordinary changes were occurring in the Canadian economy during the pre-World War I boom years. In the chapters to follow, more attention will be directed to the theoretical implications of the data, particularly as they relate to the problem of capital transfer.

[49] Royal Commission, *Report*, I, 73.
[50] W. J. A. Donald, *The Canadian Iron and Steel Industry* (Boston and New York, 1915), pp. 303–311.

PART III
VINER'S ANALYSIS OF THE PERIOD 1900–1913: A CRITIQUE

X

Viner's Presentation

Professor Viner[1] has utilized the statistical material of the main wheat-boom years in Canada to attempt what has frequently been regarded as the only adequate, complete verification of the "classical" Mill-Taussig theory of the capital transfer mechanism.[2] In Chapter 3 attention was devoted to this theory, of which Viner is an important exponent, and to some of the criticisms directed against it, in particular by those favoring emphasis upon the shifts of purchasing power. Basically it is this Mill-Taussig theory which Viner seeks to defend,[3] although he adds some modifications to it. The more important of these are the recognition of the possible substitution of short-term capital movements for the gold flows, a detailed elaboration of the type of relative price changes to be expected, and allowances for the irregular crescendo of capital importations.

This rather lengthy critique of Viner's study perhaps calls for some explanation. This might be demanded particularly by those who consider the criticism of economic literature predating

[1] Viner, *Canada's Balance of International Indebtedness, 1900–1913.*

[2] For example, Haberler, *The Theory of International Trade,* pp. 96ff.; Taussig, *International Trade,* chap. 19, especially p. 235; C. Bresciani-Turroni, *Inductive Verification of the Theory of International Payments* (Egyptian University Publications, 1932), p. 3.

[3] Viner, *Canada's Balance,* preface. "This study is intended primarily as an inductive verification of the general theory of the mechanism of international trade."

Keynes' *General Theory* to be analogous to the flogging of a dead horse. The following points may be made:

(1) International trade theory, while greatly influenced by Keynesian theory, has by no means been brought to a definitive state by this influence, and it remains in an unsatisfactory state of flux. Viner's study has been very influential, and it has led to a great amount of controversy which cannot be resolved along simple Keynesian and anti-Keynesian lines. Much of this literature has involved misinterpretation and error, and has generally dealt only with certain limited aspects of the problems raised. Viner has had an opportunity to reply to his critics, successfully countering many of their arguments and clearing away much of the ambiguity in his earlier statement, but in my view many important questions have remained unanswered. In an attempt to solve these problems, not only Keynesian but also Schumpeterian and other recent business cycle theories provide assistance. Throughout I have endeavored to keep in mind the general context of economic growth and development.

(2) The period 1900–1913 in Canadian history has been referred to by Taussig as an unusual case of the isolation of a single force in history. "The import of capital was so great, it overshadowed so completely all other [causes], that there can be no error in attributing to this the main economic changes which appeared." [4] This view may be an exaggerated one, but it is enough to indicate that the period may well provide a field of profitable research for investigators interested in problems of international economic equilibrium. Viner's industrious work in this field supplemented the already copious statistics provided in an important governmental report,[5] and this statistical material has been further increased in the course of subsequent investigation.

(3) The study of the transfer mechanism in the Canadian experience is rendered the more interesting by the facts that, as seen in the preceding chapter, Canada was relatively self-sufficient in the capital goods she required, and her additional import requirements were not primarily satisfied by Great Britain, the

[4] Taussig, *International Trade*, p. 235.
[5] Viner, *Canada's Balance*, pp. 22, 23; and Canada, Department of Labour, *The Rise of Prices and the Cost of Living, 1900–1914*, vol. II and synopsis.

country from which Canadian capital borrowings derived. Thus the transfer was not of the simple variety so often in evidence in previous history, where the transactions were primarily bilateral, with the capital goods and the loans both being provided by the more advanced industrial country.

(4) The Viner study is also to be distinguished by its being the only important study of a borrowing country on the gold standard. It can be seen, however, by comparison with the Canadian situation under free exchanges during the inter-war period, as borne out by the general theoretical analysis in Part I, that the fact of being on the gold standard has frequently been endowed with exaggerated significance in explanations of the transfer mechanism.[6]

(5) Part III might also be regarded as a study in the interrelationship of fact and theory. Certainly it points to the many difficulties in the path of empirical verification which Viner was attempting to follow. It is suggested that at numerous points in his argument these difficulties were not squarely faced by Viner. The critique I am attempting might also give some indication as to how much, or how little, has been learned in the field of international trade theory in the last quarter century. One point of great methodological importance does seem to be born out by our investigation, namely, that intellectual attachment to a particular theory may prove to be a very considerable handicap to empirical analysis, and unconscious prejudice may render acceptable conclusions that otherwise would be seriously questioned in view of the shaky statistical evidence on which they were thought to be founded.

VINER'S STATISTICS

Viner's initial task of building up estimates of the balance of international indebtedness of Canada is a heavy one. He defines the balance of indebtedness in what would now be regarded as an unusual way. By the term he means "the difference between

[6] Viner, *Canada's Balance,* preface. "The study of Canada's balance of international indebtedness during the war [World War I] and postwar period would encounter problems which in many respects would be essentially different from those analyzed in the present inquiry; most important of all would be the effect on the mechanism of international trade of Canada's departure from the gold standard."

the totals of Canadian debit and credit international transactions"
or, in another sense, "the tabulation of all the debit and credit
items, without special reference to the quantitative relations of
total debits to total credits." [7] Viner distinguishes between the
balance of indebtedness as consisting of all international obligations immediate and deferred, and the balance of payments as
consisting of immediate and honored obligations. [8] Viner's emphasis on the balance of indebtedness and balance of transactions
as distinct from the balance of payments leads him later to a
departure from the currently accepted procedure of tabulating
the international accounts. He records only the net balances for
noncommercial transactions (chiefly migrants' capital and remittances) on the ground that these noncommercial transactions do
not refer to the international trade of either commodities or services. "To add the noncommercial debits to the other debits, and
the noncommercial credits to the other credits, is to exaggerate
the volume of international transactions." [9]

Statistical estimates of the merchandise components of the
international accounts are chiefly based on the actual transfers of
goods through the customs, and rarely can adjustment be made
for delayed payments for goods received. For this reason estimates could not generally be made available for what Viner has
termed the balance of payments. Though logical, Viner's distinction has not proved important in practice. Fortunately, his treatment of the balance of indebtedness, in his sense of the term, con-
forms with current handling of the balance of payments, with the
relatively unimportant exception of noncommercial debits and
credits as observed in the preceding paragraph. For the term
"balance of indebtedness" we may therefore substitute "balance
of payments" and conform with current practice.

There is good reason for the substitution as a result of the fact
that common usage has associated a different meaning with the
term balance of international indebtedness. Its present accepted
meaning is that of a balance at a particular date of outstanding

[7] *Canada's Balance,* p. 21.
[8] *Canada's Balance,* p. 22n. For the definition of the international balance of payments, see Chapter II, "Definitions."
[9] *Canada's Balance,* p. 104.

claims on foreigners and liabilities to foreigners.[10] It is therefore analogous to the firm's balance sheet in private accounting parlance. The balance of international payments, on the other hand, must not be regarded as analogous to the accountant's balance sheet. It is more similar to income or to profit and loss statements in that these, too, refer to changes during a stipulated period of time.[11] Similarly, the balance of payments refers not to a moment but to a period of time.

Viner proceeds as follows in his computation of the balance of indebtedness:[12]

(1) Certain adjustments are made to the customs figures for merchandise exports and imports, notably for the gold trade. Estimates are then made for migrants' capital and remittances, the other noncommercial credits and debits being assumed as offsetting. Freight, insurance, and tourist expenditures are then estimated. The net debits and credits for all these items are then totalled. This net total represents the remainder of the balance of international indebtedness, which, if we assume there to be no unexplained residual error, includes (a) Canadian investment abroad, (b) Canadian borrowing abroad, (c) interest and dividends received from abroad, and (d) interest and dividends paid abroad. Items (a) and (d) would have negative signs attached, and items (b) and (c) positive signs.

(2) Direct estimates for Canadian investment abroad are then made.

(3) The interest due upon these is calculated, being estimated at 4 per cent of the amounts, one year preceding, of total Canadian capital abroad.

---

[10] Haberler, *Theory of International Trade,* p. 19. The balance of payments on current or income account (in the present conventional sense) is therefore the source of changes in the balance of international indebtedness (again in terms of current usage). Also see S. Enke, "Some Balance of Payments Pitfalls," *American Economic Review,* March 1951, pp. 161–164.

[11] The balance of international payments has a still closer parallel in the less familiar funds statement of private accounting which summarizes changes in financial elements between any two balance sheet dates.

[12] *Canada's Balance,* chaps. 2–6. The term balance of indebtedness is here employed in Viner's sense of the term as explained in the preceding paragraphs.

(4) The investment of foreign capital in Canada in 1900 was then estimated.

(5) Assuming an interest rate of 3 per cent, the interest payments for the first year of the period were calculated (to make an allowance for the later conversion of pre-1900 loans at higher rates, the average yield on these loans was estimated at 4 per cent after 1907).

(6) The Canadian borrowing abroad for 1900, the first year of the period, was then calculated by deducting (a), (c), and (d) from the net total of international indebtedness, the appropriate arithmetic signs being retained in the calculation.

(7) The additional interest payable on this additional investment in Canada made during 1900 was then calculated at the prevailing interest rate for 1901. The interest payments for 1901, the second year of the period, once estimated, the Canadian borrowings abroad were again assumed to be the residual, as in (6). These calculations were repeated in successive years to 1913.

(8) Following the establishment of this indirect estimate of foreign investment in Canada in each of the years 1900–1913, direct estimates of the annual foreign investments are undertaken by Viner. The two sets of estimates checked remarkably closely for the period as a whole, but as might be expected there is considerable discrepancy between the two estimates for individual years of the period (in Table 27 this discrepancy is classified as the residual). In effect the indirect estimate, by making no allowance for residual error, implicitly includes the net unexplained error in foreign investments.

THEORY — ATTEMPTED VERIFICATION

His initial task completed, in Part II of his study Viner takes up the inductive verification of the classical theory, introducing modifications where these appear to be called for by the facts. He deals first with variations in the exchanges, then gold movements, changes in relative price levels, and finally alterations in the volume of commodity imports and exports.

The variations in the exchanges were found to be very small, the movement within the gold export and import points being no more than ⅙ of 1 per cent.[13] This range was viewed as being too slight

[13] *Canada's Balance*, p. 155.

to have any effect on the volume of imports and exports. Canadian foreign exchange transactions were carried on almost solely via New York. The New York rate dominated the Canadian rate of sterling exchange, and the United States balance-of-payments situation was the primary factor in its determination.[14] The influence of the Canadian balance of payments was therefore sought in the New York rate on the Canadian dollar. It was found to be generally at a premium during the period of large capital imports, being quoted at a premium averaging between 1/64 and 1/32 of 1 per cent. This is in conformity with the theoretical expectations.[15]

With respect to the gold movements, Viner finds that a modification of the theory is necessary.[16] Loans made to a Canadian corporation, for example, result in an increase in deposits to its credit in Canada, with an equivalent increase of Canadian bankers' deposits in New York resulting directly in the case of an American loan, and indirectly with the sale of sterling exchange in New York by the Canadian banks in the case of a British loan. Ten per cent of these New York deposits would in the simplified case be drawn on to provide gold for the Canadian domestic reserves while the remainder would be lent on call in New York. In the process of a series of loans, the gold importations were proximately governed by the reserve requirements of the Canadian banks, and not by the balance of payments. In the expenditure of the loans, the gold reserves of the Canadian banks would be drawn on to provide the exchange to finance the resultant import surplus only when they were unable to provide sufficient funds from their New York reserves.

The Canadian process is as automatic as the process described in the generally accepted theory. It differs from the latter solely in that fluctuations in bank deposits and in outside reserves play the part in Canada which the classical theory attributes to gold movements.[17]

It is the variations of bank deposits consequent upon foreign borrowings which affect the relative price changes without the neces-

[14] *Canada's Balance*, p. 153.
[15] *Canada's Balance*, p. 154.
[16] *Canada's Balance*, pp. 177ff.
[17] *Canada's Balance*, p. 181.

sity of a gold movement to stimulate these variations as in the Mill-Thornton theory. Viner concludes,

But if the outside reserves are regarded as equivalent to gold in Canada, then the Canadian process of adjustment of international balances approaches more closely that set forth *a priori* in the generally accepted theory. It is probable, however, that the Canadian variation from the typical method, by preventing sudden inflows and withdrawals of gold, operated to bring about a steadier and smoother adjustment of price levels and trade balances in the face of huge and irregular borrowings abroad than would have been possible if gold movements into and out of Canada were as automatic and free as they are elsewhere.[18]

Such fluctuations in outside reserves would be classified as one type of short-term capital movements in contemporary analysis. The stressing of the analogy of these with gold movements is a significant contribution of Viner's.[19]

Viner next deals with the changes in relative price levels. He finds that wholesale prices in Canada rose more in the period studied than did world prices. British wholesale prices rose much less than the Canadian, while United States wholesale prices occupied a generally intermediate position.[20] Viner lays yet more stress, however, on the sectional price levels, the relative changes of domestic as compared to international prices. He discovers "that the rise in the prices of domestic commodities was most marked, that the prices of import commodities, which are least subject to the influence of domestic conditions, rose least, and that the rise in the prices of export commodities, which are subject to both internal and external influences, was intermediate between the rise in import prices and the rise in domestic prices." [21] The result would be a tendency to a shift of resources out of the export industries, and an increased incentive to import.

It is interesting to note that Mill and most other classical economists had devoted no more than passing attention to this variety

[18] *Canada's Balance*, pp. 181–182.

[19] In the Kindleberger classification outlined in Chapter 2, these short-term capital movements would fall in the first category, designated "equilibrating" or compensatory. There was no short-term money market available in Canada at the time, and therefore they could not be included in the category of income movements to a higher rate of interest.

[20] *Canada's Balance*, pp. 217, 220, 222, 225, 227.

[21] *Canada's Balance*, p. 229.

of price levels, confining their attention primarily to changes in the general price levels and in the terms of trade. A possible deterrent to the extension of the analysis may be found in the usual classical assumptions of constant costs and complete internal mobility of the factors of production. Cairnes was responsible for perceiving the importance of the sectional price levels for the theory of international trade, and the integration of those price changes into the "classical" analysis was effected by Taussig.[22] Viner held that the sectional price changes were closely related to the capital imports which occurred, and that there was a satisfactory basis for empirical verification of the "classical" theory as modified by Taussig.

Viner goes on to devote attention to the commodity balance of trade which, exclusive of gold, he holds to be the primary long-run dependent variable in the equilibration process resulting from a disturbing capital import. Viner observes a high degree of correlation between the commodity balance of trade and the total balance of indebtedness.[23] He concludes "that the borrowed capital was transferred to Canada mainly in the form of increased commodity imports." [24] Exports were not found to contribute to the capital transfer by an actual decline but

the increase in the value of the total exports was due almost wholly to the entrance in to the exports trade of the products of newly-exploited natural resources, where special factors kept down the costs of production. Although production in general was undergoing great expansion during this period, the exports of all but a few commodities actually decreased in terms of quantities. In some cases exports declined because their prices rose in full sympathy with the general rise in Canadian prices and therefore became too high for foreign markets. In other cases, exports declined because their prices did not rise in full sympathy with the general rise in Canadian prices, so that their production became less profitable. Prices rose most and exports declined most for those commodities which found a large part of their market in Canada. Throughout the range of the export commodities of which there was substantial consumption in Canada, there was convincing evidence of the restrictive influence on exports arising out of both the increased purchasing power acquired by a borrowing country and its relative rise in prices as compared to other countries.[25]

[22] Viner, *Canada's Balance*, pp. 210–211. See also Chapter 3.
[23] *Canada's Balance*, p. 259.
[24] *Canada's Balance*, p. 276.
[25] *Canada's Balance*, p. 274.

The descriptive analysis of Chapter 9 implied criticism of Viner in its emphasis on actual and prospective increases in wheat and other exports as facts serving to explain capital imports, rather than emphasizing these increases as facts that ran counter to the Mill–Taussig theoretical expectations that diminished exports would result from the capital import.[26] These facts would not be too disturbing to the Mill–Taussig theory, which can be qualified to state that the decline in exports need not be absolute if the borrowing country is an expanding one, nor if the borrowing is for the purpose of expanding export industries. However, it appears to me that Part I provides a better approach via a theory which explains how both increases in exports and capital imports are based upon innovations and changes in world markets. Such a theory accounts for simultaneous increases, whereas increases of exports due to a growth of the borrowing country or due to expansion of export industries with the aid of capital borrowed from abroad would lag behind the increases in capital imports. Where the lag was a matter of years, it would be too great for the relationship to serve us in analyzing the short-run process of adjustment. Yet it is to this process that our attention is directed.

Criticism of Professor Viner's approach to the facts is clearly implied in the theory I have developed. The chief points of difference I wish to emphasize there and in what follows are:

(1) Viner fails sufficiently to consider the innovational, dynamic changes in a growth situation, and so exaggerates the explanatory value of an overly abstract theory. The type of equilibrating action outlined in the Mill-Taussig theory in fact appears to play a negligible part in the adjustment of the Canadian balance of payments from 1900 to 1913.

(2) There is no thought of denying the great importance of the capital imports into Canada during the period. This has been stressed in the preceding chapter. However, this does not provide an excuse for neglecting the role of large-scale immigration and the important domestically-financed investment, the impact of

---

[26] Similar criticism is to be found in A. F. W. Plumptre, *Central Banking in the British Dominions* (Toronto, 1940), p. 340.

which can be observed in the period 1896–1905 before the large inflow of outside capital got under way.

(3) Where the capital imports were significant, the causal nexus was generally not that postulated in the Mill-Taussig theory. The emphasis should have been placed not on a changing money supply producing relative price changes, but on production function changes, and on associated variations in investment activity and in the relative levels of incomes and employment. The price changes that occurred were incidental to these latter changes, and were not to be attributed primarily to fluctuations in the quantity of money.[27]

(4) Relative price changes, by whatever means effected, appear to have been of relatively small consequence in the balance-of-payments adjustment which took place.

(5) The lesser generality of the Mill-Taussig theory is also to be found in its narrow insistence on the primacy in the causal sense of the capital movements rather than of the commodity balance. The view is more tenable that, depending upon the circumstances, either may be the causal factor, or changes in both capital movements and commodity movements may be the common effect of secular and cyclical changes in fundamental economic conditions.

(6) In what follows I will also criticize the method by which Viner attempted to verify the Mill-Taussig theory, and I will criticize the use which was made of the available statistics.

SIMILAR EMPIRICAL STUDIES

In approaching the empirical data the difficulties of either proof or disproof must be kept in mind. At the very outset we are

---

[27] The quantity of money would certainly be a limiting factor if it were restricted during an expansion, but "monetary and banking institutions have had a way of adjusting themselves (not always without serious frictions and sometimes serious social strain, it must be admitted) to the deeper *real* requirements of a dynamic community" (Hansen, *Monetary Theory and Fiscal Policy*, p. 148). There are many other similar expressions of opinion to be found; for example, in a letter to James Bonar written by Alfred Marshall the latter claimed that he was never weary of preaching in the wilderness that "the only very important thing to be said about currency is that it is not nearly as important as it looks" (*Memorials to Alfred Marshall*, ed. A. C. Pigou, 1925).

given to pause when we read that Canada from 1900 to 1914 "provide[s] one of the very few cases where adequate verification is possible." [28] Other inductive studies, for example White's study of the French International Accounts, Bresciani-Turroni's of Germany in the 1920's, and Taussig's of the United States following 1918, have not provided inductive verification for the "classical" theory.[29] These studies noted a smooth and rapid adjustment of commodity to capital flows which could not be explained on the basis of the gold flows and the price changes which were not always in the direction called for by the theory. Further, in some instances the banking system did not follow the rules of the game and the effects of the gold flows when they were in the right direction were offset. Taussig himself candidly observed:

The movement of exports and imports — the substantive course of international trade — responds with surprising promptness to the balance of payments as a whole — what is puzzling is the rapidity, almost simultaneity, of the commodity movements. The presumable intermediate stage of gold flows and price changes is hard to discern, and certainly is extremely short.[30]

The ease and immediacy of adjustment is not surprising when other equilibrating factors, such as relative income changes, are admitted to the explanation, and when the role of expectations and innovation are given prominence in the context of cyclical changes and economic development.

[28] Haberler, *Theory of International Trade,* p. 96.
[29] League of Nations, *International Currency Experience,* p. 101.
[30] Taussig, *International Trade,* p. 261.

XI

Viner's Critics

Considerable misunderstanding has arisen in certain criticisms of Viner, notably by Angell [1] and Carr. [2] These criticisms have resulted in large measure for two reasons. (1) The misinterpretation and misuse of certain statistical material in Viner's study which was not set forth by him in a sufficiently clear and unambiguous manner. In particular, in my view, Viner did not furnish a sufficiently clear treatment of the indications which short-term capital movements and the residual error might give of untransferred long-term capital imports. (2) Viner's relative neglect of the secondary expansion of bank credit (which played such an important part in "classical" theories of international adjustment), while at the same time not making clear that he was not assigning much importance to such secondary expansion.

The fact that these criticisms were inadequate and at times in error invited the onslaught subsequently made on them by Viner, and this in turn obscured the valid points of criticism which they contained. It gave Viner an opportunity to concentrate on the error of others, so that the prestige of his study was little diminished by his critics. It would be superfluous to relate the numerous defects in these criticisms which are clearly set forth by Viner, [3] and I will confine myself to a few major points.

[1] J. W. Angell, *The Theory of International Prices* (Cambridge, 1926), pp. 170ff and 505ff.
[2] R. Carr, "The Role of Price in the International Trade Mechanism," *Quarterly Journal of Economics*, 1931, pp. 710ff.
[3] Viner, *Studies . . . International Trade*, pp. 414–426.

ANGELL AND CARR — STATISTICAL DIFFICULTIES

The investigator in the "classical" tradition should keep two aspects of the problem in mind in attempting to assess the significance of the relative price changes in the adjustment mechanism. First, there is the effect upon relative price changes of the net international transfers of purchasing power related to the capital imports; second, there is the influence of the relative price changes in inducing the real transfer via a current account deficit. In *Canada's Balance,* Viner had not attempted to verify statistically any lagged causal relation of this nature. Indeed, being based solely on a calendar-year basis and subject to considerable error, the statistics would have been inadequate to verify any such relation, even assuming it to exist. Viner's critics were less cautious as well as less familiar with the statistics and so made themselves vulnerable to attack.

If the statistics were complete and free of error, we would find in the simple case that the untransferred borrowings would be represented by the net movements of monetary gold and short-term capital in the period concerned. The balance of payments is an accounting identity (see "Definitions," Chapter II, and Table 27). Therefore, the balance on current account must be exactly offset by the balance on account of long-term and short-term capital plus monetary gold, the residual error being eliminated by assumption. The current balance not offset (or not transferred) through long-term borrowings would therefore equal the net flows of short-term capital plus monetary gold. Viner makes a distinction between nonmonetary and monetary gold, the latter consisting of gold coin.[4] The distinction I have employed (see the Statistical Appendix) treats Canadian production less Canadian consumption and private hoarding as net exports of nonmonetary gold. Monetary gold movements then consist of all gold movements affecting the monetary reserves. Thus a capital import would be considered untransferred to the extent that external bank assets were acquired and to the extent that the domestic gold reserves were augmented. To consider a reduction in gold exports associated with an acquisition of gold reserves a real transfer,

[4] Viner, *Canada's Balance,* pp. 32–36.

while considering the acquisition of external short-term banking assets to be an indication of the lack of real transfer, would be illogical.[5]

Angell and Carr had the misfortune to select as an indicator of the untransferred borrowings the residual error, the difference between the direct and indirect estimates of the capital borrowings.[6] Angell appears to have assumed that this residual consisted largely of short-term capital movements. Unfortunately for Angell's purpose, Viner had accounted for and separately tabulated an important category of short-term capital, namely, net external bank assets, which he then included in his series for Canadian investment abroad.[7] Viner, in criticizing Angell, states: "the excess of borrowings over import surplus as computed by Angell must be regarded as meaningless except as a measure of the net error in the various estimates."[8]

The errors Viner had in mind in criticizing Angell and Carr were primarily errors with respect to allocation between years, or timing errors. Thus he continued to adhere to the earlier view expressed in *Canada's Balance* that it is the predominance of timing errors that explains the near offsetting of total residual error taking the period 1900–1913 as a whole.[9] Professor Viner, has indicated, however, that he would now incline toward the hypothesis that the net errors chanced to be offsetting. The net errors, as we shall see, have not always behaved so nicely for the investigator of the Canadian balance of payments.[10]

There are three types of errors that enter into the residual which it would be helpful to distinguish. The first type consists of the set of errors, which, if they had been pointed up rather

[5] Where the customs records for nonmonetary gold shipments were accurate, and where little gold was minted in Canada (less than $5 million during the Viner period), this difference in procedure was of relatively small importance. Gold was shipped abroad as a nonmonetary export, minted, and imported in monetary form. Viner did not rely on the customs figures for the specie imports, which were very inaccurate.

[6] Viner, *Studies . . . International Trade*, pp. 421–426.

[7] Viner, *Canada's Balance*, p. 94, table 25; and Viner, *Studies . . . International Trade*, p. 424.

[8] Viner, *Studies . . . International Trade*, p. 426.

[9] *Canada's Balance*, p. 140; and *Studies . . . International Trade*, p. 424.

[10] See Statistical Appendix.

than underestimated by Viner, would have made his criticism of Angell and Carr even more destructive. These are the errors that would be offset in time only by chance: inaccurate reporting of all the items in the balance of payments upon which the indirect estimate of loans is based, and inaccuracies in the direct estimate, particularly those attributable to the trade in outstanding securities and to the amortization of foreign loans.

The second type of error relates to long-term financing, which is recorded at the wrong date. For example, there may be an interval between the announcement of a loan and its actual flotation, with the announcement being reported as a flotation in the statistics. Or, direct investments in branch plants might be assigned at the time the plans were announced, while the actual transfer of funds and required imports might lag by a year or longer.[11]

A third type of error derives from the fact that short-term capital movements are peculiarly difficult to record. Among those that are likely to escape attention are nonbank short-term debts incurred one year and not liquidated until the next. If liquidated within the same calendar year, no error would arise in calendar-year balance-of-payments reporting. Another example is to be found in "call loans in New York by Canadian banks without agencies there made directly from and reported as of their Canadian head offices." [12] These unrecorded short-term capital movements would tend to be mutually offsetting over a period of years, except to the extent that an increasing amount of short-term debt might remain outstanding. In the instance where imports were arranged on short-term credit and later refinanced by permanent loans, the first step would be recorded in the balance of payments as merchandise imports offset by a numerically positive element in the residual error, which would reflect the unrecorded short-term capital import. The second step would be recorded as a long-term capital import offset by a numerically negative element in the residual error, which would reflect the unrecorded repayment (or export) on short-term capital account.

It was this third type of residual error that Angell and Carr

[11] Viner, *Studies . . . International Trade*, p. 423.
[12] *Studies . . . International Trade*, p. 427.

appear to have assumed constituted the main differences between the direct and indirect estimates of capital imports. Since they did not take cognizance of the recorded short-term capital movements, they seem to have regarded these differences as indicating the total volume of short-term capital flows. It strikes me that Viner, who referred to both the second and third type of residual error, emphasized the third type more than the second type in *Canada's Balance*. In his *Studies . . . International Trade*, on the other hand, it appears to me that it was the second type of error he had primarily in mind when criticising Angell and Carr.

There are some statements made by Viner respecting the residual error (the difference between the direct and indirect estimates of capital imports) and short-term capital movements which I find misleading and which may help to account for the misguided steps taken by Angell and Carr. A concluding sentence runs as follows:

The closeness of the two estimates for the entire period confirms, therefore, the hypothesis that the discrepancies between the estimates for individual years are due in large part to the differences in time between the flotation of a loan and its transfer to the borrowing country in the form of commodities.[13]

This statement and the discussion which precedes it may be taken to indicate Viner's view that unrecorded short-term capital movements were a larger part of the residual error than were inaccurate estimating of the various items and incorrect allocations as between successive years. The unwary reader might have gone further and inferred that recorded gold movements and recorded short-term capital movements (which like the unrecorded short-term capital movements reflect "differences in time between the flotation of a loan and its transfer") were also included in the differentials between the direct and indirect estimates. This, I believe, proved to be the pitfall for Angell and Carr.

Viner is obviously attracted to some aspects of the approach

[13] *Canada's Balance*, pp. 140–141. In passing it might be noted that Viner's implicit expectation that due to a lag the large negative residual of 1913 and the smaller negative residual for the entire period 1900–1913 might be wholly or partially offset by a positive residual in 1914 was in fact not realized (see Table 27). The estimates for that year (and subsequent years until 1918), which Viner did not undertake, revealed further negative residuals.

made by Angell to the problem of the capital transfer, an approach subsequently adopted by Carr. Like Angell, Viner attempts to make allowances for the transfers of funds other than those attributable to the capital borrowings in relating the monetary and the real transfers. Unlike Angell, he takes correct account of the short-term capital movements, and he considers migrants' capital and remittances that escaped Angell's attention. Thus he develops, in his *Studies . . . International Trade,* series for the "net acquisition of outside funds" and for the "amount of net economic transfer." The former is Canadian borrowings abroad, direct estimates, minus Canadian investments abroad exclusive of changes in outside reserves of Canadian banks, plus credit balances and minus debit balances of noncommercial transactions, minus net interest payments by Canada. The "net economic transfer" is then commodity import surpluses inclusive of coin and bullion,[14] plus service debit balances exclusive of interest payments. The innovation here is the treatment of noncommercial transactions, which consist of immigrants' capital and noncommercial remittances, as equivalent to capital transfers, that is, insofar as the transfer problem is concerned. Viner concludes "that there was a variable time-lag between borrowings abroad and economic transfer, with the recorded, or long-term, borrowings usually but not always preceding the economic transfer chronologically." [15] It is surprising that Viner implies that there may be any significance in such a conclusion after revealing Angell's inconclusive examination of the residual, for even though Viner takes account of recorded short-term funds, the residual which includes errors and omissions accounts for the greater part of the discrepancy between the acquisition of funds and their transfer in all but four of the thirteen years for which

[14] Professor Viner has expressed the belief that this is an appropriate treatment of gold movements, and that they were not an "untransferred" item but were "normal" given the Canadian monetary system and the expansion of Canadian activity measured in dollars. Taking the period as a whole, certainly a large proportion of the gold movements (*and of the short-term capital movements*) might be so regarded, but this is much less admissable for the year to year changes which Viner was recording, and which undoubtedly consist in large measure of compensatory adjustments.

[15] Viner, *Studies . . . International Trade,* p. 431.

he presents figures, and the discrepancies for these four years are relatively small.[16]

Angell had attempted to demonstrate that the sequence of events in the Canadian case was (1) an increase in borrowing, (2) an increase in capital imports over the import surplus — actually the residual, (3) an increase in bank deposits, (4) an increase in relative prices, (5) an increased import surplus resulting from these price changes and so offsetting the initial increase in capital loans.[17] Angell's graphic correlation did not include the price series. Carr introduced the latter along with Angell's other series and concluded that he could demonstrate the following sequence: (1) an increase in prices, (2) an increase in capital imports greater than the increase of the import surplus — that is, the residual, (3) an increase in Canadian domestic bank deposits, and (4) an increased import surplus.[18]

In neither case is the postulated correlation at all clearly demonstrated. The calendar year series are inadequate and there is the danger of spurious correlation between cyclically varying time series. In any case, the correlations become devoid of merit due to the significance erroneously attached to a residual error.

On the theoretical plane, where Angell differs from Viner, I find myself in agreement with Viner's statement that the reason is usually to be found in Angell's misinterpretation of *Canada's Balance*. For example, I agree with Viner's summary statement.

The primary expansion in Canadian deposits was neither prior to the expansion in outside reserves, as Angell claims, nor after it, the view which he attributes to me, but was, as I contended, simultaneous with it.[19]

[16] *Studies . . . International Trade,* p. 430, table 7; and pp. 428ff. Viner comments that he could have reached this conclusion on the strength of column 3, table 7, plus the general picture, without any other statistical analysis. I remain sceptical that there was "usually" any specific time lag which can be demonstrated from these calendar year statistics. How can Viner's comment be reconciled with his criticism of Angell which emphasizes the possibility of erroneous allocations in the direct estimate of long-term capital transfers as between different years?

[17] Angell, *The Theory of International Prices,* p. 508.

[18] Carr, "The Role of Price in the International Trade Mechanism," *Quarterly Journal of Economics* (1931) p. 713.

[19] Viner, *Studies . . . International Trade,* p. 419.

The primary credit expansion is the increase in domestic bank deposits stemming directly from the foreign loan and from the acquisition of gold or external bank reserves, and not from the increase in bank loans in Canada (the secondary expansion of credit).[20] Angell was able to make his conflicting claim only because he appears to have erroneously interpreted external bank reserves as being confined to those held in New York, thus excluding those held in London.[21]

Carr's contribution is in the emphasis he lays upon change, industrial growth, and the associated opportunities for profitable investment, an orientation lacking in Viner's study. He is correct, too, in assigning to prices and bank deposits a role more independent of capital imports than is found in *Canada's Balance*, but he ignores the fact that it would only be necessary to introduce expectations into the picture in order to posit a chronological precedence to price changes and bank deposit fluctuations, while retaining the causal role for the foreign loans.[22]

In examining the transfer problem and the effect of the borrowings on prices, Viner in *Canada's Balance* used the figures for gross borrowings; Angell's approach is superior in that he subtracts Canadian investment abroad (unfortunately for his analysis not realizing that this included banks' foreign short-term assets), and he subtracts interest and dividend payments as well, thus recognizing that the gross borrowings do not require transfer, but that there is some net figure to which attention should be directed.[23]

CREDIT EXPANSION

Viner's position with regard to the relative importance of primary and secondary credit expansion in Canada from 1900 to 1913 has changed since the writing of his *Canada's Balance*. In his 1937 publication he states that in his earlier study he "overemphasized the primary phase, both with reference to the facts

[20] *Studies . . . International Trade*, p. 414.

[21] *Studies . . . International Trade*, p. 415.

[22] See White, *The French International Accounts 1880–1913*, pp. 13–17; Kahn, *Great Britain in the World Economy*, p. 35; Taussig, *International Trade*, pp. 207–8; Viner, *Studies . . . International Trade*, pp. 429–430; and Haberler, *International Trade*, p. 53.

[23] Angell, *The Theory of International Prices*, p. 505.

in Canada and with reference to the classical doctrine." [24] However, quite a contrary impression of Viner's emphasis might have been derived from certain of his statements in *Canada's Balance*, which stressed the analogy between the external bank reserves and the gold movements, leading some critics to think that the analogy did extend to the secondary credit expansion.[25] Viner carefully pointed out how the chronology of the gold flows differed in the Canadian case and how "through their use of outside reserves the Canadian banks can control and regulate the movements of gold into and out of Canada, largely irrespective of the state of the balance of payments." Yet at the same time, without pointing to the limitations of the analogy with respect to secondary expansion, as should have been done, considering the view Viner admits to have taken while writing those lines, he states: "the Canadian process is as automatic as the process described in the generally accepted theory. It differs from the latter solely in that fluctuations in bank deposits and in outside reserves play the part in Canada which the classical theory attributes to gold movements.[26]

Viner's neglect of the secondary expansion of credit is associated with his belief

that the banks are powerless to break the dependence of their total liabilities on conditions and circumstances over which they themselves have no control. The banks could therefore have succeeded as they did, in maintaining their cash reserve ratios constantly at the desired level throughout seasonal fluctuations in demand liabilities and cyclical fluctuations in business conditions, only by deliberately adjusting their cash reserves to their total demand liabilities, and not vice versa.[27]

He states that the "volume of loans granted by the banks, and consequently the volume of demand deposits, had only a very limited degree of flexibility," [28] and further to this point he observes: "The Canadian banks kept their discount rates practically constant throughout the period under study. They repeatedly

---

[24] Viner, *Studies . . . International Trade*, p. 415.
[25] *Studies . . . International Trade*, pp. 415–421.
[26] Viner, *Canada's Balance*, p. 181.
[27] *Canada's Balance*, p. 177.
[28] *Canada's Balance*, p. 175. See page 180, however, where Viner qualifies his argument in pointing out that bank lending policy would vary with business optimism and depression.

claimed that no deserving request for an extension of credit was refused." [29] Apart from the fact that the latter claim was perennially made by the banks in order to deny criticism that there was any discrimination against western Canadian customers, there is evidence that the banks did exert some influence on the volume of loans. The banks certainly did not disregard their actual or potential gold supply. Cairncross notes bankers' complaints over the gold shortage in 1907 and again in 1913 and further complaints that builders were finding credit tight in Montreal in 1913.[30] In 1913 banking officials were making such statements as the following: "Throughout the year the bank exercised restraint upon their customers." Circumstances have "curtailed the loaning power of all banks and [have] checked the encouragement of new business." [31] This certainly implies that, during the other years of the period, when reserves of gold and foreign balances were ample, the credit policy followed by the banks was relatively easy and so helped to swell purchasing power and to ease the capital transfer.

The Cairncross criticism and the Viner admission of error in overemphasis on the primary credit expansion are both significant. But an erroneous impression may remain unless it be further pointed out that the credit policy of the banks is likely to be a relatively minor, permissive factor in the secondary purchasing power shifts which, as I have noted, takes two primary related forms, the expansion and contraction of bank credit and the multiplier. Much more important than banks' credit policy will be the consumption and investment induced by the primary injection into the circular flow. Here the analysis should stress the marginal propensities to consume and import, the entrepreneurs' expectations of profit, their investment plans, and the demand for credit associated directly with these plans and also indirectly as a consequence of the induced increases in incomes. In this process, while bank credit policy is not to be denied some autonomous role, the change in the supply of money is likely to

[29] *Canada's Balance*, p. 176.

[30] A. Cairncross, "Die Kapitaleinfuhr in Kanada 1900–1913," *Weltwirtschaftliches Archiv*, 46 Band (1937 II), 627.

[31] *Canadian Annual Review*, ed. J. C. Hopkins, quoting E. L. Pease, vice-president of the Royal Bank of Canada (Toronto, 1913), p. 20; and p. 24, quoting J. Galt, president of the Union Bank.

be a relatively passive adjustment to the increasing investment activity and incomes.

THE COST-OF-LIVING REPORT

Viner, as I have noted, derived much of his material from the Exhibit by the Statistical Branch, Department of Labour, prepared in connection with a Canadian cost-of-living report under the direction of R. H. Coats, who subsequently became the Dominion Statistician. While the latter's analysis was more pedestrian than Viner's and certainly did not contain any semblance of Viner's high-powered theorizing, it had the advantage of not being prejudiced in advance by the influence of any particular type of theory. A case could probably be made for the view that where Viner succeeded in emerging from the influence of the Mill-Taussig theory, his analysis of the situation improved, and further that this improvement in analysis was due in no small measure to Viner's familiarity with Coat's Exhibit. Certainly, at the one point where Viner attempted to defend his own theoretical analysis in contradistinction to that of Coats, he succeeds in demonstrating most clearly the weakness in his own approach (see Chapter 13, especially note 1).

While leaving the Viner criticism of Coats to be dealt with later, we will cite herewith some of the latter's contributions. The pages of Coats' Exhibit, incidentally, number about 1200, and a great deal of factual and statistical material is available there. Its weaknesses inhere partly in the difficulty in digesting such a mass of material and in the Exhibit's limited amount of theoretical analysis.

Coats' emphasis is "that the underlying factor in the expansion was the drawing of Canada into the world-wide market scheme as a producer of cereals and other raw materials." [32] This is a necessary corrective to the view taken by Viner of the capital movements as an autonomous, initiating factor in the situation, which leads him to an attempt to discover the restrictive influences upon Canadian exports rather than emphasizing their actual and prospective increases.

With regard to the relative price increases which took place

[32] Canada, Department of Labour, *The Rise of Prices and the Cost of Living 1900–1914*, II, 45.

in Canada, Coats pointed to the great Canadian industrialization with its accompanying construction and other forms of investment, the tremendous expansion of the labor supply, particularly in nonfood producing occupations, the rapid progress of urbanization, the shift to less self-sufficient farming and the much greater increase of industrial as compared with agricultural production during the period under study.[33] These are factors which other critics of Viner have come to emphasize.

CAIRNCROSS

Cairncross' improvement[34] on the Viner approach lies primarily in his emphasis upon the real factors in the Canadian situation, the changes in investment activity and in employment, as opposed to the undue "classical" concentration upon monetary changes and banking policies. Cairncross's assumptions are those of the investment multiplier and foreign trade multiplier analysis, namely, that investment activity and exports in general play the role of autonomous, initiating factors in changes in income and employment, while changes in imports, consumption, and savings are generally induced by fluctuations in the level of incomes.[35] He therefore directs attention to the forces which, in their turn, affected the level of home investment in Canada and the level of Canadian exports.[36] Over the period as a whole Cairncross believes the two most important factors to be the rise of agricultural prices in world markets, and the opening up of low-cost farming land and mineral deposits. The most fundamental scarcity in his view was that of Canadian export goods on world markets. This was reflected in the scarcity of capital and labor in Canada and is the basic explanation for the

[33] Canada, Department of Labour, *The Rise of Prices and the Cost of Living 1900–1914*, II, 24, 37, 39, 41.

[34] Dr. Cairncross kindly arranged to place at my disposal the English original of the German translation. He has indicated that he is far from satisfied with the translation at many critical points. A somewhat modified version of the original article is now available in A. K. Cairncross, *Home and Foreign Investment 1870–1913* (Cambridge, England, 1953), chapter 3. My footnote references are to the original article unless otherwise indicated.

[35] Cairncross, "Die Kapitaleinfuhr in Kanada 1900–1913," *Weltwirtschaftliches Archiv*, p. 621.

[36] Cairncross, pp. 617–618, 624.

capital imports and immigration during the years 1900–1913. In the short-run, Cairncross held that the three major influences were: borrowings from abroad, banking policy, and harvest fluctuations. This neglects other important factors in the short-run cyclical swings, particularly the influence of industrial fluctuations in the United States and Great Britain on the levels of Canadian exports and domestic capital formation, an influence that need not have been channeled via the capital imports from abroad. Cairncross explains that the three short-run influences to which he alludes are closely interrelated, crop fluctuations causing the demand for loanable funds, the supply of loanable funds derived from Canadian banks, and the supply of capital from abroad to vary in the same direction. It is certainly reasonable to assume that the lending policy of the banks would vary with the influence of changing levels of exports upon the balance of payments. It does not appear so reasonable to assume that such short-run changes would significantly influence the supply curve of foreign loanable funds. Any effect of harvest fluctuations on actual capital imports would more likely be exerted through shifts in the Canadian demand for short-term and long-term capital. Cairncross, in explaining the cyclical fluctuations in the period under study, lays most stress upon the variations in crop yields and grain prices.[37] I find the resultant analysis unconvincing. There were poor harvests in 1903–1904, 1907, and 1910. In 1910 the high level of investment activity was nonetheless well maintained, as Cairncross points out. The years 1903–1904 denoted ones of recession in the United States, and the depression of 1907–1908 was world-wide in extent. Canadian crop yields were only one of many significant influences in the Canadian participation in these cycles.

Cairncross's most important statistical contribution is his series for Canadian investment; Cairncross is careful to stress the limitations of the series, which is largely based upon extrapolation and interpolation of the capital value figures for two census years.[38] The best information was that available for railway

[37] Cairncross, p. 629.
[38] Cairncross, "Die Kapitaleinfuhr in Kanada 1900–1913," *Weltwirtschaftliches Archiv*, p. 606. In *Home and Foreign Investment* Cairncross formulates an improved series based upon estimates made by Dr. K. Buckley. See footnotes in Tables 5 and 10.

building, industrial and residential construction, and government
capital outlays. No estimates were available for the inventory
changes that count so heavily in short-run fluctuations. Once the
series for investment is made available, it is used in conjunction
with the capital import estimates in order to calculate the value
for domestic Canadian savings.[39]

Cairncross, while frequently stressing interdependence and
mutual causation, does not directly take issue with Viner's exposition of the Mill-Taussig thesis, and he maintains that the
difference between his analysis and Viner's is one of emphasis.[40]
His view is that home investment governed the balance of payments, but that this domestic investment activity was determined
largely by foreign borrowing. His treatment is similar to the
foreign trade multiplier analysis with its stress upon income
effects. Although at no point does Cairncross directly question
the adequacy of the Mill-Taussig thesis in its insistence upon
the primacy of relative price changes in effecting changes in the
trade balance, nor attempt to assess the importance of relative
price changes in effecting the capital transfer, implicitly his
analysis is critical.

In my judgment, Cairncross, despite his general emphasis upon
the real as opposed to the monetary factors, nonetheless exaggerates the importance of the banks' credit policy in dealing with
the mechanism and relative smoothness of the capital transfer.[41]
Other factors dealt with in Part I (especially Chapters 4, 5, and
7) loom much larger, namely, the primary shift of demand with
the foreign investment, the secondary shifts of the multiplier and
acceleration effects, and common influences in the processes of
the business cycle and economic growth working upon exports,
imports, incomes, and investment. In the total picture the influence of the credit supply on investment and incomes appears
relatively passive.

[39] Cairncross, "Die Kapitaleinfuhr in Kanada 1900–1913," *Weltwirtschaftliches Archiv*, p. 622. The Buckley estimates used by Cairncross in
Home and Foreign Investment include 5-year averages for inventory
changes, but not year to year fluctuations.

[40] Cairncross, "Die Kapitaleinfuhr in Kanada 1900–1913," 594 note.
This comment does not appear in *Home and Foreign Investment*. The
criticism of Viner remains implicit rather than explicit.

[41] Cairncross, "Die Kapitaleinfuhr in Kanada 1900–1913," *Weltwirtschaftliches Archiv*, pp. 632–633.

In the Cairncross analysis I believe we find the first realistic and theoretical analysis of Canadian economic development and the balance of payments in the period 1900–1913. In general, while in agreement at most points, I would not extend the same emphasis to harvest fluctuations or to monetary policy. And I would like to press further in the analysis of the balance-of-payments adjustment mechanism, and in assigning a role in this adjustment to the relative price changes.

KAHN

Kahn[42] contrasts the "rapid and easy" adjustment of the Canadian balance of payments to the huge capital inflow with the "muddle of reparations," and on the whole his approach to the matter is admirable. His criticisms of Angell's and Carr's arguments are similar to those of White.[43] White and Kahn agree that there is little validity in the stress on the time sequence of changes in the variables, and this quite apart from the statistical fallacies in the Carr and Angell arguments, which neither White nor Kahn mention. Kahn agrees with White that "the fact that divergence of Canadian from world prices was greatest at the end of the period need not prove, as [Carr] alleges, that this divergence could not have caused the adjustment of the trade balance. . . . Carr's error is basically the same as Viner's — the attempt to draw a single line of causation, overlooking, except initially, the basic conditioning factors behind all the changes and overlooking, too, the complete interdependence and mutual interplay of the various series."[44]

Kahn finds himself in agreement with Carr and the many others who have emphasized as fundamental to the whole situation the "high prospective marginal efficiency of capital in Canada after 1900," although here the particular date selected by Kahn should have been 1896. He goes on to state:

Whether the expansion of the [bank deposits] preceded or succeeded the capital inflows and the increase of reserves is a matter of indifference; the two had to go together. Without continuous growth of capital imports, domestic expansion would have stopped much sooner.

[42] *Great Britain in the World Economy*, pp. 34–36.
[43] *The French International Accounts 1880–1913*, pp. 13–15.
[44] *Great Britain in the World Economy*, p. 35.

Again, whether the adverse trade balance preceded or succeeded the capital imports is also a matter of indifference. The two were inseparable. Although certainly the former could not have persisted without the latter and was undoubtedly increased by it, both were the result in addition of the more basic determinants. This was precisely the reason why the enormous transfer succeeded; the flows of both capital and goods were the product of antecedent circumstances tending to that end. Changing cyclical conditions involved simultaneous and interrelated changes in the incomes, prices, interest rates, investment, international lending, and the trade balances. Because the capital flows fitted in as a necessary part of the process of differential rates of world growth and expansion, their "transfer" occasioned little pressure or distress.

And the whole was effected in an international pattern which was propitious for related reasons. The expansion of newer areas and the growth of investment therein called forth simultaneous flows of money and real capital from the world's creditors. Equipment was needed for construction, and consumer goods to satisfy the rising money incomes in regions where investment was outstripping real voluntary saving, and only foreign capital (i.e., a surplus of foreign goods over what these areas could command by current sales) could feed such expansion. This growth thus imparted a leaven to the entire world economy, and all areas, new and old, shared in the expansion. Transfers were easily effected by relatively greater inflation in the receiving countries rather than by absolute deflation of prices and incomes in the lending countries. It is extremely instructive, in this regard, that it was Canada's imports which corresponded most closely to the capital inflow, the capital being transferred by increased sales to Canada rather than by decreased purchases by the lenders. There is no presumption in the accepted theory that this should be the case. The extraordinary ease of international adjustments to the rapid changes of the years 1900–1913 was the result of a complex of interdependent dynamic world-wide cyclical and secular conditions rather than of the simple balance-of-payments adjustment to a capital flow induced by autonomous external factors.[45]

I have quoted Kahn at such length, not because the points which he makes are novel, but because they are well expressed and aptly applied to the Canadian situation. Kahn attributes the "increasingly adverse trade balance" of Canada to two factors, "the growing price differential and the faster rise of domestic income and industrial demands." [46] At another point Kahn contends that Viner's study is held to provide inductive verification,

[45] Kahn, pp. 35–36.
[46] Kahn, p. 35.

not of the Mill-Taussig theory, but of Kahn's own type of international equilibration theory which incorporates the analysis of the primary and secondary shifts of demand, the latter in its modern guise of the multiplier theory.[47] It appears that Kahn would hold the Viner analysis, while in many respects inadequate in its approach, to be a reasonably adequate explanation of the changes which took place. This I question.

In the foregoing pages I have frequently found myself at odds with other critics of Viner; there are several questions to which more definitive answers should be sought and Viner's critics in the main have avoided these questions. I will devote attention in the remaining chapters of Part III to these questions.

[47] Kahn, p. 34.

XII

Shifts of Demand

Professor Viner's reaction to the purchasing power shift approach has not been a sympathetic one. I suspect that this may be one of the important matters that Viner had in mind when he admitted that Ohlin's "persistent refusal to agree" had forced him "to revise — and perhaps even upon occasion to abandon doctrines" to which he "had been disposed to cling as long as it was possible to do so without violating the intellectual decencies."[1] At times, as we shall see, his sympathy for the "classical" Mill-Taussig theory has conflicted with his grasp of the nature of the problem in hand. The issue as it posed itself to Viner at the time of writing his 1937 publication[2] was not "whether a relative shift in demands occurs, but whether this shift in demands, *of itself and aside from its effect on relative prices,* exercises an equilibrating influence." His answer is in the affirmative. "Unless there is an extreme and unusual distortion of the relative demands for different classes of commodities from their previous proportions this shift in demands will of itself contribute to an adjustment of the balance of payments."[3] It might be pointed out that Viner is doubtless thinking in terms of the direct influence on the trade balance of relative changes in demands and

[1] Viner, *Studies . . . International Trade,* p. xiv.
[2] *Studies . . . International Trade,* p. 294n.
[3] *Studies . . . International Trade,* p. 294.

thus he is neglecting the additional equilibrating influence through subsequent rounds of expenditure of that proportion of the increased purchasing power expended domestically.[4]

In *Canada's Balance* only very qualified recognition is given to the equilibrating influence of the demand shift. Viner admits in the course of his commentary on the Taussig-Wicksell controversy that in the absence of price changes some of the proceeds of a loan will be used directly for the purchases of foreign goods, and that domestic purchases would reduce the amount of commodities available for export.[5] Viner's analysis lacks explicit admission that domestic goods may have some import content, or may compete directly or indirectly with imports which are then increased,[6] and that even if there is no such foreign competition the increased incomes, aside from the effects of the relative price changes, will lead in subsequent rounds of expenditure to increasing imports.

The foreign trade multiplier concept was not among Viner's tools of analysis, and this fact helps explain what would now be considered his exaggerated emphasis on the question of a possible increase in the ratio of imports to income (or the average propensity to import). There is no doubt but that such an increase would contribute to the transfer of capital from abroad. But very much more important is the tendency to an increase of incomes which leads to an increase of imports, even although the average propensity to import may not increase. Indeed, a decreasing average propensity to import is quite consistent with the major portion of the capital transfer being accomplished by means of the income effect rather than the price effect. However,

---

[4] This was typical, of course, of writing which preceded the Keynesian income-expenditure brand of analysis (see Nurkse in *The New Economics*, pp. 264ff.). Rather diligent searching is required even in the writing of those economists like Ohlin who stressed the income effect if one is to find a sketch of the multiplier process (see Chapter 3). This was to be expected in view of their relative neglect of cyclical change and associated changes in the volume of employment and of output. Ohlin's analysis of the purchasing power shifts is thus lacking in realism compared to the Keynesian income analysis, towards which it might be regarded as a first step.

[5] Viner, *Canada's Balance*, p. 205.

[6] See Bresciani-Turroni, *Inductive Verification of the Theory of International Payments*, pp. 91–93.

a high and increasing average propensity to import would strengthen the equilibrating income effects.

Viner has taken some pains to dispute the proposition that there will be an increase in the ratio of imports to income following an increase in purchasing power in a borrowing country (presumably not only an absolute increase, but an increase relative to other countries). It can be argued forcibly in defense of this proposition that the short-run availability of the increased amounts of products demanded will be greater in the world community than within the relatively small area in which the increase of demand occurs. The proposition appears to apply with particular force to Canada during the period which Viner was studying.

The situation for Canada was one in which a country small in population enjoyed conditions of high elasticity of supply for her imports.[7] The greater availability of the needed imports abroad does not imply, as Viner argues, that the explanation for the relative shift in buyers' purchases to foreign sources is to be found in price inducements. By far the most important reason for the shift is the increase of Canadian purchasing power. From the point of view of price, Canadian imports were relatively noncompetitive with domestic production (see Chapter 16). The foregoing argument that the income elasticity of demand for imports would be expected to be greater than unity might be expected to apply most strongly to a relatively full employment situation, such as Canada's during 1900–1913, for the difficulty of increasing domestic supplies would then be enhanced. However, there is strong empirical evidence in the studies which I am going to cite that income elasticities likewise exceeded unity through the interwar period despite prevalent underemployment.

There are additional reasons for expecting an income elasticity of demand for imports greater than unity (or an increasing average propensity to import) in the case of a country like Canada. These reasons are substantiated by statistical investiga-

[7] Table 8 reveals that between fiscal years 1900–1914 the volume in quantity terms of imports for the major categories more than doubled in every instance (and increased almost sixfold in one classification), yet price rises in no instance reached 30 per cent, and with the exception of one category were less than 20 per cent (four of the nine categories less than 10 per cent).

tion of import-income relations to the extent that the results may be relied upon.[8] A relatively high cyclical income elasticity of demand for imports might be expected for Canada in view of the fact that investment goods and high standard of living consumption goods appear to form more important components of her import list than of her domestic commodity list.[9] Chang's investigations for the years 1924–1938 reveal that the basically agricultural countries such as Canada have an income elasticity of demand for imports which exceeds the world average of 1.50, it being estimated in Canada's case as 1.75.[10] Since the income elasticity of demand is equal to the marginal divided by the average propensity to import,[11] these results indicate that the ratio of imports to income will increase with increasing income,

[8] For example, I. de Vegh, "Imports and Income in the United States and Canada," *Review of Economic Statistics*, August 1941; T. C. Chang, "The International Comparison of Demand for Imports," *The Review of Economic Studies*, 1945–46, XIII. See also Table 23, for a crude average propensity to import estimated in value terms with no attempt to separate statistically the price and income effects.

[9] See Dominion Bureau of Statistics, *The Canadian Balance of International Payments* (Ottawa, 1949), pp. 18–19, 24–25. There are numerous essential goods and services, e.g., utilities and house rents which appear almost solely in the domestic list, which serve to implement this reasoning.

[10] Chang, "The International Comparison of Demand for Imports," *The Review of Economic Studies*, xiii, pp. 64–65. This income elasticity of 1.75 is considerably lower than those for other so-called agricultural countries, such as Australia and New Zealand. This may be because Canada is relatively more industrialized than these other countries as Chang suggests. On the other hand Chang finds a price elasticity for imports of −1.34 for Canada, a figure suspiciously high considering that the negative price elasticities for nearly all other countries, agricultural or industrial, were found to be less than unity. Could it be that there are other explanatory variables which Chang has not considered and which, in being correlated with relative price changes, have led to an erroneous price-elasticity estimate? For example, decreasing investment activity (only partly accounted for in Chang's income variable) and enhanced administrative customs restrictions may have reduced imports at a time when relative price changes, partly associated with increased tariffs, were taking place. In any case, the limitations of multiple correlation analysis of a fourteen-year time series must not be forgotten. The computations for price elasticities are particularly unsatisfactory. See J. J. Polak, "Projections of the International Sector of Gross National Product," *N.B.E.R. Conference on Research in Income and Wealth* (Mimeographed), May 1951, pp. 14ff. Also see Guy H. Orcutt, "Measurement of Price Elasticities in International Trade," *Review of Economics and Statistics*, May 1950. The price elasticities would be expected to increase through time, since supply reactions, particularly, are sluggish.

[11] Nurkse, in *The New Economics*, 270n.

taking the world as a whole, and that the increases will be even more marked for agricultural countries.[12] There are additional tendencies of a secular character toward an increasing average propensity to import for a country progressing in the manner of Canada, 1900–1913. *Ceteris paribus,* a higher average propensity to import may be demonstrated[13] (1) the higher the real income per capita, (2) the more industrialized the country, and (3) the more specialized the exports of the country concerned.[14] Canada was advancing markedly with respect to export specialization and industrialization, but real income per capita may have declined.[15]

Viner failed to consider such factors as these and affirmed:

In the absence of special circumstances such as the requirement that the proceeds of the loan be used in making purchases in the lending country, and in the absence of price changes, there is no reason why borrowings abroad should disturb the proportions in which the total purchasing power in the borrowing country, including that derived from the loan, would be used in buying domestic and foreign commodities.[16]

[12] The income elasticity of demand for imports would normally be higher in the short-run fluctuations of an inventory cycle than in the longer run of a major cycle. Price elasticities, on the other hand, tend to increase through time, since supply reactions to a price change, in particular, are slow. See Polak, "Projections of the International Sector of Gross National Product," *N.B.E.R. Conference on Research in Income and Wealth,* pp. 21ff.

[13] Chang, "The International Comparison," *The Review of Economic Studies,* XIII, pp. 53–55.

[14] These propositions are best taken as tentative hypotheses that would probably best apply to a relatively dependent economy in the earlier stage of its development. For example, a contrasting downward trend has been apparent in the United States import-income ratio since the 1870's (see J. J. Polak, pp. 19–21), and the major changes in the Canadian ratio since 1914 have probably been chiefly cyclically induced and war induced. The trend in the American ratio can be partly explained by the growing proportion of income which services have come to represent, by the increasing variety of domestic production facilitated by a growing domestic market, and by the increased availability of substitutes for imports, such as synthetic rubber.

[15] See Chapter 9. Cairncross, "Die Kapitaleinfuhr in Kanada 1900–1913," *Weltwirtschaftliches Archiv,* 46 Band, p. 616, believes that the available data indicate an increase in real wages of the order of 5 per cent, but the evidence is certainly not reliable. Those groups with more stable money incomes than the wage earners would probably have suffered a decline in real income.

[16] *Canada's Balance,* p. 206.

Apparently having forgotten the admission he had made on the immediately preceding page that the purchasing power shift will have a restrictive effect upon exports, Viner added this statement: "Without a disturbance in these proportions the loan cannot wholly enter in the form of commodities."

Viner's statement that what we now refer to as the average propensity to import would be unaffected by a shift in demand in the absence of price changes was contested [17] even prior to the statistical investigations to which I have alluded. Viner, in reply, held that the meaning of his original statement would have been better expressed as follows:

The assumption that, in the absence of price changes and of known evidence to the contrary, the amounts available for expenditure in each country would after their increase or decrease be distributed among different classes of commodities in the same proportion as before still seems to me more reasonable than any other specific assumption.[18]

The analogy drawn by Viner is the probability of a marksman hitting the bull's eye at which he is aiming. Viner's position, as he has clarified it, appears to be that the probable changes in the average propensity to import following an increase in purchasing power in the absence of price changes could be represented by a particular form of probability distribution. This probability distribution would be modal at the point of the initial average propensity to import and would be skewed neither to the right nor left. The issue between us can then be clearly stated. I am maintaining that on an empirical and a priori basis the expected probability distribution would be skewed to the right. The modal average propensity to import in the distribution following the expenditure increase would be higher than the initial average propensity to import. But to repeat, such an increase would not be an essential element in the equilibration process as analysed in Part One of this book.

Viner's conclusion in his Canadian study is in support of Taussig's argument that "without gold movements and changes in price levels there is no visible mechanism whereby increased purchases by the borrowers of foreign commodities, and of those

---

[17] For example, White, *The French International Accounts 1880–1913*, pp. 20–21.

[18] Viner, *Studies . . . International Trade*, p. 325.

domestic commodities which otherwise would be exported, will
exactly equal the amount of the borrowings." [19] The foregoing
claim has been answered by the presentation of a theory alternative to the Mill-Taussig in which gold movements and relative
price changes are admitted as one of many equilibrating influences, but one that is not essential to final equilibration, and that
does not appear in my judgment to play an important role. Since
the influences which were emphasized in the theory may not
always appear as well qualified as relative price changes to bring
about exact equilibration, it might be desirable at this juncture
to point out that exact equilibration is not characteristic of the
usual balance of payments adjustment, certainly not of the Canadian case Viner selected for study, and that gold and short-term
capital movements compensate for the difference between the
total amount of transfer payments and the total amount of the
offsetting increases of commodities and services actually transferred.

[19] Viner, *Canada's Balance*, p. 205.

XIII

Relative Price Changes—Their Causes

The questions which I intend to discuss in the remaining portion of Part III include an examination of the statistics set forth in Viner's analyses and the theoretical interpretation of this statistical material. I further propose to examine more closely the degree to which the Mill-Taussig mechanism as interpreted by Viner may have participated in the actual balance-of-payments adjustment that ensued during the period under study. In this connection it would be of interest to examine the basis for the great persuasiveness and appeal of Viner's attempted empirical verification of the Mill-Taussig propositions, if, as I contend, this verification can be shown to be inadequate.

At the outset I wish to criticise a certain lack of clarity in Viner's approach to attempted verification of the Mill-Taussig hypothesis. The causal sequence in the hypothesis appears straightforward enough. The transfer of financial capital involved in the sale of securities to foreigners is held to result in the relative price changes elaborated on by Taussig and Viner. These relative price changes then induce changes in the flows of exports and imports that result in the effecting of the real transfer on current account.

There are two distinct causal nexuses here that should in my view have been separated in Viner's exposition. Therefore I propose to examine, first, the various causes of the relative price changes that occurred during the 1900–1913 period. The transfer of financial capital that took place and the changes in the Canadian money supply associated with them will be shown to be only one among many significant initiating forces. Second, I propose to examine the extent of the influence of the relative price changes that did in fact occur, for whatever reason, in bringing about the real transfer through effecting changes in the current balance. The short-run buffer adjustment is of course to be found in the movements of gold and short-term capital, particularly the latter, so that these movements must occupy much of our attention. It is recognized that empirical verification of any theory is most difficult, if not impossible, but correlative investigation of hypotheses and statistics can be most illuminating, and taken as a whole go far toward establishing a sound case against many of Viner's contentions.

In particular, the correlative testing of causal and chronological sequences must prove extraordinarily difficult. In the first place, our time series are inadequate for annual data, and this is particularly true with respect to the data for short-term capital movements. Secondly, not only annual data but monthly and weekly or even daily data would be relevant to our purpose, but generally, and for the vital short-term capital movements in particular, these are not available. Finally, an initiating factor that has prior claim in a causal sequence may alter simultaneously with the factor whose change it is responsible for effecting, or it may alter only subsequently in the chronological sequence, if anticipations of its change are operative. Strictly, the anticipations do precede the recorded change in the factor affected, but the expectations themselves are not available in recorded time series form.

Professor Viner has not favored theories that would emphasize, in explaining Canadian price changes, factors additional to the capital imports that might have been operating throughout the period under study. In particular he denies that industrialization and investment activity of themselves would be important factors.

If expansion of this sort in a given country was financed from domestic savings, it would simply mean, however, that those having purchasing power were voluntarily shifting their demand from consumers' goods to producers' goods and from labor engaged in producing consumers' goods to labor engaged in industrial developments. What might be expected to happen would be that producers' goods would rise and consumers' goods would fall in price. The general price level would not be affected by this change in the character of the demand. On the other hand, if the expansion was financed by borrowings from abroad, there would still be available the normal supply of consumers' goods, the extra supply of goods and labor necessary for the industrial development being provided directly or indirectly by the lending country. In so far as the industrial expansion per se was concerned, there would again be no obvious reason why prices should rise more rapidly in this than in other countries, and there would even be some reason for expecting a relative fall in prices.

It unquestionably was true that in general the countries in which industrial expansion was taking place at the most rapid rate were also the countries in which prices were rising at the most rapid rate. But these were also the countries which were borrowing capital from abroad in the greatest volume, notably Canada, the Argentine, Australia, New Zealand, Japan, and the United States.[1]

This passage reveals, in several respects, inadequate treatment of the problem.[2] (1) First, and most important, Viner fails to admit the possibility of domestic credit expansion (which was very considerable during the period, as Table 11 indicates) leading to a general price rise, with rises in the prices of domestic goods being particularly great in the areas where investment expenditures were concentrated. The statement that a relative fall in prices might be expected, but certainly not a relative rise, if the investment activity were to be financed by capital imports, is extraordinary. If the goods and labor are to be provided indirectly, certainly relative price rises are likely to be associated with the relative income rises in the loan-receiving country. Viner must be assuming away the transitional period with which we are directly concerned.

(2) The close analogy between domestically and foreign financed investment was seemingly not appreciated by Viner. With the former, if consumption decreases do not offset the in-

---

[1] Viner, *Canada's Balance*, p. 249. It is here that Viner is taking issue with R. H. Coats (see Chapter 11).

[2] Viner can certainly be excused on the grounds that he is being criticized partly from the standpoint of later analysis that he could hardly have been expected to anticipate. The fact that he did not so anticipate is nonetheless a weakness. One of my objectives is to demonstrate the superiority in the approach to Viner's problems made possible by recent developments in the economic literature.

creased investment, there is a change in the level of purchasing power. With the latter, if changes in the capital imports are not immediately offset by increased imports, there is also a change in the level of purchasing power, which manifests itself in increased bank deposits at home associated with increased assets (usually short-term) abroad or with monetary gold imports.

Whether the purchasing power increases are based on domestic bank credit creation or on bank deposits resulting from foreign loans is irrelevant from the point of view of the effects upon relative price levels, except insofar as the nature of the loan, foreign or domestic, may affect the direction of the expenditures. The shifts in the factors of production, the "forced savings" of those whose incomes lag behind the rising prices, the increase of goods and labor movements both from within and without the country to the areas in which the expenditures may be concentrated, are similar whether the loans are domestic or foreign. Domestic and foreign loans are likely to be associated, since they are both attracted by the same expectations of profit, and either will tend to the same cumulative processes, partly dependent on the relative and general price changes and the multiplier principle, which lead to expectations of even greater profit. Expansion on the basis of domestic loans will tend to be inhibited by the loss of gold and foreign reserves in other than a closed system, unless there were to be simultaneous foreign expansion.

The shift of purchasing power associated with the import surpluses which would develop would manifest itself in a decline in monetary gold stocks and in foreign reserves and would tend through the action of the equilibrating mechanism to quell the investment activity which was leading to the expansion. The equilibrating action would be similar in the case of any intranational region where the supply of funds from outside the region failed adequately to support the investment activity being carried out. In this case, however, local financing and activity is more likely to keep in step with the interregional flow of funds from outside than in the case of international financing, due to a variety of reasons, such as the single banking and currency system; the greater mobility of capital, labor, and goods; the superior information and manoeuvring ability of a domestic compared to an international capitalist group, and a single government. International maladjustment is therefore likely to present more acute problems. On the other hand, if foreign loans are forthcoming in adequate volume, domestically financed credit expansion, although it will in all probability take place, is not a *sine qua non* in the expansionary process.

(3) Viner, in the statement I am discussing, was thinking too much in terms of a fixed national product, in which investment could only expand at the expense of consumption or by incurring an import surplus. This was far from being the case in the Canadian situation. An indication of the expansion that took place is found in the increase of total commodity production from $943 million to $2,859 million during the period 1901 to 1913.[3] National income more than doubled.[4] Immigration swelled the Canadian population, as indicated in Table 10. From 1903 to 1914 2,513,000 persons entered Canada, or over 200,000 per annum, which was about three times the natural increase. The period 1900 to 1913 was certainly not one when constancy of output could be assumed.[5]

(4) Viner, in his argument here as elsewhere, mistakenly attempts to relate total capital imports to the relative price changes, without considering as of equivalent relevance the transfer of other funds which are not the result of relative price changes, but on the contrary, if considered independently, would require the action of the equilibrating mechanism to effect equivalent commodity transfers in the same manner as would the capital transfers. Among such transfers, the most important items are likely to be interest and dividends, and immigrants' remittances.

However, even without taking account of transfers other than capital, Viner's statement with regard to Australia in the preceding quotation proves to be invalid. From 1904 to 1911 Australia was actually exporting capital, while if interest and dividend payments are included the transfer abroad of funds is much greater.[6]

---

[3] Viner, *Canada's Balance*, p. 262, table 52.

[4] Table 23.

[5] The preceding figures are estimates of gross immigration. Emigration (gross) for the period was estimated by Viner to be about 1,753,000. For reservations regarding these estimates see Chapter 13, note 21. The shift of the population westward, and possibly other shifts within the labor force, would have been stimulating, quite apart from net immigration gains.

[6] Wilson, R., *Capital Imports and the Terms of Trade*, p. 30, table 10.

The United States did import capital during the period 1898–1914, but, net of her own capital exports the total was only one billion dollars for the entire period. Net payments abroad on account of interest and dividends, immigrants' remittances, and tourists amounted during the period to $3.0, $2.8 and $3.2 billion respectively. It seems reasonable to include the payments made by tourists abroad among payments to which the rest of the balance-of-payments account must adjust, particularly if, like Viner, one is emphasizing the type of equilibrating action that involves relative price changes. For it is unlikely that relative prices were an important factor in inducing tourist travel, except possibly to Canada, where the relative price changes of the period were a deterrent. A heavy part of the expenditures was the result of trips to Europe on the part of previous immigrants. The American problem was to maintain a large surplus on merchandise account during the period so as to transfer in real terms her very large net payments abroad.[7]

During the period 1900–1913, Great Britain was an exporter of capital, but her net investment income was greater than the capital exports, so she was actually the recipient of net sums from abroad.[8] True, a greater part of her investment income was left abroad at the end than at the beginning of the period, and a partial defense of Viner's hypothesis may be made in the light of this fact. But Viner notably fails to consider this aspect of the problem in his general international comparisons. The yearly net transfer of funds from the United States on account of the items cited above is not recorded. Judging from the surpluses on merchandise account there were some substantial fluctuations from year to year, but the trend for funds to be transferred was certainly not downward during the period. The merchandise export surplus underwent an increase from $135 million in fiscal year 1896 to an average of over $600 million in fiscal years 1900–1901. The average for fiscal years 1912–1913 was virtually identical to that of the opening of the century. All in all, it would appear that Viner cannot account for the differing price changes in

[7] C. J. Bullock et al., "Balance of Trade of the United States," *Review of Economics and Statistics,* July 1919, especially pp. 231–232.

[8] Kahn, *Great Britain in the World Economy,* p. 128, table 15.

various countries almost solely in terms of capital imports as he would like to do.

Examination of Canadian wholesale prices, both for foods and for other commodities, reveals that both series display an upward trend from 1896 on, with the increases in prices from 1896 to 1900 being of a comparable order to any of the increases in the Viner period. For example, the index for foods increased from 82 to 100 from 1896 to 1900, and from 107 to 135 during 1904–1908, a period of maximum rise during the years studied by Viner. The increases in food prices were large relative to those of Great Britain from 1896 to 1900. The index for seventy commodities indicates a rise from 83 to 100 in the first period and from 101 to 116 in the second.[9] Yet statistics reveal that 1896–1900 was a period of export surpluses, those of fiscal years 1897 and 1898 being the greatest surpluses recorded from the time of Confederation to World War I. Adjusted statistics which took account of the nonmerchandise items would perhaps indicate that there were net capital imports, but that they were certainly at an ebb.[10]

Considering all the above facts it is difficult to accept Viner's statement relating to Canada, 1900–1913, that "no factor was operating during this period, other than the import of capital, which would adequately explain a substantially greater rise in prices in Canada than in the world at large." [11] Nor does it appear that "it is significant that in general the capital-lending countries experienced the least rise in prices, and the capital-borrowing countries the greatest rise." [12] Or at least the significance must be sought in other than the simple causal relations set forth in the Mill-Taussig theory.

A concluding statement of Viner's runs as follows:

In the absence of any other conspicuous factor which could be cited in explanation of an upward movement in Canadian prices more than proportionate to the general world movement, a substantial relative rise, if it occurred, must be explained as due to the import of capital

[9] K. W. Taylor and H. Mitchell, *Statistical Contributions to Canadian Economic History* (Toronto, 1931), pp. 55–56, 87.

[10] *Canada Year Book*, 1940, p. 526. Also see Chart I.

[11] Viner, *Canada's Balance*, p. 215.

[12] *Canada's Balance*, p. 218.

and therefore must be accepted as confirmatory of the classical theory.[13]

I will cite a series of several factors, all interrelated; and if not conspicuous in every case, at any rate they are of importance in the relative price rise. These several factors might be considered as different aspects of or results of changes in the production function which would affect relative costs, and/or as associated with changes in the volume of purchasing power, whether domestic or foreign in origin, operating on the demand side.

(1) Domestically financed investment associated with credit expansion has been discussed as a possible factor in the price rise, absolute and also relative to that in other countries. Note in Table 10 that in the whole period net capital imports estimated by either the direct or the indirect method certainly accounted for a very important share of total home investment. The expansion process would certainly have been different without it. It is not my intention to deny that capital imports constituted a most important expansionary factor, taking the period as a whole. I do deny that the story is complete once capital imports have been dealt with, and I do question the adequacy of Viner's explanation of the relationship between the capital imports and the price changes. Early in the period 1900–1913 the capital imports were proportionately much less important, and I have argued that there is reason to believe that they were still less important during the period 1896–1900 when large relative price changes were in evidence.

(2) A second factor undoubtedly leading to relative price increases was innovation affecting particular industries, increasing the demand for and hence the prices of the factors of production, which in turn led to increased costs in industries not similarly advantageously affected. In Chapter 9 I dwelt for some time on the advantages accruing to the wheat industry. Wheat exports did not develop on a very large scale until late in the period, particularly 1911–1913. As Viner observes: "The production of wheat for export did not develop to large proportions until the virgin lands of the Canadian prairies, with their high yields at low cost in the first years of cultivation, were opened up to

[13] *Canada's Balance*, p. 264.

Table 10. *Economic trends, 1900–1913*

Year	Net capital balance[a] (millions of dollars) Direct estimate	Net capital balance[a] (millions of dollars) Indirect estimate	Deposit and note liabilities in Canada[b] (millions of dollars)	Total home invest-ment[c] (millions of dollars)	Immi-grant arrivals[d] (to nearest thousand)	Terms of trade[e] (1900 = 100) Viner estimate (calendar year)	Terms of trade[e] (1900 = 100) Taylor estimate (fiscal year)
1900	30	25	344	123	42	100.0	100.0
1901	35	47	374	131	56	107.1	101.5
1902	40	34	411	145	89	111.1	106.4
1903	52	54	449	175	139	105.4	106.8
1904	59	121	496	199	131	110.8	105.3
1905	109	97	551	240	141	109.9	102.5
1906	102	88	631	283	212	107.5	105.3
1907	91	141	671	336	272	108.9	104.1
1908	218	233	664	325	143	120.5	106.2
1909	249	190	786	362	174	120.8	113.7
1910	308	218	914	454	287	119.5	114.2
1911	343	355	998	532	331	124.5	111.9
1912	316	413	1122	629	376	122.2	112.6
1913	542	424	1135	628	401	117.1	111.4
Totals	2494	2440		4562	2794		

Note. The Taylor estimate for terms of trade, fiscal 1914, was 103.5.

[a] From Table 27. The indirect estimate is the capital balance plus the residual.

[b] J. Viner, *Studies* . . ., p. 428, table VI. Averages of amounts reported monthly in banking supplements of the *Canada Gazette*.

[c] Same as for Table 5. See note to Table. More recent estimates have substantially increased the over-all investment figures by more than one half. See K. Buckley, *Capital Formation in Canada 1896–1930* (Toronto, 1955), whose estimates are mainly on a quinquennial rather than an annual basis. These estimates have been utilized in A. K. Cairncross, *Home and Foreign Investment, 1870–1913* (Cambridge, England, 1953), chapter 3, especially p. 45, where he presents a revised investment series. Investigation disclosed that the relative changes and amplitude of the two series were quite similar and would effect no change in my analysis.

[d] *Canada Year Book* (1936), p. 186. Figures rounded to the nearest thousand.

[e] The Viner estimates I have calculated from the *calendar* year import and export indices, *Canada's Balance*, 230. The Taylor estimates, to be found in Taylor and Mitchell, *op. cit.*, 6, are for fiscal years ending June 30th to 1907 and March 31st from 1907 to 1913. The estimates are thus *not* for identical yearly periods.

settlement, largely during the period under study and with the aid of capital borrowed from abroad." [14] My argument has been that, although wheat exports attained prominence late in the period, the expected profitability of wheat production and of investment associated with prairie development constituted an expansionary factor of significance throughout the period, stimulating domestic and foreign investment alike. It is scarcely adequate to treat wheat merely as an exception to the general rule of

[14] *Canada's Balance*, p. 264.

capital imports exercising a restrictive effect on exports.[15] Taussig,[16] writing in the same vein as Viner, refers to the following statement of Marshall's as perhaps partly explanatory of the increased exports of wheat despite its very slow rise in price. "Sometimes . . . the new settler regards his wheat almost as a by-product; the main product for which he works is a farm, the title deeds to which he will earn by improving the land." [17] This is appreciation of land value, and is analogous to capital appreciation, a means whereby expected returns may be realized in advance. The importance of the expected profitability of wheat production is surely enhanced in such an argument, although it minimizes the importance of the immediate cost-price ratio.

(3) Innovation and investment in a particular industry, namely, in transportation, is so important, particularly in the case of Canada, that it deserves to be treated separately. Due to improved transport conditions, prices at the farm, especially in the interior, were enabled to rise proportionately more rapidly than the world prices for like products. Railway freight rates remained quite steady from 1900 to 1913,[18] while ocean freights rose only 7 per cent from 1896 to the 1909–1913 average.[19] Price rises for wheat at Winnipeg, which would be relatively much less than further west, were from 76 cents per bushel to 96 cents per bushel,[20] in the interval 1895–1899 to 1910–1914. The lion's share of price increases in the world market accrued to the farmer.

(4) The tremendous immigration indicated in Table 10 [21] and

[15] Viner, *Canada's Balance*, pp. 261ff.

[16] Taussig, *International Trade*, p. 229.

[17] A. Marshall, *Principles of Economics* (London, 1938), p. 429.

[18] Viner, *Canada's Balance*, p. 245, data for chart 12.

[19] *Report of the Royal Commission on Dominion-Provincial Relations* (Ottawa, 1939), I, 67, table B.

[20] V. W. Bladen, *An Introduction to Political Economy* (Toronto, 1941), p. 101.

[21] Cairncross, "Die Kapitaleinfuhr in Kanada 1900–1913," *Weltwirtschaftliches Archiv*, p. 617, has estimated that on the average during the period 1900–1913 for every two Canadians entering the labor market for the first time, three immigrants offered their services. The gross immigration statistics are official, but in view of the open nature of the American-Canadian border their accuracy should not go unquestioned. In the absence of official statistics on emigration Viner made his own estimates (see *Canada's Balance*, p. 57). R. Wilson, in "Migration Movements in Canada, 1868–1925," *The Canadian Historical Review*, 13:157–182 (1932), has conducted a more intensive investigation that resulted in estimates somewhat higher than

the associated increases in population are another factor in the price increases. This led to an increased demand for food and other domestic products, but not to a comparative increase in supply of these products, since the new labor supply was so largely attracted into monocultural wheat farming, construction, railway building, and heavy industries. The demand created for residential housing was particularly acute. Between 1901 and 1911 the number of families increased by 447,000, while the addition to the number of occupied dwelling houses was only 387,000.[22]

(5) Urbanization is a factor which received its impetus from several of the other factors which have been listed, notably from the investment activity, the transport development, and the increase of farming for export. Urbanization proceeds parallel with the adoption of modern industrial techniques and increased specialization. Despite the tremendous land settlement in the West between 1896 and 1913, when "one million people moved into the three Prairie Provinces and the population increased from 7 to 20 per cent of the total population of the Dominion,"[23] the population of cities (over 5,000) grew apace, not only absolutely but relatively. From 1900 to 1910 city population grew from 38 to 45 per cent of the whole.[24] Rapidly growing urban markets created demands for domestic commodities which could not be matched by increased supplies, and inflation ensued.

(6) More basic than the preceding factors is the increasing demand for Canadian export commodities in evidence from 1896 on (see Chapter 9). Without this, the large increases in capital importations and investment activity could have been expected; and of itself an increased foreign demand for exports will exert an inflationary effect, with accompanying relative price changes.

Viner's. Cairncross has pointed out that the population increase between the decennial census years of 1901 and 1911 was 1,835,000. A reasonable estimate made by Cairncross for the natural increase is 800,000, which would leave the net immigration responsible for a gain of about one million persons. Yet Viner's estimates for emigration in conjunction with the official estimates for immigration would provide a net immigration of only 650,000. Obviously the statistics relating to migration leave much to be desired.

[22] Cairncross, p. 615.

[23] Royal Commission, *Report*, I, 68.

[24] Canada, Department of Labour, *The Rise of Prices and the Cost of Living, 1900–1914*, II, 1055.

The significance of these factors[25] in the pattern of Canadian historical development in the period under study has been set forth in Chapter 9. The basic factor was the expanding European demand for imports, wheat being a particularly important one, import commodities that Canada was eminently suited to supply in increasing quantity, partly as the result of the narrowing possibilities for land settlement in the United States. The exploitation of the agricultural resources of Western Canada stimulated and in turn was made possible by the extension of transportation facilities. The actual and potential demand for Canadian products was reflected in a growing scarcity of the capital and labor required to make exports possible. Domestic supplies of both capital and labor were wholly inadequate to meet the requirements and hence large-scale borrowing and immigration ensued. Canadian manufacturing industry, along with agriculture, was growing rapidly during the 1900–1913 period. This, together with a large internal migration of the labor force, supported and supplemented by additions to the population through natural increase plus immigration from abroad, gave rise to a pressing demand for residential housing. The urbanization associated with Eastern Canadian industrialization and the rise of commercial towns and cities to serve the agrarian population of Western Canada reinforced the demand for residential housing.

These several factors that participated in the upward inpulses given to the prices of Canadian domestic goods and services were thus all interrelated. Each factor may have a certain degree of independence, and may vary in the extent to which it appears in an initiating or dominant role. To treat the process of adjustment, as Viner and Taussig have done, as an adaptation, external and internal, to a single disturbing force can only result in a caricature. Contrast with the foregoing account with its emphasis on mutual interdependence the expressed viewpoint of Viner and Taussig:

The inward movement of capital dominated all other factors in Canada's foreign trade during the period of heavy borrowings, and the variations in the inward flow of foreign capital were marked

[25] Ohlin, *Interregional and International Trade*, pp. 466–7, discusses the factors enumerated under heading (2), (3), and (4) as being possible causal influences relating to the price changes in Canada.

enough to effect sharp correlated variations in other elements in the situation. As a consequence, an inductive study of Canada's international trade during this period becomes largely a study of the adjustment of Canada's trade balance, currency and banking system, price levels, and industry in general, to a heavy import of capital.[26]

In essentials the case is of a kind rare in economic experience, in that a single force was at work under conditions which enable us to trace its effects with certainty.[27]

The various factors I have discussed are interrelated in a process which the Mill-Taussig theory held to by Viner is not designed to analyze. The approach to the analysis of such a process is clearly best made via some form of theory stressing the business cycle and economic growth.

By the time of his 1937 publication Viner had much more reason to direct his attention to the business cycle influence which had been analyzed more thoroughly since the writing of *Canada's Balance*. Viner deals with it in the space of a very few pages,[28] itself indicative, perhaps, of the fact that there had been little change in his point of view since the publication of his Canadian study. He takes an agnostic position.

It seems a mistake to assume that there is one definite pattern of relationship between business fluctuations and international capital movements.[29]

Given the disturbed — though in my opinion exceedingly promising — state of business cycle theory at the moment and the absence of the necessary inductive spadework on the international aspects of business fluctuations, it seems to me that we must await further developments in both directions before we can expect to incorporate cycle theory into the theory of international trade, or, a more important task, to apply international trade theory to cycle theory.[30]

We may grant some validity to these observations, especially at the time of writing. But they do not justify the ignoring of the cyclical influences, and in particular, once the relevance of cyclical fluctuations is admitted by Viner, it follows that the conclusions of his Canadian study, where these fluctuations were

[26] Viner, *Canada's Balance*, p. 16.
[27] Taussig, *International Trade*, p. 223.
[28] Viner, *Studies . . . International Trade*, 432–436.
[29] *Studies . . . International Trade*, p. 434.
[30] *Studies . . . International Trade*, p. 432.

largely ignored, are suspect. Surely Viner leaves an erroneous impression with his readers in concentrating on the errors of the critics of *Canada's Balance*, while failing to indicate the weakness in it which his own, more recent, analysis implies.

It is obvious that the course of the business cycle may vary considerably from one country to another for a number of reasons, of which international capital movements is merely one possibility. Thus capital imports are not the sole basis upon which one can explain differences in price levels between countries. A fact that is unquestioned today is that some goods and services are cyclically more price flexible than others. It is essential to keep this in mind in examining the sectional price changes which Viner attributed to capital imports.

XIV

Time Series Analysis

My attitude toward attempts to establish significant correlations between the annual variations in the various price series and in series derived from the balance of payments data has been critical. These attempts have been based on the Viner data, which I believe to be somewhat improved upon and somewhat better organized in my presentation. However, the data presented still suffer from the basic inadequacies of the Viner calculations on which they are largely based, and investigation discloses that they do not afford a means of escaping the type of criticism I have made.

In the light of the theory developed in Part I it would be very interesting to be able to study disequilibrium in the balance of payments as evidenced by the flow of short-term funds and gold. But to examine the transfer of funds on the one hand and the transfer of commodities and certain services on the other, certainly in view of the probable importance of short-run adjustments, accurate monthly statistics would be required. Even then it might not be possible to judge which factors, internal or external to the balance of payments, were involved in the equilibrating reaction, in view of its probable complexity. As it is, one has only to glance at Table 11, and to note the preponderant size of the residual relative to changes in external bank assets and monetary gold in six out of the thirteen years, to realize the impossibility of obtaining annual balance-of-payments statistics

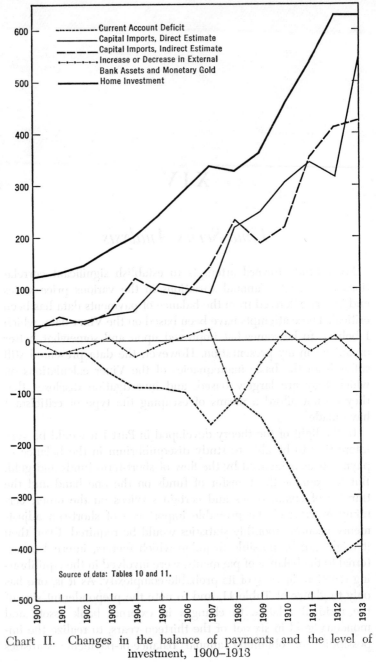

Chart II. Changes in the balance of payments and the level of investment, 1900–1913

Table 11. *Certain series relevant to the transfer problem*
(millions of dollars)

Year	Net acqui- sition of outside funds[a]	Amount of net economic transfer[b]	Increase (−) in external bank assets and monetary gold[c]	Residual[d]	Bank loans in Canada[e]
1900	4	1	0	−5	310
1901	8	5	−26	12	324
1902	16	2	−12	−6	354
1903	26	−37	8	2	408
1904	34	−64	−31	62	449
1905	74	−50	−10	−12	483
1906	63	−57	8	−14	561
1907	39	−111	21	50	630
1908	140	−32	−123	15	584
1909	172	−71	−43	−59	608
1910	225	−151	17	−90	717
1911	238	−229	−20	12	800
1912	178	−282	8	97	919
1913	370	−215	−37	−118	985
Totals	1587	−1291	−240	−54	

Note. All but the last column are derived from Table 27, and the figures carry the positive or negative sign appropriate to the balance-of-payments items from which derived. Thus the first column is dominated by capital imports and carries a positive sign, the second is dominated by the merchandise import surplus and generally carries a negative sign, while the acquisition of external bank assets or of monetary gold is equivalent to an export of capital on short term, or to an import of gold and hence is given a negative sign.

Compare the estimates made by Viner, *Studies . . . International Trade*, p. 430, table VII. The balance-of-payments series for external bank assets have been improved by new estimates by Knox, which further include, as Viner's estimates do not, foreign securities held by the Canadian banks, and deposit liabilities of the Canadian banks outside Canada. Viner does not make estimates of monetary gold similar to mine, and no estimate is included in his table 7 (*Canada's Balance*, p. 166). See the Statistical Appendix.

[a] Transfer of funds on long-term capital account; interest and dividends; other current items (includes immigrants' remittances, immigrants' capital, and transfers of funds by insurance companies which by 1926 were placed in the capital account — the first two items predominated); tourist expenditures which are included for reasons already given, which apply to Canada as well as to the United States (see Chapter 13).

[b] Net transfers of merchandise, commodity gold, and freight services. Allowing for slight error due to rounding off figures to the nearest million, the difference between *a.* and *b.* is accounted for by the external bank assets, monetary gold, and the residual.

[c] From Table 27.

[d] From Table 27.

[e] Viner, *Studies . . . International Trade*, p. 428, table VI. Averages of amounts reported monthly in banking supplements of the *Canada Gazette*.

adequate to such an examination, let alone monthly statistics. Assignments of estimates to particular calendar years have not been accurate, and although for a period as long as a year the major part of the residual could perhaps be assumed to fall to the capital account, the question of how it should be divided between short-term and long-term capital could not be safely answered. The shorter the period, the greater the latter difficulty in view of the greater importance in the short run of short-term business credit which does not show up in the statistics.

Several of the annual series (Tables 10 and 11) indicate a remarkable correspondence. Those for investment, immigration, bank loans, bank deposits and currency, merchandise imports, all show a considerable and steady rise from the beginning to the end of the period 1900–1913, with one setback in 1908 and the recovery following closely in 1909. Capital imports, the net acquisition of outside funds, external assets of Canadian banks and acquisition of monetary gold fluctuated more irregularly during the period so that their year-to-year correlation with the former series appears to have been relatively small. For example, we find in 1908, that although the first group of time series all underwent a decline, the second group increased, and so were exerting an expansionary influence. It might be argued that this liquidity due to the foreign loans, which showed itself in a much lesser decline in deposit and note liabilities in Canada than in bank loans, prevented as great a decline in Canadian prices as occurred in other countries (see Table 12). But this argument, although it doubtless has some validity, gives little assurance that it is an important explanation. Of numerous series indicating economic activity, those for exports and investment underwent the least decline, a very slight one indeed. If other countries suffered a greater decline in exports and investment activity, this might well be the explanation for their greater price decline. From fiscal 1908 to fiscal 1909 exports fell off by only one per cent, while imports slumped fully 18 per cent. The price index for exports fell by a mere fraction of one per cent, while that for imports dropped from 117.0 to 108.6.[1] This good fortune of Canada's is certainly not typical in more recent years of the exporter of cyclically price flexible agricultural commodities. There is no apparent evidence of the restrictive effect upon exports of capital borrowings at this period. It seems reasonable to assert that it was the continuing strong demand for Canadian exports as compared to industrial exports of other countries which helped to place the seal of approval on previous foreign invest-

[1] Calculated from statistics given in Taylor and Michell, *Statistical Contributions to Canadian Economic History*, II, 43, 31, 6.

Table 12. *Prices and Price Ratios, 1900–1913*
(Indices, 1900 = 100)

Year	Canadian wholesale prices[a]	Ratio of Canadian domestic to import prices[b]	Ratio of Canadian to world wholesale prices[c]	Ratio of Canadian to British wholesale prices[d]	Ratio of Canadian to American wholesale prices[e]	Ratio of Canadian to American domestic prices[f]
1900	100	100	100	100	100	100
1901	100	110	101	99	102	110
1902	104	117	101	105	102	112
1903	104	113	101	106	100	113
1904	105	119	105	105	101	110
1905	108	118	103	117	103	118
1906	114	110	102	106	100	112
1907	122	110	102	106	99	121
1908	118	128	104	109	102	121
1909	119	128	105	112	100	122
1910	121	129	106	111	100	123
1911	124	134	104	111	101	124
1912	136	129	105	113	104	124
1913	132	132	106	109	107	131

Note. All data are rounded to nearest one per cent.
[a] Viner, *Canada's Balance*, p. 226. Weighted average, chart VII.
[b] Viner, p. 252, data of chart XIV.
[c] Viner, p. 217, calculated from indices for the identical 145 commodities, data of chart IV.
[d] Viner, p. 223, calculated from indices given for 52 identical commodities, data of chart VI.
[e] Viner, p. 227, calculated from indices given for 135 identical commodities in table XLVIII.
[f] Viner, p. 240, calculated from indices given for almost the identical 23 commodities in table LI.

ment and served to attract the subsequently even greater flows of funds from abroad.

With the annual series of price indices (Table 12) and the series derived from the balance of payments (Tables 10 and 11) being notable for considerable fluctuation (as contrasted with the steady upward trend displayed by several of the series I have discussed), investigators have been tempted to find significant correlations between them. The fact that there has been disagreement among these investigators is not surprising. The general difficulties besetting their attempts may be listed as follows. (1) Imperfections in balance-of-payments data as indicated by the residual between the direct and indirect estimates of capital imports on a calendar year basis. (2) No attempt has been made to provide monthly balance-of-payments data which would be essential to an adequate investigation. (3) Other things being equal, the investigators would expect parallel movements in the price ratios which have been assembled in Table 12, all resulting from the influences of alterations in capital imports or in certain international transfers of funds, dependent upon the particular theory held. But unfortunately the movements of the series are not always parallel, and substantiation of the hypothesis is dependent on which series are selected. The differences are partly due to the differences in commodities included in the indices and to differences in weighting. The danger of placing too much reliance on the ratios between two imperfect series, both of which are showing considerable upward trends, is an obvious one. (4) There are, of course, as I have emphasized, many other important factors in the situation of which a number may be statistically nonmeasurable, and which are likely to be especially significant when we are comparing particular years rather than examining the trend for the period as a whole.

In general Viner wisely avoids this year-by-year analysis, and where it is attempted he leaves himself open to criticism. First, he attempts to relate capital imports, rather than the net acquisition of outside funds, to the relative price changes. Had direct estimates of capital imports been used, there would have been no differences in the direction of change of this series as compared to the series for the acquisition of outside funds. However, as indicated in the quotation that follows, Viner uses the indirect estimate in corroboration for three years and the direct estimate for one, and leaves the first four years out of consideration altogether.[2]

If allowance is made for probable error in the estimates of the volume of capital borrowings and for the incompletely representative character of the price indices available, Chart XIV adequately substantiates the reasoning presented here. As the rate of borrowing in-

[2] A. G. Silverman, in an unpublished dissertation in the Harvard University Library (1930), "The International Trade of Great Britain, 1880–1913," chapter 9, pp. 190ff, has similar and more detailed criticism of these particular conclusions of Viner's which he refers to as "far-fetched." He concentrates much of his attack on Viner's price indices, e.g., that for domestic prices (pages 198ff). Elsewhere in his analysis (page 56), Silverman emphasizes that capital exports are "an integral part of the business cycle" and that they are "a process of savings in which the monetary mechanism, while exceedingly important, is not in most cases the originating force."

creased, the divergency between domestic and import price levels widened. For the first four years, marked variations in the prices of the particular commodities entering into the indices, and a rate of borrowing too small to exert a distinguishable influence on the trend of prices, make inductive inference of questionable value. Marked relative increases in the rate of borrowing as compared to preceding years occurred in the years 1904, 1907, 1908, and 1911, according to the indirect estimates. In each of these years except 1907, there was a substantial widening of the divergency between domestic and import prices. According to the direct estimates, the rate of borrowing decreased in 1907, and the greatest relative increase in borrowings occurred in 1908, when there was also the greatest relative increase in the divergency between domestic and import prices. In 1912 and 1913, borrowings at the peak were accompanied by a divergency in prices very near, but not quite at, the peak, possibly because of the progressive effect of the divergency which made its appearance in the preceding years.[3]

Secondly, Viner here refers to only one of his series of price relatives, and the one selected, the ratio of domestic to import prices, is open to strong objections. As Ohlin observes, "the import price index is so unreliable that it is far from certain that any changes in the terms of exchange took place."[4] For example, comparison with an index with a much more adequate coverage, but which is for the fiscal year rather than the calendar year, as in the case of Viner's import price index, reveals quite different behavior.[5] In particular, it is a fall of 3 per cent in Viner's import price index that gives him his rise in the ratio of domestic to import prices for 1904, which he cites in the quotation I have given. The more adequate index does not decline so much as Viner's following 1900; and fiscal years (ending June 30) 1904 and 1905 indicate a rise of over 2 per cent and a decline of less than ½ of one per cent respectively. It seems probable that the rise of Viner's ratio stems from the inadequacy of his import price index. In 1904 the ratios of other indices did not conform

---

[3] Viner, *Canada's Balance*, pp. 253–254. In fairness to Professor Viner it should be pointed out that the above quotation from him is to be found in the summary portion of Chapter X, preceding which there is presented a great deal of tabulated and charted material which he believes bears out the conclusion I have quoted. Further criticism of this material follows.

[4] Ohlin, *Interregional and International Trade*, p. 468.

[5] Taylor and Michell, *Statistical Contributions to Canadian Economic History*, II, 6, table D; Viner, *Canada's Balance*, data of chart viii, p. 230; also compare with Table 10.

with the behavior of Viner's ratio in every instance, for both the ratio of Canadian to British wholesale prices and the ratio of Canadian to American domestic prices underwent a decline.

There are other instances where all the price ratios do not support Viner's reasoning, but one example is sufficient to show the danger of attaching too much importance to a particular price ratio. Further inadequacies in the Viner price indices will be dealt with later in this chapter. Viner, despite these inadequacies, goes so far as to attach significance to the size of the divergency between the two series as well as to its direction of change, as the above quotation indicates. Note that throughout his argument Viner does not distinguish between the price divergency leading to an increased import surplus, and the capital imports leading to the price divergency. Related to this is his failure, at any point in his study, to draw the line adequately between the net acquisition of outside funds and the related transfer of goods and services. Associated with this is his failure to clarify the important part played by monetary gold and short-term funds.

I will not apply the criticism levelled generally at attempted correlations to the work of Angell and Carr (Chapter 11). It is sufficient to recall that they both mistakenly assumed that the difference between the direct and indirect capital estimates consisted, not of residual error, but of short-term capital and gold flows which in fact were already included in the capital and current account estimates. We now have additional reasons for doubting the significance of their graphical correlations. It is particularly difficult to see the validity of the correlation between the steadily rising bank deposits series and the irregularly rising series for relative prices or for import surpluses, which they affirm exists on the basis of simple graphical demonstration.

Ohlin, in an ingenious piece of analysis, claims to discover a correlation between capital imports, in particular the indirect estimate of the borrowings after deduction of interest and dividends, and increases of wholesale prices in Canada relative to those in Great Britain and the United States.[6] He marks off four periods of borrowings net of interest payments ending 1903, 1906, 1910, and 1913, in which he claims levels of borrowings are clearly distinct from the level of the preceding period. Then he

[6] Ohlin, *Interregional and International Trade*, pp. 457ff.

argues that "the *second* year in each period should show a greater discrepancy between the price index figures for Canada and other countries than the last year of the preceding period, while this price discrepancy may well have been reduced towards of end of each period, when the adjustment to the then-existing inflow of capital had been carried out to a greater extent than in the middle of each period." [7] Ohlin is considering here the effect on prices of the inflow of capital, and not the influence of the relative price changes in effecting the real transfer via the import surplus. In his estimate of capital imports he takes the average of the direct and indirect estimates, an arbitrary assumption.[8] It is in the indirect estimates that the periods are clearly marked, however, and these are more likely to indicate the resultant real transfer than the supposedly initiating financial transfer. Ohlin's periods do not manifest themselves in the series for the net acquisition of outside funds. In their effects on prices, his analysis does not distinguish between capital imports which are accompanied by parallel imports of goods and services, and those capital imports which result immediately in the considerable accumulation of external bank assets and monetary gold.

Ohlin himself provides several possible criticisms of his own demonstration. In criticizing Viner he pointed to several factors other than capital imports, including rapidly increasing population and production function changes in certain industries, which could be responsible for the relative price changes.[9] Nonetheless he concludes as follows:

On the other hand, it seems likely that the changes in borrowings contributed to the relative rise in Canadian prices during the decade 1903–13. In particular it is difficult to attribute the fact that the margins between Canadian, British, and American price levels varied upward and downward to any other element than the variations in the rate of borrowings.[10]

[7] Ohlin, p. 464.

[8] The assumption would be correct if one half the residual error represented an error in the estimate of long-term capital imports. Viner recognizes the possibility of errors of allocation between years here, but it is dubious if the long-term capital imports should carry such a large share of the possible error. For example, the difficulties in estimating short-term capital movements were greater.

[9] Ohlin, pp. 463–7.

[10] Ohlin, p. 464.

Unfortunately Ohlin, in his general neglect of cyclical influences, disregards the possibility that relative differences between the three countries in domestic investment activity could be productive of these price changes, and that such changes, while possibly induced by international borrowings, are more likely to be the initiating factor, especially in the case of Britain and the United States. Nor does he take sufficient note of the inadequacy of the Viner indices.

Ohlin has a series of only ten years on which to base his conclusions, since like Viner he discards the early years of the period 1900–1913. "The first clearly marked period" of capital borrowings does not substantiate his conclusions. In the subsequent three periods Ohlin notes one exception in the British compared to the Canadian wholesale price changes, and another in the American as compared to Canadian domestic price changes, which he is forced to attribute to "other circumstances." [11] A further exception unmentioned by Ohlin occurs in 1913 when the differential between the Canadian and foreign prices increases rather than decreases as Ohlin's theory would have it (Table 12). Such exceptions, when there is such limited corroborative evidence, are obviously very damaging to Ohlin's thesis.

Ohlin is certainly not dogmatic in his argument. He admits that "such calculations have a limited value as verification," and points out that if the direct rather than the indirect estimate had been used in order to divide the whole period into smaller periods the results would not have been corroborative. But he does not think this to be "very damaging to the analysis in the text, for the direct estimate is likely to show *too late* the increase of the buying power in Canada in some cases." [12] It may also show it too early. Ohlin here commits the error that has been criticized in others of attributing too much significance to a mere residual (see Chapter 11).

An adequate explanation of the differences in the relative price changes of the three countries would require a detailed explanation for the relative differences in the changes in investment activity and national incomes. I will do very little more than to indicate that in some instances there were international differences in the

[11] Ohlin, pp. 464, 465.
[12] Ohlin, p. 465n.

impact of the business cycle, which appear to be associated with the relative price changes. Further, the relative price changes appear to have been associated at times with the erratic price movements of certain commodities.

The first notable fact to observe is that whereas Canadian wholesale price changes differed considerably from the British during the period under study, they did not differ so markedly from the American (Table 12). Therefore we may infer that there were common influences operating within both the rather closely associated economies of the United States and Canada tending to increase prices relative to those of Great Britain. I have already pointed out that transfers of capital (immigrants' remittances and interest and dividend payments included) to the United States were not in the direction that theory would require them to be if they are to be assumed as the basis for the relative price changes. There is no doubt that the flow of capital to Canada was much more important than to the United States at this time. Are there any differential effects to be observed which stem from this fact? The emphasis, it seems, must be laid on the comparison of American and Canadian prices if Ohlin's and Viner's theories are to be substantiated. The difference between American and Canadian wholesale prices is not a marked one, and Ohlin has contrasted the series for domestic prices. For Britain and Canada, the wholesale prices are compared, but as I have indicated, there is no reason for assuming capital movements to have been an important influence in the price differentials between the two countries. Relatively small increases in transport costs for Canadian exports, and relatively large investment and population increases (reciprocally stimulating each other), could provide the chief bases for the relatively greater Canadian price increases.

Let us examine the changes in the ratio of Canadian to American domestic prices, 1900–1913 (Table 12). Note first that the index is primarily composed of agricultural and food products, many of them perishables, and that all but a very few of these products would fall into the cyclically price flexible group.[13]

[13] Viner, *Canada's Balance*, p. 230n. For discussions of cyclical price flexibility see The National Resources Committee, *The Structure of the American Economy*, Part I (Washington, 1939), pp. 35ff.; and A. H. Hansen, *Fiscal Policy and Business Cycles* (New York, 1941), chapter 15.

Also note that there are five commodities of the 23 in the Canadian index which are not included in the American index (Viner assures the reader that this omission is of little consequence).[14] As indicated by the ratio, Canadian and American domestic prices vary quite uniformly throughout the period with the exception of four years (1901, 1905, 1907, and 1913), which we will consider separately.

Viner claims that the sharp rise of the Canadian price index in the first few years is attributable to the quotations for salt mackerel and potatoes.[15] I find that the first of these products increased 75 per cent from 1900 to 1901 in the Canadian price index, while it decreased by over 20 per cent in the United States index. Such erratic and extreme behavior as this is not such as to inspire confidence in Viner's index.

From 1904 to 1905, the Canadian index took a sharp rise relative to that of the United States. Presumably for these years Viner regards the index as being fairly reliable, since it is only the first four years that have been excluded for the purpose of deductive inference, the exclusion being made because of the relatively small capital borrowings and the "marked variations in the prices of the particular commodities entering into the indices." [16] It is therefore disturbing to find that in the years 1904–1905 the price index for potatoes in Canada rose from 148 to 188, but in the United States fell from 195 to 108. Even if there were significant changes in the general price indices of the two countries, there are two factors apart from capital movements to assist us in explaining a decline in the United States domestic price level while that of Canada rose slightly. Agricultural conditions are more important for Canada and there were considerable crop increases in the year 1905. More significant, the depression of that year appears to have been considerably more severe in the United States than in Canada.[17]

---

[14] Viner, *Canada's Balance*, p. 240n.

[15] The price quotations, like those of Viner's, derive from Canada's Department of Labour, *The Rise of Prices and the Cost of Living, 1900–1914*, II, 250ff.

[16] Viner, *Canada's Balance*, p. 253.

[17] For a comparison of cyclical influences in different countries see W. L. Thorp, *Business Annals* (New York, 1926), pp. 75ff; and Haberler, *Prosperity and Depression*, pp. 266–267.

Potatoes and salt mackerel again help to explain the relatively greater increase in Canadian domestic prices in 1907. A further basis for the general price changes which took place may be found in the relatively greater depression suffered by the United States in that year.

In 1913 the increase in the ratio is accounted for by the decline in American domestic prices while the Canadian remained virtually stable. To the extent that this was general, it may be explained by the lag in the impact of depression on the Canadian as compared to the American economy. Canada had enjoyed greater prosperity than had the United States during 1910–1913, construction, especially of railways, and other forms of investment being at a very high level, while grain prices were good and exports reached new heights.[18] Capital imports were merely one of a number of interrelated factors that operated actively or permissively in the wheat boom that brought great prosperity to Canada after decades of relative stagnation. In the United States, on the other hand, large-scale settlement within national boundaries was virtually at an end, while the important investment outlays associated with street railways reached a peak during 1900–1909.[19]

Admittedly the preceding analysis does not fully explain the variations in the price indices used by Ohlin and Viner. That could be achieved only through a detailed investigation of the changes in the prices of the individual commodities involved in the indices and of the various factors involved in the international differentials of the Canadian, American, and British cyclical processes. Tentative investigation does disclose, however, the shaky basis for the inductive inferences drawn by Viner and Ohlin.

[18] Cairncross, "Die Kapitaleinfuhr in Kanada 1900–1913," *Weltwirtschaftliches Archiv,* p. 625.

[19] Hansen, *Fiscal Policy and Business Cycles,* pp. 40, 45. I would not claim that this is more than a tentative hypothesis for the explanation of the United States lapses from prosperity in 1910–1911 and later in 1913–1914. Schumpeter, *Business Cycles,* I, 425–427, finds that the latter downturn falls in with his cyclical schema but he is unable to account for the relative inactivity of 1910–1911 in terms of his schema, and attributes it to "the after effects of preceding irregularities." For an interesting analysis of the close relation between transportation and construction in the cycle, see W. Isard, "Transport Development and Building Cycles," *The Quarterly Journal of Economics,* LVII, 1942, No. 1.

Professor Viner, in commenting on my manuscript, offered the following argument in his defence. "If greater buoyancy of business in good years and less recession in bad years were demonstrated to me to be closely associated with relative price divergencies, I would not have regarded that as a refutation of my thesis, since as I recall it was my thesis that capital imports would tend to have just such consequences." He then suggests that the reason for the increase in the ratio of Canadian to American domestic prices in 1913 following the absolute decline in the American index may be found in the fact that the United States was not importing capital heavily.

First, as to the facts, capital movements into the United States showed no trend either upward or downward during the period 1900–1913. In the fiscal year ending June, 1914, there was a decline in the U.S. export surplus from $683 million to $495 million, which suggests that an indirect estimate for capital imports would probably have shown an increase in 1913. The available evidence does not support the view that the distinctive changes in United States prices could be explained in terms of changes in capital imports. Rather the evidence suggests that there is a strong positive year-to-year correlation between prices and incomes and domestic investment activity. The facts do not indicate a similar short-run correlation between cyclical fluctuations and United States capital imports. Both empirical investigations and a priori analysis support the view that the likelihood of a positive correlation between cyclical fluctuations and capital imports tends to diminish for an economy as it becomes more industrially advanced, as in the case of the United States in the first decade of the century. It is worth noting that Viner himself claimed that on a priori grounds no consistency in the relationship could be posited.[20]

Where there is a positive correlation between the capital inflow of a developing country and its business fluctuations, as in the case of Canada during the 1900–1913 period, the relation is significant for the period as a whole rather than in the short-run fluctuations from year to year. For example, capital imports *increased* in the recession years of 1908 and 1913. As far as may be determined by the data, the annual changes in relative prices

[20] Viner, *Studies . . . International Trade*, p. 435.

and their international comparisons are best explained with reference to cyclical fluctuations and economic growth, and not with reference to international flows of capital with which no consistent relationship has been revealed. This accords with my emphasis that even in the case where capital imports are highly significant they should be regarded as only one of many elements in the cyclical fluctuations, and that their role is more likely to be a permissive than an actuating one. This would also appear to be generally true in the case of long-run economic development.

XV

The Terms of Trade

Much more attention is devoted by Viner to a demonstration of the changes in the domestic versus the international sectional price levels than to the important corollary of the "classical" theory that the terms of trade shift in favor of the borrowing country during a period of capital imports, which is inadequately and summarily treated. This is true despite the following statement by Viner. "Adequate inductive verification of this proposition is supplied by the demonstration already made that export prices rose relatively to import prices."[1] But no series for the terms of trade is presented, nor is any careful analysis of the relation between capital imports and the changes in terms of trade attempted. Indeed, it is suggested later by Viner that the export-import price ratio is an inadequate measure and the ratio of domestic to import prices is put to the novel use of measuring the terms of international exchange.

[1] Viner, *Canada's Balance*, p. 295. The sketchiness of Viner's treatment of the terms of trade is not justified in the light of his own viewpoint as expressed in *Studies . . . International Trade*, pp. 325 and 327. There he emphasizes that "the existence of domestic commodities is not essential to any valid theory of the general mechanism of adjustment of international balances to disturbances." In an attack on a study by R. Wilson, which minimized the shifts in the terms of trade while emphasizing the changes in domestic relative to international prices, Viner stated: "That this proposition is incorrect can be sufficiently shown by the *reductio ad absurdum* to which it would lead if there were no domestic commodities."

The relative degree of rise in the domestic price level as compared to import prices measured the degree to which the shift in the terms of international exchange *temporarily* lowered to Canada the cost of the goods purchased abroad with the proceeds of the borrowings. But the degree of profit accruing to Canada from the exchange of her exports for foreign products on more favorable terms was not nearly so great. This reasoning is verified by the evidence presented in an earlier chapter to the effect that the prices of export commodities did not rise in nearly the same degree as did domestic prices. It is further verified by the evidence presented in the preceding chapter to the effect that Canada's export trade would have been seriously checked, had it not been for the operation of special circumstances which made possible the profitable export of a few important products at prices relatively little higher than the import prices.[2]

The costs of goods purchased abroad certainly did not decrease absolutely, and surely the fact that domestic goods rose relatively in price compared to internationally traded goods need have nothing to do with the terms of international exchange. The relatively greater elasticity of demand and supply of internationally traded goods than of domestic goods presumes greater relative changes in the latter's price. Criticism of the overemphasis of classical theorists on the terms of trade is surely called for, rather than an attempt to measure the changed terms in a novel, and what appears to me, an unjustifiable manner.

As I have indicated, Viner's import price index is too inaccurate to serve as a basis for the "adequate inductive verification" he claims of the classical theorem on the terms of trade. Nor does resort to more adequate statistical material support Viner's thesis.[3] The terms of trade (export prices as a percentage of import prices) were at an ebb around 1900 (note that the figures of the source cited apply to fiscal years), after having reached a peak in fiscal 1895. This was partially due to the increased world demand for industrial materials, some of which was associated with the Boer War. The improvement in terms of trade enjoyed by Canada in the early years of the century could hardly be explained on the basis of capital imports, which remained

[2] *Canada's Balance*, pp. 298–299.
[3] Taylor and Michell, *Statistical Contributions to Canadian Economic History*, II, 6, table D. Calculations of the terms of trade from Viner's series have also been made and are compared with the Taylor estimates in table 10. For pre-1900 terms of trade see Table 2 and Chart I.

relatively unimportant until the increase of 1904, but could probably be explained partially as a deflationary reaction from the earlier period of rise in import prices. The greatest improvement in terms of trade takes place from fiscal 1908–1909. There was indeed a large accumulation of external bank assets and monetary gold reserves which was sustained by the capital imports. But cyclical fluctuations dominate and complicate the situation. The altered terms of trade are probably best explained, as previously suggested, on the grounds of a world slump in the demand for investment and other manufactured goods in 1908, while the demand for agricultural commodities was only very slightly abated. As has been noted, this was exceptional cyclical behavior.

Compare Kahn, who is observing from the British point of view.

For the considerable improvement of British terms of trade, 1905–1907, despite expanding capital exports, and their deterioration 1907–1909, one must look again to the great cyclical increase and decrease in the demand for British goods. British capital exports were often the least rapidly responding part of the pattern rather than the independent outside initial cause.[4]

Kahn does however find that the British terms of trade operate in accordance with classical theory in the longer run, deterioriating from perhaps 1700, and certainly from 1800 to 1860, and improving from 1880 to the 1930's.[5] Kahn might be criticized for the concentration of attention on British terms of trade to the exclusion of any consideration of sectional price levels. But domestic commodities play a less important role in Britain, it seems safe to say, even than in Canada, especially since foods are not for Britain a typically domestic commodity, as Viner's analyses seems to imply.[6] Furthermore, the study of British terms of trade comes much closer than in the case of the Canadian terms of trade to a study of the terms upon which industrial countries and agricultural, raw-material producing countries exchange their products, and this is particularly true of the nine-

[4] Kahn, *Great Britain in the World Economy*, p. 151n.
[5] Kahn, p. 145.
[6] Viner, *Canada's Balance*, 253.

teenth century. The Canadian terms of trade alterations are best analyzed in the light of this broader picture.

Kahn, referring to important reactions or plateaus in the improving British terms of trade, includes 1900–1913, as well as 1873–1880 and 1924–1929. Of 1900–1913 in particular he concludes that "it is difficult to make of the period anything worse than a plateau in the long-run development, for by 1911–1913 the trade terms were almost back at their extremely (and abnormally) high 1899–1900 level. . . . Nevertheless, this leveling off of a marked earlier improvement was an important phenomenon, with important effects." [7] The Canadian terms of trade, whose reaction would tend to be reciprocal of the British, barely exceeded the 1895 level in the peak fiscal years of 1909–1910, while fiscal 1914 (covering three quarters of 1913) indicated a drop below all other fiscal years in the period with the exception of 1900–1901, and 1905. This occurred despite peak capital imports in 1913 which were accompanied by a considerable accumulation of net external bank assets and monetary gold. Long-run development of the Canadian trade terms shows improvement during fiscal 1872–1895, deterioration during fiscal 1895–1900, improvement during fiscal 1900–1910, and deterioration during fiscal 1910–1915, a trend terminated by World War I. Taken in historical context, it is not easy to see that the terms of trade were dominated by capital imports, and so verified the Mill-Taussig theory, as Viner claimed. Part of the explanation may be as Viner claimed, but after due regard for transport and other costs, the changing terms of trade are best related to world demand and supply dispositions, as in the Kahn analysis. These, if they alter in a manner favorable to Canada, tend to improved terms of trade, and they may also lead to capital imports as well as to domestically financed investment. Capital imports might appear to improve the terms of trade without being the causal factor at all.[8]

Frequently there is not even prima facie support for the Mill-Taussig theory regarding the terms of trade. Increasing capital

[7] Kahn, p. 148n.
[8] For example, Kindleberger, *International Short Term Capital Movements*, p. 153.

exports to agricultural countries have on numerous occasions been associated with increasing demands for industrial products on such a scale that the terms of trade have shifted in favor of the capital exporting country.[9] There are instances of this in the Canadian situation, for example 1870–1872, when there were substantial increases in the import surpluses and the terms of trade declined substantially, although this was perhaps largely a reaction to a sharp improvement from 1869 to 1870, when, incidentally, the import surplus was declining.[10]

The improving terms of trade following 1872 are at first associated with an increasing import surplus, as Canadian exports declined more than her imports. This increased import surplus is not necessarily to be associated with larger capital imports, which may well have preceded the import surpluses. The causal relationship is in all probability not at all the Mill-Taussig one. The reason for import surpluses and the altered terms of trade is to be found in the onslaught of the "great depression" in 1873, the influence of which only gradually extended to Canada which enjoyed relative prosperity until 1875.[11] This reasoning is borne out by the fact that, although the import surpluses declined following 1875, the terms of trade continued to improve.

There is little to be said for the Taylor and Michell contention[12] that the improvement which occurred in the Canadian terms of trade during the periods 1872–1878, 1882–1888, and 1900–1912 bears out the "classical" theory. Reasons for holding an agnostic, if not an opposing, point of view with regard to the first and the latter of these periods are stated in the foregoing pages. Prima facie, the second period supports the Mill-Taussig analysis, but the case is weakened by the fact that while the import surplus increased still further after 1886, remaining at a high level until 1891, the terms of trade deteriorated. Then, as the import surplus declined, they improved again (Table 3 and Chart I).

It should be pointed out that such instances as these do not disprove the classical theory as a statement of tendencies, which may be said to be outweighed by other factors in the specific

[9] C. Clark, *Conditions of Economic Progress* (London, 1940), p. 454.
[10] *Canada Year Book*, 1940, p. 526, and Taylor and Michell, *Statistical Contributions to Canadian Economic History*, II, 6.
[11] Thorp, Business Annals, p. 300.
[12] *Statistical Contributions to Canadian Economic History*, II, 7.

situation. There is enough here to make us skeptical, however, and the evidence is certainly damaging to those who have held that empirical verification has been achieved. Were it not for the number of such attempts, and the stress that has been laid, I think mistakenly, on the terms of trade of particular countries by innumerable theorists, I should not have directed much attention to them. So many factors may influence the export-import price ratios that there is a great risk in attaching particular significance to any given change in the ratio. In conclusion I will enumerate several of the factors involved in shifts in the terms of trade as calculated in the Canadian case.

Production function changes may be a very important factor, leading to changes in the terms of trade which would be unaccounted for in the simplified version of the Mill-Taussig analysis. Particularly significant here are the changes in international transport costs. Since transport services are not included separately with the commodities entering into the export and import indices, it is quite conceivable for the terms of trade to improve for all participating countries if transport costs decline. Such shifts as these in the terms of trade may be very considerable, and may overshadow any possible changes due to gold and short-term capital flows and the associated fluctuations in demand. In other words, changes in costs may dominate the situation.

Tariffs may affect the wholesale price level of imports, and hence the terms of trade, quite apart from any purchasing power shifts.

The most important shifts in the terms of trade and other relative prices, stemming from demand, tend to be associated with the wide fluctuations in purchasing power in the business cycle. The various factors in such relative price changes have already been discussed (Chapter 13).

Thus whatever effects there may be on the terms of trade that are directly attributable to the shifts in purchasing power associated with a transfer of capital are likely to be swamped by all these other influences on the terms of trade which I have mentioned. In any event, the terms of trade need not improve with an import of capital, as the "classical" theory argues. They may move in the other direction.[13] Ohlin expects very little change in

[13] See, for example, Ohlin, *Interregional and International Trade*, pp. 484ff.

the terms of trade due to a capital transfer since he emphasizes the normally high elasticity of demand for any one country's export goods.[14] In the case of Canada, Ohlin has particular reason for anticipating a negligible change in the terms of trade due to the relative unimportance of the Canadian as compared to the world supply of most of her export commodities. Also, Ohlin points to the fact that Britain, the capital exporter, did not supply most of the Canadian import needs, and that Canadian demands directed toward the United States would tend to increase United States export prices and so worsen rather than improve Canadian terms of trade.[15] Ohlin might have added that this tendency would in fact have been negligible due to the relative insignificance of the Canadian import demand as compared to the world and United States domestic demands for similar commodities.

Finally, the effect of the changed terms of trade on the export and import values is likely to be more influential than the effect on the qualities exported and imported. Such changes, not necessarily directly induced by the import of capital, may either assist or inhibit its transfer. In the Canadian case, *if* the terms of trade had turned very markedly in Canada's favor, the quantity of imports necessary to accomplish the transfer of capital would have been greater, and the ease of the transfer might have been diminished, and not enhanced, as implied in the "classical" theory.

Once the trade terms are viewed in this light and the infinite possibilities of cause and effect are emphasized, the danger of assuming any particular theoretical relationship and the even greater danger involved in statistical verification become apparent.

[14] Viner had also emphasized the high elasticity of demand for Canadian exports, *Canada's Balance*, p. 298. Further, in *Studies . . . International Trade*, p. 333f, Viner defends the classical writers against Ohlin by emphasizing that where changes in relative prices and the terms of trade are small, they may be nonetheless highly significant if price elasticities are high. The difficulties of statistical verification would be enhanced, however, if the price movements were small. My own criticism of the "classical" approach is directed toward its emphasis both upon price changes and high price elasticities.

[15] Ohlin, *Interregional and International Trade*, pp. 468–470.

XVI

Relative Price Changes—Their Importance

In the preceding chapters I have concluded that capital imports are likely to be of small importance in explaining relative price changes in comparison with other influences. I have also concluded that where relative price changes may have tended to bring about equalizing imports of commodities and services, these relative price changes were probably not brought about by the capital imports, or, if associated with capital imports, were probably associated in a manner differing from that indicated in the Mill-Taussig theory. I have had to emphasize the complexity of any theory which could attempt to account for the complex reality. Each historical situation is distinctive with regard to the degree with which various factors are operative in effecting adjustment. I have further been forced to emphasize the difficulties in drawing conclusions from the empirical data.

PRICE CHANGES AND THE CAPITAL TRANSFER

The question now to be answered is, what was the degree of importance of the relative price changes in effectuating the real transfer of goods and services? As compared with other peacetime price changes, those for Canada during 1900 to 1913 were undeniably considerable in magnitude. If it can be shown that even in this particularly favorable historical set of circumstances they were relatively insignificant in influence, then the conclusion may be justifiable that under most conditions they should not be assigned more than a very small role in the equilibration mechanism.

In his chapter on "The Mechanism of Adjustment," Viner's explanation of the transfer equilibration is categorically stated:

The inductive results of this chapter confirm the general proposition which has been laid down on deductive grounds, that the adjustment of the balance of trade to a newly introduced or increased disturbing factor is brought about through the influence of diverging price levels on the quantitative ratio of exports to imports.[1]

But I find that elsewhere Viner modifies this conclusion and introduces equilibrating factors other than the relative changes in price levels without indicating that this weakens the theory he is attempting to verify.

Viner takes the stand that the merchandise elements in the balance of payments play by far the most important equilibrating role. The explanation for this viewpoint seems to be his overemphasis on capital movements as the initiating factor operating via changes in the money supply and his exaggeration of the role of relative price changes in the equilibrating mechanism. The facts, however, reveal that nonmerchandise elements in the current account had a very significant part in the actual adjustment.

The commodity balance of trade is by far the most important single factor in the final adjustment of international balances of indebtedness to more or less permanent disturbing factors. . . . Gold imports and exports . . . exert their main influence, not through the effect on the balance of payments of their own value as debits and credits, but by their influence on price levels and through them on the remaining items in the commodity balance of trade.

Prices exert little direct influence on the volume of international transactions in services. . . . Interest payments are dependent simply on the amounts of capital borrowings, the rates of interest originally agreed upon, and the extent to which the debtors fulfill their contractual obligations.

Non-commercial transactions, such as immigrants' remittances, gifts, and the movements in and out of a country of migrants' personal effects, because they are non-commercial in character, are wholly free from the direct influence of capital borrowings or changes in price levels, and in the main are not appreciably affected by them even indirectly. A possible exception is in the case of capital brought in by immigrants, for an increase in capital borrowings abroad tends to create in the borrowing country a situation favorable to labor, and thus stimulates immigration.[2]

[1] Viner, *Canada's Balance,* p. 254.
[2] *Canada's Balance,* pp. 256–257.

Viner goes on to present as confirmatory of his reasoning the facts that the commodity balance of trade (excluding gold) shows a much higher degree of correlation with the total debit balance of international indebtedness (i.e., the net current account deficit) than does the gold coin balance, the debit balance of service transactions, or the debit balance of noncommercial transactions.[3] This is scarcely surprising, since the debit commodity balance forms the major proportion of the total debit balance of which it is a widely fluctuating component. There is also a high correlation with the service transactions, due partially to the dependence of freight charges on the volume of imports and exports, as Viner points out.

Quite apart from the small number of the variates, and the possible errors in them, these correlations are of little theoretical value. It is not a correlation with the direct estimate of net long-term capital borrowings, nor is it even a correlation with the indirect estimate, which would equal the current deficit only after the latter had been adjusted for the partial offset of short-term capital movements, i.e., net changes in external bank assets. Such a correlation would have been much less confirmatory. For example, in the years 1908 and 1913, when both the current deficit and the commodity import surplus turned down, the direct and indirect estimates of long-term capital imports turned up, as did all the noncommodity elements of the balance of payments. I have, however, expressed reasons for not attaching too much significance to similar correlation results. The presence of a large residual error in the estimates must not be overlooked. It would therefore not be worth while to pursue the matter further.

It can be demonstrated that Viner erred in thinking that the balance of payments adjustment was confined almost solely to the commodity items. To a considerable extent all the nonmerchandise elements of the balance of payments were participating in the equilibration. Taking the period 1900–1913 as a whole, it may be seen from Table 13 that little more than one half of the net capital imports were offset by net transfers of commodities and services which might be construed as responsive to relative price changes. Of the other offsets, interest and dividends predominated, while acquisition of external bank assets and of monetary

[3] *Canada's Balance*, p. 259.

gold in the net amounts of $86 million and $154 million respectively was also an important item.

Table 13. *Offsets to net capital imports into Canada, total, 1900–1913:*
annual averages 1900–1901 and 1912–1913
(to nearest million dollars)

Offsets	*1900–1913*	*1900–1901*	*1912–1913*
Tourists	+5	+2	−6
Interest and dividends	−869	−32	−118
Other current items	−41	+5	−32
Monetary gold and external bank assets	−240	−13	−15
Residual	−54	+3	−6
Total	−1199	−35	−178
Amount of net economic transfer[a]	−1295	+3	−249
Capital imports (direct estimate)	+2494	+32	+428

Note. Calculated from Table 27.
[a] Freight and shipping, merchandise, including nonmonetary gold.

The averages in Table 13 for the two years at the beginning and end of the period under study indicate the changes which took place in the size of the offsetting items, and suggest whether or not they may be considered as equilibrating.

The changes in monetary gold and external bank assets have been regarded as the indicators of disequilibrium, and of course they are at the same time compensatory short-term balancing items which fill the gaps occasioned by the disequilibrium. However, it should be pointed out that the "movements" of monetary gold and external bank assets were not indicators of disequilibrium to the extent that they were satisfying the changing requirements of an expanding economy for reserves in gold and in liquid foreign assets. To this extent the offsets were no different from those due to merchandise imports, except that as banking reserves they provided a basis for credit expansion, and that they surely could not be hypothesized as imports induced by relative price changes. The absolute increase in price levels, as well as the increase in output and foreign trade led to the expansion in banking requirements. Insofar as decline in output and price deflation would decrease the banking requirements and make possible the "export" of monetary gold and external bank assets, the "movements" would be reversible. These "movements" come into the pictures as equilibrating movements,[4] and due to their further impact upon the credit supply, they exert, unlike imports and exports of commodities and services, equilibrating influences of a secondary order. The equilibrating influences of nonmonetary gold (the exports of which are assumed to be equal to the domestic production — see the Statistical Appendix) in contrast to those of monetary gold, are due in some measure to the changes in relative prices which Viner was emphasizing. As a commodity the price of which failed to rise with the rising trend of other prices and costs, its production declined during the period 1900–1913 (see Table 27). The most important reason for this decline, however, was the fact of short-lived high production early in the period consequent upon the Yukon gold strikes.

Interest payments were very much more important than dividend payments in the period under discussion.[5] Since interest is a fixed, contractual payment it is of little account in short-run year to year equilibration, but the period 1900–1913 is sufficiently long that it assumes great importance. Throughout the period (see Table 27) interest payments coupled with the relatively unimportant dividend payments were providing very considerable offsets to the flow of capital imports. At the outset of the period these payments more than offset the capital imports, while with capital imports at their peak in the last two years of the period, they nevertheless offset more than one quarter of the annual inflow. This was certainly a very important means of effecting the transfer of capital which was independent of the relative price changes.[6]

Other current items consist primarily of immigrants' capital and of noncommercial remittances sent abroad chiefly by recent immigrants.[7] A relatively small portion consists of transfers on account of insurance companies. Early in the period the immigrants' capital predominated and there was a net transfer to Canada, but

[4] That is, they reduce the required amount of compensatory movements for the remainder of the gold and short-term capital.

[5] Viner, *Canada's Balance*, pp. 98–99.

[6] See the analysis of the role of debt servicing in the adjustment process in J. J. Polak, "Balance of Payments Problems of Countries Reconstructing with the Help of Foreign Loans," *Quarterly Journal of Economics*, February 1943.

[7] Viner, *Canada's Balance*, pp. 85–86.

as the period wore on the remittances abroad more than offset the immigrants' capital, and from 1907 on there is a net transfer of funds out of Canada. This difference between the annual averages at the beginning and end of the period is $37 million, a change from a credit to a debit item which indicates more importance in offsetting the increasing capital imports than the total net offset for the period as a whole reveals. To the extent that capital imports made immigration possible, undoubtedly to an important degree, they led to later equilibrating offsets in the form of immigrants' remittances home, a further type of equilibration independent of the relative price changes. The change from a net credit to a net debit on tourist account, though relatively minor, can be classed to a large extent as an equilibrating change on the same grounds as the change in other current items. For as the period proceeded, the expenditures of earlier immigrants returning for a visit to their native lands became an increasing offset against the expenditures of persons classed as visitors or tourists from abroad.[8]

There remain merchandise, freight and shipping, and nonmonetary gold which might figure in the Mill-Taussig sequence of capital imports causing relative price changes, which in turn led to increased debits on commodity and service accounts. To what extent this was true it is impossible to say with absolute accuracy or certainty. I have argued that the classical theory provides an element of the explanation for the decline in the nonmonetary gold export. Similarly, rising costs in the face of less rapidly rising world market prices must have been partly responsible for the decline or the failure to expand significantly of many other exports. Production usually contracted much less than in the case of gold, for domestic markets replaced the foreign to a larger, generally more than compensating, extent.[9] But the restrictive influences upon exports derive from other expansionary influences as well as from capital imports, and neither these influences nor capital imports operate primarily through relative price changes, although they often tended to produce such relative price changes. The factors we have examined included investment of domestic resources financed by credit expansion; in-

[8] *Canada's Balance*, p. 61.
[9] Viner, *Canada's Balance*, pp. 273–274.

novation affecting various industries, particularly the transportation system; immigration and an expanding population; and urbanization. These factors, which were essential elements in the substantial economic growth of the period, cannot be separated in the Canadian situation of 1900–1913 from the foreign investment, with which there were reciprocal causal relations, but neither can they be excluded in an explanation of balance of payments or price changes.

The same factors that tended to reduce exports tended to increase imports, so that again importations of capital and relative price changes must not be overplayed in the explanation. The import list is most varied (see Table 7) and it is difficult to state with much conclusiveness how important or unimportant relative price changes were. But examination of the list does reveal important imports, e.g., fruits, nuts, and rubber, unavailable in a northern climate and so not entering into price competition with domestically produced commodities. Others, such as fresh vegetables, were not available seasonally. Still other imports, such as coal and petroleum products, were due to a limitation of the Canadian natural resources. Manufacturing production, which more than doubled in value from 1900 to 1910,[10] involves many almost technologically fixed requirements which could not be satisfied domestically. These include producer goods and high standard of living consumer goods for which the income elasticity is high, and which would consequently tend to increase the average propensity to import in an investment boom.

Quite apart from the consideration of the components of the import list, there are reasons for holding that one would expect, under the circumstances of 1900–1913, an increasing average propensity to import for Canada whether or not relative price changes were encouraging to this development. These reasons, which have been enumerated in an earlier chapter, support the view that both cyclical changes and longer-term structural changes related to economic development, such as occurred in Canada 1900–1913, would have tended to produce a higher average propensity to import, without regard to the relative price changes which Viner insists are essential.

[10] W. A. MackIntosh, *Economic Background of Dominion Provincial Relations* (Ottawa, 1939), p. 29, table 4.

Viner's analysis of restrictive influences upon exports is not at all confirmatory of the Mill-Taussig theory, since the causal mechanisms referred to are not confined to relative price changes, which indeed are relegated to a subordinate position in some of Viner's conclusions. Viner continues to err in minimizing expansionary factors other than capital imports in his analysis, seemingly on the basis of his view that these borrowings from abroad were the only major force in the expansion.

It is difficult to explain the decline in the percentage of exports to total commodity production, without reference to the capital borrowings from abroad. Some of the relative decline in exports was undoubtedly due to the increasing extent to which Canadian raw materials were being manufactured in Canada for Canadian consumption, instead of being exported in their crude form in exchange for imported manufactured goods. But this increase in manufactures would not have been possible in nearly the same degree had it not been for the foreign investments of capital in Canadian manufacturing enterprises. The expansion of manufacturing not only absorbed an increased proportion of the Canadian production of raw materials, but it withdrew labor, from the production of the raw materials which otherwise would have been exported, to the construction of plant and equipment and the fabrication, from imported raw materials, of manufactured commodities for domestic consumption. The development of roads, towns, and railroads, made possible by the borrowings abroad, absorbed a large part of the immigration of labor, and these consumed considerable quantities of Canadian commodities which would otherwise have been available for export. Changes in relative price levels resulting from the capital borrowings were also an important factor in restricting exports, operating coordinately with the factors explained above.[11]

The fact that Viner on occasion accords greater significance to the increases in incomes than the theory he is attempting to verify also seems to be borne out in the following statement: "Throughout the range of export commodities of which there was substantial consumption in Canada, there was convincing evidence of the restrictive influence on exports arising out of both the increased purchasing power acquired by a borrowing country and its relative rise in prices as compared to other countries." [12]

Viner subsequently states:

[11] Viner, *Canada's Balance*, pp. 262–263.
[12] *Canada's Balance*, p. 274; also see p. 270.

Except for commodities for which there is no important domestic demand, the volume of export will probably respond more conspicuously to changes in domestic demand, either for the products themselves or for labor, arising out of the capital borrowings, than to changes in relative prices.[13]

It might be added that those "commodities for which there is no important domestic demand" were the type the export of which increased during the period, and for which Viner argues the restrictive influence via relative price changes was negligible for special reasons such as the exploitation of virgin soil and the discovery and development of mineral resources.[14]

It follows that if the adjustment of the trade balance is to be brought about "through the influence of diverging price levels on the quantitative ratio of exports to imports," which is the thesis Viner is claiming to have verified, such influence of relative price changes must relate chiefly to imports. I have suggested reasons for believing that relative price changes were in fact an unimportant factor in the large commodity import increases which took place. Astoundingly enough Viner makes not the slightest effort to investigate the influence of the relative price changes, if any, upon the large import increases which occurred. He occupies himself with a misleading statistical demonstration of the significance in the capital transfer of the commodity import increases.[15]

Viner's conclusion is "that the borrowed capital was transferred to Canada mainly in the form of increased commodity imports." [16] Yet the tabulation of Table 13 revealed that almost one half of the offsets to the capital imports are to be found in the nonmerchandise items, which were responsible for a very considerable proportion of the debit balance increase from the beginning to the end of the period. The nonmerchandise items were only slightly less important than the merchandise items, and should certainly not be neglected. In seeking to demonstrate his proposition, Viner commits an error similar to that criticized earlier. He correlates variations in the volume of gross imports (not the import sur-

[13] *Canada's Balance*, p. 275.
[14] *Canada's Balance*, pp. 263–270.
[15] *Canada's Balance*, pp. 274–276.
[16] *Canada's Balance*, p. 276.

plus) and the variations in the current account deficit, again erroneously treating the latter as if it represented long-term capital imports.[17] In this way he has given at least some readers the very misleading impression that the increases in commodity imports have more than accounted for the capital import increases, which the debit balance is supposed to represent, for his figures show a greater sum of annual increases for the former than for the latter.[18] This neglects the fact that there were greatly increased credits, notably for commodity exports, during the period, which the increased debits on account of imports, etc., must offset before a net balance will result. A substantial part of the equilibration cannot be explained in terms of commodity imports. Viner's table and comments seem to imply that the increases in imports of commodities are more than sufficient to account for the capital borrowings, but this is clearly not the case. Viner suggests that some of the import increase might be allowed as due to two factors which are components in a cyclical upswing in which capital imports are merely one element. Then he attempts to reach a conclusion regarding the importance of the changes in one debit, commodity imports, relative to one credit, capital imports (of which the debit balance, i.e., the current deficit, is erroneously taken to be a measure), without explicitly taking account of the variations in other debits and credits in the balance of payments.

Some of the increase in the value of the imports was undoubtedly due to the rise in the prices of the import commodities and to the increase in population. Even if generous allowance is made for these two factors, there still remains an increase of imports sufficient to account for a large share of the capital borrowings. In spite of the operation of other factors in the adjustment of the balance of indebtedness, there is apparent a substantial measure of correlation between the variations in imports and the variations in net capital borrowings.[19]

[17] *Canada's Balance*, p. 276, table 55.

[18] This procedure of Viner's has been referred to as a "pairing-off fallacy." To quote R. O. Hall, *International Transactions of the United States* (New York, 1936), p. 30, "Such pairings-off are sometimes useful for comparing the magnitude of items on opposite sides of a balance of payments; but rarely do they show a cause-and-effect relationship, especially when absolute amounts are considered."

[19] *Canada's Balance*, p. 276. See also Chapter 13.

The limitations of Viner's line of reasoning may be illustrated in the following hypothetical case. Assume that over the period of time under consideration both exports and imports rise *pari passu*. There would be a higher correlation between merchandise imports and capital imports than in the Canadian case. Yet no increase in the import surplus would accompany the increase in capital imports. We must look away from the merchandise account to discover other possible vehicles for the transfer of capital. The transfer could be completed by the development of a deficit on nonmerchandise account equal to the increase in borrowings from abroad, while the merchandise trade (in this hypothetical illustration) contributed not a whit.

In conclusion, Viner neglects in his consideration of the real transfer the important contributions made by the elements of the nonmerchandise current account, the most important of these being net payments abroad of interest and dividends. In such adjustments as these, relative price changes certainly played an insignificant role.

In Viner's examination of the relations of the merchandise account to the capital importations he does not succeed in demonstrating that the latter was autonomous and the former induced. Nor does he succeed in demonstrating that any significance whatsoever attaches to the relative price changes operating on the merchandise account so as to produce the required import surplus. Viner's own interpretations of what actually took place are at times sufficiently realistic as to give much weight to the role of the relative shifts of purchasing power in influencing the Canadian trade accounts. But no revision is made of the original proposition he persistently claims to have verified: "The adjustment of the balance of trade to a newly introduced or increased disturbing factor is brought about through the influence of diverging price levels on the quantitative ratio of exports to imports." [20] One of Viner's former students has suggested to me that Viner may well have been surprised when, during the course of renewed controversy over the comparative importance in the adjustment mechanism of price changes and shifts in purchasing power, the examination of his account in *Canada's Balance* re-

[20] *Canada's Balance*, p. 254.

vealed such extensive emphasis upon the purchasing power shifts. Viner does not appear to have been aware of the contradictory nature of the Mill-Taussig thesis when tested against several of the statements recently quoted from him in which income effects, and not price effects, were stressed.[21]

GENERAL CONCLUSIONS

Viner has attempted to demonstrate that Canadian development during the period 1900–1913 can best be analyzed as an adjustment by the Canadian economy and particularly the Canadian trade balance to a single disturbing force, namely, capital imports from abroad. He has stressed in the adjustment process changes in the money supply as the result of the foreign loans, and resultant changes in relative price levels that in turn induced the real transfer through their influence upon the trade balance.

My analysis has, on the other hand, emphasized the mutual interdependence and reaction to common influences that appear characteristic of actual historical secular and cyclical developments. Monetary and credit expansion and relative price changes appear more generally as relatively passive induced variables rather than as active causal forces in the processes of economic change under investigation. The migration of labor, increases of population, the growth of capital formation, and the propagation of incomes have all contributed more in my analysis than the relative price changes and alterations in the supply of money. Viner, at times verging if not entering upon contradiction, seems to be close to this point of view. (A reservation, however, should be made for the fact that, writing at the time he did, Viner did not distinguish between that aspect of the income effect I have termed the primary shift in purchasing power, and the propaga-

[21] See P. T. Ellsworth, "Comparative Costs, the Gains from Trade, and Other Matters, Considered by Professor Viner," *The Canadian Journal of Economics and Political Science*, 5:242 (May 1939), where an analogous alleged bias in favor of the older theory appearing in Viner's *Studies . . . International Trade* has been noted: ". . . is it too much to hope that in Professor Viner's next book the doctrine of comparative costs will be accorded treatment only as a stage in the development of economic thought? And is it not perhaps true that Professor Viner's reluctance to cast this doctrine overboard is attributable more to the fact that it is an old and trusted friend than to any intellectual requirements of the theory of the gains from trade?"

tion of incomes dealt with in connection with the secondary shifts of purchasing power or the multiplier sequence.) At such times the Mill-Taussig theory which Viner set out to verify empirically seems to disappear into the background of his thoughts.

It is only fair to stress that much of our criticism of Viner has been made possible as a result of theoretical developments that have occurred since the time of Viner's writing. What is interesting methodologically is how Viner convinced himself and a host of other economists of the validity of a theory while giving it what I hope I have shown to be a very tenuous basis of fact. This seems to the writer to be a very striking example of what William James referred to as the "will to believe." It is also a tribute to the high order of Viner's ability in providing a very convincing demonstration in favor of a theory for which there was little supporting evidence.

Great admiration is due Viner for his industrious work on the balance-of-payments estimates for the years 1900–1913. Subsequent investigators have made much use of his estimates and his procedures. However, as Viner makes no attempt to conceal, much of the estimating is merely intelligent guesswork, and recent revisions of Canadian balance-of-payments estimates following 1926 have indicated how far astray such estimating may go. Nonetheless, it is on the use of the Viner statistics rather than on their possible inaccuracies that I have based my criticisms. For it is my view that this type of brave statistics is better than nothing, and that if we are but mildly perfectionist in a historical balance-of-payments analysis we must produce little in the way of results.[22] The knowledge of the statistical inadequacies, however, should counsel us to avoid dogmatic conclusions.

At the risk of considerable repetition, I will summarize my view of the adjustments which took place in the Canadian balance of payments during the period 1900–1913. Viner's tenet that the period is illustrative of the Mill-Taussig mechanism whereby relative price changes operate on the export-import quantities to equilibrate them to the capital inflows I find unacceptable. In the first place, the period must be set in the context of the favorable world cyclical conjuncture which commenced about 1896 — a new surge of economic growth. Many of the relative price

[22] See Viner, *Studies . . . International Trade*, p. 424.

changes which Viner was relating to capital imports got under way at that time, although capital importations themselves did not assume very great significance until the years following 1905.

Canada rose to prominence in these prosperous years as "the last best west." Increasing demands for her exports, particularly of grains, created a favorable atmosphere for domestic and outside capital. The demand for labor and for farmer settlers rose along with the demand for capital. Population and incomes expanded. Industrialization and urbanization further stimulated investment activity. All this was combined in the one process in which prospects of increasing returns and larger profits provided a major incentive. The simultaneity of the increased demands for outside capital and for imports must be emphasized. It is not unlikely that this type of simultaneous adjustment may provide the greater part of the explanation for the equilibration effected. In my view, the process of lagged income propagation as dealt with in dynamic foreign trade multiplier analysis provides an important explanation for the remaining adjustment which took place. Once induced investment, the acceleration principle, variable time lags, and heterogeneity in the causal interrelationships are introduced, this process of income propagation may merge logically with the simultaneous "common cause" type of adjustment.

In the Canadian case we find miscellaneous types of adjustment assuming importance which might normally account for little. A steady swelling of interest and dividend payments provided large offsets to the capital inflows, and to a lesser extent immigrants' remittances and transfers on account of tourists were also equilibrating.

Marginally, banking policy and relative price changes may have assisted to some degree in the equilibration, but there is certainly no evidence that they were of any considerable importance. If the adjustment were a very fine one, there might be more reason to attach importance to them.[23] The adjustment was, how-

---

[23] Professor Viner has commented on my manuscript at this point that he could not see what difference this makes for the theory. Yet, as we have seen, he himself stressed the important role of the relative price changes in a model assuming exact equilibration. Also, we have seen that determinate disequilibrium may be a feature of the model that relies upon relative income changes alone for adjustment.

ever, inexact, the failure to equilibrate being indicated by the very substantial flows of monetary gold and short-term capital.

Finally, it might be pointed out that my approach in analyzing this particular period in Canadian economic life has been as much historical as theoretical. I have striven to set the period in its historical setting and to take adequate account of the historical specificity of the Canadian economy and of its relations to other countries during a period when its development was proceeding at an unusually great pace.

PART IV
THE INTERWAR PERIOD

XVII

Economic Development and Commercial Policy

The interwar period contrasts considerably with the years 1900–1913. The latter had been cited as the unusual case of the near isolation of a single force in history,[1] a force represented by an "import of capital . . . so great, it overshadowed so completely all others, that there can be no error in attributing to this the main economic changes which appeared."[2] In preceding chapters I took exception to this point of view. I emphasized that powerful growth processes which were not subsidiary to capital importations from abroad dominated the Canadian economy in the period 1896–1913, and that the shorter cyclical swings were subordinated to this secular trend. Capital borrowings from abroad were not the initiating factor but acquired great importance in the second half of the period. The chief contrast to be found in the interwar period is that the secular growth processes no longer are continually in predominance. The outstanding characteristic of the various economic time series is the postwar prosperity and the subsequent depression. Nor are international capital movements of comparable importance for Canada in the years 1919–1939.

The interwar period finds Canada yet further removed from the position of one of a group of agricultural, raw-material producing countries to which unidirectional flows of capital from

[1] F. W. Taussig, *International Trade* (New York, 1927), pp. 222ff.
[2] *International Trade*, p. 235.

more mature countries were a *sine qua non* of a pulsating economic development. International capital flows play a much less important part. They are not unidirectional, and at times Canada is on balance a net exporter of capital, with considerable repatriation of former debts. In other words, domestic savings are at times more than adequate to finance domestic investment activity.

Increased Canadian self-sufficiency in part provides the basis for a departure from the traditional positive correlation between cyclical upswings and capital imports that marked the earlier phases of Canadian development. In its place there appears in the 1930's an increasing net capital export as an accompaniment of an expanding national income.[3] More detailed statistics are available for the many various elements of the current and capital accounts that reveal a disconcerting variety of behavior patterns. This complexity makes it much more difficult than in the 1900–1913 period to move beyond description to a theoretical analysis.

Exchange rate fluctuations, changes in tariff levels, and other trade restrictions also enter to complicate the interwar picture. The appearance of alterations in foreign exchange rates and in tariff levels provides the investigator with an added opportunity for examining the influence of relative price changes as compared with income effects.

Finally, there are important changes in the fabric of the Canadian economy associated with the growth of export-producing regions rivaling those of the prairie west. Despite the significant changes in the structure and institutions of the Canadian and world economies, and the new phase in Canadian economic development, I would argue that similar tools of analysis are applicable to earlier and later periods, and that intercomparison is fruitful. The contrasts are so apparent that there is danger of their being exaggerated.[4]

[3] See, for example, the case of Sweden, discussed earlier. In the Canadian case the fact that the expansion commenced from low levels of income and employment was also highly significant. Partly as a consequence of excess capacity, a large induced increase in investment activity, with its characteristically high import content, did not occur, so that export increases were not matched by import increases. (See Chapters 7 and 19.)

[4] See A. F. Burns, "Current Research in Business Cycles — Discussions," *American Economic Review*, May 1939, p. 81. "While there is a greater

Despite the number and complexity of the forces operating on and within the Canadian economy, and the strong externally and internally derived shocks to which it was subject, there was a surprising degree of balance-of-payments equilibrium without the extensive fluctuations in the exchange rate, or default on liabilities to foreigners, or measures of governmental control to which so many other countries were subject. It is the large measure of balance-of-payments adjustment rather than the failure to adjust that generally calls for explanation. The principles of balance-of-payments analysis elaborated on in the foregoing chapter will again serve to throw light upon the major forces operating toward equilibrium, although the actions of some forces will remain obscure or appear a matter of mere chance.

ECONOMIC DEVELOPMENTS

Little attention will be given to wartime developments as such, although the influence of world wars, past and prospective, must be recognized as very important in the interwar period. This influence, which is difficult to segregate analytically, will not be dealt with other than in passing.

World War I, following as it did on the boom years of high investment activity, may well have averted a serious depression. I have noted shifts in the terms of trade consequent on declining export prices as early as 1913, while between 1913 and 1914 the value of construction contracts awarded in Canada declined by 37 per cent. A small wheat crop aggravated the situation for the short run.[5] As Professor Knox has pointed out, the opinion that the break in 1914 was due to the cessation of the import of capital receives little or no support in the statistics.[6] Capital imports, although reduced from their peak in 1913, continued at a high level through 1916, while a greater falling off of payments than

continuity in business-cycle experience before and after World War I than many students realize, there can be little doubt that certain structural changes in world economy did occur around that time."

[5] Canada, Royal Commission, *Report on Dominion–Provincial Relations*, I, 90.

[6] F. A. Knox, "Canadian War Finance and the Balance of Payments," *The Canadian Journal of Economics and Political Science*, May 1940, p. 299. The erroneous view is to be found, e.g., in Royal Commission, *Report*, I, 90; Taussig, *International Trade*, p. 223; and Ohlin, *Interregional and International Trade*, p. 451.

of receipts on current account indicated a reduction of Canadian foreign exchange requirements. In addition to other sources of outside capital there was resort to $24 million in special advances from the United Kingdom government. That such advances were sought by the Canadian government was due to the absence of any domestic capital market in Canada at the time, plus the weakening of governmental finances consequent upon the decline of the main revenue source, namely, customs duties. Merchandise imports remained below the levels of the period 1911–1913 until 1916.

The war facilitated adjustment primarily by inflating overseas demands for Canadian exports. Although the past had seen secularly increasing Canadian exports accompanying the secularly increasing demands of importing countries, there were periods, after heavy investment programs, when exports declined or increased only very slowly over a period of years, e.g., the years following the boom of 1868–1875.[7] The war prevented any such possible recurrence. The result was that expansion in many lines proceeded further than might otherwise have been expected.

In the main, expansion continued in the same industries which had been growing rapidly in the prewar period. . . .

Wheat-growing, in the Prairie Provinces, was greatly extended by the reduction of acreage in the importing countries of Europe, by the cutting off of Russian and Danubian exports, and by the high freight rates which discouraged expansion in Argentina and Australia.[8]

Great gains were also recorded in the exports of pulp and paper which rose from $19 million in 1913 to $105 million in 1919. Further rises in the exports of pulp and paper and of wheat took place in the 1920's. This was in contrast to other important wartime export increases, where the values recorded, after being greatly diminished in the postwar depression of 1920–1921, were never regained in the subsequent prosperity. Increases in production for the domestic market were also notable during the war. Additions to the tariffs on imports, increased shipping costs, and overseas supply difficulties while Canadian demands were swelling provide part of the explanation. These supplied a stimulus

[7] See Table 3.

[8] Mackintosh, *The Economic Background of Dominion-Provincial Relations*, p. 31.

to manufactures, but an even greater one came from the British requirements for munitions and war equipment.[9]

Another important factor serving to sustain the Canadian economy during the early war years was the continued momentum of railway construction that had been initiated in the prewar period. Railway mileage in operation continued its rapid rate of expansion into 1917. The increase from 1913 to 1917 was some 9,000 miles of track as compared with about 11,600 for the period 1900–1913.[10] The continued expansion of Canadian railroads in large measure explains the continuing large import of foreign capital. Other forms of construction, on the other hand, fell off markedly in 1915.[11] Simultaneously, immigration, another factor of great significance in the prewar expansion, dwindled away to small proportions.[12]

The strong trend toward urbanization noted in the 1900–1913 period has continued through war and peacetime to the present day. In the seventy years following Confederation in 1867 the urban population had increased 8.7 fold while the farm population had only increased 1.8 fold.[13] Paradoxically it is the expanding wheat economy, along with increasing industrialization, that has been one of the factors hastening the relative decline of agriculture. As the productivity of the mechanized, monocultural wheat farm has risen, it has become increasingly dependent upon the urban community for its supplies of equipment, consumer goods, merchandising, and transport services.[14]

Industrialization proceeded apace during the war years. The net value of production of manufactures, which had increased from $214 million to $564 million during the period 1900–1910, more than doubled once again by 1923 when it reached a figure of $1,304 million.[15] The greatest increases appear to have oc-

[9] Royal Commission, *Report,* I, 91.
[10] *Canada Year Book* (1945), p. 652.
[11] *Canada Year Book* (1945), p. 168.
[12] *Canada Year Book* (1945), p. 450.
[13] W. B. Hurd, "Demographic Trends in Canada," in the "Features of Present-Day Canada" volume, *Annals of the American Academy of Political and Social Science,* September 1947, p. 12.
[14] V. C. Fowke, "Agriculture in the Postwar World," *The Annals,* September 1947, p. 45.
[15] Mackintosh, *The Economic Background of Dominion–Provincial Relations,* p. 29, table 4.

curred during the years 1916 and 1917, when national income attributable to manufacturing is estimated to have increased 47 and 65 per cent respectively.[16] Since there was no annual Census of Manufactures until 1917, these estimates are none too firmly based. The chief gains of the interwar period were established between the years 1925 and 1929 when the annual net value of manufactures increased almost $600 million, or by approximately 50 per cent.[17]

The preeminently cyclical character of the fluctuations in most important series is demonstrated in Tables 20 and 24 in the series for national income, investment, and wholesale prices.

One major contrast provided by the war and postwar booms, when compared with that for 1896–1913, is that in the early period investment was based on actual or potential increases in wheat production to a much greater extent than it was in the later periods. During the war years, construction, which had been associated so largely with the opening up of the Canadian West, declined from its 1913 peak of $275 million to an average of $60 million for the years 1916–1918.[18] It was on the basis of previous investment that wartime expansion was possible. The increase from 1913 to 1919 in the area devoted to field crops was equal to the increase which took place in the twenty years prior to 1913. "While the expanding market for wheat was a major factor in the economic growth of Canada during the twenties, other forces were perhaps more important." [19]

The resources of British Columbia and of the northern areas of Ontario and Quebec became the basis of large staple industries. In addition to the agricultural frontier on the prairies, Canada acquired new frontiers on the Pre-Cambrian Shield. The exports of pulp and paper and non-ferrous metals rose to 30 per cent of total exports in 1929 compared with 19 per cent in 1920. . . . The large fixed equipment represented by central electric stations, pulp and paper factories, smelters and metal refineries was the major factor in the exploitation of these resources. . . .

[16] Estimated from J. J. Deutsch, "War Finance and the Canadian Economy," *Canadian Journal of Economics and Political Science,* November 1940, p. 538, table 1.

[17] *Canada Year Book* (1941), p. 306.

[18] Deutsch, "War Finance and the Canadian Economy," *Canadian Journal of Economics and Political Science,* p. 538, table 1.

[19] Royal Commission, *Report,* I, 115.

Another technical innovation which called forth large capital outlays in the post-war years was the automobile. It gave rise to new automobile factories, petroleum refineries, service stations, repair shops and, what was most important, a greatly extended and improved system of highways and streets. . . .

The heavy capital expenditures involved in the development of the primary industries and transportation stimulated investment in manufacturing, in distribution facilities, in community equipment and housing. . . .

The northward extension of wheat growing on the prairies required a substantial increase in costly transportation facilities. New branch lines were built, main lines improved and canals and harbours enlarged in accordance with the national policy of all-Canadian transportation.[20]

The political and economic consequences of these changes were of the greatest importance.

The nature of the development during this decade modified the simple unity of the Canadian economy which rested on the rising production and exportation of wheat. Prior to the War, there was one predominant export area, the Prairie West, whose growth under the influences of the national policies built an integrated transcontinental economy. During the twenties new important export staples emerged in two other regions. Formerly the economy had but a single important external contact; now there were several. One promoted East-West cohesion; the others emphasized North-South relationships and regional economic independence.[21]

The two new export areas were Central Canada and British Columbia. Their exports of forest products and nonferrous minerals found their chief markets in the United States, in contrast to the Prairie export of wheat, which found its way to overseas markets in Britain and Europe. This development was further enhanced in the thirties with the decline of wheat exports, particularly to Europe, and by further increases in nonferrous metal

[20] Royal Commission, *Report*, I, 115–116. Total railway mileage in operation expanded, however, by about 3000 miles of track during the twenties, which compares with an increase of 14,000 miles in the preceding decade. The facts that fewer men were required for agricultural and railway building and that much of the Canadian development of the twenties focused upon extractive industries requiring relatively little manpower help explain the larger emigration than immigration during some years of the period. For net emigration figures to 1925 see R. Wilson, "Migration Movements in Canada," *Canadian Historical Review*, 13:181.

[21] Royal Commission, *Report*, I, 125.

exports to the United States, particularly of gold. There were partial offsets in the growing markets found in Britain for non-ferrous metals, and by innumerable other instances of increasing intra-imperial trade.

In closing this summary survey of the most significant Canadian interwar economic developments, a note of caution might be sounded on the interpretation of the global statistics relating to manufacturing. Listed in order of gross value of product, the seven leading manufacturing industries in 1937 were nonferrous smelting and refining, pulp and paper, slaughtering and meat packing, automobiles, flour and feed mills, butter and cheese, and sawmills.[22] Apart from automobiles, which were the manufacture of a branch plant industry and to a large degree assembled from imported parts, these industries were not in a highly advanced industrial category. They were representative of the more important type of Canadian manufacture which entailed the further processing of raw materials. This has significance for the export list where the increased proportion of fully and partly manufactured products of the twenties and thirties as compared with the years immediately preceding World War I reflects in large measure the increasing importance of newsprint and nonferrous metals while wheat suffered a relative decline.[23]

COMMERCIAL POLICY [24]

The tariff level cannot be definitively and satisfactorily measured and its measure is not an indication of the protectionist effect of the tariff. Such measures as have been attempted indicate that "the Canadian tariff from 1879 to 1930 was comparatively stable. There was no pronounced upward movement and, though difficult to measure, there was probably some downward trend."[25] Partly this has resulted automatically from a rising

[22] *Canada Year Book* (1939), p. 425.

[23] D. H. Fullerton, "Survey of Canadian Foreign Trade," *The Annals,* September 1947, p. 144.

[24] For more detailed accounts see O. J. McDiarmid, *Commercial Policy in the Canadian Economy* (Cambridge, 1946), chapters 11 and 12; K. W. Taylor, "The Commercial Policy of Canada," *Canadian Marketing Problems,* ed. H. R. Kemp (Toronto, 1939); and J. F. Parkinson et al., *Canada in World Affairs* (Toronto, 1941), part II, for the years 1935–1939.

[25] Mackintosh, *The Economic Background of Dominion–Provincial Relations,* p. 83.

price level which reduced the weight of specific duties. The tendency had been to attempt to combine reductions in duties with the least possible sacrifice of protection or, in some cases, with increases in protection. Characteristic Canadian devices for accomplishing this were special concessions of low duties, free import, or "drawbacks" on commodities for use in Canadian manufactures; the reduction of rates on noncompetitive items; and "reduced preferential rates which . . . raised the preferential producer's price rather than the Canadian importer's duty-paid price."[26]

For what it is worth the Canadian tariff level of 1925 was computed by the World Economic Conference of 1927 to be 23 per cent as compared with 37, 29, and 27 per cent for the United States, Argentina, and Australia, respectively. This was a level slightly less than that estimated for the new countries of Central Europe, slightly higher than that of France, Italy, and Germany, and very much higher than that of Sweden, Holland, Belgium, and Switzerland.[27]

There is a particularly strong reason for not regarding the tariff level as an adequate indication of protection in the case of Canada. This is to be found in her use of tariff-making by administration, the antimonopoly and antidumping clauses of which dated from the nineteenth century, and which during the period 1930–1935 in particular was perhaps carried further in Canada than in any other country.[28]

Until 1930 this relatively stable tariff level, together with ingeniously designed loopholes in the tariff structure and protectionist administrative provisions, served to implement the traditional commercial policy which consisted of (1) protection of domestic manufactures, (2) encouragement of diversified exports through trade treaties and information services, and (3) the encouragement of export staples chiefly through government expenditures or statutory controls of railway rates.[29] While no general tariff revision took place during the 1920's, there were a

[26] Mackintosh, p. 84.

[27] W. A. Mackintosh, "Canadian Tariff Policy," Canadian Institute of International Affairs, Canadian Papers (Toronto, 1933), p. 14.

[28] McDiarmid, Commercial Policy in the Canadian Economy, p. 306.

[29] Taylor, "The Commercial Policy of Canada," Canadian Marketing Problems, p. 7.

number of important changes with respect to individual items.[30] In the years 1919, 1922, and 1924, duties on farm machinery were substantially reduced. The year 1926 saw the reduction of the tariffs on less expensive automobiles with larger drawbacks being accorded in offsetting relief to the Canadian manufacturer. In 1923 the Maritime ports and Montreal were favored in their competition with New York when a reduction of 10 per cent of the preferential rates was granted on goods shipped directly to a Canadian port. During the twenties the trade treaty policy was further extended, in particular with France, Italy, and Belgium.

In the year of 1930, Canada retaliated in kind to the Hawley-Smoot high tariff schedule introduced by United States legislation.[31] The Canadian Prime Minister, Mr. R. B. Bennett, cited a number of reasons, other than retaliation, which he regarded as favoring higher tariffs. These included the relief of unemployment, the prevention of emigration, the prevention of dumping, the development of Canadian resources, and the furthering of Canadian economic independence.[32] A notable omission is the use of the tariff to bolster the balance of payments, which due to Canadian borrowings abroad was in a relatively strong position that particular year. The government did not appear to regard the tariff as a desirable future support for the balance of payments, nor as an alternative to floating loans in New York. "The government would have been surprised had anyone suggested that the Canadian dollar needed support." [33]

The increased tariffs were supplemented by the use of such administrative devices as were already available. The antidumping provision, which permitted the use of fixed or arbitrarily determined exchange rates in assessing the value of imports from countries with depreciated currencies, was particularly important after 1931, as it was applied to imports from Great Britain in that year. "Very few countries, indeed, used their tariffs more

[30] Mackintosh, *The Economic Background of Dominion–Provincial Relations*, pp. 51–52.

[31] J. M. Jones, *Tariff Retaliation: Repercussions of the Hawley-Smoot Bill* (Philadelphia, 1934), chapter VI.

[32] Jones, p. 187.

[33] F. A. Knox, *Dominion Monetary Policy, 1929–1934* (Ottawa, 1939), p. 14.

energetically or showed more ingenuity in developing supplementary controls in the same field.[34]

The Ottawa Agreements for the extension and increase of British imperial preferential tariff margins were entered into during the depths of the depression in 1932.

Since the Canadian administration regarded protection as an instrument for national development and recovery, the idea pervading the Anglo-Canadian negotiations was to make concessions to the manufacturing interests of the United Kingdom at the expense of foreign rather than Canadian manufacturers. Canadian duties upon those goods which Canada genuinely desired to protect remained, for the most part, at prohibitive levels, even though the British producer was accorded a margin of preference equivalent to 10 to 20 per cent of the duty to which foreign foods were subjected.[35]

One study has arrived at the conclusion that the treaty was responsible in the year following its initiation for the diversion of $15 million of imports, or 5 per cent of total Canadian imports, from other countries to the United Kingdom. Of this, $12 million was estimated to have been gained by Britain at the expense of the United States.[36] The chief products affected were chemicals, textiles, primary iron and steel, and anthracite coal. The more important gains made by Canadian exporters in the British market were due to the preferences on lumber, apples, and bacon. Since there were British Commonwealth surpluses of most important agricultural products, many other preferences accorded, such as that on wheat, were ineffective.[37]

[34] McDiarmid, "Canadian Tariff Policy," *The Annals*, September 1947, p. 153.

[35] McDiarmid, *Commercial Policy in the Canadian Economy*, p. 286. The principle of binding the preferential margins, rather than the rates themselves, was introduced in 1932. At Geneva, in 1947, Canada obtained a release from this provision from the United Kingdom, but the provision has continued to apply to trade with other British Commonwealth countries and has handicapped Canada in negotiating tariff reductions with the United States. See the *Financial Post*, July 7, 1951, p. 13, for an article by Kenneth R. Wilson.

[36] D. Annett, *British Imperial Preference in Canadian Commercial Policy*, p. 126 (a dissertation, Harvard University Library, 1947, published under the auspices of the Canadian Institute of International Affairs, Toronto, 1948), citing conclusions of A. C. Annis, "A Study of Canadian Tariffs and Trade Agreements," unpublished dissertation, Cornell University (1936).

[37] Royal Commission, *Report*, I, 159.

It is no easy matter to assess the value to Canada of the preference.[38] Of total Canadian exports, 27 per cent are subject to the preferential rates. The most important of these go to markets in the United Kingdom. The preference on one third of the Canadian exports to the United Kingdom (over one eighth of total Canadian exports) was stated by the Minister to be "of great value." From this we may infer that imperial preference was probably of greater advantage to Canada than to Britain.[39] However, the difficulty in disentangling the effects of increasing British and world prosperity upon Canadian trade from the effects of imperial preference must make us wary of the claims made with regard to it.

There were important revisions involved in each of the three major commercial policy objectives of the newly elected Liberal Government of 1935. These objectives comprised (1) assistance of the depressed export regions by decreasing tariffs on manufactured goods, especially where these had been imposed by the predecessor Conservative government; (2) increasing foreign markets for the staple exports through a system of trade agreements; and (3) improving trade relations with the United States.[40] Under the United States–Canadian Trade Agreement of 1935, increased outlets were obtained for Canadian exports of lumber, cattle, fresh and frozen fish, whiskey, and potatoes. The United States had obtained tariff concessions on farm implements, certain classes of automobiles, electrical apparatus, gasoline, many kinds of machinery, and had won the very important abolition of arbitrary valuations on a long list of items.[41]

[38] The following statistics were given by J. A. MacKinnon, the Canadian Minister of Trade and Commerce, speaking before the Chamber of Commerce in London, England, on January 22, 1946.

[39] See the Ottawa Supplement, *The London Economist*, October 22, 1932; W. Beveridge et al., *Tariffs: The Case Examined* (London, 1932); H. Feis, "The Future of British Imperial Preference," *Foreign Affairs*, July 1946. In the years immediately following World War II the relative advantage of the preference appears clearly to have swung away from Canada. Restrictive controls have been applied by Commonwealth countries to imports from the dollar area, including Canada, so as to reduce substantially the favorable influence of the preference upon Canadian exports. Canadian quantitative restrictions, on the other hand, have had the effect of restraining imports almost only from the United States.

[40] Parkinson, *Canada in World Affairs*, p. 195.

[41] Royal Commission, *Report*, I, 159–160.

A thorough-going revision of the 1932 Canadian–United Kingdom Trade Agreement took place in 1937.[42] Preferential margins were increased almost entirely through preferential tariff decreases, in contrast to 1932 arrangements, when many of the increases were secured by raising foreign tariff rates (83 out of 304 items affected).[43] The items affected were relatively insignificant in United Kingdom exports ($28 million of her exports for 1935–1936), being mainly items not in the list of tariff concessions to the United States in 1935. The new preferences granted to Canada were negligible, the agreement by the United Kingdom to maintain free entry for important Canadian exports being the primary concession. A foundation was laid for subsequent tariff concessions to the United States by relaxing the provisions for bound preferential margins. In general the preferences accorded were 10 per cent, and they were rarely over 15 per cent ad valorem. Parkinson considers it doubtful if the general margin of preference remaining after the Treaties of 1935 and 1937 was as high as that of 1929.[44]

A series of treaties with other countries were concluded by the Liberal Government in which the intermediate rates were usually accorded. The higher general tariff schedule was thereby left with a very limited applicability.

The second Canadian–United States Trade Agreement was signed in 1938, after triangular negotiations which led in addition to a treaty between the United Kingdom and the United States.[45] An example of the multilateral character of the discussions is to be found in the arrangement for improved treatment of United States lumber in the United Kingdom in return for lower tariffs on Canadian lumber entering the United States. Other Canadian exports receiving favorable treatment were cattle, fish, and a number of agricultural products. Canada granted tariff reductions on numerous commodities in the iron and steel group, on cotton products, and on many articles used in the construction and building trades. Possible competitive advantages enjoyed by Canada in the United Kingdom market

[42] Parkinson, *Canada in World Affairs*, pp. 200ff.
[43] McDiarmid, *Commercial Policy in the Canadian Economy*, p. 284.
[44] Parkinson, *Canada in World Affairs*, p. 208.
[45] Parkinson, chapter 13.

were reduced when it was agreed to decrease the bound preferential margins on wheat, lumber, apples, pears, and salmon.

With this series of treaties the Liberal Government went some distance in reducing the high tariff barriers erected during the early 1930's.

In conclusion, I might anticipate the results of later investigations and indicate my impression that commercial policy has generally been overrated in its influence on the balance of payments, particularly in the short run. Both the changes in tariff levels and in the balance of payments are frequently best explained as the result of relative income changes. The protectionism of the thirties and the fluctuations during the period of exports and imports seem primarily attributable to the wide variations in the levels of national incomes.

As another example, there are many reasons apart from imperial preference which will adequately explain the lesser decline of national incomes in the United Kingdom and in the British Commonwealth than in the United States and other countries. This lesser decline of incomes was almost certainly much more important than the preference in increasing the relative importance of intra-European trade, though here protectionist policies of other countries must also be admitted as a significant factor.

On the other hand, the predepression agricultural protectionism of many European countries had disastrous consequences for Canada. Again, the Canadian tariff helped to foster the expansion of United States branch plants in Canada, which exported a large proportion of their products to the protected British Commonwealth markets. These examples are sufficient to indicate that while our attention should be focused upon the relative income changes when we are considering the problems of short-run equilibration from month to month or year to year, commercial policies may assume considerable significance over a period of years, and in the Canadian case it has provided shocks to which the economy must perforce adjust.

XVIII

Structural Changes in the Balance
of Payments

The more important structural changes in the Canadian economy which occurred subsequent to the outbreak of World War I were outlined in the preceding chapter. I propose to examine these and other relatively long-run changes insofar as they are reflected in the statistics for the balance of payments. The method of examination selected is that of comparison of three relatively prosperous years, one pre-World War I, another in the prosperous twenties, and the third the most prosperous year in the prewar thirties.

It is perhaps unnecessary to observe that no one year, nor any average of a number of years, can be completely representative of any period, and the three years selected are not without their idiosyncrasies. The year 1913 was one of large capital imports, with imports at a much higher level than exports, the culminating year of a period of heavy borrowings abroad. The year 1928 rather than 1929 was selected as representative of postwar prosperity because of the disappointing grain crops and exports of the latter year, although investment activity was such as to prevent any decline of national income in 1929. In view of the great importance of grain exports in the Canadian postwar prosperity, 1928 was regarded as a more representative selection. The selection of 1937 was made because it was the peak year of a recovery which was cut short late in that year, leaving 1938 relatively depressed, while the subsequent more prosperous year of 1939 saw the beginning of World War II. The recovery of national income in 1939 beyond the 1937 level, despite a continuation of the decline of agricultural prices and a worsening of the terms of trade, was in large measure the result of increased demands stemming from war or from the preparation for war.

In the comparisons of 1913, 1928, and 1937, it should be remembered that whereas 1913 was a year of heavy capital imports, both 1928 and 1937 were years of considerable capital exports with merchandise export surpluses. The comparisons of the three years have been made in value terms without adjustment for the changing price level. In the instances where price

Table 14. *Index numbers of wholesale prices of exports and imports, calendar years 1913, 1928, and 1937*
(1926 = 100)

Group	Exports			Imports		
	1913	1928	1937	1913	1928	1937
Agricultural products	60.6	88.8	87.2	78.0	94.0	79.7
Animals and products	61.3	111.3	76.5	92.3	132.0	89.9
Fibers and textiles	63.2	95.3	73.1	63.3	94.7	72.1
Wood, wood products, paper	58.3	98.7	72.1	—	—	—
Iron and products	73.9	91.9	95.2	75.7	94.8	114.5
Nonferrous metals	89.0	87.5	79.9	93.6	99.7	93.6
Nonmetallic minerals	98.7	83.8	69.7	61.9	88.4	82.8
Chemicals and allied products	75.3	98.2	72.1	51.9	92.3	85.1
Average—all groups	64.7	94.2	81.1	73.0	96.1	89.8

Source. Compiled from *Prices and Price Indexes, 1913–1939*, the Dominion Bureau of Statistics (Ottawa, 1941), page 51.

changes are relevant to the analysis, reference will be made to Table 14, which indicates alterations in the export and import price indices.

CURRENT CREDITS

The following analysis of the current accounts is based upon the data presented in Tables 6 and 15. For the detailed analysis of the merchandise account the basis is to be found in Tables 7 and 16.

Table 15. *The distribution by country of the Canadian balance of payments,
current account, calendar years 1928 and 1937*
(all figures to nearest million dollars)

Transactions	United Kingdom	Other Common- wealth	United States	Other foreign	All countries
			Exports or credits		
1928					
Tourists	9	1	163	4	177
Interest and dividends	2	2	20	22	46
Freight and shipping	11	5	68	12	96
Nonmonetary gold	—	—	40	—	40
Other credits	13	—	69	6	88
Total nonmerchandise and gold	35	8	360	44	447
Total merchandise	288	95	507	451	1341
Total current credits	323	103	867	495	1788
1937					
Tourists	11	2	149	5	166
Interest and dividends	2	3	31	38	76
Freight and shipping	38	9	45	22	112
Nonmonetary gold	—	—	145	—	145
Other credits	8	—	42	3	53
Total nonmerchandise and gold	59	14	412	68	552
Total merchandise	385	105	391	157	1041
Total current credits	444	119	803	225	1593
			Imports or debits		
1928					
Tourists	19	2	72	5	98
Interest and dividends	100	2	169	4	275
Freight and shipping	10	2	92	12	116
Other debits	21	3	73	25	122
Total nonmerchandise	150	9	406	46	611
Total merchandise	194	62	810	143	1209
Total current debits	344	71	1216	189	1820
1937					
Tourists	16	2	65	4	87
Interest and dividends	85	2	211	4	302
Freight and shipping	43	4	68	22	137
Other debits	17	2	73	19	111
Total nonmerchandise	161	10	417	49	637
Total merchandise	148	87	463	78	776
Total current debits	309	97	880	127	1413

Table 15. (*Continued*)

Transactions	United Kingdom	Other Common-wealth	United States	Other foreign	All countries
	Net current credit (+) or net current debit (−)				
1928	−21	+32	−349	+306	−32
1937	135	+24	−77	+98	+180

Source. For the major part of the table, statistics are derived from the Dominion Bureau of Statistics, *The Canadian Balance of International Payments, 1926–1944* (Ottawa, 1945). The division between other commonwealth countries and other foreign countries was not available for the year 1928, however, only the total for the two being given. The division of the merchandise account, the most important item, was based upon the proportions given in the Bank of Canada, *Statistical Supplement* (Ottawa, 1946), p. 118. Estimates of the division on nonmerchandise account are not large amounts relative to the merchandise account, and are made on the basis of proportions known to exist for the years 1933 on.

Between 1913 and 1928 the total credits multiplied more than threefold, but the geographical distribution of the increase was quite uneven. The credits with the United Kingdom increased by less than one half — that is, an increase of the order of that of the price rise of merchandise exports — while the credits with other Commonwealth countries were increased fourfold, with the United States three and one half, and with "other foreign countries" about sevenfold. Of the increase of total credits from 1913–1928 of $1224 million, nonmerchandise and gold credits represented the smaller portion, some $326 million. Of these, $272 million was acquired with the United States, largely due to increased expenditures of American tourists in Canada and to increased freight receipts payable to Canada by the United States.

The remaining $898 million of the $1224 million increase in current credits between the years 1913 and 1928 is attributable to the merchandise account. Approximate increases totalled $350 million with the United States, $390 million with other foreign countries ($360 million with Europe), and only $85 and $70 million with the United Kingdom and other Commonwealth countries respectively. It should be noted here that there was a considerable exaggeration of the extent of trade with the United Kingdom prior to the recent revisions of Dominion Bureau of

Table 16. *The distribution by country of Canadian merchandise exports and imports, excluding gold, calendar years 1928 and 1937*
(millions of dollars)

Group or product	1928			1937		
	United Kingdom	United States	All countries	United Kingdom	United States	All countries
			Exports			
Agricultural and vegetable products	226	58	651	133	38	245
Animals and their products	49	88	163	80	49	144
Fibers and textiles	1	5	10	3	3	14
Wood, wood products, paper	21	238	289	44	180	263
Iron and its products	8	9	71	15	7	66
Nonferrous metals	15	46	93	101	45	195
Nonmetallic minerals	2	17	27	3	19	31
Chemical and allied products	4	9	18	5	10	22
Miscellaneous	1	4	6	4	7	13
Total	327	476	1329	389	357	993
Wheat	156	12	434	83	1	124
Total grains	185	13	483	90	4	137
Living animals	—	17	17	1	18	20
Bacon and ham	7	1	9	32	1	33
Cheese	23	2	25	12	1	13
Fish and fishery products	4	16	36	5	1	10
Planks, boards	7	36	48	24	15	45
Newsprint	10	122	141	5	103	126
Wood pulp	2	38	46	4	33	41
Pulpwood	—	15	15	—	12	12
Agricultural machinery and implements	—	3	14	1	—	10
Autos, trucks, parts	5	—	36	2	—	29
Aluminum and products	1	4	9	11	3	21
Copper and products	1	20	24	34	8	56
Nickel and products	4	12	22	29	18	59
Asbestos and products	1	7	11	1	7	15
			Imports			
Agricultural and vegetable products	27	103	210	19	44	148
Animals and their products	6	44	70	6	13	32
Fibers and textiles	76	77	202	53	39	115

Table 16. (*Continued*)

Group or product	1928			1937		
	United Kingdom	United States	All countries	United Kingdom	United States	All countries
			Imports			
Wood, wood products, paper	5	49	57	4	27	34
Iron and its products	39	295	344	32	174	213
Nonferrous metals	1	32	40	7	30	46
Nonmetallic minerals	12	130	162	13	105	136
Chemical and allied products	5	25	37	8	23	37
Miscellaneous	8	28	45	6	30	38
Total	179	784	1167	148	485	799
Fruits and nuts	1	34	42	—	16	27
Grains and milled products	—	12	23	—	7	18
Rubber	—	22	24	1	5	19
Alcoholic beverages	13	—	21	5	—	8
Tea and coffee	7	1	19	3	—	14
Hides and leather	3	23	26	3	4	12
Furs	1	12	17	1	4	8
Cotton and products	14	46	61	12	26	41
Silk and products	2	11	30	1	5	8
Wool and products	39	3	53	20	—	35
Paper and printed matter	4	23	29	—	—	22
Sheets, plates, hoops, bands, and strips	—	—	33	—	—	37
Agricultural implements, machinery	—	40	40	1	16	17
Motors vehicles and parts	—	—	90	—	48	49
Engines, locomotives, and boilers	1	17	18	1	9	11
Other machinery	3	53	57	4	41	46
Electrical apparatus	2	21	24	2	12	16
Coal and products	3	58	61	6	34	42
Petroleum and products	—	52	62	—	47	59

Source. The data are available in Dominion Bureau of Statistics, *Trade of Canada* (Ottawa), for the calendar years 1928 and 1937. The figures are adjusted by the exclusion of gold, settlers' effects, and overcharges on alcoholic beverages, and by estimates for the diversion of wheat from the United Kingdom to other countries. Adjustments were also made for certain non-commercial items and for the unrecorded import of ships. No adjustment was made for administrative overvaluation of imports for duty purposes, since the adjustment estimate was available only for the global total of imports, and not for the various groups or commodities. Despite these adjustments to bring the customs data more in line with that used in the balance-of-payments estimates, there was still lack of conformity between the two sets of estimates, as may be seen by comparing the totals for merchandise trade in Tables 15 and 16. The disparity is not so great as to invalidate the analysis based on the tables, however. For further information, reference should be made to the Statistical Appendix.

Statistics estimates which took account of the diversion of wheat from Britain to other countries.[1]

Over 50 per cent of the increase of 1928 merchandise credits with the United States over the 1913 level occurred in the wood, wood products, and paper group. Newsprint alone accounted for $128 million of the $193 million increase of this group. Wheat bulked heavily in the additions to the exports of 1928 over the 1913 level going to the United Kingdom and the foreign countries other than the United States, the respective increases being $75 and $250 million.

The change in the distribution of merchandise credits between 1928 and 1937 was such as to reduce the proportion derived from other foreign countries to the 1913 level. The proportion due to credits with the United Kingdom was considerably augmented, but at 28 per cent it was still a long way from regaining the 1913 proportion of 39 per cent. Current credits originating in transactions with the United States again displayed a small proportional increase, as they had between the years 1900 and 1913, and between 1913 and 1928.

Between 1928 and 1937 there was a decline of $195 million in total current credits, smaller from the point of view of percentage than the 15 per cent price decline in export prices during the period. There were important offsetting shifts within the global totals. Geographically the important decline was in credits with foreign countries other than the United States. This was $270 million, which was approximately the decline in credits with Europe. The 1913–1928 increase in wheat exports to other foreign countries was largely offset by the 1928–1937 drop in their value of $226 millions. Compare this decline with the over-all decrease of $300 million in merchandise exports, and its outstanding importance becomes apparent. The increase of current credits with the United Kingdom amounted to $120 million, of which almost $100 million was due to merchandise export increases which took place despite a decline of $50 million in agricultural products shipped to Britain. Note that only a very minor fraction of the declines in the exports of agricultural products (including wheat)

[1] See the Statistical Appendix. The revised statistics have made it possible to correct some prevalent misconceptions regarding the Canadian trading position vis-a-vis other countries.

is the result of a price decline, 1937 prices being almost as high as those of 1928. Current credits with other Commonwealth countries were up somewhat, while those with the United States fell by $64 million. The most important changes with regard to the latter country were a drop in the value of merchandise exports of $116 million ($75 million of which was due to animals and their products and to newsprint), and an offsetting increase in nonmonetary gold exports of $105 million. A significant rise in the export of other nonferrous metals was the chief factor promoting the increase of exports to Great Britain which occurred despite the substantial decline in the value of agricultural products imported from Canada.

CURRENT DEBITS

Imports were already running at a high level in 1913, as were interest and dividend payments, and it is not surprising that the total current debits were less than doubled by 1928. During the interval, the merchandise import price level had risen by one third and so accounted for much of the increase. While the proportion of total current debits incurred with the United States increased from 56 to 67 per cent, the proportion incurred with Great Britain declined from 31 to 19 per cent.

Of an increase in total current debits of $869 million between 1913 and 1928, $554 million is accounted for by merchandise imports. Of the increase in merchandise imports, $396 million was gained by the United States, but only $51 million by the United Kingdom. The United States also figured predominantly in the increases between 1913 and 1928 in the nonmerchandise debits. The increased reliance on capital imports from the United States resulted in the whole of the increase in debits due for interest and dividends accruing to the United States. The latter country also received $72 million of the $87 million increase in freight and shipping payments, and $54 of the $61 million increase in expenditures by Canadian tourists. In a typical year, freight charges on coal shipments from the United States accounted for approximately one half of the total freight and shipping debits.[2]

[2] Dominion Bureau of Statistics (hereafter referred to as D.B.S.), *The Canadian Balance of International Payments, A Study of Methods and Results* (Ottawa, 1939), p. 96.

The merchandise imports which were considerably increased in value in 1928 as compared with 1913 constitute a varied list that makes summary treatment difficult. Instances of the type of imports derived mainly from United States sources and which increased substantially from 1913 to 1928 include: fruits and nuts, rubber and its products, raw and manufactured cotton, agricultural implements and machinery, motor vehicles and parts, engines, locomotives and boilers, other types of machinery, electrical apparatus, coal and its products, and petroleum and its products. The list includes the most important categories of Canadian imports. In it we find the investment goods and durable consumer goods which have a notably high cyclical income-elasticity.

In 1937 we find that the trend to greater proportional current payments to the United States has been reversed, while Britain, along with other Commonwealth countries, enjoys relative gains. Factors contributing to this change are increased Canadian protectionism and self-sufficiency in certain lines, increased preferential margins applying to many Commonwealth products, and, most important, a lower level of investment activity and incomes in 1937 as compared with 1928, with consequently reduced imports from the United States of producers' material and equipment and of goods representing a high standard of living. The decrease in total current debits of $407 million is explicable almost entirely in terms of the merchandise import decline, which amounted to $433 million. In nearly every import group there is evidence of declines between 1928 and 1937 which weigh more heavily on United States exports than on those of other countries. Only one instance need be given, that of the group iron and its products. Many producers' goods are to be found in this group, the imports of which fell by $131 million, United States exports suffering to the extent of $121 million.

CAPITAL ACCOUNT

The triangular adjustment entailed during the period 1900–1913, when capital imports into Canada from Great Britain were transferred mainly through import surpluses with the United States, has already been commented upon and contrasted with earlier bilateral transfers of the nineteenth century.[3] "Commencing about 1910 the United States began to take a greater interest in the public issue of our securities."[4] The transition toward dependence upon New York in Canadian borrowings abroad was speeded by World War I. The British capital market continued to be important until 1915, the large issue of 1916 being merely the refunding of a floating debt.[5] The year 1915 marked the change in the primary source of capital inflow from abroad, and the United Kingdom was rarely to figure significantly from that date forward as a net lender to Canada.

The statistics available for breaking down the capital account into its constituent elements by country are much less adequate than similar statistics for current account. Prior to 1926 only broad generalizations can be made. In the ten years 1916–1926 it is known that there was considerable repatriation of capital from the United Kingdom.

There is no doubt that the outstanding bonded indebtedness of Canada to Great Britain has been considerably reduced. In the immediate post-war period, that is to say, from 1919 to 1924, sterling exchange was at a considerable discount relative to the Canadian dollar. This gave Canadians an excellent opportunity to repurchase sterling and optional payment securities at bargain prices, and they were not slow in availing themselves of the chance. There is abundant evidence of this type of repurchasing during the period. Journals published currently estimated that as much as $100 million of such securities were repurchased by Canadians in a single year. So great was the outflow of capital from Canada that an attempt was made to check it by Sir Henry Drayton, the finance minister of the time, because of some undesirable repercussions on internal financial conditions connected with Victory loans. The effort involved a semi-official embargo in that it took the form of voluntary cooperation on the part of dealers. There was a good deal of opposition and the effort fell short of complete success. It is also known that a considerable portion of the repurchases of this period were afterwards resold to the United States.[6]

[3] See chapter 9.

[4] D.B.S., *The Canadian Balance . . . A Study*, p. 23. Although it might be noted that, due largely to the relatively greater participation of the United States than Great Britain in direct investments in Canada, the British share in outside capital investment in Canada did not exceed the American until 1903. See Viner, *Canada's Balance*, p. 282.

[5] F. A. Knox, "Canadian War Finance and the Balance of Payments," *The Canadian Journal of Economics and Political Science*, May 1940, p. 230.

[6] D.B.S., *The Canadian Balance . . . A Study*, p. 23.

The presumption is that the net inflow of capital from the United States was even greater than the total capital inflow from all countries of $773 million from 1920 to 1924. The result of this new dependence upon the New York capital market is the primary reason for the sixteenfold increase in interest and dividends payable to the United States between 1913 and 1928, while those payable to the United Kingdom, despite increased average returns on capital between the two years, remained stable.

Direct estimates made of British and foreign capital investments in Canada bear out the foregoing inference.[7] The estimates are based upon the capital employed in the industry, and since the valuations fluctuate cyclically, changes from year to year could not be expected to correspond exactly with the net imports or exports of capital.

From the beginning of World War I the value of United States investments increased rapidly in comparison with the value of the British investment in Canada, advancing from $780 million in 1913 to $3464 million in 1926, while British investments declined from $2793 to $2355 million in the same period, having attained their peak value of $2840 million in 1916. From 1926 to 1930 both British and United States investments increase in value, but the latter much more than the former, while through the 1930's capital depreciation and repatriation led to large reductions in the value of the British and United States investments.[8]

It is interesting to compare the current and capital account balances, although the inaccuracies of the basic estimates must not be forgotten. In Table 17 the addition of the surpluses and deficits on nonmerchandise current account would probably decrease the surplus with the United Kingdom by approximately $100 million per annum and increase the deficit with the United States by something of the order of $50 million per annum, while effecting little change in the surplus with other countries taken as a whole. As an example of the changes effected by the addition of the nonmerchandise items, compare the two estimates for 1926

[7] H. Marshall et al., *Canadian-American Industry* (New Haven, 1936). See appendix by F. A. Knox, pp. 299–300.

[8] See appendix by Knox in *Canadian-American Industry*, pp. 299–300; and D.B.S., *The Canadian Balance of International Payments, 1926–1944* (Ottawa, 1945), p. 50.

Table 17. *Merchandise surpluses and deficits, 1919–1926*

Year	United Kingdom	United States	Other countries	All countries
1919	408	−252	193	349
1920	190	−418	189	−39
1921	142	−220	93	15
1922	134	−162	160	132
1923	126	−190	177	113
1924	165	−130	99	34
1925	185	−128	304	361
1926	162	−198	305	269

Source. Dominion Bureau of Statistics, *Condensed Preliminary Report, Trade of Canada, 1939* (Ottawa, 1941). Adjustments for wheat diversions were applied to the published figures (see the Statistical Appendix). Minus sign indicates deficit.

in Tables 17 and 18, the first of these being for the merchandise account alone, and the second for the entire current account. The current account surplus with the United Kingdom during the years 1920 to 1926 appears to have been less than $100 million per annum, while from 1927 to 1932 an actual deficit was developed.

The popular notion of transactions with the United Kingdom serving as a source of United States exchange for Canada appears to be exaggerated due to failure to take account of the diversion of wheat from the United Kingdom to Europe and to failure to consider the Canadian deficits on nonmerchandise and capital accounts. If repatriation is considered among the factors determining the demand and supply of sterling in United Kingdom–Canadian transactions, the net supply of other currencies provided for Canada in her dealings with Britain must have been rather small, while from 1927 to 1932 Canada was a supplier of other currencies to Britain (see Table 18) on both current and capital accounts. Canada arrived at a balancing of her international accounts from 1920 to 1932 mainly through the current deficit with the United States being offset by capital imports from that country plus current surpluses with countries other than Great Britain. Wheat exports, as we have seen, figured prominently in the building up of these current surpluses.

In 1933, however, there developed a surplus on current and

Table 18. *Surpluses and deficits on current and capital accounts,*
by country, 1926–1940

| | Current account | | | Capital account | | |
Year	United Kingdom	United States	Other countries	United Kingdom	United States	Other countries
1926	58	−231	300	—	—	—
1927	−19	−248	257	−15	48	−52
1928	−21	−349	338	−49	−59	−60
1929	−99	−437	225	−14	100	−6
1930	−106	−344	113	−21	335	1
1931	−54	−205	85	−30	43	−10
1932	−14	−168	86	−36	−4	−9
1933	26	−113	85	98	−147	−8
1934	46	−80	102	98	−189	−5
1935	62	−29	92	−49	−120	5
1936	122	−1	123	−32	−222	−2
1937	135	−77	122	−9	−187	10
1938	127	−149	122	−53	−59	—
1939	137	−116	105	−83	−53	—
1940	343	−292	98	−132	−53	—

Source. Current account statistics are from Dominion Bureau of Statistics, *The Canadian Balance of International Payments, 1926–1944* (Ottawa, 1945), and capital account statistics are from D.B.S., *The Canadian Balance of International Payments, 1939.* The capital account estimates for the years 1938–1940 are not strictly comparable, being for Commonwealth countries and non-Commonwealth countries, but the United Kingdom and the United States predominate within these two groups, and there is little error in assuming that other countries do not participate. The 1938–1940 estimates derive from D.B.S., *The Canadian Balance of International Payments, 1926–1945* (Ottawa, 1947).

It should be noted that the 1926–1937 estimates are not closely comparable with recent revisions. They have been employed, despite their lesser accuracy, because of the breakdowns by category of capital and by country which are not available in the more recent estimates. In particular it should be noted that the latter estimates have considerably altered the figures for direct investment and trade in outstanding securities.

External bank assets have been deducted from the capital estimates.

Minus sign indicates deficit.

capital accounts with the United Kingdom, which, despite the renewed repatriation of capital in 1935, was continued through increasing surpluses on current account into the post-World War II years. Relatively more depressed economic conditions and low rates of induced investment in Canada as compared with those in the United Kingdom, the construction boom and the growth of new industries, and growing military preparations in the latter country were all factors encouraging a current account surplus in the 1930's.

In view of the not infrequent approximation to a bilateral balance in the transactions between the United Kingdom and

Canada, and the large participation in Canadian trade of countries other than the United States and Great Britain, the triangular aspects of the Canadian balance of payments should not be exaggerated but should be set in their proper perspective. There are many examples of failure to do this, of which I cite one from an otherwise generally excellent historical study.

Thus American economic isolation had forced Canada, and Great Britain also, into distortions of a triangular movement of goods and money which had been advantageous to all three countries in the past.[9]

Professor Brebner uses unadjusted merchandise figures to support his case, comparing years 1929 and 1933. Apart from the tremendous cyclical decline in trade, which cannot be attributed to increased American tariffs as the author suggests, the striking change is from a current deficit with both the United Kingdom and the United States, which was offset by current surpluses with other countries and a capital import from the United States (the latter being understated in Table 18 with regard to trade in outstanding securities, as explained in the Statistical Appendix), to a current surplus with the United Kingdom, a decreased deficit with the United States, a decreased current surplus with other countries, and a repatriation of capital from the United States.

[9] J. B. Brebner, *North Atlantic Triangle* (New Haven, 1940), p. 292. Kahn, *Great Britain in the World Economy*, pp. 232–233, falls into similar error.

XIX

The Problem of Adjustment — Current Account

In the preceding chapters economic and commercial policy developments and structural alterations in the balance of payments have been examined as a prelude to an investigation into the equilibrating changes in the interwar balance. Many such changes are of a short-run nature, and a study of the year-to-year changes in the balance of payments is required. Changes taking place over a shorter period than a year are also without doubt very relevant to the analysis, but they cannot be adequately considered because of the lack of statistical material.

With regard to the theoretical approach in the investigation to be undertaken it is proposed to proceed upon the basis of the eclectic theory developed in Part I. The inadequacy of the "classical" theory is even more apparent in relation to the facts of the interwar period than in relation to the facts of the boom period preceding World War I. Much of our case regarding Viner's attempted inductive verification of the classical Mill-Taussig theory of capital movements rested on the view that the changes in the terms of trade, sectional price levels, and wholesale prices cited by Viner in support of the classical theory were associated primarily with the cyclical upswing and economic growth of the period, an upswing that could not be explained as being mainly a resultant of Canadian borrowings from abroad.

There was a correlation between capital imports and the high rate of investment of some of the later years of the 1896–1913 prosperity which lent some plausibility to Viner's argument. In the interwar period such correlation did not exist. There was even less support to be found for the "classical" relation between capital movements and relative price changes, e.g., the terms of trade, than pre-World War I.

Table 19. *Capital imports, the terms of trade, and net movements of monetary gold and external bank assets, 1919–1940*
(millions of dollars)

Year	Capital imports[a]		Terms of trade (1926 = 100)	Net movements of monetary gold and external bank assets
	Direct estimate	Indirect estimate		
1919	−10	−29	96.6	−24
1920	143	281	99.6	61
1921	138	13	110.1	167
1922	237	20	94.3	−45
1923	142	−38	85.0	42
1924	113	−122	91.1	−40
1925	−50	−180	99.0	−109
1926	54	−77	100.0	−51
1927	—	1	100.1	9
1928	—	−104	98.0	136
1929	—	186	97.8	125
1930	—	373	92.5	−36
1931	—	113	83.6	61
1932	—	55	77.9	41
1933	−41	−28	75.6	30
1934	−91	−45	79.2	−23
1935	−150	−123	79.8	−2
1936	−244	−247	84.0	3
1937	−158	−164	90.3	−13
1938	−105	−93	94.6	−7
1939	−136	−126	89.3	−27
1940	−185	−146	86.4	−3

Source. All series are derived from Table 27 with the exception of that for the terms of trade, which is derived from W. A. Mackintosh, *The Economic Background of Dominion-Provincial Relations* (Ottawa, 1939), pp. 25, 41; and Dominion Bureau of Statistics, *Prices and Price Indexes, 1913–1940* (Ottawa, 1942).

[a] The direct estimates were not utilized for 1927–1932. See the Statistical Appendix.

Table 19 indicates that the terms of trade did increase with the increased capital imports of 1919–1921, but this is explicable in terms of differential price changes and lags during the postwar boom and depression rather than in terms of capital imports.

This interpretation is borne out by the deterioration of the terms of trade from 1921 to 1923, despite continuing high capital imports. The period 1923–1927 was one of diminishing capital imports, yet improving terms of trade, while 1929–1933 was a period of increased capital imports and deteriorating terms of trade, and the following period of 1933–1938 was one of capital repatriation accompanied by improving terms of trade. Particularly in the

Table 20. *Index numbers of wholesale prices in the United Kingdom,*
the United States, and Canada, 1919–1940
(1926 = 100)

Year	United Kingdom	United States	Canada
1919	—	138.6	134.0
1920	203.7	154.4	155.9
1921	133.1	97.6	110.0
1922	106.9	96.7	97.3
1923	107.0	100.6	98.0
1924	102.2	98.1	99.4
1925	107.2	103.5	102.6
1926	100.0	100.0	100.0
1927	95.6	95.4	97.7
1928	94.7	96.7	96.4
1929	92.2	95.3	95.6
1930	80.7	86.4	86.6
1931	70.9	73.0	72.1
1932	69.1	64.8	66.7
1933	69.2	66.0	67.1
1934	71.1	75.0	71.6
1935	71.8	80.0	72.1
1936	76.2	80.8	74.6
1937	87.7	86.3	84.6
1938	81.8	78.6	78.6
1939	83.0	77.1	75.4
1940	110.2	78.6	82.9

Source. *Dominion Bureau of Statistics, Prices and Price Indexes,*
1913–1939 (Ottawa, 1941); and *1946 Supplement; Bank of Canada*
Statistical Summary (Ottawa, 1946). The United States series is
that of the Bureau of Labor Statistics, while that for the United
Kingdom is the Board of Trade series converted from base 1930
to base 1926.

thirties the terms of trade followed a clear cyclical pattern common to agricultural, raw-material producing countries, a pattern at odds with the expectations of "classical" theory in view of the capital movements which took place.

Wholesale price changes for Canada, Britain, and the United States are primarily cyclical in character. Governmental exchange rate policy may be partly reflected in the reduction of the United Kingdom price level relative to that of the United States and Canada in the 1920's, but it was also doubtless a reaction to a price level which had risen more in wartime than in the other two countries. Also there was reason, additional to the over-valuation of the pound, for depression in the British export trades.[1] Governmental policy may also have played a part in the relatively greater increases of United States wholesale prices in the years 1933–1935. The make-up of the various price indices

Table 21. *Net national incomes, Great Britain, United States, and Canada, 1919–1940*
(indices, 1926 = 100)

Year	Great Britain (millions of pounds)	United States (billions of dollars)	Canada (millions of dollars)	Great Britain	United States	Canada
1919	—	68.2	3816	—	89.0	84.5
1920	5583	69.5	4598	145.0	90.6	100.9
1921	4396	51.7	3507	114.1	67.5	76.7
1922	3801	59.5	3671	98.6	77.6	81.3
1923	3789	69.5	3847	98.0	90.6	85.3
1924	3863	69.1	3865	100.3	90.1	85.7
1925	3923	73.7	4238	101.9	96.1	93.8
1926	3858	76.6	4507	100.0	100.0	100.0
1927	4086	75.9	4738	106.2	99.0	104.9
1928	4094	78.7	5269	106.4	102.8	116.9
1929	4118	{ 83.3 / 87.4	5272	107.0	108.8	117.0
1930	3900	75.0	4452	101.2	93.5	98.6
1931	3613	58.9	3580	93.6	73.3	79.4
1932	3517	41.7	2813	91.3	51.9	62.3
1933	3675	39.6	2723	95.4	49.3	60.4
1934	3825	48.6	3147	99.4	60.5	68.8
1935	4050	56.8	3371	104.0	69.5	74.6
1936	4325	66.9	3827	112.2	83.3	84.8
1937	4550	73.6	4368	118.1	91.6	96.9
1938	4610	67.4	4288	119.7	83.9	95.0
1939	4960	72.6	4570	128.9	90.4	101.3
1940	5922	81.3	5391	153.9	101.1	119.4

Source. For the sources of the national income data, see the Statistical Appendix.

[1] Kahn, *Great Britain in the World Economy*, chapters 5 and 6.

Chart III.   Net national income, Great Britain, United States, and
Canada, 1919–1940

which differs between the three countries may be a partial explanation for the differentials between the three series. The
price changes, however, in large measure will be related to the
relative movements of national income for the three countries.
These movements, reflecting the differential incidence of the
business cycle, can certainly not be accounted for in the light of
international capital movements. Even where the empirical data
do not conflict with the "classical" Mill-Taussig theory they cannot substantiate it, and further investigation along these lines
would prove fruitless. Note in the price and in other economic
series the effects in all three countries of the postwar slump of
1920, the recovery from 1920–1929, the great decline from 1929–
1933, the recovery from 1933–1937, and the recession of 1938. The
pattern was a common one, but in Great Britain the twenties were
relatively less prosperous than in the other two countries, while
the thirties were relatively less depressed, with the national income of the latter years of the period exceeding that of 1929.
Canadian and American national incomes did not reach that level
until the war years.[2]

[2] Table 21 and Chart III.

In common with many other countries, Canada remained on the gold standard for only a relatively few of the interwar years, namely, 1926–1929.[3] The theory developed in Part I emphasized the similarity in the adjustment mechanism of the gold and paper standards. The analogy between the role played by gold and by short-term capital flows in connection with the transfer of purchasing power was already manifest in the prewar Canadian situation as described by Professor Viner. In the interwar period, while usually not freely purchasable and salable at a fixed price for the purposes of effecting international payments as in gold standard practice, gold continued to serve as monetary reserves domestically and internationally, and monetary as well as nonmonetary gold movements continued to play an important role in the balance of payments. In this connection note that monetary gold movements must be defined somewhat arbitrarily for balance of payments purposes, as is explained in the Statistical Appendix.

With the Canadian currency freed from gold standard restrictions for the greater part of the interwar period, the possibility of significant variations in the exchange rate was realized. As discussed in Chapter 6, these variations might be equilibrating or disequilibrating in effect and are analogous to other price fluctuations in this respect. Despite the possibility of variation, it is interesting to note that the Canadian dollar remained relatively close to the standard par quotations with the United States dollar and the British pound throughout a major part of the interwar period. The prewar level was regained in 1925, departed from in the currency upheavals of 1931, was restored in 1935, and again disrupted at the outbreak of World War II.[4]

The attainment by Canada of greater industrial and financial maturity had numerous implications for the balance of payments. With the growth of security markets in Canada there developed

[3] See *Canadian Investment and Foreign Exchange Problems*, ed. J. F. Parkinson (Toronto, 1940), p. 69. Even when nominally on the gold standard during 1929–1931 gold was not always freely made available and the exchanges moved outside the gold points.

[4] See Table 22. For a critical examination of exchange rate policy in Canada during the thirties, see Chapter 21.

Table 22. *The exchange relations of the Canadian
and United States dollars and the pound sterling*

Year	The pound sterling in Canada	The American dollar in Canada
	(yearly averages)	
1919	$4.63	$1.04
1920	4.07	1.12
1921	4.29	1.12
1922	4.50	1.02
1923	4.66	1.02
1924	4.47	1.01
1925	4.83	1.00
1926	4.86	1.00
1927	4.86	1.00
1928	4.87	1.00
1929	4.89	1.01
1930	4.87	1.00
1931	4.71	1.04
1932	3.98	1.14
1933	4.61	1.09
1934	4.99	.99
1935	4.93	1.01
1936	4.97	1.00
1937	4.94	1.00
1938	4.92	1.01
1939	4.61	1.04
1940	4.45	1.11

Source. The data are estimated from the Federal Reserve
System, *Banking and Monetary Statistics* (Washington, 1943),
pp. 665, 681.

a very considerable trade that cut across international boundaries.
The increased supply of funds available in domestic capital markets and the greater reliance of corporations on self-financing
made for lesser dependence on borrowings from abroad. Thus, in
the interwar period as compared with the prewar, receipts on
current account have become relatively much more important
for Canada, while net receipts on capital account have become
relatively much less important, and in many years they have been
superseded by net outward movements of capital. This changed
situation is clearly reflected in the estimates of Table 23. Capital

Table 23. *Canadian national income, investment, current credits, merchandise imports, and capital imports (direct estimate), for selected years*
(millions of dollars)

	1903	1911	1913	1922	1928	1931	1937	1950	1956
Income	1140	2085	2359	3671	5269	3580	4368	14308	23054
Investment	175	532	628	800	1222	763	923	3968	6774
% of income	15.3	25.5	26.6	21.8	23.2	21.3	21.2	27.8	29.3
Current credits	267	395	564	1177	1788	972	1593	4297	6621
% of income	23.8	18.9	23.8	32.1	33.8	27.2	36.4	29.9	28.8
Capital imports	52	343	542	237	−104	113	−158	823	1416
% of income	4.6	16.4	23.0	6.5	2.9	3.2	3.6	5.7	6.1
% of investment	29.8	64.5	86.1	29.6		14.8		23.5	20.9
Merchandise imports	252	506	655	745	1209	580	776	3129	5565
% of income[a]	22.1	24.2	27.8	20.3	22.9	16.2	17.8	21.8	24.2

[a] Or average propensity to spend,

Note. The figures for the years prior to 1928 are far from exact estimates, but it is not too much to expect that the proportions are of the correct order of magnitude. A negative sign indicates a capital export.

Source. The estimates for current credits, merchandise imports, and capital imports are from Table 27, and the investment figures for the earlier years may be found in Table 10. The figures for investment for 1928, 1931 and 1937 are for total domestic capital formation (excluding changes in grain in commercial channels and farm inventories) and, as in the prewar estimates, depreciation is not allowed for, nor are repairs and maintenance included. The statistics may be found in Dominion-Provincial Conference on Reconstruction, *Public Investment and Capital Formation* (Ottawa, 1945), table 1c, item 5, pp. 32–33. As in Table 24, the investment estimates for 1922 is based on construction contracts awarded, investment being assumed as the same percentage of the 1926 level in 1922 as were construction contracts in 1922 relative to their level in 1926. The national income estimates from 1922 on are from Table 21. Those for 1911 and 1913 are made by J. J. Deutsch, "War Finance and the Canadian Economy, 1919-20," *Canadian Journal of Economics and Political Science*, November 1940, p. 538. That for 1903 is based on an estimate of C. Clark, *Conditions of Economic Progress*, p. 109, which was expressed in terms of constant prices, and which was therefore adjusted to the 1903 price level, deflating by the Dominion Bureau of Statistics official series for the wholesale price level. The figures for investment (gross) and national income (at factor cost) are from Dominion Bureau of Statistics, *National Accounts, Income, and Expenditure, Revised Preliminary Report, 1950* (Ottawa, 1951). Net income figures were employed, since estimates for gross national product were not available for the earlier years. Recent data are to be found in D.B.S., *Canadian Statistical Review*.

imports, which in 1913 had risen to an exceedingly high proportion of total investment (doubtless somewhat exaggerated since the indirect estimate of capital imports is lower than the direct estimate), had dropped to a considerably lesser proportion of total investment even in a peak year of borrowings abroad in the 1920's such as 1922. Funds available for investment, in addition to satisfying the domestic needs, were in many years of the interwar period available for the reparation of capital previously obtained from abroad; in other words, a net export from Canada took place,

These are important changes with important implications for the level of investment and income, the relations of which to the current and capital balance will be examined. However, from the narrow viewpoint of adjustment in the balance of payments the dissimilarity of shifts of purchasing power on current and capital account can be exaggerated. For example, merchandise exports, and exports of bonds or securities, both tend to create a flow of expenditure in the form of investment and consumption, and this expenditure tends to flow into offsetting imports on both current and capital account. Merchandise exports of course tend to be associated with a proportion of investment-to-consumption expenditures which differ greatly from the higher investment-to-consumption proportion associated with the capital imports, and this in turn may have important repercussions on the balance of payments. Furthermore, if the import of capital represents the sale to a foreigner of an outstanding security rather than a new issue, the probability of a resultant injection into the income stream is much reduced. A somewhat analogous situation may arise in the short run with respect to exports of merchandise where the exports are accompanied by a reduction in domestic inventories of the exported product.

The variations in receipts on current account in the interwar period inflicted shocks on the Canadian economy such as were not suffered in connection with the likewise exceedingly variable receipts on long-term capital account in the years 1900–1913 (see Table 27). The reasons are clear enough. The trend of real capital formation was continuously on the upgrade apart from the very slight setback of 1908, and doubtless a national income series, if available, would display a similar contour. The irregular movements of monetary gold and external bank assets reflected both the smooth utilization of irregularly provided capital from abroad and the fact that the proceeds of the capital imports might be held idle and not immediately injected into the income stream, as is likely in the case of merchandise exports proceeds. As has been shown, the economic situation was such as to require vastly augmented supplies of labor and capital and these requirements dovetailed well in the process of economic development. A vast investment program and great structural changes in the Canadian economy were possible without overly disturbing shifts of the factors of production because of the tremendous increments of new capital and new labor. Not all the consequences were welcome, as the governmental investigation into the increased cost of living clearly demonstrates, but in an atmosphere of expansion the disadvantages were rendered more tolerable. The impact of increased receipts on current account was likewise absorbed with relative comfort in the years of war and postwar expansion. The contraction of current receipts at the end of the decade of the 1920's, on the other hand, was a shock at odds with the basic requirements of the economy, since the absorption of the shock involved large-scale underemployment and unemployment of capital and labor.

The treatment of capital imports as a relatively autonomous factor, to which other elements in the balance of payments adapted, has been criticized. Such a view as I have attacked would be much less defensible in the interwar period when borrowings abroad played a role of much lesser prominence. As in the years preceding World War I we will find common influences operating on both current and capital accounts to effect offsetting changes. But, and this is not surprising in view of the greatly increased relative importance of the receipts on current account, changes in the current balance more frequently and more clearly appear to have been the dominant basis for alterations in the flow of capital to or from Canada rather than vice versa.

Before attempting to give a composite picture of adjustments taking place in the interwar balance of payments, an examination of the behavior of the various elements of the current and capital accounts is desirable.

MERCHANDISE ACCOUNT [5]

The analysis of structural changes in the balance of payments in Chapter 18 has already established the importance of changes in the merchandise account. These changes are of even greater relative importance in the short run. Of the tremendous drop in current credits of $980 million between 1928 and 1932, merchandise exports accounted for $846 million. They represented $467 million of a current credit decline of $491 million from 1920 to

[5] D.B.S., *Canadian Balance . . . A Study*, pp. 55–60; and *Canadian Investment and Foreign Exchange Problems*, ed. J. F. Parkinson, pp. 17–20.

Table 24. *Canadian net national income, gross investment,*
and merchandise exports, 1919–1940
(1926 = 100)

Year	Income	Investment	Exports
1919	84.5	51.0	99.7
1920	100.9	68.4	100.1
1921	76.7	64.4	63.2
1922	81.3	89.0	69.8
1923	85.3	84.2	79.4
1924	85.7	74.5	81.7
1925	93.8	78.8	98.1
1926	100.0	100.0	100.0
1927	104.9	110.1	96.5
1928	116.9	130.0	105.3
1929	117.0	142.1	92.5
1930	98.6	126.2	69.1
1931	79.4	88.4	47.3
1932	62.3	50.3	38.8
1933	60.4	32.9	41.8
1934	68.8	55.3	50.9
1935	74.6	62.6	57.5
1936	84.8	72.6	74.9
1937	96.9	101.5	81.8
1938	95.0	88.8	66.3
1939	101.3	88.0	71.2
1940	119.4	121.0	94.6

Source. Net income and merchandise exports are from Tables 21 and 27 respectively. The indices for gross investment are based on Dominion-Provincial Conference on Reconstruction, *Public Investment and Capital Formation*, Table 3a, p. 34, item no. 10, which includes repairs and maintenance but excludes changes in grain in commercial channels and farm inventories, and also excludes the net current international balance of payments. Estimates for net investment were not available for the years prior to 1938. In default of any estimates for investment earlier than 1926, the series used was for construction contracts awarded as compiled by MacLean Building Reports, Ltd., and tabulated in *Canada Year Book* (Ottawa, 1945), p. 450. This is an obviously inadequate measure of investment, but it has been used as an index for this purpose by W. A. Mackintosh, *The Economic Background of Dominion-Provincial Relations* (Ottawa, 1939), p. 41, and is certainly preferable to the absence of any indicator of the level of investment. It is reassuring to note that its behavior from 1926 on is more volatile but otherwise similar to our gross investment series' behavior and has like turning points.

1921 (these merchandise figures are exclusive of gold exports). These reductions are greater proportionately than the reductions that occurred in the nonmerchandise items. There is an analogous predominance of merchandise imports within the current debits.

In the preceding section of this chapter it was shown how the receipts on current account had become more important for Canada in the interwar period. Of these receipts, those on merchandise account predominate, and they participate more than proportionately in the cyclical fluctuations. It is through merchandise exports that the shocks administered via the balance of payments seem to be mainly transmitted, and the greater part of the adjustment in the balance of payments to these fluctuations of exports occurs within the sphere of merchandise imports.

The fluctuations of other items, particularly on capital account, are nevertheless very important. This is indicated by the fact that the fluctuation of merchandise exports relative to merchandise imports during the period 1925–1929 was greater than for most other countries (see Table 1). But for the moment attention will be directed to the merchandise account.

In the light of the theory developed in Part I we should expect a close relation between the flow of purchasing power, as indicated by the national income index, and exports and imports. We would expect increased exports to result in increases of income and consequential increases of imports. Some of the increased income induced by the increase of exports may be due to a rise of investment encouraged by the growth of exports and incomes. Much of the investment may be autonomous, so that changes in income and imports may also stem from this as an independent source as well as from exports.

Chart IV reveals that the correlation between Canadian income, investment, current credits, and current debits supports the analysis. Note that an increase of investment in 1929 helps sustain income and debits despite the decline in credits. Note also that there was a better recovery of income and current credits in the 1930's relative to the peaks of the late 1920's than of investment and current debits. Investment must be included with exports as a determinant of national income,[6] and it might also

[6] T. C. Chang, "A Note on Exports and National Income in Canada," *Canadian Journal of Economics and Political Science,* May 1947, criticises

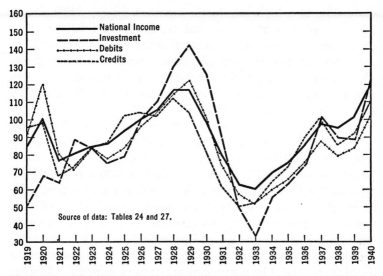

Chart IV.   The fluctuations of Canadian income and investment, and balance-of-payments current credits and debits, 1919–1940

be treated separately from the consumption component of national income as a determinant of imports. The nature of the relation will vary with the type of current credit, with the type of investment activity, and the phase of the business cycle. Let me attempt to illustrate the complex nature of the relationship.[7]

The family farm wheat producers had a high propensity to consume and in prosperous times an eager demand for credit which can then be satisfied. The repercussions of increased wheat exports are felt not only in the wheat-producing West, but in other parts of Canada which supply transportation for the wheat as well as other important goods and services to the western consumer. During the twenties there was high induced investment, not confined to the West, in farm equipment, harbors, elevators, and transport facilities. Construction and other forms of investment, for example in the pulp and paper industry, were also

---

E. Munzer, for the latter's neglect of investment in his article "Exports and National Income in Canada," *Canadian Journal of Economics and Political Science,* February 1945.

[7] See A. F. W. Plumptre, *Central Banking in the British Dominions* (Toronto, 1940), pp. 355–356.

proceeding at a high rate in the twenties. In the 1930's wheat exports were regularly so low that net agricultural disinvestment must have been general. The income of individual enterprisers in agriculture in the Province of Saskatchewan, the heart of the wheat economy, struck by a combination of drought and low wheat prices, was reduced from a peak of $228 million in 1928 to a net loss of $8 million in 1931.[8]

In 1936 and 1937 the income figures were still only $28 and $57 million respectively. The buoyant influence of increasing exports was partially diminished by a decline in grain stocks (chiefly wheat) of $178 and $105 million in 1936 and 1937.[9] The pulp and paper industry was able to utilize excess capacity for the greater part of its production increases from the low points of the 1930's. The propensity to consume in mining is relatively lower than in the case of wheat farming, returns to both domestic and outside capital being quite high. In view of depletion much of production must be considered as return of principal. Comparing 1932 and 1937, we find that the nonferrous metals (especially gold) and pulp and paper exports contributed heavily to the recovery. There was no increase in the value of wheat exports between the two years. Relatively large exports to the United States had occurred in 1936, but this was a temporary increase attributable to drought conditions in the American Midwest. Also contributing considerably to the rise in exports between 1932 and 1937 were autos, trucks and parts, and other products of United States direct investments, a high proportion of which was stimulated by the more favorable preferential rates on Commonwealth products. But the favorable influence of these increased exports was reduced by the allocation of branch plants' gross revenue to returning previously invested capital to the parent concern. Note in Table 27 that the inflow of direct investments ceased in 1932, becoming a heavy outflow. Such factors as these make for inconstant, unpredictable relations between exports, investment, and income, and discourage the search for stable multipliers.[10]

[8] D. C. MacGregor, et al., *National Income* (Ottawa, 1939), p. 55.

[9] O. J. Firestone and M. C. Urquhart, *Public Investment and Capital Formation, 1926–1941* (Ottawa, 1945), p. 31.

[10] Plumptre, *Central Banking in the British Dominions*, pp. 355ff, emphasizes this point.

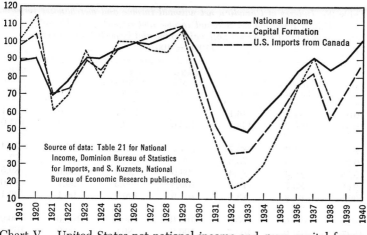

Chart V.   United States net national income and gross capital formation related to imports from Canada

In Chart V the relation between United States' net national income, gross investment, and imports from Canada is depicted. The income elasticity of United States demand for imports[11] has been calculated at 1.27, considerably higher than unity, and higher than the United Kingdom's (1.10), but considerably lower than the world average of 1.50.[12] The income elasticity of demand for Canadian exports equals 1.52, approximately the world average. Since the income elasticity of demand for Canadian foodstuffs, mainly directed to countries other than the United States, would be low, it is probably a safe inference that the American income elasticity of demand for Canadian produce is much higher than for imports from other countries, and probably higher than the world average. Forest and mineral products, for which there is a relatively high income elasticity of demand, help to explain the situation. The prices of Canadian exports to the United States would tend to move with the American national income and to be cyclically very flexible in price in most instances, so that fluctuations in values of exports to the United States relative to American incomes would be further amplified.

[11] See R. Nurkse, "Domestic and International Equilibrium," in *The New Economics*, ed. S. E. Harris (New York, 1947), pp. 270–271.
[12] For the statistical estimates, see T. C. Chang, *Cyclical Movements in the Balance of Payments* (Cambridge, England, 1951), pp. 42, 50.

Table 25. *Indexes of Canadian net national income and merchandise imports, United Kingdom net national income and imports from Canada, and United States net national income and imports from Canada*
(1926 = 100)

Year	Canadian income	Canadian imports	United Kingdom income	United Kingdom imports	United States income	United States imports
1919	84.5	96.1	—	149.1	89.0	98.1
1920	100.9	144.2	143.0	129.0	90.6	104.0
1921	76.7	83.7	114.1	80.8	67.5	70.4
1922	81.3	75.3	98.6	83.0	77.6	73.3
1923	85.3	89.4	98.0	86.0	90.6	89.5
1924	85.7	79.9	100.3	96.5	90.1	84.0
1925	93.8	83.6	101.9	106.2	96.1	96.1
1926	100.0	100.0	100.0	100.0	100.0	100.0
1927	104.9	108.7	106.2	86.0	99.0	102.8
1928	116.9	124.1	106.4	91.5	102.8	106.7
1929	117.0	131.0	107.0	71.1	108.8	109.0
1930	98.6	100.0	101.2	54.6	93.5	84.0
1931	79.4	59.6	93.6	44.1	73.3	53.4
1932	62.3	40.9	91.3	47.3	51.9	35.5
1933	60.4	37.8	95.4	59.6	49.3	37.2
1934	68.8	49.7	99.4	74.2	60.5	47.5
1935	74.6	54.1	104.0	81.9	69.5	59.8
1936	84.8	62.9	112.2	108.6	83.3	75.0
1937	96.9	79.7	118.1	122.1	91.6	82.0
1938	95.0	66.6	119.7	103.9	83.9	56.4
1939	101.3	73.3	128.9	102.2	90.4	72.4
1940	119.4	108.9	153.9	172.0	101.1	89.0

Source. See the Statistical Appendix for the derivation of the national income series. The post-1925 merchandise trade series are indices based on Canadian trade statistics in *The Canadian Balance of Payments, 1926–1944* (Ottawa, 1945). Pre-1926 statistics for Canadian imports are to be found in the appendix, *Dominion Monetary Policy* (Ottawa, 1939). Statistics for Canadian exports of domestic produce to the United Kingdom and the United States for pre-1926 calendar years derive from *Condensed Preliminary Report of the Trade of Canada, 1939* (Ottawa, 1940), p. 56, the adjustment for wheat diversions being estimated and applied to these unadjusted published figures. See the Statistical Appendix for further information.

Certain of the deviations in the behavior of imports from Canada from the behavior of the national income may be due to divergence of the United States investment from its normal relation to consumption in the United States national income series. One striking fact to note is the upturn in 1932–1933 of Canadian exports to the United States along with American investment

prior to the increase of American national income.[13] Another
analogous instance is the decrease in both the level of American
imports from Canada and American domestic investment in 1924
while United States national income remained virtually stable.

The relation between British income and imports from Canada
is not nearly so close as the other income-import relations I have
been demonstrating. This is indicated in Chart VI. A considerable

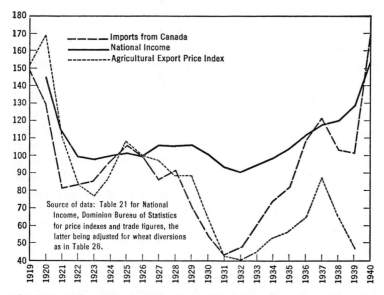

Chart VI.   The imports of the United Kingdom from Canada related
to United Kingdom net national income and the price index of Canadian agricultural exports

part of the explanation is to be found in the behavior of the
prices of agricultural exports to the United Kingdom which is a
function of world commodity markets upon which British income
is only one of many influences. In order to give an approximate

---

[13] The end of prohibition in the United States and the addition of alcoholic
beverages to the official list of imports from Canada provide a partial
reason for the increase. This, however, accounts for only $12 million of the
$51 million increase in the total of Canadian exports to the United States.
A sizable proportion of the remainder was accounted for by increases in
exports of mineral, wood and paper, and animal products.

indication of the importance of these changes, the price index of
Canadian exports of agricultural and vegetable products is included in the chart. This group in 1928 constituted 69 per cent
by value of total exports to the United Kingdom, although by
1937, due primarily to its relatively greater price decline and to
the increased importance of nonferrous metal exports, the proportion had been reduced to 34 per cent. The price fluctuations of
agricultural commodities help to account for the declines in the
value of exports to the United Kingdom after the peak year of
1925, despite the fact of rising British income. They also serve to
explain the tremendously low trough in exports in the thirties
despite the relatively small decline in the United Kingdom's
national income. Again, continued weakness in agricultural prices
in 1939 tended to prevent a revival of export values. There is, of
course, a great deal more to the story and I have no intention of
leaving a contrary impression. Depreciation of the pound may
have contributed to the continued decline of agricultural export
prices and of exports to Britain in 1931 (the Canadian dollar
retained an intermediate position between sterling and the United
States dollar — see Table 22), but in the year of greatest average
depreciation this decline appeared to be halted. The depreciation
and low agricultural prices were undoubtedly favorable factors
influencing British incomes and tending to prevent a further
drop.[14]

Numerous Canadian exports reflect the contrasting behavior of
income and investment (particularly construction) in Britain and
the United States.[15] The influence of tariffs was also tending to
increase Canadian exports to the United Kingdom relative to
those to the United States, but this was probably a lesser influence than that of the relative incomes. As an example we may
take lumber, planks, and boards, the exports of which were relatively greater to the United States markets in 1928, and to the
British markets in 1937. Similar behavior is recorded for exports
of copper and nickel and their products (Table 16).

In dealing with structural changes in the balance of payments

[14] S. Harris, *Exchange Depreciation* (Cambridge, 1936), pp. 1ff; and A. H.
Hansen, *Fiscal Policy and Business Cycles* (New York, 1941), p. 101.
[15] Hansen, *Fiscal Policy and Business Cycles*, chapter 5.

in Chapter 18 the significant role played by wheat was emphasized. Its part is no less striking in the very short-run changes and their shock effects upon the Canadian economy. The tremendous decline of 50 per cent in the value of wheat exports from the fiscal year 1929 (ending March 31) to fiscal 1930 was in large measure due to a short crop. The facts of the crop being small and of high quality were one deterrent to the immediate growth of pessimism which mounted only after the break in October in the United States security markets. As we have seen, despite the resultant decline in exports, investment and income continued at high levels through most of 1929. But prices continued their downward movement from the 1925 peak while exports continued at a low volume, especially to the European markets. The impact on Canadian incomes of the substantial drop in wheat exports must have been very severe indeed.

The seriousness of Canada's agricultural export problem was multiplied manyfold in the world depression. The decline of American investment, first foreign, then domestic, had tremendous repercussions throughout the world. The disappearance of American foreign lending and the great contraction of her imports was shattering in its effect upon the "network of world trade," leading almost inevitably to autarchic policies throughout the world.[16] But it should be emphasized that the blows fell on commodity markets that were already showing signs of a basic weakness and that the Canadian position was particularly vulnerable.[17] This weakness was closely related to the marked increase of grain cultivation in "the big four," the United States, Canada, Australia, and the Argentine, during World War I, and to a lesser extent in the 1920's and even in the 1930's. These increases were intimately associated with the fall of one fifth in

[16] For an analysis of the repercussions of the United States on the world economy, see H. B. Lary and Associates, *The United States in the World Economy*, Department of Commerce Economic Series No. 23 (Washington, 1943), especially pp. 27–35.

[17] See D. A. MacGibbon, *The Canadian Grain Trade* (Toronto, 1932), pp. 418ff; Bank for International Settlements, *16th Annual Report*, pp. 47ff.; Wheat Advisory Committee of the Canadian Royal Grain Inquiry Commission, Memorandum 1, *World Demand for Imported Wheat* (Ottawa, 1938), pp. 17ff.; *Royal Commission on Dominion Provincial Relations*, I, 115.

European production of grains during the war, and the virtual disappearance of Russian grain exports from world markets. The average annual exports of "the big four" rose from 345-million bushels to 706-million bushels from 1909–1914 to 1923–1928. Canada captured the lion's share, amounting to 202-million of the 361-million bushel increase. Her exports more than tripled in the process, while the exports of none of her three main competitors so much as doubled. A primary advantage over Argentina and Australia was the relatively short Atlantic route to Europe which in wartime was economical of shipping and escort vessels. Canadian wheat producers were in an excellent position to take advantage of their opportunities following the western settlement and expansion of transport facilities which had taken place in the period 1900–1916. As the twenties wore on, the relatively liberal tariff policy with respect to wheat, which was in large measure a reflection of postwar shortages, was modified by an increasing number of European countries. From 1927 to 1929 wheat carry-overs of the "big four" rose from 266- to 325-million bushels. The situation was certainly one to cause concern quite apart from the international repercussions of a serious depression in the United States. The grievous effects of the latter were felt doubly because of the already fundamentally unstable international grain markets.[18]

NONMERCHANDISE ACCOUNT

Nonmonetary gold [19] exports are treated separately from the merchandise trade because of their somewhat arbitrary definition as approximating current gold production (see the Statistical Appendix), and because of gold's monetary qualities which have given it a distinctive behavior pattern in the trade cycle. Its price in terms of Canadian dollars has fluctuated only in the case of depreciation or appreciation of the currency. Therefore, if the exchanges remain stable, gold production and exports tend to be curtailed in periods of rising prices and costs, and to expand when

[18] See Royal Commission, *Report*, I, 115.
[19] See D.B.S., *The Canadian Balance . . . A Study*, pp. 60–62, and *Canadian Investment and Foreign Exchange Problems*, ed. J. F. Parkinson, pp. 20–21.

prices and costs are falling. Thus, in a prosperity stimulated by increasing capital imports or by increasing exports, the decline of gold production and exports might well play an equilibrating part analogous to import increases. There are numerous other factors affecting the production of gold, such as gold discoveries and new techniques, which may well be more important. However, the failure of significant expansion to materialize in the period 1900–1913 or in the war years is to some extent an illustration of the type of equilibrating action I am discussing. Again, in the 1930's, export decreases and lower prices were associated with increased gold exports, which were given added uplift by the American revaluation of gold from $20.67 to $35.00 an ounce and the accompanying rise in the Canadian price. Another example is to be found where increasing production and prices during World War II were factors contributing to the decline in the volume of gold which was mined.

Tourist expenditures[20] affecting the balance of payments in the interwar period are no longer, as in 1900–1913, closely related to overseas immigration. Preponderantly they arise from the growing stream of Canadian and American tourists across the international boundary, the flow of which was vastly augmented with the growing use of the automobile. The early figures of the 1920's prior to 1926 are almost certainly in error,[21] the estimates for the tourist receipts being particularly subject to correction. The break in the trend in the year 1926 is fictitious, therefore, and it seems safe to say that we have on tourist account until the 1930's a secularly increasing source of credits which has only partially been offset by Canadian tourist expenditures abroad. In the 1930's it was indicated that tourist expenditures may be disequilibrating and a source of pressure on the balance of payments, for credits declined more than debits in both 1929–1933 and 1937–1938. It appears that expenditures of American tourists in Canada were more elastic with respect to income than the expenditures of Canadian tourists in the United States.

[20] See D.B.S., *The Canadian Balance . . . A Study,* pp. 62–70; and *Canadian Investment and Foreign Exchange Problems,* ed. J. F. Parkinson, pp. 21–22.
[21] See the Statistical Appendix.

Interest and dividend payments[22] were a secularly increasing debit until 1930, which was only partially offset by relatively minor receipts by Canadians. These receipts have risen to a larger proportion of payments as repatriation has proceeded and as Canada has grown as a source of capital for other countries. In 1939 Canadian long-term investment abroad was greater than that of the United States (excluding war debts), when calculated on a per capita basis, being approximately $112 as compared to $77.[23] It is an interesting fact that despite the tremendous American direct investments in Canada, Canada's direct investments south of the border were even larger in proportion to her wealth and population.

There was no short-run equilibrating action of net interest and dividends in 1921, 1930, or 1938, the net payments increasing in each case despite a weakening balance of payments. In the case of the first two years, borrowing was continuing at a high level and serving to augment the net interest payments. Dividends tend to be maintained in the early part of a depression, and in 1938 depression did not strike Canadian industry so heavily as it did American. Fixed interest-bearing securities form a large proportion of Canadian external debt, interest payments amounting to approximately one half the total interest and dividend payments in the period 1927–1937.[24] There is therefore a large element of cyclical inflexibility in the net interest and dividend payments. The reduction which did occur in the 1930's was primarily attributable to repatriation, which in turn was partly attributable to a balance-of-payments position that had been strengthened due to the operation of other factors. There would have been a greater contraction of net payments had American investments, notably in mining and in branch plants favored by the Ottawa agreements, not fared relatively well in the thirties.

[22] See D.B.S., *The Canadian Balance . . . A Study*, pp. 97–102; and *Canadian Investment and Foreign Exchange Problems*, ed. J. F. Parkinson, pp. 23–24.

[23] Estimated from Lary, *The United States in the World Economy*, p. 123; and D.B.S., *The Canadian Balance of International Payments, 1926–44* (Ottawa, 1945), p. 56.

[24] Calculated from D.B.S., *The Canadian Balance . . . A Study*, p. 191; and from Table 27.

Freight and shipping transactions[25] are a separate element in the Canadian balance of payments which increases in importance through the fact that the customs valuations of exports and imports are, like the American, largely f.o.b., and not c.i.f., as in the case of most other countries. Thus international payments on account of freight and shipping must be estimated separately. The relations between the debits and merchandise imports are closer than between the credits and exports.[26] Freight payments on coal imports, which amount to approximately one half the total inland freight payments to the United States, were almost equal in value in 1936 to the coal itself. Similarly, payments for shipping are closely related to imports from overseas.

Credits received from freight transactions are less closely related to the total export trade because of the important earnings of railways in Canada from in-transit traffic and because most inland freight on exports of grain is already included in the value of grain exports. . . . Earnings from in-transit traffic are dependent upon factors external to Canada, such as economic conditions in the United States and the foreign trade of that country.[27]

The depressing influence of these external factors coupled with the fairly rigid volume of debits arising from the coal imports serve to explain the increased net debits deriving from freight and shipping in the thirties, while simultaneously net credits on merchandise account were growing. The freight and shipping items therefore tended to be a cyclically disequilibrating element in the balance of payments.

Other current items[28] are a miscellany in which no one item is very large, although the total is quite considerable. This heterogeneity contrasts with the relative simplicity of the 1900–1913 period when first migrants' capital and later immigrants' remittances dominated the aggregate. This is partly due to the fact that there has been a growing number of items covered in this

[25] D.B.S., *The Canadian Balance . . . A Study*, pp. 70–97; and *Canadian Investment and Foreign Exchange Problems*, ed. J. F. Parkinson, pp. 22–23.
[26] D.B.S., *The Canadian Balance . . . A Study*, pp. 95–96.
[27] D.B.S., *The Canadian Balance . . . A Study*, pp. 95–96.
[28] See D.B.S., *The Canadian Balance . . . A Study*, pp. 102–107; and *Canadian Investment and Foreign Exchange Problems*, ed. J. F. Parkinson, pp. 24–25.

category, which, since 1926, when there is an important change in the series, has included:[29] immigrants' remittances and receipts; government expenditures and receipts; charitable and missionary contributions; advertising transactions; motion picture royalties, etc., capital of immigrants and emigrants; earnings of Canadian residents employed in the United States and of American residents employed in Canada; net payments for entertainment services, royalties, etc., not included above; and exchange, London and New York, on interest and retirement. During war years very substantial debits have arisen in this category due to expenses incurred with regard to Canadian Expeditionary Forces overseas.

The series for the years following 1926 indicate that the net total of "other current items" added to the weakening of the balance of payments in 1929–1930 and 1938, but that in the main the declines in credits during the thirties were offset by an almost equal fall in the debits. In the recovery of the thirties Canadian credits did not fare as well as the debits, and the net debit had increased considerably by 1937 as compared to 1928. Let us examine which of the other current items were responsible for these changes.[30]

Of a $41 million decline in credits between 1928 and 1937, a drop in the earnings of Canadian residents in the United States chiefly due to legislative restrictions accounted for $16 million; a falling off in imports of immigrants' capital accounted for $13 million ($10 million of this related to U.S. immigrants); immigrants' remittances from the United States declined by $8 million; and expenditures by governments in Canada fell $4 million.

Other current items debits declined by only $15 million between 1928 and 1937. Canadian government expenditures abroad and expenditures on films from abroad were both maintained, while expenditures for entertainers from abroad actually in-

[29] Viner assumed that in the absence of data relating to several of these items they could safely be assumed to be offsetting and so neglected. See his *Canada's Balance*, pp. 87–88. The "relative simplicity" of the earlier period is at least partially the result of a statistical void.

[30] The statistics on which the following analysis is based derive from D.B.S., *The Canadian Balance . . . A Study*, tables 40–50, pp. 216–239. Note that in more recent D.B.S. statements the totals have again been altered somewhat, though not so much as to significantly affect our analysis.

creased by $4 million. Immigrants' remittances abroad and exports of immigrants' capital were primarily responsible for the net decline, falling off by $11 million and $8 million respectively. The changes taking place in the other current items category must be considered largely fortuitous in relation to the question of balance-of-payments adjustment. To some extent the increased debits might be considered as an adjustment to the increased credits derived from increasing Canadian exports. This might be a reasonable hypothesis with respect to the expenditures on movies and entertainment from abroad which we might expect to find associated with the large expansion of nonagricultural exports and incomes in the thirties.

XX

The Problem of Adjustment —
Capital Account

Net movements of capital into Canada after World War I were relatively much less important than prewar ones. The gross movements on capital account are much greater in volume, but offsetting movements, e.g., of outstanding securities and of new issues and retirements in refinancing operations, reduce the net amounts of such movements very considerably.

NEW ISSUES AND RETIREMENTS [1]

Retirements fluctuate widely from year to year, being primarily determined by the security issuance contract, although in the case of certain issues there is the optional repayment of principal. Some of these optional redemption operations may escape recording under retirements and may be included with outstanding security movements.[2] Retirements had become a very large item by 1919, and their bunching in certain years may be a considerable influence in the balance of payments.[3] The association of large new issues and retirements in refinancing operations

---

[1] See D.B.S., *The Canadian Balance . . . A Study* (1939), pp. 111–125; and *Canadian Investment and Foreign Exchange*, ed. J. F. Parkinson, pp. 25–29.

[2] D.B.S., *The Canadian Balance . . . A Study*, p. 118.

[3] F. A. Knox, *Dominion Monetary Policy, 1929–1934* (Ottawa, 1939), p. 6.

becomes very significant, net borrowing by Provinces, for example, being very much lighter than their new issues suggest.[4] It is, however, often difficult to classify retirements as to whether external refinancing operations are reflected. There may be a lag from one year to the next between a new issue and the retirement of an old issue, as in the instance of the $100 million Dominion government loan floated in 1930 in New York, $88 million of which was used for redemptions in that market in 1931.[5]

Despite increasing redemptions, new issues predominated (though only by a very slight margin in 1925 and 1928) until the early thirties. From 1933 on repatriation of capital from the United States definitely swung the balance the other way, in spite of considerable net new issues in the United Kingdom during 1933–1934. In the 1920's there had been consistent net retirements of capital held in Britain which had been more than offset by the capital inflow from the United States.

An unpleasant fact, often emphasized in depression, is that borrowing abroad may be least feasible when the balance of payments is suffering the most strain. Canada in the thirties was relatively fortunate in this regard. Issues net of retirements increased as exports fell off in 1929 and 1930, reaching the highest level in 1930 since 1914. As mentioned above, part of the large total was devoted to redemptions in the subsequent year, however. Through the stiffening of interest rates in New York in 1928 and 1929, some Canadian borrowing may have been diverted to London,[6] thus exacerbating the British balance of payments problem, but net retirements of British capital continued, albeit at a reduced rate, while the net inflow continued to come from the United States, where Canadian credit standing remained high, as the following description of foreign borrowing in the United States would indicate.

The decline in foreign underwriting, especially noticeable for German securities, was general. . . . Canadian issues were an exception, registering a net increase in 1929 over 1928. This increase was largely in the Government guaranteed group, high-class securities that fluctuate less in value than securities of lower grade, and which undoubt-

[4] D.B.S., *The Canadian Balance . . . A Study*, p. 116.
[5] D.B.S., *The Canadian Balance . . . A Study*, pp. 119, 122; and Knox, *Dominion Monetary Policy, 1929–1934*, p. 12.
[6] D.B.S., *The Canadian Balance . . . A Study*, p. 117.

edly have a fairly substantial and constant institutional market in this country. . . .

An improvement in the bond market occurred in the closing months of 1929, and, for domestic bonds, continued for about a year. . . . Stimulated by easier market conditions, foreign flotations — chiefly by Canada, Germany, and Argentina — were fairly substantial in the first half of the year. Thereafter, falling prices for foreign bonds in the United States, world-wide business depression, unfavorable fiscal situations, especially in Latin American countries, and disturbed political conditions in Bolivia, Brazil, Germany, and elsewhere served to curtail foreign financing in this market. The year 1931 witnessed the beginning of widespread defaults, which drove foreign-bond prices to extremely low levels . . . and marked the end of an era of foreign underwriting in the United States. Since that time foreign issues have been insignificant in amount and have consisted largely of refunding issues. The Canadian and Argentine Governments have been the principal borrowers.[7]

The inflow of capital from new issues net of retirements was undoubtedly one of the factors serving to support the balance of payments and maintain the exchanges at a time when most agricultural exporting countries had no alternative but to depreciate.[8] No support was forthcoming from this source in 1931 and 1932, when the Canadian dollar was depreciated along with sterling, but there was no substantial repatriation until 1933 when it was strengthening again, large surpluses on merchandise account having virtually erased the current account deficit. Large current account surpluses followed from 1934 on, to which the repatriation of capital was doubtless partly an equilibrating adjustment.

Exchange rates[9] do not appear to have played an important part in affecting the volume of new issues in the thirties. The low level of new issues abroad during the years 1932 to 1938 is adequately accounted for by a domestic cheap money program, a depressed demand for investment funds accompanying the increased domestic supply, increased reliance upon corporate self-financing, and governmental restrictions upon the floating of loans in the United States.[10] The strengthened pound of late

[7] Lary et al., *The United States in the World Economy*, p. 100.
[8] Knox, *Dominion Monetary Policy, 1929–1934*, p. 13.
[9] Table 22. Also see Chapter 6.
[10] See *Canadian Investment and Foreign Exchange Problems*, ed. J. F. Parkinson, p. 27.

1933 and 1934 may, however, have been one consideration leading to the sterling issues of the Dominion government in London, which produced the first net inflow of capital from Britain for many years. With regard to retirements, exchange rates may have been more influential, for voluntary as opposed to contractual retirements are a very significant proportion of the total in certain years, and the fact that depreciation of the currency would increase the expense of redemption and thus should discourage it is doubtless an equilibrating influence.[11]

OUTSTANDING SECURITIES[12]

This is one of the most difficult items in the balance of payments to analyze. Yet if not suppressed through exchange control, gross outstanding security movements may represent values exceeded by only one other category in the Canadian balance of payments, namely, merchandise trade.[13] The net movements, it is true, may be relatively very small.

One difficulty which immediately confronts the analyst is the unavailability or inadequacy of the statistics. The United States and Canada have been exceptional in separating outstanding securities from other forms of long-term capital movements.[14] In the Canadian case the statistics have a very tenuous basis until 1933. Theoretical analysis of outstanding security movements has been very inconclusive. One investigator has this statement to make regarding the cyclical pattern of outstanding securities movements:

While there are, *a priori*, several conceivable patterns, yet in view of the complexity of these movements, and the differing and often conflicting motives involved, I cannot find any one pattern which would seem to be the most likely.[15]

[11] D.B.S., *The Canadian Balance . . . A Study*, pp. 119, 123.

[12] See D.B.S., *The Canadian Balance . . . A Study*, pp. 125–139; and *Canadian Investment and Foreign Exchange Problems*, ed. J. F. Parkinson, pp. 29–31. Also see A. I. Bloomfield, "The Significance of Outstanding Securities in the International Movement of Capital," *The Canadian Journal of Economics and Political Science*, November 1940.

[13] See Table 27. The gross estimates are available for the years 1933–1939.

[14] Bloomfield, *The Canadian Journal of Economics and Political Science*, November 1940, p. 496.

[15] Bloomfield, p. 524.

This is very understandable, since we are faced with all the difficulties inherent in analysis of domestic stock market activity plus additional difficulties related to the international nature of the transactions.

In order to confine what will be in any such case a cursory analysis I intend to restrict my attention to certain of the more important aspects of the Canadian transactions in outstanding securities. If the statistics are accurate, they indicate that purchases by Canadians outweighed the purchases from abroad until 1930. It is interesting to observe that the largest net capital exports on this account appear to have occurred from 1926–1928. This is compatible with the viewpoint that outstanding security movements are primarily related to short-run considerations of capital appreciation,[16] for it coincided with general and large foreign purchases of American common stocks "induced by progressively rising stock prices and the resultant opportunities for capital profits. . . ."[17] Other motives which may have induced the continuing net purchases of outstanding securities through the twenties are the desire to take advantage of the relatively high returns available on many United States investments, the desire to diversify investment portfolio, and the desire to hedge against possible depreciation of the Canadian dollar.[18]

It should be noted that the stresses in the international balance may be exacerbated in the case of net capital movements via outstanding securities. As is well known, an example is provided in the flight of capital to the United States in the 1930's, a transfer only accomplished through large gold movements. The fact that the final purchases velocity of the foreign investment funds may be negligible inhibits the transfer in the form of goods and services. However, it is possible for some tendency to adjustment to be induced indirectly by means of capital appreciation acting as a stimulus to increased consumption or through the influence of a decreased interest rate in stimulating new investment.[19] Any

[16] Bloomfield, p. 517.
[17] Lary, et al, *The United States in the World Economy*, p. 109.
[18] Lary, p. 110.
[19] Bloomfield, *The Canadian Journal of Economics and Political Science*, November 1940, pp. 521–522; and D.B.S., *The Canadian Balance . . . A Study*, pp. 137–138.

increased consumption or capital formation induced would then tend to produce higher commodity and service importations.

From 1930 to 1947, with the sole exception of a minor reverse movement in 1937, there has been a continuing net capital import on outstanding securities account. The Canadian net sales of securities contrasted with the repatriation of outstanding securities by most other debtor nations, which repurchased their securities at low prices which were in large part attributable to a strained balance of payments situation, default, and the operations of their exchange controls.[20] In the case of Canada, national credit standing continued high,[21] there was no exchange control, and there was no general defaulting. A hypothesis to explain the net sales of outstanding securities which commenced in 1930 could include as explanatory factors the loss of interest in the New York stock market on the part of Canadians and the liquidation of their previous investments there, which would be particularly significant factors in the early years of the period; the improving position of certain Canadian industries, such as mining, which attracted outside as well as domestic capital into Canadian stocks; the depreciation of the Canadian dollar relative to the American and an expected rebound which encouraged stock purchases during 1931–1934; and finally, flights of capital from Europe due to currency and war scares which contributed to the purchases by outsiders of Canadian securities. The continued importance of the factor of expectations of capital appreciation may be attested by the fact that 1937 was the only year in the thirties in which there were net sales of outstanding Canadian securities by foreigners, while it also marked a serious recession in the prices of Canadian stocks. In 1937 the liquidation of New York holdings by Canadians does not appear to have been the important factor it was in the early thirties.[22] The change from a net export of capital to a net import in 1930 did in fact serve to adjust the balance of payments, but whether it could be classified as an

[20] Bloomfield, pp. 506–508.

[21] Lary, *The United States in the World Economy*, p. 100.

[22] Canadian purchases of American securities were restricted after the imposition of exchange control in 1939. This helps to explain the substantial net sales of Canadian securities to foreigners during the war and immediate postwar years, as well as the net liquidation during the years of a lagging stock market, 1947 and 1948.

equilibrating type of action which could be depended upon on other occasions of the weakening of the balance of payments is no easy matter to decide.[23]

It is perhaps impossible to move beyond such general hypotheses as those set forth above without a preliminary and thorough investigation which would take account of the various types of securities which participate in the international movements, and which would consider all the various factors affecting the psychology of the investors in the main participating countries, obviously a colossal task. One study that has gone into some detail especially with regard to the influence of exchange rates on the monthly Canadian international trade in securities for the years 1933–1938, has revealed the difficulty in obtaining any conclusive results.[24] It was found that "variations in foreign exchange rates must be quite pronounced before their effects upon the broad course of trade are apparent." [25] Even when the variations in exchange rates were pronounced, movements were not always in accordance with the expectation that purchases would be stimulated by a low exchange rate and discouraged by a high exchange rate. As we know, prospective purchasers could well be discouraged at the time of a low exchange rate, which might be associated with an unfavorable or a worsening economic position. The study concluded that factors other than the exchange rate dominated the international security transactions between the United States and Canada, and between the United Kingdom and Canada for the later years of the period. No attempt was made to analyze these "other factors," and indeed it might have been an impossible task.

The Dominion Bureau of Statistics study remarks on the relatively small net movements of outstanding securities which it attributes to the parallel movements of stock prices in the United States and Canada based upon similar market conditions in both countries.[26] The net movements from month to month are at

---

[23] See, however, Chapter 21, where the proposition is supported that in 1930 the capital import was at least partly induced by changes on current account.

[24] D.B.S., *The Canadian Balance . . . A Study*, pp. 133ff.

[25] D.B.S., *The Canadian Balance . . . A Study*, p. 133.

[26] D.B.S., *The Canadian Balance . . . A Study*, p. 138.

times relatively larger.[27] It may well be that much of the short-run stability in the Canadian exchange rate may be attributed to the international security dealings, especially in the multicurrency bonds formerly so important in Canadian financing.[28] But the statement made in the D.B.S. report regarding equilibration to an export of capital through the purchase of outstanding securities is applicable here: "It would be idle to attempt to analyze the effects in any detail, as to make such refined speculations would require more details than are available regarding the continually changing complex circumstances." [29]

OTHER CAPITAL MOVEMENTS [30]

This category includes those capital movements connected with direct investments, trust companies, and insurance companies. The most important element here has generally been the movement of funds between Canada and other countries arising from British and foreign direct investments in Canada. Until 1928 this provided an inflow of funds, whereas there was a crescendo of capital outflow from then on through the thirties as returns grew on the original parent company investments.[31] Note that profits from the direct investments, when reinvested in Canada were not recorded on the grounds that this did not directly affect the balance of payments.[32] Certainly this corporate policy regarding the reinvestment of profits had important indirect consequences for the balance of payments, which was strengthened as a result of such reinvestment. In the interwar period Canadian direct investment abroad was less than one quarter of the value of direct investments of other countries in Canada, so that the transfer of funds on this account was a much less important element. However, due to the preponderance of a few large firms, there may be

[27] D.B.S., *The Canadian Balance . . . A Study*, pp. 202–203.
[28] *First Annual Report of the Bank of Canada* (1936), p. 13.
[29] D.B.S., *The Canadian Balance . . . A Study*, p. 138.
[30] See D.B.S., *The Canadian Balance . . . A Study*, pp. 139–161; and *Canadian Investment and Foreign Exchange Problems*, ed. J. F. Parkinson, pp. 30–32.
[31] D.B.S., *The Canadian Balance . . . A Study*, p. 145.
[32] D.B.S., *The Canadian Balance . . . A Study*, p. 144. The International Monetary Fund (see its *Balance of Payments Manual*, 1950, p. 2) has changed its official view and decided in favor of recording reinvested profits.

net transactions of greater significance than the relative value of the investments would indicate.[33]

The movements of capital related to Canadian trust companies are considerable and erratic. In the thirties a large part of the net capital exports in the "other capital movements" category is attributable to trust company transfers.

Capital movements stemming from insurance transactions are not so large as the size of their operations might suggest, since their policy is to build up assets corresponding to their liabilities abroad.[34] The net movements are usually a substantial proportion of the gross movements, and not very predictable.[35]

The net result of the changes in these various elements of other capital movements was a continuing import of capital into Canada until 1932, when a reverse movement began which contributed to the repatriation of capital during the thirties. This is certainly a type of repatriation which departs from the usual meaning of the term and which must be given separate attention with regard to its significance for balance-of-payments adjustment. The movements of trust and insurance company funds are so irregular that it is probably impossible to accord them any functional role in the balance-of-payments equilibration. However, there appears to be more rationale to the movements of branch plant funds which, fortunately for the purposes of analysis, are the dominant element in the category of other capital movements. During the 1920's, as during the period of 1900–1913, profitable investment opportunities attracted branch plants as well as other forms of capital, and the commodity imports which were required in connection with the establishment of these branch plants provided an adjusting offset for the capital inflow. In the 1930's branch plants played an important part in the recovery from the depression, and proved a source of export commodities and of funds for the parent concern which were offsetting in the balance of payments.

Bryce[36] has argued that repatriation of capital may serve as

[33] D.B.S., *The Canadian Balance . . . A Study*, p. 147.
[34] D.B.S., *The Canadian Balance . . . A Study*, pp. 152–153.
[35] D.B.S., *The Canadian Balance . . . A Study*, p. 160.
[36] R. B. Bryce, "The Effects on Canada of Industrial Fluctuations in the United States," *The Canadian Journal of Economics and Political Science*, August 1939, p. 385.

an "investment outlet" stimulating to incomes. This is certainly not true in the conventional multiplier sense. Bryce reasoned that an increased export surplus would be induced by the depreciation of the Canadian dollar. The depreciation, he held, would be effected by the augmented demand for foreign exchange resulting from the repatriation of capital. Presumably the reasoning would also apply to the outflow of capital implied in much of the return of funds by Canadian branch plants to the parent concerns.

Bryce's argument does not appear to be a strong one for several reasons: (1) the price effects of exchange rate fluctuations are unlikely to be very effective in inducing an increased export surplus; (2) as I view the situation, the export surplus seems more likely to have been the relatively autonomous variable, with the repatriation of capital being induced through the increase in incomes and funds available for investment; (3) the transfer of purchasing power abroad from Canada will have been depressive in effect. This is more clearly the case in the instance of branch plant funds. If the entire incomes arising from the branch plants were available only to Canadian consumers and investors, then surely the contribution to domestic income propagation would have been greater, unless we wish to make the implausible assumption that the direct gains to Canada through foreign repercussions more than offset the losses through the transfer of purchasing power abroad.

GOVERNMENT LOANS

This is a category of the balance of payments which I will mention only in passing. It arose from various intergovernmental war and postwar financial transactions, such as loans and reparations. They helped to support a weak Canadian balance of payments in the years succeeding World War I.

EXTERNAL BANK ASSETS AND MONETARY GOLD [37]

This category is the closest statistical approximation available of the gold and short-term capital movements upon which so much attention was focused during the course of previous theore-

[37] See D.B.S., *The Canadian Balance . . . A Study*, pp. 61, 161–165; and *Canadian Investment and Foreign Exchange Problems*, ed. J. F. Parkinson, pp. 32–33.

tical discussions. The approximation, as might be expected, is far from adequate. Monetary gold movements are distinguished from the nonmonetary as being those which effect an alteration in Canadian banking reserves.[38] Changes in external bank assets are a record of the net change in banks' foreign assets less foreign liabilities from December 31 of one year to December 31 of the next. The major foreign assets include:[39] gold and subsidiary coin held elsewhere than in Canada; government and bank notes other than Canadian; amounts due by banks and correspondents elsewhere than in Canada; securities other than Canadian; call and short loans elsewhere than in Canada; and current loans elsewhere than in Canada. Foreign liabilities include: deposits elsewhere than in Canada; deposits by and balances due banks and correspondents elsewhere than in Canada; and bills payable. It is important to observe that some short-term assets and liabilities have not been included because of the absence of complete information. These include:

. . . foreign deposits in the Canadian banks when these are in Canadian currency, and some short-term foreign assets and liabilities of Canadian individuals, corporations, and governments when these are not held through the medium of Canadian banks. Examples are provided by the Canadian currency deposits of foreign "fugitive" capital in Canadian banks, some deposits of Canadians in United States banks, money loaned on call in the New York money market by Canadian corporations, bills drawn on buyers abroad by Canadian exporters and not discounted at Canadian banks, "frozen" merchandise credits, etc. It should be pointed out, however, that probably the bulk of the international transfers of funds of many Canadian companies are recorded elsewhere in the capital account of the balance of payments. Among these concerns are insurance companies, transportation companies, Canadian companies with direct investments abroad, companies or branches which are directly controlled in Great Britain, the United States, or elsewhere, and trust companies.[40]

An important additional limitation in the statistics derives from the fact that Canadian banks pursue a considerable banking business abroad. "A considerable proportion of the external assets and

---

[38] See the Statistical Appendix.

[39] D.B.S., *The Canadian Balance . . . A Study*, p. 163, lists these foreign assets and liabilities, but indicates that certain modifications are made for balance-of-payments purposes. These modifications are not enumerated.

[40] D.B.S., *The Canadian Balance . . . A Study*, pp. 163–164.

liabilities of the Canadian chartered banks are the direct result of the business of foreign branches and not the result of any movement of funds from Canada." [41] However,

changes [in net external bank assets] have been principally in the assets rather than in the liabilities and this in itself throws a certain amount of light upon the general explanation for the reduction in net assets. The reduction has evidently been due to other reasons than a reduction in the foreign branch business.[42]

Changes in external bank assets, therefore, while they are the best indicator of short-term capital movements available, are far short of the ideal. This fact and the presence of a large residual error in many years means that we must proceed with caution in analyzing the relation between the current and capital balances and the movements of short-term capital and monetary gold.[43]

It seems safe to say, in view of the large changes in monetary gold and external bank assets, that the latter played an important part as a stopgap where the current and capital accounts failed to adjust to each other.[44] It is suggestive that during the period 1919–1940, changes in monetary gold and external bank assets in twenty of the twenty-two years bore an opposite sign to the net current account and so were offsetting. The two years in which the annual change in external bank assets and monetary gold were not of opposite sign to the current account were, significantly enough, the years of greatest net capital imports and greatest net capital exports, 1930 and 1936 respectively.[45] During the period 1900–1913, on the other hand, the change in external bank assets and monetary gold was offsetting to the current account in only four of fourteen years.[46] On first appearance it

[41] D.B.S., *The Canadian Balance . . . A Study*, p. 162.
[42] D.B.S., *The Canadian Balance . . . A Study*, p. 164.
[43] See Table 27.
[44] In the Kindleberger terminology (see Chapter 2), these stopgap movements of short-term capital would be initially "equilibrating" for the most part, but where bank policy affected the movements through taking account of the income on the capital or of possible exchange rate fluctuations, they would be income or speculative movements. For example, where short-term assets were maintained abroad in lieu of obtaining gold in order to obtain some return on the capital, we would have an income movement of short-term capital.
[45] See Chart 7 in connection with this and the subsequent analysis.
[46] See Table 27.

might appear that virtually all the shocks relating to the balance of payments during 1919–1940 registered on current account rather than on capital account, and were partially absorbed by changes in monetary gold and external bank assets. However, the direction of these changes must also be examined. The examination reveals that the direction of change of monetary gold and external bank assets is opposite to the direction of change in the net current account eight years during the period 1919–1940, is opposite to the direction of change on net capital account eight of the years, and is opposite to the direction of change on both current and capital accounts in five of the years. This seems to indicate what we should expect a priori, namely, that any change in the flows either on current or on capital account is likely to produce adaptive alterations in the flows of monetary gold and short-term capital.

Examples of this may be seen in Chart VII where there may be noted adaptive alterations in the flows of monetary gold and

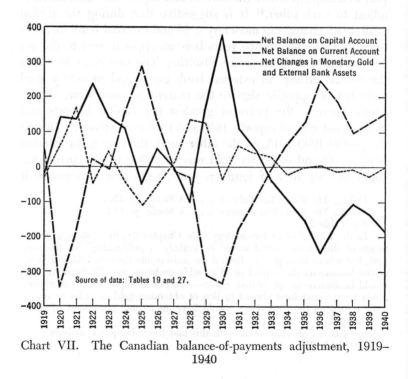

Chart VII. The Canadian balance-of-payments adjustment, 1919–1940

short-term capital accompanying the large current deficits of 1920–1921, the large current surplus of 1924–1926, the high capital importations of 1922, the capital exports and current deficit of 1928, the large current deficit of 1929, the peak capital imports of 1930, the current deficits of 1931–1933, and the current surplus of 1934.

In the 1930's there was a notable decline in the net movements of monetary gold and external bank assets. One can only hazard a guess at some of the reasons for this. A Canadian central bank first commenced operations in March 1935, and the policy of one institution replaced the several policies of the individual commercial banks with regard to the holding of external assets. The latter were placed in the position of being able to rely on the Bank of Canada for supplying the means of foreign payments, and no longer felt compelled to provide a secondary reserve abroad. The incentive for either commercial or central banks to hold such secondary reserves was furthermore diminished as a consequence of the fluctuating exchange rates of the 1930's. To quote the central bank's first report:

> In times past, New York call loans and bankers' acceptances were, to a large extent, regarded as the secondary reserve of Canadian banks. Fluctuating exchange rates have practically ruled out these items as a means of employment of that portion of a bank's Canadian assets which need not be kept in cash, but which must be convertible into cash, in large volume and without sacrifice, at a moment's notice.[47]

These may have been partly the reasons for the failure to build back to the level of the large reserves of the late 1920's when the current surpluses of the 1930's developed. The easy money and government deficit financing policy, with its domestic lending, to some extent replaced the lending abroad on short term. The low Canadian interest rates encouraged domestic loan flotations and repatriation of capital which in this way may have replaced the accumulation of external bank assets and of monetary gold as an offset to the current account surplus.[48] During World War II and the years immediately following, the fluctuations in monetary

[47] The Bank of Canada *First Annual Report* (1936), p. 17.
[48] See Canada, House of Commons, Standing Committee on Banking and Commerce, *Memorandum and Tables Respecting the Bank of Canada*, Ottawa, 1939, p. 37, where Governor Towers of the Bank of Canada ex-

gold and other liquid assets, the control of which had been assumed by the Foreign Exchange Control Board, again came into
prominence, thus indicating the continuing importance of their
stopgap role. This reversion after the advent of exchange control
might also signify that certain capital movements which would be
restricted or discouraged by the exchange control had been
fulfilling a stopgap role similar to that of gold and recorded external bank assets.

---

pressed the view that if the interest rate had been maintained at a higher
level and if there had been a tendency to less repatriation of capital as a
consequence (instead of an inflow of gold and short-term capital taking
place, the possibility which I suggested), the decreased demand for foreign
exchange would have appreciated the Canadian dollar and this would have
led to the repatriation of capital, despite the tighter domestic credit policy.
This serves to indicate the speculative nature of the discussion. Also see
Bryce, *The Canadian Journal of Economics and Political Science,* August
1939, p. 385, according to whose reasoning we should expect a reduced
export surplus to be the chief result of the appreciation, not an increased
repatriation of capital. See also Chapter 21, where it is argued that capital
repatriation was achieved at the expense of unemployment that resulted
partly from the lack of an effective monetary fiscal and exchange rate policy.

XXI

A Composite Picture

A summary account of balance-of-payments adjustments for Canada during the period 1919–1940 is much more difficult to achieve than for the period from 1896 through World War I. Partly this is due to the fact that the earlier period was dominated by a strong upward burst of economic growth that was not interfered with more than briefly by short-run business fluctuations. In contrast, the interwar picture is one of overwhelming dominant cyclical movements influencing Canadian and world economic conditions. Furthermore, as has been noted, because of increased Canadian industrialization and independence, an enhanced export potential, an excess capacity and a low level of domestic capital formation, there was no longer the simple positive correlation between prosperity and increased capital imports characteristic of newly developing regions. Also, the comparative wealth of statistical data in the interwar years has made it possible to glimpse complex relations involving the finer classifications that had been made available of the current and capital accounts. The story told in preceding sections, of the varied behavior of the different elements in the balance of payments, reveals an embarrassment of riches. Simple straightforward theories are much more readily related to simple facts, and are obviously less tolerable in the face of the interwar data than they might have been in the face of the relatively limited material available for the period of Viner's study. Yet the very wealth of statistics forces us to admit that we are not always able to account very satisfactorily for the heterogeneity of the behavior patterns revealed to us.

Nonetheless the theory of balance-of-payments equilibrium developed in Part I has proven of great interpretative value. Particularly has this been true with respect to the merchandise account, whose fluctuations may best be explained in terms of relative income changes. Interdependence and the common influence of business fluctuations have been emphasized in analyzing the relations of the current and capital accounts to each other, thus following the example set for the pre-World War I period. Where conclusions have been more tentative for the interwar period, the reasons are sometimes found in the new importance of outstanding capital movements — and the significance for these of stock market speculation — and in the enhanced importance in the thirties of flights of capital, especially from Europe. Expectations unrelated to relative rates of profit and interest assume more prominence than in the years preceding World War I.

Much of the contrast of the interwar period with those earlier years may be explained by comparing the role of the newly dominant United States in the world economy with that of British leadership in the nineteenth century. In the earlier period the world gained from the complementarity between Britain and the areas to which she was exporting capital. The world suffered as the result of the relative self-sufficiency of the United States and of the tendency to autarchic policies that her relative independence encouraged. Cyclical fluctuations in the earlier period centered primarily in the newly developing areas of the world. There was not only the strong growth trend but also the shift to less profitable opportunities for domestic investment in Britain to serve as buffers in a cyclical decline. Compare the interwar period when world cyclical movements appear to have centered in the wide fluctuations of United States domestic incomes and investment. This, coupled with the fact that security markets were better developed throughout the world, served to attract capital from the relatively capital-poor countries to the capital-rich United States. No doubt the greater importance of common shares as compared to fixed-return types of securities was a significant element in this contrasting behavior of capital movements. In depression the substantial decline in American investment and incomes, coupled with an income elasticity of demand for imports that was higher than Great Britain's, dealt a severe blow to other countries.[1] Added to the tremendous decline in imports into the United States in the thirties was the shift from an American capital exporting to a net capital importing position. The flight of capital from other countries was produced by fears of war, currency depreciation, and was supplemented by the repurchase by foreigners of their own securities at bargain prices.

Canada occupied a peculiar role in the world economy in that she was not only a recipient of flight capital as a result of her relatively strong currency and of her advantageous geographical position from the military point of view, but she also participated in the repatriation of her securities that were held abroad.[2] These conflicting tendencies have been analyzed within the aggregate of net capital movements. The geographical proximity of Canada to the United States and the unique intimacy of their economic and social interrelations have made Canada peculiarly subject to the influence of United States psychological vagaries, particularly those associated with the stock markets. The basis for anticipating that fluctuations in the United States economy will influence Canada, if not directly via changes in United States purchasing power for Canadian exports, then indirectly through her preponderant influence upon the world economy is, however, a rational one. A suggestion to the contrary has been put forward by R. B. Bryce.

It is difficult to draw precise conclusions from this review of the major channels of influence of American business conditions on those in Canada. Broadly it would appear that the effects by way of trade are real and substantial, but not so preponderant that they could not be outweighed or substantially counteracted by movements in our trade with other countries. On the other hand, the influences by way

[1] T. C. Chang, "The International Comparison of the Demand for Imports," *Review of Economic Studies*, XIII (1946–1947), estimated the two elasticities at 1.27 and 1.10 during the interwar period. I suspect that a still lower estimate for Britain would result if it were possible to calculate the British income elasticity for the period before World War I.

[2] The effect of the reverse flow of funds from Canadian branch to parent plants was the same as repatriation, as far as the balance of payments was concerned.

of investment are more indirect and intangible, but no less effective. In part, they rest on a belief in themselves, on a belief that the dependence of Canadian business and finance on the United States is more complete than really is the case. The similar course of business in the two countries during the past fifteen or twenty years affords some basis for that belief. But I suggest that in part this similarity has been, if not accidental, then at least a result of unusually universal conditions, and that it is not at all impossible to picture a fair divergence between the course of business in the two countries. If that should come about, it might itself reduce somewhat the dependence of our investment on American conditions, and thus reinforce itself.[3]

The question is whether Bryce gives sufficient weight to the indirect influence of the United States on Canadian trade from the point of view of volume and price, though he considers this at some length.[4] The influence of the United States on world markets might well be preponderant in view of the wide fluctuations of her domestic activity and the high income elasticity of her demand for imports.[5] If this be the case, there would be much more ground for the expectations of Canadian business men than Bryce was disposed to grant.

Throughout the period under study there were important offsets of current and capital accounts which would have been closer to equalizing had the statistics been less in error.[6] The large current deficits of 1920–1921 were partly counteracted by increasing capital imports, and we may surmise that the increases on both current and capital account were due in large part to a common cause, namely, the boom in economic activity following the war. The current deficit was so large that pressure on the balance of payments was evident in both losses of monetary gold and external bank assets and in a heavy discount of the Canadian relative to the American dollar. The period 1922–1928 inclusive was one of merchandise export surpluses, with surpluses on current account as well, for four of the seven years and negligible current deficits in the other three. They were accompanied by

[3] Bryce, *The Canadian Journal of Economics and Political Science,* August 1939, p. 386.

[4] Bryce, pp. 381–382.

[5] Lary, *The United States in the World Economy,* especially pp. 27–31; and R. Nurkse, "Domestic and International Equilibrium," *The New Economics,* ed. S. Harris (New York, 1947), p. 271.

[6] See Table 27 and Graph VII in connection with this and the succeeding analysis.

declining credits on capital account which were a product of a net decrease from 1922–1928 in the excess of new issues over retirements plus increasing net purchases of outstanding securities. Without breakdowns in the outstanding security totals being available for these years we can only surmise that there was an increasing flow of funds from Canada to the New York stock market. This appears to be a fortuitous part of the adjustment, being stimulated by the excessive New York stock market boom, which cannot be related to changes in other items in the balance of payments. However, to an important degree the rationale for the adjustment of current and capital accounts may be found in the mechanism whereby increasing export surpluses led to increasing incomes which provided a greater volume of domestic funds for investment purposes. It is notable that throughout the twenties the adjustment between the current and capital accounts was in any case far from a fine one, and that the stopgap flows of monetary gold and external bank assets were very considerable.

Poor wheat crops in 1929 and the onslaught of the depression brought mounting current deficits in 1929–1930. The losses of gold and external bank assets, which had been induced in 1928 by the virtual cessation of net new issues, and rising imports continued into 1926. In 1930, the largest net new issues of the interwar period relieved the strain on the balance of payments. It seems logical to assume that the large net transfer of funds abroad on account of the current deficit were rendering conditions inauspicious for the domestic flotation of loans. The presumption that capital imports in 1930 were at least partly induced by the current account deficit is a strong one. The loss of gold and outside reserves had already been so large during 1928–1929 that Canada had remained only nominally on the gold standard during 1929, when restrictions on gold exports were accompanied by a depreciation of the currency below the gold point. The banks could not have been favorably disposed towards a large expansion of domestic loan flotations in view of the pressure upon their reserves.[7]

[7] I have noted that the Dominion Government was not influenced directly by the balance-of-payments situation in undertaking new borrowings in New York, but the balance of payments may have exerted considerable indirect influence through causing the loss of banks' foreign and domestic reserves.

The low net capital issues of 1928 must either be regarded as fortuitous or be explained in terms of an American shortage of investable funds that handicapped Canadian more than American borrowers. Judged in terms of Canadian income and capital formation, which were increasing more rapidly than the American, the Canadian requirements for investable funds would have been more intense than those in the United States. The heavy drain on foreign reserves reflected the unsatisfied need for funds from abroad. It is a fact that Canadian issues were viewed in an exceptionally favorable light relative to other foreign issues on the New York security market, and that net new issues of Canadian securities in the years 1929–1930 were very large.[8] However, it may still be possible that conditions did not favor Canadian flotations relative to American in 1928.

From 1930 to 1936 the picture was one of decreasing current deficits that altered in 1934 to mounting current surpluses. On capital account there was an offsetting movement with a trend from net capital imports to net capital exports. The primary components in this trend on capital account were net new issues and a net outflow of funds on direct investment account. Both may be regarded as an equilibrating reaction to the increasing export surpluses which become possible partly on the basis of the investments of the twenties. Since excess capacity was prevalent in the thirties, the increased exports did not entail large industrial imports for purposes of new investment. A large volume of funds was thus released for the domestic refinancing of loans previously floated abroad (a cheap money program reflecting the easy supply of funds), and funds also became available for their return to foreign parent plants, and to a lesser extent for Canadian direct investment abroad. Running counter to this trend were the international transactions in outstanding securities, which resulted in a shift from net exports in the twenties to net imports in the thirties. It might be thought that the plethora of Canadian funds available for investment in the thirties, which had resulted in large net retirements, would also have tended to effect large net purchases of outstanding securities by Canadians. This tendency must have been offset partly by stock market in-

---

[8] See Chapter 20, "New issues and retirements."

fluences with a strong interest being taken by the American investor in certain Canadian stocks, such as golds, which fared well in the thirties, and partly by Canada sharing with the United States in receiving flight capital from Britain and continental Europe.

The years 1937–1938 saw a cyclical decline in the export surplus attributable in the first year to a greater increase in imports than exports as investment and incomes swelled, and in the second year to a greater cyclical decline in exports than in imports. The adjustment of the capital and current accounts was perhaps to a large extent one where the decreasing current surplus tended to reduce the funds available for the domestic refinancing of earlier foreign flotations.

The inference to be drawn from the behavior of current and capital accounts during the interwar period is that, in a period of underemployment and excess capacity, a rising national income is likely to be associated with a tendency towards current account surpluses and an export of capital. This also appears to be the tendency during the war years. On the other hand, during peacetime periods of prosperity, the outcome is much less certain. If capital formation is proceeding at a pace that is not relatively less than that abroad, particularly in the United States, the prosperity is likely to be associated with a current account deficit and capital imports. It is not justifiable to take the behavior of the 1930's as representative.[9] The result appears not to be dependent solely upon the relative intensities of the Canadian and foreign business cycles. The tendency to current account deficits will be enhanced if the fluctuations occur when important sectors of the Canadian economy are operating near full capacity.

[9] This is a criticism I would direct against T. C. Chang, *Cyclical Movements in the Balance of Payments* (Cambridge, England, 1951), chapter 12. Chang, incidentally, did not obtain the latest official balance-of-payments data to support his investigations, and the data he supplies for capital movements, particularly for the 1920's, do not correspond with the official estimates supplied more recently. For example, he refers (p. 206) to a net outflow of capital during the later prosperous years of the 1920's, when there was actually a small net inflow. Chang notes exceptions to his generalizations (which are based upon the period 1924–1938) in the years 1927 and 1928 when there were small current account deficits rather than surpluses. Such exceptions become all too frequent when we observe behavior beyond the short period he selected for observation.

One striking fact in the balance-of-payments adjustment of the 1930's which we have had occasion to observe is the very small part played by movements of monetary gold and external bank assets as compared to the 1920's. Hypotheses were suggested in the preceding chapter to account for this lesser role, but there was left unanswered the question as to how minor short-run adjustments were effected in the absence of the continuing intervention of gold and external assets holdings.

There are many types of short-term capital movements that do not fall into the category of external bank assets, some recorded and some unrecorded, which might accompany the purchasing power shifts and fulfill the same equilibrating stopgap function, and which might be either "equilibrating," speculative, or income movements, these terms being employed in the Kindleberger sense. As examples of the recorded categories which might participate, there are branch plant, insurance company, and trust company funds, all recorded under other capital movements, and international exchanges of outstanding securities. I noted one investigation (Chapter 20) of the relation of the latter to exchange rate differentials which produced inconclusive results. The influence of exchange rates, despite the lack of empirical verification, may be of some year-to-year equilibrating importance on current and capital account, and hence may reduce the movements of monetary gold and external bank assets. Empirical evidence may be inconclusive for several reasons: (1) certain short-term movements may be disequilibrating due to expectations of a continuing depreciation or appreciation of the exchanges, although the net movements over a longer period may be equilibrating; (2) if statistics were available for all the capital movements influenced by exchange rate fluctuations, the aggregate might indicate equilibrating movements whereas the analysis of outstanding securities alone might not; (3) if there had not been exchange rate fluctuations, the capital movements might have been even more disequilibrating. In any event, with regard to the 1930's, it is only the marginal importance of such adjustments with which we are concerned, for the major adjustment of the capital account relating to the net current account changes certainly occurred in the category of new issues and retirements.

I have offered a tentative hypothesis to account for this adjustment, but the reason for the exactness of the equilibration must remain mysterious, unless we assume that there were certain "equilibrating" or speculative short-term capital movements which minimized the movements of monetary gold and external bank assets. It must not be forgotten, however, that I have investigated only the latter's year-to-year changes and that shorter-run changes may have been relatively more important.

My study of the adjustments undergone by Canada in the world economy during the interwar years has necessarily at many points been less conclusive than my study of the period 1900–1913. The complex nature of the balance-of-payments equilibration is evident. It is also evident that many of the topics touched upon are worthy of additional investigation, although whether individual or even governmental research could uncover many of the necessary relevant facts for past years is a matter for considerable doubt. Questions, the answers for which might require, for example, the distinguishing of capital movements with regard to the use of funds by the borrower and the purpose of the investor, and the provision of certain statistics for shorter than annual periods, must in all probability wait the results of future statistical investigation of current changes. And in view of the historical individuality that has been observed with respect to different balance-of-payments adjustments, it might well be dangerous to apply the results of any future investigation to the interpretation of earlier, less detailed data.

My investigations have revealed the complexity of the changes in the balance of payments and the necessity for uncovering the heterogeneity often concealed within the broad classifications. The cyclical fluctuations of the interwar period and the dominance of the United States with respect to the Canadian and world economies were seen to be of overriding importance, but the relations between the various balance-of-payments series, and the widely fluctuating income and investment series, are not always easy to see. With regard to the merchandise account, however, the income-import relationship seems to provide sufficient explanatory value that the factors of relative prices, tariffs, and exchange rates appear insignificant in comparison. This is particularly true with regard to the shorter-run cyclical changes. Over a period of several years, protectionist policy — and particularly we should note imperial preference and its influence upon Canadian investment and exports — tends to assume greater importance. The influence of protectionist policy may be greatly exaggerated when it has been to a large extent a product of declining incomes, as in many examples following 1929, or when it has been associated with a national income which was increasing for reasons independent of commercial policy, as in the instance of British imperial preference and the ameliorating intra-imperial national incomes from 1933 on.

GOVERNMENT POLICIES

Exchange rate fluctuations certainly have had considerable significance for the Canadian economy, but this related more to the aggravation or improvement of area incomes and of sectional price levels — for example agricultural versus industrial and mineral products — than to the short-run equilibration of the international accounts. Agricultural and most forest products suffered from a greater cyclical price flexibility than industrial products, and the price weakness of the depression was aggravated by the selling in competition with countries whose currencies were more greatly depreciated than the Canadian, and by selling into markets where the currencies were also more greatly depreciated. Mineral and newsprint producers tended to gain from the depreciation of the Canadian dollar relative to the American, while agricultural producers tended to suffer from the appreciation relative to Australia, the Argentine, and Great Britain. The heavier relative debt and taxation burdens of the wealthier Eastern provinces signified that they stood to gain from resistance to depreciation that would increase service on the Canadian debt, which in the early thirties was chiefly payable in terms of American dollars. The divergent interests of the Prairie Provinces, exporting to and in competition with countries whose currencies were more greatly depreciated than the Canadian, and of Ontario and Quebec (and to a lesser extent British Columbia), exporting to the United States whose currency was appreciated relative to the Canadian, were bound to lead to political controversy. Commercial policy also produced its regional conflicts, for the increased tariffs of 1930 further increased the burdens of the Prairie Provinces, which were buying in protected domestic markets and selling into unprotected foreign markets. Add to this the relatively greater cyclical price flexibility of the goods the Western farmer sells as compared with what he buys, and the basis for a most uneven economic impact of the depression is clearly revealed. "The resulting pattern of economic consequences may best be described as in the nature of a 'whip saw,' for the West had its income reduced at a time when its burdens had increased." [10]

Canadian monetary, fiscal, and exchange rate policies taken as a whole can be explained, and to that extent excused, in the light of the then prevailing inexperience and ignorance, but they can hardly be justified in terms of ideal standards. A cheap money policy was initiated by the federal Department of Finance shortly before a Canadian central bank was finally established in 1935.[11] This policy was continued by the Bank of Canada. Unfortunately this monetary policy was not only belated but was not effective to any great extent outside the high-grade bond market, especially the market for governments. It is well known that there was a similar difficulty elsewhere, for example in the United States, yet Canadian customer and call-loan rates were sometimes decreased only to meet the competition of the cheaper American money.

The fiscal policy of the federal government was not actively countercyclical in the early thirties. There were increased deficits and a partly automatic stabilizing influence as a result of decreasing revenues and salvaging operations entailing increased expenditures in certain directions. But public investment followed the same broad trend as private investment prior to World War

[10] Manitoba, The Government of the Province of, *Manitoba's Case — A submission presented to the Commission on Dominion-Provincial Relations,* part 3, "The Effects of Federal Monetary Policy on Western Canadian Economy" (Winnipeg, 1937), pp. 5–6. This submission is the work of A. R. Upgren with the assistance of H. C. Grant, and the manuscript was read by J. Viner and A. H. Hansen.

[11] See A. F. W. Plumptre, *Central Banking in the British Dominions* (Toronto, 1940), especially pp. 142–143, where interest rates in Canada are discussed.

II, and thus served to intensify rather than to alleviate the intensity of the cyclical fluctuations.[12]

The fact that Canadian monetary and fiscal policy was not strongly and effectively antidepressive accounts in large measure for the comparative strength of the Canadian dollar on the foreign exchanges that was witnessed during the thirties. Equilibrium in the Canadian balance of payments with net capital imports was obtained at the price of a low level of incomes and employment in Canada which held down the demand for imports. Alternatively, it could be fairly alleged that the repatriation of Canadian securities proceeded at the expense of greater unemployment than necessary.

Canadian policy must be criticized largely on the grounds that it was negative or passive, rather than that it was positive and perverse. Such criticism must, of course, be borne by most other governments, particularly during the early thirties. The theory of compensatory fiscal policy was generally misunderstood, ignored, or unacceptable, and the hazards confronting such a policy were in any event greatest for a country with a high marginal propensity to import. The difficulty in adjusting all rates of interest downwards was a general one, while the machinery for introducing appropriate monetary policies was introduced to Canada only at a late date. Criticism can legitimately be directed toward the tardiness with which a central bank was established. The most feasible effective policy perhaps lay in the sphere of exchange rates. Here, as well as in connection with monetary and fiscal policy, it could be argued that experimentalism with untried techniques was extremely inviting to disaster for a country so traditionally dependent on foreign capital and confidence. The position of the Conservative government is clearly expressed in the budget speech of March 1933, in which the Minister of Finance stated:

. . . let the sponsors of inflation never forget that apart from the other difficulties and dangers involved in their program, one inevitable result would be a flight from our dollar, a withdrawal on a large

[12] Canada, Department of Trade and Commerce, Economic Research Branch, *Investment and Inflation* (Ottawa, 1949), pp. 33, 161, 164. This was a report to the Royal Commission on Prices prepared under the direction of Dr. O. J. Firestone.

scale of the capital invested by foreigners in this country in the form
of securities and bank deposits. There are also to be considered internal
reactions to any steps which might impair confidence in a country's
currency. Against policies which might lead to such dangers, this
government has resolutely set its face.[13]

The government had evidently not learned the lesson to be
derived from the British experience of the preceding several
years that financial conservatism does not necessarily provide
the appropriate answer where exchange rate policy is concerned.
The stressing of the danger of capital flight was uncalled for in
view of the fact that the market rate for Canadian exchange was
above the rate at which relatively full employment was feasible.
Speculative capital flight that served to depress the rate would
have been desirable. On other occasions opponents of further depreciation inconsistently argued that without central banking
machinery further depreciation could not have been effected.[14]

Proponents of depreciation gave too much credit to other countries, such as Australia, for having followed desirable and intelligent policies. Analysis of such policies indicate that this was
far from the truth and that, characteristically, it was despite
great precautions that an uncontrolled depreciation got under
way.[15] The reaction of the Canadian dollar to any depreciation
of the pound sterling had typically been to occupy a position
intermediate between the pound and the American dollar. An
intermediate depreciation of the Canadian currency would tend
to improve the trade balance vis-a-vis the United States so as to
offset the deteriorated trade balance vis-a-vis Great Britain that
the more greatly depreciated pound would tend to induce.[16]

In general natural equilibrating forces operated to buoy up
the Canadian dollar on the exchanges. The most important of

[13] Canada, *House of Commons Debates*, Session 1932–33, III, 3208, cited
by F. A. Knox, *Dominion Monetary Policy 1929–1934* (Ottawa, 1939), p.
33.
[14] See Knox, *Dominion Monetary Policy 1929–1934*, pp. 61–63.
[15] Plumptre, *Central Banking in the British Dominions*, pp. 391–392.
Plumptre points to the only exception among the British Dominions as
being New Zealand in 1933.
[16] Plumptre, pp. 414–417. These price effects on merchandise trade were
probably much less significant than the expectations of speculators whose
action affected the capital account, and still more important the relatively
greater declines of Canadian incomes as compared to the British.

these were, however, the undesirable declines in income and employment induced by the decrease in Canadian exports and investment. By taking little action via fiscal or monetary policy to increase incomes, and by preventing a further depreciation of the exchanges by borrowing abroad, particularly heavily in 1930, and by discouraging speculation on the possibility of further depreciation rather than resumption of parity with the American dollar, the Canadian government contributed to further deterioration of the employment situation. The Canadian experience has revealed the strong support given the Canadian currency because of close ties with the United States affecting the balance of payments on both current and capital account. It has indicated the importance, as one element in a countercyclical program, of an exchange rate policy designed to resist undesirable equilibrating forces. Such a positive exchange rate policy has been adopted by Canada in post-World War II years as both a counterdeflationary and counterinflationary device.[17]

In weighing the pros and cons of exchange depreciation in times of depression, the important secondary effects stemming from increased incomes of exporters, and from the upward stimulus given the price level, should not be forgotten. Nor should one ignore the advantage given a cooperant monetary and fiscal policy through the tendency of exchange depreciation to diminish the marginal propensity to import. The marginal propensity to

[17] Further reference to the subject of exchange depreciation may be found in S. Harris, *Exchange Depreciation* (Cambridge, 1936), and J. S. Allely, "Some Aspects of Currency Depreciation," *Canadian Journal of Economics and Political Science,* August 1949. Analysis supporting the view that exchange depreciation is likely to have favourable effects for smaller countries may be found in J. Tinbergen, *The Dynamics of Business Cycles* (Chicago, 1950), pp. 311–316, and "Some Measurements of Elasticities of Substitution," *Review of Economic Statistics,* August 1946. In my view Knox, *Dominion Monetary Policy 1929–1934,* pp. 61ff., is too pessimistic regarding the possible beneficial results of a further Canadian depreciation in the thirties. In particular (page 64) Knox's conclusion that wheat producers might benefit little from depreciation appears unjustified. Tinbergen found the elasticity of substitution for wheat to be relatively high. Knox observed that Canadian Cooperative Producers Ltd., with government backing, was supporting the price of Canadian wheat above normally competitive world prices. His suggestion that there would be little to gain from reducing the sterling price does not correspond with Tinbergen's findings, and the increasing of the price in terms of the Canadian dollar would probably have lessened the selling agency's incentive for price maintenance.

import has been estimated at about one third for Canada,[18] and the prominence of this leakage accounts for the relatively low Canadian investment and export multipliers, each being approximately one and one half.[19] There is reason to believe that the leakage through imports had been somewhat reduced through increased tariffs in the early thirties, and probably more significantly through the failure of private capital formation, with its relatively high import content, to respond positively to income increases in the thirties, partly as a result of excess capacity. For this reason, and if government investment were designed so as to reduce its import content as much as possible, the multiplier attached to government expenditures might have been greater than the above estimate would indicate. A desirable form of depreciation would have been a substantial once-and-for-all exchange rate change that would have reduced the incentive to withdraw capital from Canada. At the same time the depreciation of the Canadian dollar would have diminished the incentive to repatriate capital, particularly from Britain, and thus would have provided a source of foreign exchange for the increased imports that would have resulted from an expansionary policy.

I wish to emphasize that I am not now taking a position contradictory to my previous arguments. I continue to maintain that income effects are much more weighty than price effects. It is true that the exchange rate policy which I have supported depends for its effectiveness largely on price effects. But it was recommended as only one element in an antidepression policy coordinate with monetary and fiscal policy. Countercyclical policy offers tremendous obstacles for an economy such as the Canadian, very subject to influences from abroad, and having a high marginal propensity to import with its serious implications for the balance of payments. Freedom of action for Canadian policy makers and, more important, the effectiveness of this action, may be severely limited unless undesirable controls and extreme changes in the now dependent and specialized structure of the Canadian economy are introduced. If such controls and

[18] T. C. Chang, "The International Comparison of the Demand for Imports," *The Review of Economic Studies,* 1945–46, XIII.
[19] T. C. Chang, "A Note on Exports and National Income in Canada," *Canadian Journal of Economics and Political Science,* May 1947.

extreme changes with their probable adverse repercussions on the efficient allocation of resources are to be minimized in Canadian countercyclical policy, then every possible vehicle of action must be seized on and operated as effectively as possible. Opposing pressures are likely to be tremendous, but this does not furnish us with a rationale for *laissez faire*, or an excuse for failing to deploy all the forces at our disposal.

Policy making is an art, and the dangers of generalization should be apparent. The policy we have been considering relates to what might be termed a peripheral economy, with important markets and sources of supply in the key currency countries of Great Britain and the United States. Such a country as Canada must hope to implement policies that will enable it to weather the cyclical disturbances and possible storms that may emanate from abroad without being able to control the disturbances, or in all probability without being able to completely offset them, if a relatively free enterprise economy is to be maintained. For Canada, then, the income effects stemming from the propagation of purchasing power from abroad must be taken as given. The most effective contribution to a solution of the problems of Canadian employment and low prices of agricultural, forest, and other products, would have been the maintenance through fiscal, monetary, and other policies of a high level of incomes and employment in the United States. (For a dominant clearing country such as the United States, depreciation of the currency would be generally both ineffective and undesirable.) The circumstances of the thirties were those in which strong and effective antidepression policies were not pursued in the United States. Effective palliative policies were not adopted in Canada, and the Canadian national income accompanied the American national income in its decline to levels relatively lower than those for almost any other country.

In order to retain our perspective regarding exchange rate policy, then, it must be remembered that it has been advocated at a time of severe depression in the most influential economy in the world, when countries similar to Canada were depreciating. Further, depreciation for Canada has been argued as a complement to an appropriately direct monetary and fiscal policy, and partly with a view to decreasing the leakages from the additions to the Canadian income stream generated by the latter.[20] Part of the efficacy of depreciation was attributed to its anticipated favorable effects on those incomes and prices most severely affected in the depression, and to the fact that the elasticity of demand with respect to price of certain Canadian exports such as wheat would be relatively high. And, in order to keep the price effects in perspective, it should not be forgotten that a portion of the favorable effects of depreciation in reducing leakages through imports are attributable to induced income effects, namely, those resulting from the reduction of purchasing power in real terms as import prices (in Canadian dollars) rise.

I do not wish to slight the dilemma that may arise where fluctuating exchange rates are permitted. Depreciation may bring about desirable short-run effects, but may create additional uncertainties for the foreign investor that may prove a deterrent to future imports of capital, thus handicapping the long-run economic development of the country. This particular influence on the foreign investor can be overrated, however. Much more significant are the prospects for convertibility of the earnings of the capital invested and of the principal itself. More important, too, are earning prospects of the firms to which the capital is directed, especially where equity capital is concerned, and these prospects in many cases are improved by depreciation. The deterrent would be greater where government bonds are concerned. A greater premium for risk would be demanded in foreign markets, and the government would be confronted with the prospect of having to offer a higher interest return on its obligations. This might be a low price to pay for the gains of depreciation, but there would doubtless be a tendency for the government to overrate the cost, as in the recent Treasury Department-Federal Reserve controversy over interest rate levels in the United States. However, taken together with the difficulty of foreseeing the increased degree of independence of the Canadian capital market

[20] In view of the extreme seriousness of the situation, a strong case could have been made for the imposition of exchange control and quantitative restrictions upon imports if the expansionary policy had resulted in a severe drain of foreign reserves. Such a step would have been even more unpalatable politically than exchange depreciation.

from foreign funds, there were considerable, though undoubtedly exaggerated, grounds for the Canadian government following the passive line with respect to its exchange rate policy.

In undertaking the foregoing analysis of the interwar period, it has been my view that it was profitable to approach the period in a broad historical setting while attempting throughout to use the theoretical principles of interpretation which primarily emphasize production function changes, the income approach, and the influence of industrial and agricultural fluctuations in a context of economic growth. There is little doubt, however, that portions of the period studied and aspects of the problems faced may deserve more detailed analysis than my broad approach has permitted.

The experience has been a common one — the further the investigation was pursued the less validity there appeared to be in the broad type of generalization; and the recognition of historical individuality has demanded a rather descriptive form of analysis. I have furnished evidence as to how easily one may run into error in balance-of-payments analysis and how readily one may submit statements on insufficient grounds. However, I have not myself foresworn theorizing of a speculative nature in attempting to interpret the facts; there is no intent to deny its usefulness, but only to recommend caution in recognizing it for what it is. Advancement of the analysis will perhaps depend more on the improvement and greater detailing of the factual and statistical material with which the investigator must cope than on the bettering or addition of theoretical tools of analysis. Since important sections of the factual material must relate to such complex or nebulous factors as the incentives of bankers and businessmen, one is always handicapped at this level of investigation by the lack or inadequacy of data. There will doubtless always be room for speculation as to the facts in addition to speculation regarding their interrelationships. A most important advance in international trade theory has been the movement away from a focusing on a single causal nexus toward the acceptance of multifarious possibilities in the theoretical relations. This is a notable accomplishment and clears the way toward the new insights which can be expected to accompany new factual relations. Though the basis for great optimism may have been undermined, it may justifiably be concluded that there is no reason for extreme pessimism, and that there is good reason to expect slow but steady progress in the field of balance-of-payments analysis.

XXII

Postscript: Following World War II

In this chapter, without attempting a thorough or detailed analysis, I wish to draw attention to some recent changes in the Canadian balance of payments and to make some comparisons with earlier periods.[1] The period 1946–1957 has been marked by a gratifying world recovery from wartime dislocations, and by subsequent advances to record levels of production. Canada's economic progress and advances in national output have been striking. From 1951 to 1956 Canada's population has had one of the fastest rates of growth in the world, to over 16 million, the increase of 2 million being a 15 per cent increase for the five years.[2] Population increases, and backlogs which had developed

[1] This chapter is based largely on data and information taken from Dominion Bureau of Statistics official reports on the balance of payments and national income, and on the annual reports of the Bank of Canada and Foreign Exchange Control Board, all of which may be consulted for further information. See Table 27 for the balance-of-payments data. Some of the merchandise trade statistics on which the analysis was founded were drawn from the *Canada Year Book* and *Trade of Canada,* and in this task I had the help of Mr. Charles Meyerding, now on the faculty of Washington University, St. Louis, Missouri.

[2] In absolute numbers, but not in percentage terms, this increase was greater than for any previous ten-year period, except for 1941–1951 when the population grew by some 2½ million, including the accession of 345,000 in the Newfoundland population in 1949. Immigration at 783,000 was as large as in the late twenties, but not as large as in the boom period before World War I (see Table 10). Emigration was relatively small, and as a result net migration was larger than any past five-year period taken in absolute terms.

during a war which succeeded adjustment to underemployment levels of income, provided great expansionary stimuli. Demand for housing, pressure against industrial capacity (contrasting with the 1930's), and the drive to develop additional mineral and petroleum resources, led to substantial capital formation accompanied by considerable imports of capital from abroad. In contrast to the 1900–1913 period of rapid development and large capital imports, resources have been developed more for Canadian and American markets, and relatively less for British and European markets. Canada has provided a much greater proportion of capital formation from her own resources, and the borrowings from abroad have been even more preponderantly American than in the earlier period they were British.

The advance of the Canadian gross national product, marked by pauses in 1949 and 1954, was from $12.0 billion in 1946 to $29.9 billion in 1956. This increase of nearly 150 per cent compares with an increase in GNP for the United States from $209.2 to $412.4 billion, or 97 per cent. The role of capital formation in the expansion of Canadian incomes was very much more important during the period than was that of exports. For example, capital formation during the period 1945–1956 rose from $0.6 to $6.1 billion, and exports from $3.7 to $4.8 billion. Capital formation has been a larger proportion of income in Canada than in the United States, and has been a larger proportion than in the previous boom years of 1913 and 1928, taking 1950 as an example (see Table 23).

Features of the boom common to the years of prosperity preceding World War I—the brief surge upward before the depression of 1921, and the late years of the 1920's—were the high levels of investment activity and incomes and the need for expanding capacity. This was in marked contrast to the peak years of the later 1930's, when, with less pressure on output capacity, there was a tendency to increasing current account surpluses and capital exports accompanying increasing prosperity. Instead, in the postwar years and in the comparable periods cited, there has been a general tendency toward a current account deficit and capital imports.

The tendency for imports to increase with incomes is revealed in the statistics, but in the early postwar years import and exchange control restrictions together with foreign supply limitations were restraining factors. For example, as a result of the Emergency Exchange Conservation program introduced in November 1947, the volume of imports was actually reduced in 1948. The increase in the value of imports that had taken place by 1950 as compared with 1947 was perhaps entirely the result of price increases. The proportion of imports to income in 1950 was somewhat lower than in 1928, and while this proportion was surpassed in 1956, it was lower than that for 1913 (see Table 23).

The tendency for exports to rise with foreign incomes was likewise hampered by restrictions, particularly for an exporter from the dollar area, in the early postwar period. The increase in their value during 1946–1950 could be largely accounted for by price rises. Within the aggregate there were marked changes in the direction of exports, gains being exhibited in trade with the United States and losses being registered in exports to the United Kingdom as compared with prewar. This displays an upsurge in a trend I have observed in operation since the beginning of the century toward a growing proportion of Canadian transactions being conducted with the United States at the expense of the United Kingdom (see Tables 6 and 15). It reflects the abundant opportunities offered through high American incomes and expanded markets, compared with the relatively restricted opportunities in countries short of dollar exchange. More basically, perhaps, it reflects the regression of the United Kingdom in the world economy relative to the United States, a trend accelerated once again by World War II. The trend with respect to merchandise exports excluding gold had been temporarily reversed during the depression of the thirties, when the United Kingdom once again became the leading recipient of Canadian exports. By 1946 only 27 per cent of Canadian exports were directed to the United Kingdom compared to 38 per cent to the United States. By 1950 these proportions had been altered further to 15 and 65 per cent.[3] Once the leading importer of Canadian produce, the United Kingdom was now dwarfed by the United

[3] In 1956 these proportions were 16.8 per cent and 58 per cent respectively. Between 1938 and 1950 the proportion of exports going to Commonwealth countries other than the United Kingdom fell from 11.7 to 5.8 per cent of the total. The decline in the proportion destined for Europe was from 8.7 to 6.5 per cent during the same period.

States. Relatively high American incomes were one factor in this shift of proportions, but it was obvious that in the early postwar years incomes were of decreased significance as an explanatory variable. It might be noted that exports to the United States were not so adversely affected by the recession of 1949 as to reduce the annual average for that year (a fact partly to be explained by the trend of growing availability of many Canadian exports to the American market, exports which had been in relatively short supply and the demand for which was not adversely affected by the American inventory recession). However, the United States recession, with its adverse effects on dollar earnings of other countries, supplies us with one good reason for the falling off of Canadian exports in other directions.

When the detailed merchandise export classifications are examined, they reveal the changed weighting within the prosperous export industries as compared with the late twenties. Wheat and the entire class of agricultural and vegetable products, typically consigned to the United Kingdom and to Europe, have become a much smaller proportion of the total, while forest products and nonferrous metals, comprising a large share of the exports to the United States, are now a substantially larger proportion. But Canada remains very dependent on exports of agricultural, forest, and mineral products, the prices of which would doubtless undergo considerable declines in the event of a serious American depression.

One interesting aspect of the Canadian balance of payments during the early postwar period was the existence of a shortage of United States dollars, despite the fact that a surplus was maintained on current account up until 1950. It was not an ordinary balance-of-payments problem, but was the result of (1) inability to convert sterling and other currency earnings freely into American dollars, and (2) a program of lending to reconstructing European economies that was certainly ambitious for a peripheral, open economy of the Canadian type,[4] and that was per-

---

[4] Post-war credits to the United Kingdom and Europe were initiated in the first two years after World War II to the extent of $1,850 million. Equivalent credits for the United States relative to her national income would have totalled roughly $33 billion. See R. B. Bryce, "Some Aspects of Canadian Economic Relations with the United States," in *Foreign Economic Policy for the United States*, ed. S. E. Harris, Cambridge, 1948, pp. 138–139.

haps partly based on the then prevalent assumption that a depression in the United States was imminent, and that a program of loans would be one useful technique for sustaining Canadian exports and incomes. The convertibility problem was eventually eased and the Canadian dollar became a stronger currency relative to the American through (1) a marked reduction in Canadian lending abroad, (2) off-shore purchases which made Marshall Plan dollars indirectly available to finance Canadian exports to Europe, (3) increasing exports to the United States, and (4) the import of capital from the United States on private account, which reached such dimensions as to raise the Canadian dollar above parity with the American.

Thus, in 1946 and 1947, when the transition from a wartime to a peacetime economy was taking place with less friction and unemployment than had been generally anticipated, economic problems were centering on Canada's international transactions. Exports fell off from the high levels of the latter war years, at which they had been so largely supported by aid contributed to allied countries. The substantial postwar loans, referred to above, partially substituted for the war aid, but drawings on these loans of over $1 billion in 1946–1947 were associated with net declines in reserves of the same order. Contributing to the difficulties of these years was a considerable repatriation of Canadian capital from abroad through retirements. A foreign exchange crisis was the result.

In the years 1948–1949 the foreign lending and the repatriation of capital became insignificant and the credits earned on current account were thus enabled to eventuate in a rebuilding of Canadian foreign exchange reserves to a less uncomfortable level. We have seen that the tendency in the direction of a current deficit has been a general one when there are prosperous peacetime North American economic conditions without much excess capacity. This tendency asserted itself in reducing the current account surplus, and from 1950 to 1958 — with the exception of 1952 — a current deficit had become an annual feature. In 1952 an alteration to the surplus side occurred, associated largely with a marked improvement in the Canadian terms of trade, and also with a growth of exports stimulated to a large extent by the Korean war. During 1950–1951, substantial capital imports were attracted to a situation that was making higher levels of capital formation attractive while, with foreign exchange difficulties overcome, the Canadian dollar appeared undervalued. These capital imports financed, as well as further stimulated, the growing deficit, and in addition facilitated a continued growth in reserves and a growing contribution to NATO. Variations of components within the capital account have been substantial in the postwar period with, for example, outstanding securities predominating in the inflow of 1950, and new issues and direct investment in 1951.

The year 1953 saw a return to a current deficit with capital imports again providing an offset for the deficit plus contributions to NATO. This situation has continued, the recession of 1953–1954 being very moderate in its effect. As the boom reached new heights, the merchandise account, however, drew additional attention. Until 1955, exports had generally been sufficient to offset imports and, indeed, in the earlier postwar years had provided for a substantial surplus. A considerable part of the adjustment in the Canadian balance of payments was derived through exports and imports growing together in response to rising consumption and investment at home and abroad. In 1956, however, with imports exceeding those of 1955 by $1 billion, exports rose approximately only one half this amount, and the result was a current deficit substantial enough to give rise to concern. This enlarged deficit rose further into 1957. Capital imports also increased, and were quite adequate to sustain the inflated deficit, so that the Canadian dollar actually strengthened on the exchanges. But fears arose in many quarters that American investment, influence, and control might be unduly high in the process of developing Canadian resources.

Some very interesting aspects of the postwar situation relate to exchange rate policy, where Canadian authorities have displayed great flexibility and ingenuity. Appreciation of the Canadian dollar by 10 per cent was undertaken largely as an anti-inflationary measure in mid-1946. The appreciation advanced the Canadian dollar to par with the American, i.e., at the official rate, and not on the free market, where it was at a discount. At par it remained until the widespread devaluations of September 1949. The Canadian dollar was then depreciated by only 9 per cent compared with the sterling devaluation of 30 per cent. During the interwar period, the depreciation of the Canadian dollar percentage-wise had ordinarily been about one half that of sterling from the American dollar. The lesser depreciation of the Canadian dollar than sterling in 1949, and the subsequent appreciation in 1950, may be taken as an indication of the deterioration of the British economic position relative not only to the American but also to the Canadian position. It reflected the closer affiliation of the American and Canadian economies, the similar strong exporting capacities of the two countries, and the confidence of the foreign investor in the Canadian economic future.

The Korean war was bullish in its implications for the Canadian economy. There would be little fear of deficient demand for Canadian exports in a world of high-employment defense or war economies. The Korean incident was superimposed on a situation in which the Canadian balance of commodity trade had already improved vis-a-vis the United States, an improvement accelerated during the American recovery from the 1949 recession. One result was the inflow of American capital into Canadian outstanding securities. Some of it was induced by the prospect of increasing profits, for example, in the base metal and newsprint industries, and the related expectations of capital appreciation. Some of the capital went into obligations such as Canadian government bonds payable in Canadian currency, being influenced by the view that the Canadian dollar was undervalued and would eventually appreciate. The inflow was embarrassingly large from the standpoint of the monetary authorities, since it was increasing the supply of money and adding fuel to the inflationary fires. Some offsetting was accomplished through sales on the open market of government securities by the Bank of Canada. It was decided that only appreciation of the Canadian dollar would quell the speculative inflows.[5] However, it was agreed that the most desirable rate could not be soundly adjudged. To return once again to par from the 9 per cent discount might result in such profit-taking by speculators as to drain Canadian foreign exchange reserves to the point where devalution once again was necessary. Here was a situation in which the International Mone-

[5] See D. B. Marsh, *World Trade and Investment* (New York, 1951), pp. 439–440.

tary Fund Agreement calling for exchange rate parities within narrow limits did not appear to meet the test. The Canadian decision which took effect in September 1950, and which was sanctioned for the time being by the Fund, was to allow the free market mechanism to determine the rate, as it had been permitted to do following the departure from the gold standard in 1931.[6] This course of action was in line with various other steps that were taken to liberalize Canadian international transactions.

The results were apparently favorable. During the first year of operations on the free exchange rate (an oddity in a world of controlled exchanges), the market moved in a narrow range of 4–7 per-cent discount from parity with the American dollar. Subsequently the Canadian dollar strengthened and from 1952 on has been at a premium varying up to 6 per cent with the American dollar. Since 1952 the policy of the Canadian Exchange Fund Account has been to smooth out excessive short-term fluctuations, but not to attempt to reverse persistent trends. Private individuals and firms have been encouraged by this policy to take positions on their own account. Private short-term capital movements have provided a balancing factor of increased importance. (In Table 27 they consist of the greater part of other capital movements less direct capital movements. An important element is changes in receivables and payables not directly recorded, for which the residual in the balance of payments has provided an estimate.) These short-term capital movements appear on the whole to have reduced rather than to have exaggerated the exchange rate fluctuations.[7]

The Canadian experience appears in some measure to justify the philosophy underlying the Tripartite Agreement of 1936 between Britain, France, and the United States, and the advocacy by Professor John H. Williams of a "key currency" approach to

[6] It might be argued that a fixed intermediate exchange rate of, say, 5 per cent discount would have been satisfactory. But to forecast market reactions within such a narrow range is obviously not an easy task. An argument for any particular rate put forward after the official Canadian decision was taken would almost inevitably be affected by hindsight. As subsequent developments have shown, further decisions on still greater appreciation would have been almost inevitable.

[7] See S. I. Katz, "Two Approaches to the Exchange-Rate Problem: the United Kingdom and Canada," *Essays in International Finance,* August 1956, Princeton, N. J.

the international monetary problem. The International Monetary
Fund should possibly encourage complete freedom of the exchange rates within a broader range, say 20 per cent, for peripheral, nonclearing countries such as Canada. One advantage in
the Canadian situation has been the tendency of the Canadian
dollar to strengthen during periods of maximum capital imports
and inflationary pressures. This should have tended to act as a
brake on capital imports and exports, and so to reduce the inflationary pressures. The movement in the opposite direction of the
exchange rate, of course, would tend to counter the recession.

What does the future hold with respect to developments in the
Canadian balance of payments. The following quotation (from a
manuscript I completed in 1951) appears to me still applicable.[8]

Tremendous hazards pertain to crystal-gazing amidst the uncertainties of future economic and political developments and it might
be foolhardy to attempt an estimate. There are, however, bases for
future trends which are currently amenable to observation, and which
are worthy of note. The recent intense pace of Canadian resource
development may offer some concern in the short run. The current
account deficit, both over-all and with the United States, deteriorated
further during the first half of 1951. However, the possibilities of being able to continue to cover the deficit by importing capital from the
United States are favorable, and in the longer run the prospects of
saving on imports from the United States or expanding exports thereto
appear excellent. There is, it appears to me, an outlook for the viability
of the Canadian economy and ease in servicing her foreign investments
which is superior to the outlook viewed by Professor Viner shortly
after the First World War. Grounds are to be found for this optimism
in the steadily increasing volume of production associated with resource development, notably with respect to petroleum, iron ore,
newsprint and other forest products, aluminum and other nonferrous
metals. As long as the national output of the United States continues
to increase, whether it is devoted to raising the standard of living or
to the purposes of defense or war, marketing prospects for the products
mentioned would appear to be favorable.

Hindsight influences the judgment, but it seems reasonable
to accord the type of investments considered above better prospects than the often overlapping rail construction early in the

[8] See also Viner, *Canada's Balance*, pp. 303–306; and G. S. Watts, "Some
Longer-Term Factors in the Canadian Balance of Payments," *Canadian
Journal of Economics and Political Science*, February 1950.

century, and the investment in facilities for producing staple grains for overseas markets.

Considerable concern has recently been evinced in Canada respecting the increased American participation in the investment picture. This in general relates to the degree of the participation and does not involve a denial that the ability to draw on American sources to supplement Canadian savings has been an advantage. It is certainly an implied favorable commentary on Canadian economic prospects that capital was made available to Canada at a time when there has been such a large demand for it from within the United States.

Some historical comparisons may perhaps serve to keep matters in perspective. In 1914 the United Kingdom owned the preponderant part of nonresidential investment in Canada, 72 per cent as against 23 per cent for the United States. In 1956 the roles were reversed, the figures being 76 and 17 per cent. But the total of nonresidential investment had increased only fourfold during this period 1914–1956, while national income had increased over ten times. The net balance due abroad on interest and dividend account had increased in the same period only from $164 million to $390 million. Even if we allowed for an estimated reinvestment of direct capital of $500 million, the net return on nonresidential investment has probably increased less than fourfold during the years 1914–1956. Also, capital imports relative to investment and income in 1956, at 20.9 per cent and 6.1 per cent, have been much less preponderant than in the peak years prior to World War I. In 1913, for example, the proportions were 86.1 and 27.8 per cent (see Table 23).

There are, of course, possibilities that my earlier optimistic view will not continue to prove justified. The major risk is the possibility of underemployment in the United States, and it may be admitted that an important basis for an optimistic outlook for Canada is an expected continuing high level of defence expenditures in the United States. Canada's economic fate is much more closely tied to that of the United States than it was before World War II, yet the influence of the American economy in the interwar period was already enormous, as my study has shown. One cost to Canada has been lessened geographical diversity in her export markets. However, overseas markets are not independent of swings in the American economy. Undoubtedly it is wise to continue to encourage exports to areas other than the United States, but substantial shifts upward in the proportion of Canada's trade with the United Kingdom appear unlikely. From the point of view of the prospects for Canadian welfare it is indeed fortunate that continuing high levels of employment and relative stability for the United States do not appear beyond the bounds of achievement.

LESSONS IN ECONOMIC DEVELOPMENT

What can we learn from the Canadian experience that might be useful in the context of the current great interest in the problems of the economically underdeveloped areas of the present-day world? Canadian economic development is best understood as analogous to the development of a region (or better, several regions) of the United States, and in fact we are confronted more with dissimilarities to present backward countries than with similarities.

Flows of capital between the United States and Canada (and in earlier years between Britain and Canada) have been unusually free. Doubtless there has at times been greater mobility of capital internationally toward Canada, than toward certain regions of the United States, such as parts of the less developed South. In the days of the nineteenth century gold standard, risks of unconvertibility of capital, from the point of view of currency, were of course low, but because of Canadian policy in encouraging foreign investment, the Canadian association with the strong dollar area, and the relative strength of the Canadian economy and its exports when the United States economy was not unduly depressed, there has been less risk of inconvertibility of the Canadian dollar than of the currencies of most backward countries. More significantly, security for the investor was provided in the fact that political stability and a high regard for the sanctity of financial obligations have minimized the risks of default or confiscation.

Part of the reduced risk related in an important way to the similarities of the Canadian and American cultures and ways of doing business (and to a lesser extent similarities with the British from which the Canadian and American so largely derived). Parenthetically, it might be observed that differences of culture and outlook were greater intranationally between leading business men of Canada and the less prosperous French Canadian business men, and between the leading business men of the industrial American North and Southern business men (at least until recent decades), than were the international differences between the business leaders of the two countries. Business men not only understood one anothers' outlook in the two countries and trusted one another, but they expected to obtain equal treatment in one anothers' law courts in the Anglo-Saxon tradition. Related to these factors was the generally relatively mild objections on the part of Canadians to American technical workers or executives participating in their economy. Further, because of the relatively advanced state of the business outlook and education in Canada, the Canadian supply of executives and technical labor was adequate. Americans would tend to view the employment of a Canadian branch plant manager rather similarly, for example, to the employment of a Texan in a similar capacity in Texas.[9]

In the nineteenth century, when governmental services were expanding, it was fortunate for Canadians that relatively low fixed interest bearing securities were attractive investments to the security minded British investor. Private sources for such foreign investment today are virtually dried up. Later, when direct investment from the United States became significant, Canadians were favored by the cultural and other similarities and geographical proximity to the United States, a relatively high income consumers' market which could be developed with techniques (such as advertising) similar to the American, and which was supplemented (partly with the aid of Imperial Preference) by additional export markets. In more recent years, beginning with World War II, the most important basis for the tremendous Canadian expansion has been similar to that of the American: the

[9] Recent years have shown more Canadian sensitivity to American influence and control in the Canadian economy. As Professor F. H. Soward observed to me, difficulties arise for the very reason that Americans may incline to treat Canadians as if they did not have a distinct nationality.

mounting pressures of consumption and investment demands, partly related to war and defense needs, against the large but not unlimited natural resources of North America.

One marked advantage of the Canadians, not shared by the typical underdeveloped country, has been a high savings and investment philosophy so vital to capitalist development, and a margin above conventional consumption requirements which would permit this to take effect. Developing along a path parallel with the more advanced countries of the world, there was not in evidence the tendency we find today of attempting initially to imitate consumption standards of much more advanced countries, without first stressing and taking the vital short-run sacrificial steps of long-term investment. Also related to Canada's development parallel with the more advanced countries has been the greater ability to benefit from American and European research and techniques directed to relatively high wage economies.

Further marked advantages in Canadian development were the plentiful natural resources, particularly the favorable land-population ratio, and the important role that would be played through the individual initiative of the small business and agricultural entrepreneur, once provided with essential transportation and government services. In the relatively optimistic Canadian environment, there was not the tight race between population and food supply, population and productivity, that today makes the situation of so many underdeveloped countries look almost hopeless. Yet with the current state of the world and the competition of rival Communist techniques for economic development, speed in economic improvement appears essential. And unfortunately, rapid economic change in the cultural settings of most underdeveloped countries is likely to cause much more social disturbance than it has in the Canadian setting.

An outstanding Canadian advantage has been the availability of domestic or foreign capital on a substantial per capita scale. Comparison with heavily populated underdeveloped countries is most striking. India, as the most important economically underdeveloped country attempting development with democratic methods, will serve as an illustration. Peak figures for per capita capital imports into Canada during the period 1900–1913 reached over $50 in a single year. Without even allowing for the decreased purchasing power of currency, this would be equivalent to a capital import for India of the fantastic size of $20 billion, not too far below her total national income. Simple arithmetic demonstrates the necessity for countries like India and China directing much more attention to improving the utilization of their major resource, labor, while in the industrialization process. The tragic waste of the labor resource, its unemployment and underemployment, is all too apparent to the traveler through rural and urban India. Western experience may well lead to the exaggeration of the possible role of capital in the early stages of economic development. Application of western capital-output ratios to countries like India can be very misleading. The tremendous volumes of capital these ratios imply may generate a defeatist outlook.

Another striking contrast between Canada and the underdeveloped countries is to be found in the latters' extraordinarily low standard of living and lack of education among the vast mass of the population. The resulting lack of initiative is coupled with nothing resembling the vast opportunities opening out to the initiating individual in Canada, opportunities that were cumulative and educative. The opportunities available to the rural as well as to the urban entrepreneur have been of overwhelming importance.

The impact of western capitalism upon an underdeveloped country has often had the tendency to create islands of relative economic advancement within urban areas, leaving the vast masses of the population comparatively unaffected. A relatively few individuals will in the course of this development reach standards of living that are similar to those of the west. The striking inequality, the lavish use of servants and display of luxury, can be demoralizing in an impoverished setting. The relative lack of opportunities and the associated economic and social immobility aggravate the situation. Contrast the circumstances of North America, where not only have inequalities been less striking, but, more important, emulation of the successful has been more feasible for oneself or one's offspring. The inequality and the abysmally low incomes help to explain the widespread graft, corruption, and cheating in the sales of goods and services to be found in so many underdeveloped countries. These factors in turn make for inefficiency in government, and increase the risks and costs of business, while generally adversely affecting morale.

Problems of inflation have beset the Canadian people in the course of economic development, an interesting period in this respect preceding World War I. Such problems are more acute for the underdeveloped country today, especially when attempting to develop along democratic lines. With all these difficulties and problems it seems not unreasonable to suggest that the pressures involved in attaining an adequate pace of economic development would be no less than those of a democratic society involved in a world war. Yet in India and other underdeveloped countries the discipline associated with modern western production, even in peacetime, is lacking. The dilemma may be somewhat similar to that confronting the democracies in wartime. This was resolved in the west without devastation of the democratic setting, techniques, and values. But victory over economic backwardness cannot be achieved as rapidly as victory in war.

The experience of communist as well as western countries should be examined for possible lessons, and the prospects of adaptation to a democratic setting considered. Variations occur between communist as well as other countries. Some factors I have considered, such as resource-population ratios, and to a lesser extent living and production standards, would place Soviet Russia closer to North America in the course of economic development than to India and China. The basic economic problems of the latter two countries display striking similarities.

There is no need to elaborate here the criticisms directed to the Chinese Communist techniques of economic development, in particular the loss of individual liberties, the threat to the institution of the family, the stress upon material values as opposed to cultural ones. But the realist cannot afford to ignore the fact that China has coped with many of the problems of economic development, inflation, increasing the accumulation of capital, developing agriculture and industry, more effective use and organization of a vast labor supply in conjunction with a relatively low volume of capital, with what appears to be more than a fair degree of success. True, the historical background and social and cultural conditions in India and other economically backward countries differ from China's. But it is not sufficient to adopt the position that the price paid by the Chinese for material advance cannot and will not be incurred by other countries. Advance need not be parallel, but over a period of decades, a poor performance of production and other indices would lead to overwhelming pressures upon the country concerned. The revolution of mounting expectations, and the prevalent comparisons with economic conditions in other countries, are most important in this connection.

India is pioneering along democratic lines, with able central planning for economic development, both urban and rural. It is the problems of implementation of government policy, especially outside urban industrialized sectors and through to the 500,000 villages in rural areas, that are most difficult to solve. With popular support, India and many other countries have adopted a course which follows neither the capitalist nor the communist prescription. Increasingly now the test of practical considerations has to be met, how to affect desired social and economic changes, and how to get things done.

An appraisal, both realistic and sympathetic of the problems of India (and other underdeveloped countries), requires first that we recognize that the difficulties and problems confronting her are so very different in kind and in degree from western peacetime experience. Foreign aid and advice can be of only marginal assistance, while the main effort, labor and intelligence, must be national in character. But Western influence is considerable, and there is great danger in our underestimating difficulties, negatively viewing Communist accomplishments that might be adopted in a relatively democratic setting, and in advocating what may be irrelevant, too little, or too late.

Statistical Appendix, Bibliography, and Index

Statistical Appendix

Statistics of the merchandise trade of Canada[1] extend back to Confederation in 1867,[2] but they do not furnish us with anything approaching a homogeneous series. The statistics are to be found in several publications; Department of Customs Reports, *Trade of Canada* (Dominion Bureau of Statistics, Ottawa), and *Canada Year Book* (Dominion Bureau of Statistics, Ottawa), the latter being entitled prior to 1905 the Statistical Year Book of Canada. Until the appearance of *Trade of Canada*, 1928, the merchandise breakdowns are unfortunately not prepared on a calendar year basis, but relate to the fiscal year (ending June 30 before 1907 and March 31 thereafter).

Various adjustments of the merchandise trade figures have been effected in order to approach more closely to an account of the transfer of funds most relevant for balance-of-payments purposes.[3] These adjustments are global and therefore a detailed

[1] There is nowhere to be found a complete intercomparison of the various balance-of-merchandise and balance-of-payments series. A more detailed analysis of some aspects of the problems involved may be found, however, in Dominion Bureau of Statistics, *The Canadian Balance . . . A Study;* F. A. Knox, *Dominion Monetary Policy, 1929–1934* (Ottawa, 1939), appendix; H. Marshall et al., *Canadian-American Industry* (New Haven, 1936), appendix by F. A. Knox; and H. Marshall, "Recent Developments in Balance of Payments Statistics," in *Essays in Transportation,* ed. H. Innis (Toronto, 1941), to all of which the following summary account is in part indebted.

[2] Statistics for the separate provinces of Upper and Lower Canada prior to 1867 may be found in *Sessional Papers of Canada.*

[3] Official Dominion Bureau of Statistics adjustments are available only for years from 1926.

analysis of the merchandise account, even although we wish to relate it to changes in the balance of payments, must still be based on the unadjusted figures for commodities in the *Canada Year Book* or *Trade of Canada*.

A primary weakness in the import and export values as derived from customs figures, which can be allowed for only partially, is that the recorded values are for duty purposes, and do not necessarily indicate monetary receipts and expenditures relevant for balance-of-payment purposes. Freight and shipping credits in connection with exports are separately recorded in the Canadian balance-of-payments statement. Yet an investigation conducted as recently as 1940 disclosed that there was not a consistent basis for the declaration of export values, less than 50 per cent of a sample of 89 firms using the proper f.o.b. factory classification.[4] The Foreign Exchange Control Board insisted on an improvement of this reporting. The erroneous classifications would have tended to overstate the values of exports.

Arbitrary customs valuations occur on occasion, one example of these being those valuations placed on imports or exports dispatched on consignment. Administrative overvaluation of Canadian imports has been a very significant source of error, especially in the years 1930–1935. The more important instances where this occurs relate to:[5]

(1) Goods not of class or kind made in Canada.

(2) The application of special duties, e.g., antidumping duties with associated high valuations on imports.

(3) The application of arbitrary valuations which are apparently protective in intent.

(4) The valuations of imports by the conversion of foreign depreciated currencies at higher than the market rate.

(5) The nonallowance of freight deductions allowed by exporter to importer.

(6) The use of the higher valuation where the price drops between the time of export and the time of purchase despite the fact of an allowance for this being made for the importer by the exporter.

The only adjustments for these overvaluations made in the bal-

---

[4] Marshall in *Essays in Transportation*, ed. H. A. Innis, p. 147.

[5] Marshall, *Essays in Transportation*, p. 148.

:ance-of-payments estimates relate to the artificial exchange values placed on foreign currencies and affecting the United Kingdom and other countries' exports in the years following 1930.

Other important adjustments in the merchandise estimates as recorded by the customs relate to the gold trade. One example of error is the recording of gold movements on account of the Bank of England. Several statistical adjustments are involved for this and other reasons.[6] In Table 27 I have followed the Bank of Canada and recent Dominion Bureau of Statistics procedure in separating gold movements into monetary and nonmonetary categories. Net exports of nonmonetary gold consist of Canadian production less Canadian consumption and private hoarding.[7] The assumption has been made that all nonmonetary gold exports go to the United States,[8] since it is with that country that there has been a constant deficit which requires offsetting and since in fact even the small portion of the Canadian gold exports which have not gone directly to the United States has tended to find its way there indirectly. Monetary gold movements are all gold movements which affect the Canadian monetary gold reserves. Thus, for example, a purchase of Canadian produced gold for monetary purposes would be an import of monetary gold, it having first been classified automatically on its production[9] as an export of nonmonetary gold.[10] For the years preceding 1926 there are no estimates available of the division into monetary and nonmonetary gold. In view of the fact that an increment of gold to Canadian monetary reserves prevents the gaining of an export

[6] See Viner, *Canada's Balance*, pp. 33ff; D.B.S., *The Canadian Balance . . . A Study*, pp. 60ff.; and Bank of Canada, *Statistical Summary*, September 1939, p. 152.

[7] This is the most important departure from the principle of recording in the balance of payments only transactions between foreigners and residents. It is now a procedure sanctioned by the International Monetary Fund. See the Fund's *Balance of Payments Manual* (Washington, 1950), p. 31.

[8] D.B.S., *The Canadian Balance of International Payments, 1926–1945* (1947). This publication separates gold into monetary and nonmonetary classifications for the years 1926 and following.

[9] There is an unimportant exception in the instance where the gold first moved in, then out of private consumption and hoarding, and finally into monetary reserves. On moving out of consumption it would be classified as a nonmonetary gold export.

[10] Some official reports denote this classification as "gold available for export."

credit and is equivalent to a reimport of gold, I have felt it worth while to prepare estimates for these earlier years. In the preparation of these estimates it was assumed that the entire Canadian gold production[11] without a deduction for estimated domestic consumption and private hoarding was an export of nonmonetary gold. No data were discovered for domestic consumption and private hoarding during the period 1900–1926 and there is reason to believe that the neglected adjustments were very small. Viner has stated with regard to the period 1900–1913; "Available data indicate that less than $2 million of Canadian gold coin remained outside the Canadian gold reserves." [12] Comparison between nonmonetary gold exports and production value figures for the years subsequent to 1926 reveals only small differentials between the two series.

Other corrections applied to the customs merchandise figures include an addition for the unrecorded import of ships, deduction from recorded imports of settlers' effects and other noncommercial items, corrections for the overvaluation or undervaluation of certain currencies to which a previous exchange rate had been applied in the valuation of imports, a small adjustment for silver and other coin, and deductions for the overvaluation of alcoholic beverages imported from Great Britain due to the inclusion of the excise tax in the customs figures.[13]

The recorded merchandise statistics are even less adequate when geographical distribution is to be taken into account. Imports may be recorded as deriving from the United States or the United Kingdom, although these latter countries may have originally imported them from elsewhere. As an example of this note the commodity tea, which is recorded in Table 16 as coming from the United Kingdom, rather than from the country of origin. The same type of error arises in the case of some Canadian exports.

---

[11] For statistics see *Canada Year Book,* 1916–1917, p. 268; and 1939, p. 336.

[12] Viner, *Canada's Balance,* p. 34.

[13] With regard to the latter item see Condensed Preliminary Report, *Trade of Canada,* 1933, p. 13. Correspondence with C. D. Blyth, Chief, International Payments Branch, Dominion Bureau of Statistics, reveals that this correction was first applied in D.B.S., *The Canadian Balance of International Payments, 1926–1944* (1945). For details of the other adjustments applied to the years 1926–1937 see *The Canadian Balance . . . A Study* (1939), tables 40–51.

One of these is of very great importance, namely, that of designating all grain shipped in bond through the United States as an export to the United Kingdom. Actually, in the course of one year, forty-seven countries (chiefly European) received shares.[14] Further error arose due to shipments consigned to the United Kingdom being reexported or diverted en route. No balance-of-payments adjustments had been published for this type of error until the year 1945, when adjustments for wheat exports were applied.[15] These adjustments are tabulated in Table 26, and an

Table 26. *Approximate adjustments for the customs overvaluation of wheat exports to Great Britain, 1919–1939*
(millions of dollars)

Year	Customs figures	Adjusted figures	Extent of overvaluation
1919	122	79	43
1920	73	151	78[a]
1921	120	75	45
1922	192	87	105
1923	178	97	81
1924	189	114	75
1925	270	124	146
1926	252	118	134
1927	245	101	144
1928	260	118	142
1929	140	83	57
1930	107	53	54
1931	65	34	31
1932	80	50	30
1933	113	55	58
1934	113	52	61
1935	133	57	76
1936	155	100	55
1937	96	83	13
1938	51	41	10
1939	40	44	4[a]

Note. The estimates for 1923–1932 derive from the Condensed Preliminary Report, *Trade of Canada*, 1933, p. 15. See footnote 16 for the explanation of the method of calculation.
[a] Undervaluation.

[14] D. A. MacGibbon, *The Canadian Grain Trade* (Toronto, 1932), p. 437.
[15] D.B.S., *The Canadian Balance, 1926–1944* (1945).

explanation of the method of estimation is made available below.[16] Whereas recent balance-of-payments estimates have taken
account of this error, the merchandise trade statistics in *Trade
of Canada* and the *Canada Year Book* have not. As I have pointed
out, this has frequently given rise to confusion and error.[17] The
adjustments were very large in certain years, especially in the late
twenties.

[16] See Table 26. The adjusted figures of wheat imports into United Kingdom from Commonwealth and foreign countries and from Canada, 1923
to 1932, have been computed by adding the difference between the excess
of United Kingdom imports of wheat from the United States, and United
States exports to the United Kingdom (Canadian wheat) and the amount
of United States wheat shipped to the United Kingdom via Canada, to the
United Kingdom imports from Commonwealth countries and Canada,
and deducting the same amount from United Kingdom imports from
foreign countries. That the difference between United Kingdom wheat
imports from the United States and United States wheat exports to the
United Kingdom represents Canadian wheat is borne out by a special com-
pilation made by the United Kingdom showing imports of wheat into the
United Kingdom: by (1) country of origin; (2) country of purchase; and
(3) country of consignment, for the year 1931. In this year, the only year for
which statistics are available on this basis, the difference between imports of
wheat from Canada based on (1) origin and (2) consignment (6,246,000
bushels) approximately agrees with the difference between United Kingdom
wheat imports from the United States and United States wheat exports to
the United Kingdom (6,983,000 bushels).

For the years 1933–39 the exports of American wheat via Canada and
of Canadian wheat via the United States were small enough to be neglected
and the records of imports of Canadian wheat into the United Kingdom
were used as a measure of Canadian wheat exports to that country. These
records may be found in Great Britain, Board of Trade, *Accounts Relating
to the Trade and Navigation of the United Kingdom*. For the years prior to
1923 the estimate was made by adding to the United Kingdom official imports from Canada the difference between the United States official exports
of wheat to Britain (published in United States, Bureau of Foreign and
Domestic Commerce, *Foreign Commerce and Navigation of the United
States*) and the British official imports of wheat from the United States. As
has been indicated, the latter has been found to exceed the former by the
amount of reexports of Canadian wheat. These early estimates are probably not very reliable. The undervaluation of 1920 might be explained by
large reexports of United States wheat through Canada.

Where calendar year statistics were not available, averages were taken
of overlapping fiscal years. Translations from tons into bushels were necessary in the case of the British figures. Valuations were applied to the quantity figures by using the Canadian yearly average wheat export price. Prior
to 1930 this was taken as the average price for the nearest fiscal year.

[17] For a further discussion see a series of articles by Sanford Evans,
Winnipeg Free Press, editorial page, April 8–12, 1949.

The Dominion Bureau of Statistics calendar year series for the balance of payments employ adjusted merchandise trade figures which differ from the presentation of the calendar year merchandise trade series in *Trade of Canada* and the *Canada Year Book* in that they make the wheat export and other adjustments whereas the latter series do not. The fiscal year series of the *Canada Year Book* and *Trade of Canada* also take no account of the adjustment with respect to wheat.

Prior to an analysis of the unadjusted series for the merchandise trade on which it was necessary to rely, adjustments were effected in order to bring it more into line with the adjusted balance-of-payments series. Considerable differentials yet remained between the two series which I was not altogether able to explain but which were not so substantial as to hamper my analysis. Part of the differential was due to the fact that one series was on a fiscal and the other on a calendar year basis, so that the series for fiscal year $(n + 1)$ extended three months beyond the series for calendar year n. No adjustment was effected in this instance, nor was there an adjustment made for the overvaluation or undervaluation of imports from countries with fluctuating currencies, the correction for the latter being available only on a global basis. Calendar year series, were, as I have noted, available for the years 1928 and following.

BALANCE OF PAYMENTS

The series 1900–1946 in Table 27 derive chiefly from F. A. Knox, *Dominion Monetary Policy,* for the years prior to 1926 and from *The Canadian Balance of International Payments, 1926–1945,* which is brought up to date annually.

Knox bases his statistics on those of Viner from 1900 to 1913, the chief differences being that he deducts reexports from the merchandise trade, separates gold movements from the other commodity trade, and reestimates net movements of external bank assets. As indicated, I have made a further separation of monetary and nonmonetary gold movements. The calculations for the years 1914–1925 inclusive are Knox's own, but his methodology, with the exceptions indicated, was Viner's.

Knox has made certain improvements in his estimates of *Dominion Monetary Policy* over those of his Appendix to *Canadian-American Industry*. The latter, however, while being less detailed for the capital account, do offer finer breakdowns for the current account. For instance, my freight and shipping series, 1900–1925, is drawn from *Canadian-American Industry*. The latter publication takes the balance-of-payments series to 1934 and the former to 1937, so we are able to make comparisons with the Dominion Bureau of Statistics improved series which commences in 1926. Important improvements in *Dominion Monetary Policy* estimates relate to the years 1914–1920. Current account debit items totalling $595 million have been added to cover more adequately the expenses of Canadian forces overseas, and there are also revisions on capital account. The result is that an earlier residual error on the credit side of $1,011 million for 1914-1919 has been reduced to negligible proportions. Residuals are offsetting in the years 1917 and 1918, and again in 1920 and 1921, as might be expected if there were erroneous allocations of transactions to given calendar years.[18]

The large residual errors of 1920 to 1926 inclusive amount to a cumulative debit of $962 million in the Knox estimates in *Dominion Monetary Policy*. Knox finds this disturbing, and is unable to offer an explanation.[19] A significant revision in the D.B.S. balance-of-payments estimates has been made in recent years. They reduce Knox's estimated net credit for tourist expenditures by approximately 50 per cent in each year. The estimates of receipts by Canada on tourist account had previously been much overestimated, and in many years of the 1930's the estimates of payments on account of Canadian tourists were too low. The overestimation of tourist revenue arose in connection with both rail and automobile traffic, so that we should expect the error to apply also to the early 1920's, when there was a smaller

[18] Knox, *Dominion Monetary Policy*, p. 88.
[19] *Dominion Monetary Policy*, p. 88; and Marshall, *Canadian-American Industry*, pp. 322–324. In correspondence, Professor Knox explained that he had not made comparisons with the recent Dominion Bureau of Statistics revisions and admitted that there might be some merit to the suggestions I am advancing, although he doubted whether such a large proportion of the residual error could be accounted for in this way.

relative volume of automobile traffic.[20] The net credits from tourist expenditures 1920–1926 as stated by Knox were $477 million, so that a 50 per cent reduction of these, if justified in the light of the experience of later years, would reduce the negative residuals by $238 million.

Another significant alteration in the recent D.B.S. estimates relates to other current items. (In Knox's *Dominion Monetary Policy* this classification differed from that of D.B.S. and *Canadian-American Industry* by including freight and shipping transactions. Insurance transactions were included only to 1926 in the *Monetary Policy* estimates, D.B.S. procedure being followed thereafter, while they were included throughout in his earlier estimates of *Canadian-American Industry* which were classified as "sundry small items.") The D.B.S. revision resulted in a net debit of $38 million as compared with a net credit of $11 million in the Knox estimate for 1926 (deducting freight and shipping and insurance transactions in order to put the estimates on a more even footing). A number of small items appear responsible for this change, of which immigrants' remittances seem to be the most important. Thus the error on the debit side for other current items for 1926 is $49 million, and if we assume it to average $40 million per annum, the total addition to current debits would be $280 for the seven-year period. If there is anything to this rough guesswork with regard to tourist expenditures and other current items, the negative residual of $962 million for 1920–1926 would be reduced by a total of $518 million.

Write offs of exported merchandise for bad debts, unrecorded flights of capital to the United States at a time when Canada was not enjoying a similar degree of prosperity, and unrecorded purchases of securities from the United Kingdom which the Dominion Government was attempting to discourage are further possibilities which may have led to the residual. Knox admits that there may be "a source of error of considerable dimensions" [21] in the estimates for outstanding securities trade. But he remained

[20] Many of the facts and statistics utilized in this argument regarding the residual have not been published but were generously furnished by C. D. Blyth and F. A. Knox in private correspondence.

[21] Marshall, *Canadian-American Industry*, p. 323.

puzzled because this was unlikely to account for the whole of the residual, and, too, during the war years, when security trading was relatively unimportant, there was also a very large negative residual. With the reduction of this war period error as indicated above, and with the discovery of alternative contributing sources of error, there is less room for bewilderment. Nonetheless the reasoning has been of a very speculative nature and may not indicate the right answer to the problem. There does seem, however, to be a basis for the reestimation of some of the elements in the balance of payments, a time-consuming task which I have not undertaken. What this whole discussion should serve to emphasize is the tenuous basis of balance-of-payments statistics. Before the advent of the recently improved methods of direct estimation, one had only to vary one's rough guesses with regard, for example, to the amounts of capital brought in by individual immigrants or the amounts expended by individual tourists in order to affect the residuals.

The essential inaccuracy of the early estimates is emphasized by the fact that, once the D.B.S. adjustments for 1926 are applied, the Knox residual is very considerably reduced from its high level of $214 million, but a high negative residual of $131 million still remains unexplained. This makes the procedure of using the residual as a measure of the transactions in outstanding securities for the years 1927–1933 a somewhat dubious one.[22]

---

[22] Considerable guesswork and arbitrariness is justifiable in balance-of-payments estimates. For example, one working rule is that any guess not more than twice the true amount is better than none. As long as the guess is less than twice the true amount the residual would be reduced. See R. O. Hall, *International Transactions of the United States* (New York, 1936), p. 22. The practice of allocating the residual, especially to a single item in the balance of payments, is less justifiable. I would prefer the practice of reducing the number of omissions as far as possible by guesswork, then publishing the various estimates, even where it may be difficult to justify them, and publishing the residual as well. The residual serves as a guide to possible directions in which to look for an improvement of our estimates, and also serves as a reminder of the inevitable imperfection of the estimates. In order to reduce the strong tendency towards unjustifiable arbitrariness and bias, if we are influenced by a set of residuals to reestimate, we should establish new and justifiable standards for reestimates, and these should be applied over the entire period for which we are supplying data, if this is at all possible. To vary the procedure for a few years only with the object of reducing the residual would be a very questionable course of action.

Correspondence has revealed that new direct estimates for the trade in outstanding securities had been made which were at variance with the earlier estimates as published by D.B.S. and Knox. These new direct estimates were "dependent on personal judgment as well as on the incomplete records," and there was a reluctance to use them, but since the residuals "were not widely different from the direct estimates in most years" it was "decided that the best basis of covering these transactions in the aggregate was to assume that the balancing item roughly measured the net movement of capital on securities account." [23]

The Canadian Balance of International Payments, 1926–1945 (Ottawa, 1947) has been the source of virtually all the current account estimates for 1926–1945 in Table 27. *The Canadian Balance of International Payments: A Study of Methods and Results* (Ottawa, 1939) has additional and more detailed information, but many estimates, notably for wheat, gold, and tourists, were considerably revised in the interim between the two publications. It is from the earlier publication that the estimates of net insurance transactions for 1927–1937 are obtained.

The detailed breakdowns on capital account to 1945 are available in the 1946 Supplement, *Bank of Canada Statistical Summary, 1946*, pp. 119 and 125. There were two changes which were effected in Table 27, namely, separating (a) net loans and advances by the Canadian government to other countries and (b) monetary gold movements from other capital movements, as recorded in the Bank of Canada publication. The first of these items is recorded in Knox, *Dominion Monetary Policy*, p. 93, and the second is recorded in the D.B.S. *Canadian Balance, 1926–1945* publication. Both capital and current account items have been brought up to date by referring to subsequent D.B.S. official balance-of-payments statements.

The difficulties of geographical allocation have already been referred to in connection with the merchandise account, and in particular adjustments with respect to the allocation of gold and wheat exports were dealt with. Even greater problems arise in

[23] Letter from C. D. Blyth, December 22, 1947. The error in the initial estimates appears to have applied primarily to transactions between Canada and the United States.

the case of some of the "invisibles" and of most of the items on capital account.[24] The general consequence is an overstating of transactions with the United Kingdom and the United States relative to those with other countries, but to what extent it is impossible to say. For example, retired securities shown as held in the United Kingdom or in the United States may have changed hands to nationals of other countries.

For further information regarding the classifications of Table 27 the reader is referred to Chapters 19 and 20 where they are analyzed in some detail.

NATIONAL INCOME

The net national income series for the United Kingdom, the United States, and Canada are tabulated in Table 21 and depicted in Graph III. Those for the United Kingdom were not published for the years prior to 1938 but were furnished by Mr. R. Stone of Cambridge University. The years subsequent to 1938 are available in the White Paper on National Income.[25] Those for the United States are the Department of Commerce series available in the *Survey of Current Business*, July 1947, for 1929–1940, and the S. Kuznets, *National Income and its Composition* series for 1919–1928. The Canadian series is published in the *Canada Year Book* and is the least reliable of the three series. For the years 1938 on there is a better and more comparable series which I have utilized, *National Accounts, Income and Expenditure, 1938–1945*, published by the Dominion Bureau of Statistics in 1945.

A more reliable series than the *Canada Year Book* series employed prior to 1938 is available in *National Income*, an appendix to the *Report on Dominion-Provincial Relations, 1939*, but this unfortunately does not include corporate savings, being a survey of payments to individuals only. There was no adequate series of business savings whereby this might have been adjusted.

An intercomparison of all the series then available is made in *National Income*, pages 10ff. The chief criticisms against the

[24] *The Canadian Balance . . . A Study* (1939), p. 169.
[25] *National Income and Expenditure for the United Kingdom, 1938–1946.* Command Paper 7099 (London, 1947).

Canada Year Book series were in connection with its assumption that the three eighths of the population engaged in the service industries were equally as productive on the average as were persons employed in other industries, its lack of direct estimates of service industry production, and its duplication (arising chiefly out of inadequate allowance for expenses) in the estimate of total net production in other industries. The result was a considerable exaggeration of the value of net national income, especially in the twenties.

Certain improvements were made over the *Canada Year Book* series in a study by the Bank of Nova Scotia, where calculations were likewise made along the lines of the "income produced" method. The resultant values were considerably lower than the original estimates of the *Canada Year Book*.

There have been revisions in the series appearing in the *Canada Year Book* which give yet lower values than the Bank of Nova Scotia estimates, so that presumably the charges laid against the earlier calculations have had effect.[26] These estimates have, however, been advanced on by the even more improved estimates for 1938–45 in *National Accounts*, etc., also prepared under the aegis of the Dominion Bureau of Statistics. These give values lower by 8 per cent in 1938 than the revised *Canada Year Book* series. Compared to the *National Income* appendix series, the revised *Canada Year Book* series declines relatively more in the depression of the 1930's, as one might expect, since it includes the widely fluctuating element of business savings, whereas the *National Income* series does not. However, despite its taking account of business savings, the revised *Canada Year Book* series rises only 17 per cent from 1926–1929, compared with 16 per cent for the *National Income* appendix series, thus indicating the possibility that the amplitude of the former series is not sufficiently great. However, despite this possibility and the error in the absolute level, all the series compare favorably with regard to direction of change and they do not differ greatly in their measurement of changes from year to year. It would appear, then, that for the purposes of the sort of comparison we are interested in

---

[26] *Canada Year Book* (1945), p. 905. No details regarding the method of estimation are made available.

making between the national income series of the three countries, the revised *Canada Year Book* series is a quite acceptable measure.[27]

[27] Since undertaking the analysis based upon the revised Canada Year Book series, improved estimates have been made available in D.B.S., *National Accounts, Income and Expenditure, 1926–1947* (Ottawa, 1948). Intercomparisons revealed only one difference in the direction of change, from 1928 to 1929, when the new D.B.S. series decreased by approximately 1 per cent, while the series I employed increased from an index of 116.9 to 117.0. This was a small differential and the differences in amplitude for the years studied was also small so that the estimates and analysis based upon the earlier series were permitted to stand.

TABLE 27

THE CANADIAN BALANCE OF PAYMENTS, 1900–1957

(millions of dollars)

Note. See the Statistical Appendix for an examination of the bases of these statistics. All figures have been rounded to the nearest million dollars.

[a] Included in IIA to 1913.

[b] Figures for 1957 provisional.

[c] The residual was estimated to have been a good indication of (B) net trade in outstanding securities, 1927–32. See Statistical Appendix.

TABLE 27½(cont.)

	1900	1901	1902	1903	190₄
I. *Current account*					
A. Merchandise trade—					
Exports (adjusted)	156	170	190	202	17℄
Imports (adjusted)	−177	−183	−203	−252	−24℈
Balance	−21	−13	−13	−50	−7℈
B. Other net receipts or payments					
(a) Tourist expenditures—					
Receipts	7	8	11	10	1℈
Payments	−6	−6	−7	−7	−℈
Balance	1	2	4	3	4
(b) Interest and dividends					
Receipts	4	4	5	5	℈
Payments	−36	−37	−39	−41	−4℈
Balance	−32	−33	−34	−36	−38
(c) Freight and shipping—					
Receipts	4	4	4	4	4
Payments	−9	−10	−10	−11	−1℈
Balance	−6	−6	−6	−6	−℈
(d) Nonmonetary gold trade	28	24	21	19	1℈
(e) Other current items—					
Receipts	11	13	22	25	2℈
Payments	−7	−9	−16	−18	−1℈
Balance	5	4	6	7	℈
Net balance on current account—					
Receipts	210	223	254	267	23℈
Payments	−234	−245	−276	−329	−328
Balance	−24	−22	−22	−62	−89
II. *Capital account*					
A. New issues (less commissions and discounts)					
Retirements					
Balance (includes some amounts not in new issues and retirements up to 1925)	6	11	16	27	34
B.[a] Outstanding securities—					
Sales					
Purchases					
Balance					
C. Net loans and advances by Canadian government to other countries					
D. Balance of other capital movements	23	24	24	24	25
Net balance on capital account	30	35	40	52	59
III. *Monetary gold*	−12	−1	−10	−12	−8
IV. *Net change in external bank assets* (after 1939 includes monetary gold)	12	−25	−2	20	−23
V. *Official Canadian contributions*					
VI.[c] *Residual*	−5	12	−6	2	62

TABLE 27 (cont.) [339]

1905	1906	1907	1908	1909	1910	1911	1912	1913	1914
205	254	254	249	269	281	284	352	443	369
−264	−312	−363	−283	−340	−429	−506	−626	−655	−471
−58	−58	−109	−33	−71	−148	−222	−274	−212	102
13	17	16	19	20	25	26	29	30	35
−11	−15	−16	−18	−20	−25	−29	−33	−37	−42
2	2	0	1	0	0	−3	−4	−7	−7
5	6	6	5	8	10	9	9	9	17
−47	−52	−57	−76	−84	−92	−101	−117	−137	−181
−42	−46	−51	−71	−76	−82	−92	−108	−128	−164
5	5	5	5	6	6	6	7	9	41
−13	−15	−15	−14	−15	−19	−23	−28	−29	−80
−8	−10	−10	−9	−9	−13	−17	−21	−19	−39
14	11	8	10	9	10	10	13	17	16
33	39	44	41	49	57	60	58	55	32
−28	−34	−45	−49	−51	−58	−70	−84	−92	−31
5	5	−1	−8	−2	−1	−10	−26	−37	1
276	332	333	329	361	388	395	467	564	510
−363	−429	−495	−440	−509	−623	−729	−889	−951	−805
−87	−97	−162	−111	−148	−235	−334	−422	−387	−295
									197
									−5
69	63	52	173	209	202	255	236	463	298
									−3
									24
40	40	39	45	40	106	88	80	78	1
109	102	91	218	249	308	343	316	542	321
0	−5	−5	−24	−11	−16	−29	0	−21	7
−10	13	26	−99	−32	33	9	8	−16	21
−12	−14	50	15	−59	−90	12	97	−118	−54

TABLE 27 (cont.)

	1915	1916	1917	1918	1919
I. *Current account*					
A. Merchandise trade—					
Exports (adjusted)	614	1072	1555	1209	126?
Imports (adjusted)	−447	−762	−996	−922	−95?
Balance	167	310	559	287	31?
B. Other net receipts or payments					
(a) Tourist expenditures—					
Receipts	37	46	55	67	7?
Payments	−29	−29	−31	−35	−5?
Balance	8	16	24	32	2?
(b) Interest and dividends					
Receipts	13	24	28	32	4?
Payments	−173	−190	−204	−214	−21?
Balance	−160	−167	−176	−182	−17?
(c) Freight and shipping—					
Receipts	71	92	84	84	8?
Payments	−101	−145	−139	−144	−12?
Balance	−30	−54	−55	−60	−3?
(d) Nonmonetary gold trade	19	19	15	15	1?
(e) Other current items—					
Receipts	20	23	26	25	3?
Payments	−47	−118	−201	−200	−12?
Balance	−27	−94	−175	−175	−8?
Net balance on current account—					
Receipts	774	1275	1765	1432	151?
Payments	−798	−1245	−1572	−1515	−146?
Balance	−24	30	193	−83	5?
II. *Capital account*					
A. New issues (less commissions and discounts)	237	315	196	56	23?
Retirements	−54	−56	−69	−66	−21?
Balance (includes some amounts not in new issues and retirements up to 1925)	179	254	127	−13	2?
B.ª Outstanding securities—					
Sales					
Purchases					
Balance	−5	−8	−10	−10	−4?
C. Net loans and advances by Canadian government to other countries	60	−53	−113	−119	−2?
D. Balance of other capital movements	0	8	12	6	3?
Net balance on capital account	235	202	16	−136	−1?
III. *Monetary gold*	−34	−8	−16	2	−?
IV. *Net change in external bank assets* (after 1939 includes monetary gold)	−113	−130	11	−28	−2?
V. *Official Canadian contributions*					
VI.ᶜ *Residual*	−64	−95	−203	246	−1?

TABLE 27 (cont.) [341]

1920	1921	1922	1923	1924	1925	1926	1927	1928	1929
1267	800	884	1004	1033	1241	1272	1215	1341	1178
−1429	−828	−745	−885	−790	−872	−973	−1057	−1209	−1272
−162	−27	139	119	243	369	299	158	132	−94
91	98	110	131	149	170	152	163	177	198
−62	−57	−57	−62	−68	−70	−99	−100	−98	−108
29	41	53	69	81	100	53	63	79	90
47	47	40	40	40	40	32	41	46	61
−213	−234	−230	−254	−242	−251	−240	−257	−275	−322
−166	−187	−190	−214	−202	−211	−208	−216	−229	−261
114	84	79	89	83	87	96	97	96	92
−170	−116	−94	−121	−99	−106	−105	−109	−116	−130
−56	−32	−16	−32	−16	−20	−11	−12	−20	−38
16	19	26	26	31	36	30	32	40	37
46	41	38	46	48	53	83	85	88	80
−50	−34	−27	−19	−24	−40	−121	−120	−122	−125
−4	7	12	28	24	14	−38	−35	−34	−45
1581	1090	1177	1336	1385	1628	1665	1633	1788	1646
−1924	−1270	−1153	−1341	−1223	−1337	−1538	−1643	−1820	−1957
−343	−180	24	−5	162	289	127	−10	−32	−311
221	246	293	156	281	240	326	301	207	297
−61	−144	−88	−51	−146	−231	−166	−160	−200	−150
154	124	210	110	143	13	161	141	7	147
−55	−40	−20	−40	−50	−80	−135	−171	−126	−2
31	28	47	64	21	2	2	10	6	4
13	26	0	9	0	15	26	21	9	37
143	138	237	142	113	−50	54	1	−104	186
19	23	−72	55	−24	−16	1	−7	49	37
42	144	27	−13	−16	−93	−52	16	87	88
138	−125	−217	−180	−235	−130	−131	...	...	...

net direct investment } included in IID { 35 21 18
net insurance transactions } { −15 −12 19

TABLE 27 (cont.)

	1930	1931	1932	1933	1934
I. *Current account*					
A. Merchandise trade—					
Exports (adjusted)	880	601	495	532	648
Imports (adjusted)	−973	−580	−398	−368	−484
Balance	−93	21	97	164	164
B. Other net receipts or payments					
(a) Tourist expenditures—					
Receipts	180	153	114	89	106
Payments	−92	−71	−49	−44	−50
Balance	88	82	65	45	56
(b) Interest and dividends					
Receipts	59	48	37	38	57
Payments	−348	−330	−302	−264	−268
Balance	−289	−282	−265	−226	−211
(c) Freight and shipping—					
Receipts	70	54	38	44	52
Payments	−103	−79	−66	−66	−79
Balance	−33	−25	−28	−22	−27
(d) Nonmonetary gold trade	39	57	70	82	114
(e) Other current items—					
Receipts	69	59	54	44	43
Payments	−118	−86	−89	−89	−71
Balance	−49	−27	−35	−45	−28
Net balance on current account—					
Receipts	1297	972	808	829	1020
Payments	−1634	−1146	−904	−831	−952
Balance	−331	−174	−96	−2	68
II. *Capital account*					
A. New issues (less commissions and					
discounts)	400	200	104	134	111
Retirements	−110	−202	−105	−166	−169
Balance (includes some amounts not in					
new issues and retirements up to 1925)	290	−2	−1	−32	−58
B.[a] Outstanding securities—					
Sales				289	321
Purchases				−238	−312
Balance	56	45	85	51	9
C. Net loans and advances by Canadian					
government to other countries	6	1	0	0	0
D. Balance of other capital movements	21	69	−29	−60	−42
Net balance on capital account	373	113	55	−41	−91
III. *Monetary gold*	−36	33	3	6	−4
IV. *Net change in external bank assets*					
(after 1939 includes monetary gold)	0	28	38	24	−19
V. *Official Canadian contributions*					
VI.[c] *Residual*	...	...	...	13	46
net direct investment ⎱ included in IID ⎰	37	10	−28	−59	−45
net insurance transactions	9	34	−1	−1	3

TABLE 27 (cont.) [343]

1935	1936	1937	1938	1939	1940	1941	1942	1943	1944
732	954	1041	844	906	1202	1732	2515	3050	3590
−526	−612	−776	−649	−713	−1006	−1264	−1406	−1579	−1398
206	342	265	195	193	196	468	1109	1471	2192
117	142	166	149	149	104	111	81	88	119
−64	−75	−87	−86	−81	−43	−21	−26	−36	−58
53	67	79	63	68	61	90	55	52	61
64	75	76	66	57	52	60	67	59	71
−270	−311	−302	−307	−306	−313	−286	−270	−261	−264
−206	−236	−226	−241	−249	−261	−226	−203	−202	−193
68	80	112	95	102	138	185	221	288	322
−82	−97	−137	−105	−119	−132	−167	−228	−294	−252
−14	−17	−25	−10	−17	6	18	−7	−6	70
119	132	145	161	184	203	204	184	142	110
45	47	53	46	59	77	166	308	437	345
−78	−91	−111	−114	−112	−133	−229	−345	−688	−1567
−33	−44	−58	−68	−53	−56	−63	−37	−251	−1222
1145	1430	1593	1361	1457	1776	2458	3376	4064	4557
−1020	−1186	−1413	−1261	−1331	−1627	−1967	−2275	−2858	−3539
125	244	180	100	126	149	491	1101	1206	1018
117	106	90	89	155	0	0	0	146	92
−256	−270	−170	−151	−251	−191	−229	−351	−322	−200
−139	−164	−80	−62	−96	−191	−229	−351	−176	−108
302	423	506	369	322					
−251	−415	−511	−340	−241					
51	8	−5	29	82	5	38	148	272	198
0	0	0	0	0	0	0	−700	18	57
−58	−88	−74	−72	−122	1	262	123	−427	83
−150	−244	−158	−105	−136	−185	71	−780	−313	230
−2	0	0	In IV from 1940. No data 1938–39.						
0	3	−13	−7	No data	−3	−568	674	−364	−278
							−1002	−518	−960
27	−3	−8	12	10	39	6	7	−11	−10
−44	−62	−64 net direct investment							
−18	−26	−10 net insurance transactions	} included in IID						

TABLE 27 (cont.)

	1945	1946	1947	1948	1949
I. *Current account*					
A. Merchandise trade—					
Exports (adjusted)	3657	2393	2723	3030	2989
Imports (adjusted)	−1442	−1822	−2535	−2598	−2696
Balance	2215	571	188	432	293
B. Other net receipts or payments					
(a) Tourist expenditures—					
Receipts	165	221	251	279	285
Payments	−83	−135	−167	−134	−193
Balance	82	86	84	145	92
(b) Interest and dividends					
Receipts	76	70	64	70	83
Payments	−253	−312	−337	−325	−390
Balance	−177	−242	−273	−255	−307
(c) Freight and shipping—					
Receipts	340	311	322	336	303
Payments	−222	−219	−278	−279	−253
Balance	118	92	44	57	50
(d) Nonmonetary gold trade	96	96	99	119	139
(e) Other current items—					
Receipts	301	274	289	313	290
Payments	−912	−417	−344	−337	−374
Balance	−611	−143	−55	−24	−84
Net balance on current account—					
Receipts	4635	3365	3748	4147	4089
Payments	−2912	−2905	−3661	−3673	−3906
Balance	1723	460	87	474	183
II. *Capital account*					
A. New issues (less commissions and discounts)	91	214	92	147	101
Retirements	−211	−526	−357	−112	−145
Balance (includes some amounts not in new issues and retirements up to 1925)	−120	−312	−265	35	−44
B.[a] Outstanding securities—					
Sales					
Purchases					
Balance	355	219	−12	−4	30
C. Net loans and advances by Canadian government to other countries	−250	−656	−454	−62	−102
D. Balance of other capital movements	−6	49	−34	93	27
Net balance on capital account	23	−700	−765	62	−89
III. *Monetary gold*		In IV from 1940			
IV. *Net change in external bank assets* (after 1939 includes monetary gold)	−666	337	716	−513	−88
V. *Official Canadian contributions*	−1041	−97	−38	−23	−6
VI.[c] *Residual*	7	In item IID			
Net direct investment in IID		26	67	86	107

TABLE 27 (cont.) [345]

1950	1951	1952	1953	1954	1955	1956	1957[b]
3139	3950	4339	4152	3929	4332	4837	4909
−3129	−4097	−3850	−4210	−3916	−4543	−5565	−5488
10	−147	489	−58	13	−211	−728	−579
(Mutual aid for NATO)							
57	145	200	246	284	222	157	107
275	274	275	302	305	328	337	363
−226	−280	−341	−365	−389	−449	−498	−525
49	−6	−66	−63	−84	−121	−161	−162
91	115	145	165	147	160	142	149
−475	−450	−413	−404	−423	−483	−523	−593
−384	−335	−268	−239	−276	−323	−381	−444
284	351	383	318	313	398	457	431
−301	−354	−375	−374	−356	−415	−502	−506
−17	−3	8	−56	−43	−17	−45	−75
163	150	150	144	155	155	150	147
288	326	366	410	387	477	541	519
−438	−493	−499	−556	−573	−634	−712	−769
−150	−167	−133	−146	−186	−157	−171	−250
4297	5311	5858	5737	5520	6072	6621	6625
−4569	−5674	−5478	−5909	−5657	−6524	−7800	−7881
−272	−363	380	−172	−137	−452	−1179	−1256
208	408	296	312	298	118	649	767
−276	−181	−89	−145	−201	−167	−141	−132
−68	227	207	167	97	−49	508	635
399	53	−82	−9	70	−4	219	131
24	68	56	87	72	69	69	50
468	417	−242	178	283	547	627	513
823	765	−61	423	522	563	1423	1329
−489	−248	−103	20	−90	133	−57	71
−62	−154	−216	−271	−295	−246	−187	−144
In item IID							
258	289	269	363	311	343	479	455

Selected Bibliography

BOOKS

Abramowitz, M. "Economics of Growth," in *A Survey of Contemporary Economics*, ed. B. F. Haley. Homewood, Ill., 1952.

Angell, J. W. *Investment and Business Cycles*. New York, 1941.

—— *The Theory of International Prices*. Cambridge, Mass., 1926.

Annett, D. "British Imperial Preference in Canadian Commercial Policy" (Harvard Ph.D. thesis, 1947). Published under the auspices of the Canadian Institute of International Affairs, Toronto, 1948.

Annis, A. C. "A Study of Canadian Tariffs and Trade Agreements," unpublished dissertation, Cornell University, 1936.

Balogh, T., et al. *The Economics of Full Employment*. Oxford, 1945.

Beach, W. E. *British International Gold Movements and Banking Policy, 1881–1915*. Cambridge, Mass, 1935.

Beveridge, W. H. *Full Employment in a Free Society*. London and New York, 1945.

—— et al. *Tariffs: The Case Examined*. London, 1932.

Bidwell, P. W. *Our Trade with Britain, Bases for a Reciprocal Tariff Agreement*. New York, 1938.

Bladen, V. W. *An Introduction to Political Economy*. Toronto, 1941.

Bloomfield, A. I. *Capital Imports and the American Balance of Payments, 1934–1939*, Chicago, 1949.

—— "Foreign Exchange Rate Theory and Policy," in *The New Economics*, ed. S. E. Harris. New York, 1947.

Brady, A. *Canada*. London, 1932.

—— and F. R. Scott. *Canada After the War*. Toronto, 1943.

Brebner, J. B. *North Atlantic Triangle*. New Haven, Toronto, London, 1945.

Breckenridge, R. M. *The Canadian Banking System 1817–1890*. New York, 1895.

Bresciani-Turroni, C. *Inductive Verification of the Theory of International Payments*. Egyptian University Publication, 1932.

Britnell, G. E. *The Wheat Economy*. Toronto, 1939.

Brown, W. A. *The International Gold Standard Reinterpreted*. New York, 1940.

Buchanan, N. S. "International Investment," in *A Survey of Contemporary Economics,* ed. B. F. Haley. Homewood, Ill., 1952.

Buckley, K. *Capital Formation in Canada, 1896–1930.* Toronto, 1955.

Burton, F. W. "Staple Production and Canada's External Relations," in *Essays in Honour of E. J. Urwick,* ed. H. A. Innis. Toronto, 1938.

Cairncross, A. K. *Home and Foreign Investment, 1870–1913.* Cambridge, England, 1953.

Chamberlin, E. H. *The Theory of Monopolistic Competition.* Cambridge, Mass., 1933.

Chang, Tse Chun. *Cyclical Movements in the Balance of Payments.* Cambridge, England, 1951.

Clark, C. *Conditions of Economic Progress.* London, 1940.

——— *The National Income of Australia.* London, 1938.

Condeliffe, J. B. *The Commerce of Nations.* New York, 1950.

——— *The Reconstruction of World Trade.* New York, 1940.

Daane, J. D. "The Fifth Federal Reserve District, A Study in Regional Economics," unpublished dissertation, Harvard University.

Donald, W. J. A. *The Canadian Iron and Steel Industry.* Boston and New York, 1915.

Duesenberry, J. S. *Income, Saving, and the Theory of Consumer Behavior.* Cambridge, Mass., 1949.

Duffett, W. E. "The International Trade Position of Canada 1913–1933," unpublished M.Sc. thesis, London School of Economics, 1935.

Ellis, H. S. *Exchange Control in Central Europe.* Cambridge, Mass., 1941.

——— ed. *A Survey of Contemporary Economics.* Philadelphia, 1948.

Ellsworth, P. T. *The International Economy.* New York, 1950.

Enke, S., and V. Salera. *International Economics.* New York, 1947.

Farrell, M. W. "Canada's Balance of International Indebtedness 1919–1925," unpublished master's thesis, Queen's University, 1943.

Feis, H. *Europe, the World's Banker, 1870–1914.* New Haven, 1930.

Fellner, W. *Monetary Policies and Full Employment.* Berkeley, 1946.

Fleetwood, E. E. *Sweden's Capital Imports and Exports.* Geneva, 1947.

Frankel, S. H. *Capital Investment in Africa — Its Course and Effects.* London and New York, 1938.

Gibson, J. D., ed. *Canada's Economy in a Changing World.* Toronto, 1948.

Gilbert, Milton. *Currency Depreciation and Monetary Policy.* Philadelphia, 1939.

Goodwin, R. "The Multiplier," in *The New Economics,* ed. S. Harris. New York, 1947.

Gordon, M. S. *Barriers to World Trade.* New York, 1941.

Gordon, R. A. *The Dynamics of Economic Activity* (selected chapters reproduced by California Book Co. Ltd.). Berkeley, 1948; later published as *Business Fluctuations.* New York, 1952.

Graham, F. D. *The Theory of International Values*. Princeton, 1948.

Haberler, G. *Prosperity and Depression*. Geneva, 1941.

————— *The Theory of International Trade*. London, 1936.

Haley, B. F., ed. *A Survey of Contemporary Economics*. Homewood, Ill., 1952.

Hall, Ray O. *International Transactions of the United States*. New York, 1936.

Hancock, W. K. *Survey of British Commonwealth Affairs*. Vol. II, *Problems of Economic Policy, 1918–1939*, Parts 1 and 2. London, New York, Toronto, 1940.

Hansen, A. H. *America's Role in the World Economy*. New York, 1945.

————— *Fiscal Policy and Business Cycles*. New York, 1941.

————— *Monetary Theory and Fiscal Policy*. New York, 1949.

Hansen, M. L. *The Mingling of the Canadian and American Peoples*. New Haven, 1940.

Harris, S. E. *Exchange Depreciations*. Cambridge, Mass., 1936.

————— ed. *Foreign Economic Policy in the United States*. Cambridge, Mass., 1948.

————— ed. *The New Economics*. New York, 1947.

Harrod, R. F. *International Economics*. Cambridge, England, 1939.

Hartland, P. "Balance of Interregional Payments of New England 1929–1939," unpublished Ph.D. thesis, Radcliffe, 1945.

Hasler, W. J. "The Boom and Depression in Canada 1924–1935," unpublished M.Sc. thesis, London University, 1936.

Hawtrey, R. G. *A Century of Bank Rate*. London, New York, Toronto, 1938.

Hayek, F. A. *Monetary Nationalism and International Stability*. London, 1939.

Higgins, B. H. *The War and Post-War Cycle in Canada 1914–1923*, Report to Advisory Committee on Reconstruction, Ottawa.

Hilgerdt, F. *Industrialization and World Trade*. Geneva, 1945.

Hobson, C. K. *The Export of Capital*. London, 1914.

Innis, H. A. *The Fur Trade in Canada*. New Haven, 1930.

————— *Problems of Staple Production in Canada*. Toronto, 1933.

————— and M. L. Jacobson. *Agriculture and Canadian American Trade*. Toronto, 1934.

————— and A. W. Plumptre, eds. *The Canadian Economy and Its Problems*. Toronto, 1934.

Innis, M. Q. *An Economic History of Canada*. Toronto, 1943.

Iverson, C. *Aspects of the Theory of International Capital Movements*. London, 1935.

James, F. C., et al. *Canada in the Markets of Tomorrow*. Montreal, 1944.

Jenks, L. H. *The Migration of British Capital to 1875*. New York and London, 1927.

Jerome, Harry. *Migration and Business Cycles*. New York, 1926.

Jones, J. M. *Tariff Retaliation: Repercussions of the Hawley-Smoot Bill.* Philadelphia, 1934.

Kahn, A. E. *Great Britain in the World Economy.* New York, 1946.

Kalecki, M. *Essays in the Theory of Economic Fluctuations.* London, 1939.

Kemp, H. R., and K. W. Taylor, eds. *Canadian Marketing Problems.* Toronto, 1939.

Keynes, J. M. *The General Theory of Employment Interest and Money.* London, 1936.

——— *A Treatise on Money.* New York, 1930.

Kidner, F. L. *California Business Cycles.* Berkeley, 1946.

Kindleberger, C. P. *International Short Term Capital Movements.* New York, 1937.

——— *The Dollar Shortage.* New York, 1950.

Klein, L. R. *The Keynesian Revolution.* New York, 1949.

Knox, F. A. *Dominion Monetary Policy 1929–1934.* Ottawa, 1939.

Kuznets, S. *Economic Change.* New York, 1953.

——— "Toward a Theory of Economic Growth," in *National Policy for Economic Welfare,* ed. R. Lekachman. New York, 1955.

Lary, H. B., and associates. *The United States in the World Economy,* Department of Commerce Economic Series No. 23. Washington, 1943.

Laureys, H. *The Foreign Trade of Canada.* Toronto, 1930.

League of Nations. *Network of World Trade.* Princeton, 1942.

League of Nations. *International Currency Experience.* Princeton, 1944.

Lindahl, E., E. Dahlgren, and K. Kock. *National Income of Sweden, 1861–1930,* Part I. Stockholm Economic Studies 5A. London, 1937.

Loveday, A. *Britain and World Trade.* London, 1931.

McDiarmid, O. J. *Commercial Policy in the Canadian Economy.* Cambridge, 1946.

MacGibbon, D. A. *The Canadian Grain Trade.* Toronto, 1932.

MacGregor, D. C., et al. *National Income.* Ottawa, 1939.

Machlup, F. *International Trade and the National Income Multiplier.* Philadelphia, 1943.

MacKay, R. A. and E. B. Rogers. *Canada Looks Abroad.* Toronto, 1938.

Mackintosh, W. A. "Canadian Tariff Policy," *Canadian Institute of International Affairs,* Canadian Papers. Toronto, 1933.

——— *Economic Background of Dominion Provincial Relations.* Ottawa, 1939.

——— *Economic Problems of the Prairie Provinces.* Toronto, 1935.

——— and C. Martin, eds. *Dominion Lands Policy.* Vol. II, *Canadian Frontiers of Settlement.* Toronto, 1938.

McWilliams, Margaret. *This New Canada.* Toronto, 1948.

Malach, V. W. *International Cycles and Canada's Balance of Payments, 1921–1933.* Toronto, 1954.

Marcus, E. *Canada and the International Business Cycle, 1927–1939.* New York, 1954.

Marget, A. W. *The Theory of Prices.* New York, 1938–1942.

Marsh, D. B. *World Trade and Investment.* New York, 1951.

Marshall, A. M. *Money, Credit and Commerce.* London, 1923.

—————— *Memorials to Alfred M. Marshall,* ed. A. C. Pigou. London, 1925.

—————— *Principles of Economics.* London, 1938.

Marshall, H., F. Southard, and K. Taylor. *Canadian-American Industry.* New Haven, 1936.

Marshall, H. "Recent Developments in Balance of International Payments Statistics," in *Essays in Transportation,* ed. H. A. Innis. Toronto, 1941.

Martin, C., ed. *Canada in Peace and War.* London, Toronto, and New York, 1941.

Masters, D. C. *The Reciprocity Treaty of 1854.* New York, 1937.

Mill, J. S. *Principles of Political Economy.* London, 1920.

Mosak, J. L. *General-Equilibrium Theory in International Trade.* Bloomington, 1944.

Neisser, H. *Some International Aspects of the Business Cycle.* Philadelphia, 1936.

Nurkse, R. "Conditions of International Monetary Equilibrium," in *Essays in International Finance,* No. 4. Princeton, 1945.

—————— "Domestic and International Equilibrium," in *The New Economics,* ed. S. Harris. New York, 1947.

—————— *Problems of Capital Formation in Underdeveloped Countries.* New York, 1953.

Ohlin, Bertil. *Interregional and International Trade.* Cambridge, 1933.

Pandit, Y. S. *India's Balance of Indebtedness, 1898–1913.* London, 1937.

Parkinson, J. F., ed. *Canadian Investment and Foreign Exchange Problems.* Toronto, 1940.

—————— et al. *Canada in World Affairs.* Toronto, 1941.

Plumptre, A. F. W. *Central Banking in the British Dominions.* Toronto, 1940.

Political and Economic Planning. *Report on International Trade.* London, 1937.

Reynolds, L. G. *The Control of Competition in Canada.* Cambridge, 1940.

Robertson, D. H. *Essays in Monetary Theory.* London, 1940.

Robinson, J. *Essays in the Theory of Employment.* London, 1937.

Rostow, W. W. *British Economy of the Nineteenth Century.* Oxford, 1948.

—————— *The Process of Economic Growth.* New York, 1952.

Royal Institute of International Affairs. *The Problem of International Investment.* London, New York, and Toronto, 1937.

Scott, F. R. *Canada Today.* London, Toronto, New York, 1938.

Schumpeter, J. A. *Business Cycles.* New York, 1939.

–––––– *The Theory of Economic Development.* Cambridge, 1934.

Silverman, A. G. "The International Trade of Great Britain 1880–1913" unpublished Ph.D. thesis, Harvard University, 1930.

Skelton, O. D. *General Economic History, 1867–1912.* Vol. IX, Part I, *Canada and Its Provinces,* ed. A. Shortt. Toronto, 1914.

Soward, F. H., ed., et al. *Canada in World Affairs: The Pre-War Years.* Toronto, 1941.

Stokes, M. L. *The Bank of Canada.* Toronto, 1930.

Taussig, F. W. *International Trade.* New York, 1927.

–––––– *Explorations in Economics* (Essays in Honour of F. W. Taussig), New York and London, 1936.

Taylor, K. W., and H. Michell. *Statistical Contributions to Canadian Economic History,* II. Toronto, 1931.

Thorp, W. L. *Business Annals.* New York, 1926.

Tinbergen, J. *International Economic Co-operation.* Amsterdam, Brussels, London, New York, 1945.

–––––– *Statistical Testing of Business Cycle Theories,* Geneva, 1939.

–––––– and J. J. Polak. *The Dynamics of Business Cycles.* Chicago, 1950.

Triffin, R., G. Haberler, and L. Metzler. *International Monetary Policies.* Federal Reserve System Post-War Economic Studies No. 7. Washington, 1947.

Upgren, A. R., and J. A. Stovel. "International Financial Institutions and the Foreign Investment Outlook," in *American Financial Institutions,* ed. H. V. Prochnow. New York, 1951.

Viner, J. *Canada's Balance of International Indebtedness, 1900–1913.* Cambridge, 1924.

–––––– *International Economics.* Glencoe, Ill., 1951.

–––––– *International Trade and Economic Development.* Glencoe, Ill., 1952.

–––––– *Studies in the Theory of International Trade.* New York and London, 1937.

Wallich, Henry C. *Monetary Problems of an Export Economy.* Cambridge, 1950.

White, H. D. *The French International Accounts 1880–1913.* Cambridge, Mass., 1933.

Williams, J. H. *Argentine International Trade Under Inconvertible Paper Money, 1880–1900.* Cambridge, Mass., 1920.

–––––– *Post War Monetary Plans and Other Essays.* New York, 1947.

Wilson, Roland. *Capital Imports and the Terms of Trade.* Melbourne, 1931.

Wilson, R. "The Import of Capital," unpublished Ph.D. thesis, University of Chicago, 1930.

Wilson, T. R., "Imperial Preference in the United Kingdom Since the War," unpublished doctoral thesis, Georgetown University.

Wood, G. *Borrowing and Business in Australia.* London, 1930.

PERIODICALS

Allely, J. S. "Some Aspects of Currency Depreciation," *Canadian Journal of Economics and Political Science*, August 1939.

Barber, C. L. "The Instantaneous Theory of The Multiplier," *Canadian Journal of Economics and Political Science*, February, 1950.

Bastable, C. F. "On Some Applications of the Theory of International Trade," *The Quarterly Journal of Economics*, IV, 1889.

Beattie, J. R. "Some Aspects of the Problem of Full Employment," *Canadian Journal of Economics and Political Science*, August 1944.

Benham, F. C. "Full Employment and International Trade," *Economica*, August 1946.

Beveridge, W. "Mr. Keynes' Evidence for Overpopulation," *Economica*, IV, 1924.

Bloomfield, A. I. "Induced Investment, Over-Complete International Adjustment and Chronic Dollar Shortage," *American Economic Review*, September 1949.

———— "The Significance of Outstanding Securities in the International Movement of Capital," *Canadian Journal of Economics and Political Science*, November 1940.

Blyth, C. D. "Some Aspects of Canada's International Financial Relations," *Canadian Journal of Economics and Political Science*, August 1946.

Bryce, R. B. "The Effects on Canada of Industrial Fluctuations in the United States," *Canadian Journal of Economics and Political Science*, August 1939.

Bullock, C. J., J. H. Williams, and R. S. Tucker. "The Balance of Trade of the United States," *The Review of Economic Statistics*, July 1919.

Cairncross, A. "Die Kapitaleinfuhr in Kanada 1900–1913," *Weltwirtschaftliches Archiv*, 46 Band (1937 II).

Carr, R. "The Role of Price in the International Trade Mechanism," *Quarterly Journal of Economics*, August 1931.

Chang, T. C. "A Note on Exports and National Income in Canada," *Canadian Journal of Economics and Political Science*, May 1947.

———— "The International Comparison of the Demand for Imports," *The Review of Economic Studies 1945–46*, XIII.

Chipman, J. S. "The Generalized Bi-System Multiplier," *Canadian Journal of Economics and Political Science*, May 1949.

Clarke, W. C. "Business Cycles and the Depression of 1920–21," *Bulletins of the Department of History and Political and Economic Science*, No. 40. Queen's University, August 1921.

Coats, R. H., ed. "Features of Present Day Canada," *The Annals of the American Academy of Political and Social Science*, vol. 253, September 1947.

Cover, J. H. "The Significance of Regional Business Cycle Analysis," *Journal of American Statistical Association*, Supplement, March 1929.

Deutsch, J. J. "War Finance and the Canadian Economy," *Canadian Journal of Economics and Political Science,* November 1940.

De Vegh, I., "Imports and Income in the United States and Canada," *Review of Economic Statistics,* August 1941.

Dexter, G. "Canada and the Building of Peace," *Canadian Institute of International Affairs,* Toronto 1944.

Domar, E. D. "The Effect of Foreign Investment on the Balance of Payments," *American Economic Review,* December 1950.

Elliot, G. A. "The Theory of International Values," *The Journal of Political Economy,* vol. LVIII, February 1950.

———— "Transfer of Means of Payment and the Terms of International Trade," *Canadian Journal of Economics and Political Science,* II, 1936.

Ellsworth, P. T., et al. "Some Aspects of Exchange Stability," *The Review of Economics and Statistics,* vol. XXXII, February 1950.

———— "Comparative Costs, the Gains from Trade, and Other Matters, Considered by Professor Viner," in a review article of "Studies in the Theory of International Trade," *The Canadian Journal of Economics and Political Science,* vol V. 1939.

Feis, H. "The Future of British Imperial Preference," *Foreign Affairs,* 1946.

———— "The Mechanism of Adjustment of International Trade Balances," *American Economic Review,* December 1926.

Frisch, R. "Forecasting a Multilateral Balance of Payments," *American Economic Review,* September 1947.

Gordon, R. A., and T. C. Koopmans et al. "Current Research in Business Cycles," *American Economic Review,* vol. XXXIX, May 1949.

Haberler, G. "A Survey of International Trade Theory," *Special Papers in International Economics,* Princeton University, 1955.

———— "The Market for Foreign Exchange and the Stability of the Balance of Payments," *Kyklos,* vol. III, 1949, Fasc. III.

———— and J. J. Polak. "The Foreign Trade Multiplier," *American Economic Review,* Dec. 1947.

Harberger, A. C. "Currency Depreciation, Income, and the Balance of Trade," *The Journal of Political Economy,* vol. LVIII, February 1950.

Harris, S., G. Haberler, and A. H. Hansen et al. "A Symposium," *Review of Economic Statistics,* November 1944.

Hartland, P. "Private Enterprise and International Capital," *Canadian Journal of Economics and Political Science,* February 1953.

Ingram, J. C. "Growth and Canada's Balance of Payments," *American Economic Review,* March 1957.

Isard, W. "A Neglected Cycle: The Transport Building Cycle," *Review of Economic Statistics,* November 1942.

———— "Transport Development and Building Cycles," *The Quarterly Journal of Economics,* vol. LVII, November 1942.

Kilduff, V. R. "Economic Factors in the Development of Canadian American Trade," *Southern Economic Journal*, vol. VIII.

Knapp, J. "The Theory of International Capital Movements and Its Verifications," *The Review of Economic Studies*, Summer 1943.

Knox, F. A. "Canadian War Finance and the Balance of Payments," *The Canadian Journal of Economics and Political Science*, May 1940.

Leontieff, W. "Exports, Imports, Domestic Output and Employment," *Quarterly Journal of Economics*, February 1946.

London Economist. "Ottawa Supplement." October 22, 1932.

Malach, V. W. "Internal Determinants of the Canadian Upswing, 1921–1929," *Canadian Journal of Economics and Political Science*, May 1950.

———— "External Determinants of the Canadian Upswing, 1921–1929," *Canadian Journal of Economics and Political Science*, February 1951.

Meade, J. E. "National Income, National Expenditure and the Balance of Payments," *Economic Journal*, 1949.

Meier, G. M. "Economic Development and the Transfer Mechanism," *Canadian Journal of Economics and Political Science*, February 1953.

Metzler, L. "The Transfer Problem Reconsidered," *Journal of Political Economy*, June 1942.

Mitchell, W. C. "The International Pattern in Business Cycles," *Bulletin de l'Institut International de Statistique*, Tome XXVIII (1935), 2ème Livraison.

Mikesell, R. F. "International Disequilibrium," *The American Economic Review*, vol. XXXIX, June 1949.

Morgenstern, O. "On the International Spread of Business Cycles," *The Journal of Political Economy*, vol. LI, August 1943.

Munzer, E. "Exports and National Income in Canada," *Canadian Journal of Economics and Political Science*, February 1945.

Neisser, H. "The Significance of Foreign Trade for Domestic Employment," *Social Research*, Sept. 1946.

Ohlin, B. "Transfer Difficulties, Real and Imagined," *Economic Journal*, June 1929.

Orcutt, G. H. "Measurement of Price Elasticities in International Trade," *The Review of Economics and Statistics*, vol. XXXII, May 1950.

Pentland, H. C. "The Role of Capital in Canadian Economic Development Before 1875," *The Canadian Journal of Economics and Political Science*, November 1950.

Plumptre, A. F. W. "The Nature of Political and Economic Development in the British Dominions," *Canadian Journal of Economics and Political Science*, November 1937.

Polak, J. J. "Balance of Payments Problems of Countries Reconstructing with The Help of Foreign Loans," *Quarterly Journal of Economics*, vol. LVII, February 1943.

Polak, J. J. "Projections of the International Sector of Gross National Products," *National Bureau of Economic Research Conference on Research in Income and Wealth*, May 1951.

Rasminsky, L. "Anglo-American Trade Prospects, A Canadian View," *Economic Journal*, June-September 1945.

Robertson, D. H. "Mr. Clark and the Foreign Trade Multiplier," *Economic Journal*, June 1939.

Rostow, W. W. "Investment and the Great Depression," *Economic History Review*, May 1938.

de Scitovsky, T. "A Reconsideration of the Theory of Tariffs," *Review of Economic Studies*, Summer 1942.

Shortt, A. "Construction and National Prosperity," *Transactions of the Royal Society of Canada*, December 1914.

Slater, D. W. "Changes in the Structure of Canada's International Trade," *Canadian Journal of Economics and Political Science*, February 1955.

Stolper, W. F. "Notes on the Dollar Shortage," *American Economic Review*, June 1950.

—— "Volume of Foreign Trade and the Level of Income," *Quarterly Journal of Economics*, February 1947.

—— and P. A. Samuelson. "Protection and Real Wages," *Review of Economic Studies*, November 1941.

Stone, R. "The National Income, Output and Expenditure of U.S.A., 1929-41," *Economic Journal*, June-September 1942.

Taussig, F. W. "International Trade under Depreciated Paper," *Quarterly Journal of Economics*, vol. 31.

Tinbergen, J. "Some Measurements of the Elasticities of Substitution," *Review of Economic Statistics*, August 1946.

Viner, J. "International Finance in the Post-war World," *Journal of Political Economy*, April 1947.

Vining, R. "The Region As A Concept in Business-Cycle Analysis," *Econometrica*, July 1946.

—— "Location of Industry and Regional Patterns Of Business-Cycle Behavior," *Econometrica*, January 1946.

—— "Regional Variation in Cyclical Fluctuation Viewed As A Frequency Distribution," *Econometrica*, July 1945.

—— and P. Neff et al. "Interregional Variations in Economic Fluctuations," *American Economic Review*, May 1949.

Wansbrough, V. C. "Implications of Canadian Iron Ore Production," *Canadian Journal of Economics and Political Science*, August 1950.

Watts, G. S. "Some Longer Term Factors in the Canadian Balance of Payments," *Canadian Journal of Economics and Political Science*, February 1950.

Whale, P. B. "International Short Term Capital Movements," *Economica*, February 1939.

Wicksell, K. "International Freights and Prices," *Quarterly Journal of Economics,* vol. 32.

Williams, J. H. "The Theory of International Trade Reconsidered," *Economic Journal,* June 1929.

Wilson, R. "Migration Movements in Canada, 1868–1925," *The Canadian Historical Review,* vol. XIII, 1932.

Young, A. A. "Increasing Returns and Economic Progress," *Economic Journal,* December 1928.

OFFICIAL REPORTS, GOVERNMENT PUBLICATIONS, ANNUAL REVIEWS

Bank of Canada. *Annual Reports.*

———— *Statistical Summary* (monthly and 1946 Supplement). Ottawa, 1946.

Bank for International Settlements, *Annual Reports.*

Canada, Department of Labour, Statistical Branch. *The Rise of Prices and the Cost of Living, 1900–1914.* Ottawa, 1915.

Canada, Department of Trade and Commerce, Economic Research Branch. *Investment and Inflation, with Special Reference to the Immediate Postwar Period, Canada, 1945–1948,* Ottawa, 1949. Prepared by O. J. Firestone.

Canada, Dominion Bureau of Statistics. *Canada — the Official Handbook of Present Conditions and Recent Progress.* Ottawa, annually from 1930.

———— *Canada Year Book.* Ottawa, annually.

———— *Canadian Statistical Review.* Ottawa, monthly.

———— *Export and Import Price Indexes, 1926–1948.* Ottawa, 1949.

———— *National Accounts Income and Expenditure 1938–1945.* Ottawa, 1946. There have been other publications dealing with single years and other periods, e.g. 1926–1947 and 1942–1949.

———— *National Income of Canada, 1919–1938,* Part I. Ottawa, 1941.

———— Prices Branch. *Prices and Price Indexes.* Ottawa, monthly.

———— *Review of Foreign Trade, First Half Year, 1949.* Ottawa, 1950.

———— International Payments Branch. *Sales and Purchases of Securities between Canada and Other Countries.* Ottawa, monthly.

———— *The Canadian Balance of International Payments 1926–1945.* Ottawa, 1947. Other publications deal with later periods, e.g., 1926–1948 and 1946–1952.

———— *The Canadian Balance of International Payments, A Study of Methods and Results.* Ottawa, 1939.

———— *The Canadian Balance of International Payments.* Ottawa, annually.

———— External Trade Branch. *Trade of Canada.* Ottawa, annually.

———— *United States Direct Investments in Canada,* Ottawa, 1949.

Canada, Dominion-Provincial Conference on Reconstruction. *Public Investment and Capital Formation, 1926–1941.* Ottawa, 1945.

Canada, Foreign Exchange Control Board. *Annual Reports to the Minister of Finance.*

358 **Selected Bibliography**

Canada, House of Commons, Standing Committee on Banking and Commerce. *Memorandum and Tables Respecting the Bank of Canada*. Ottawa, 1939.

Canada, Royal Commission. *Report on Dominion-Provincial Relations*. Ottawa, 1939.

Canada, Wheat Advisory Committee of the Canadian Royal Grain Inquiry Commission. Memorandum No. I, *The World Demand for Imported Wheat*. Ottawa, 1938.

Canadian Institute for International Affairs. *Canadian Papers*. Toronto, 1933.

Federal Reserve Board. *Banking and Monetary Statistics*. Washington, 1943.

Great Britain, Command Paper 7099, *National Income and Expenditure for the United Kingdom, 1938–1946*. London, 1947.

Great Britain, Board of Trade. *Accounts Relating to the Trade and Navigation of the United Kingdom*. London, monthly.

Great Britain, Statistical Office, Customs and Excise. *Annual Statement of the Trade of the United Kingdom with Foreign Countries and British Possessions*. London, annually.

Hopkins, J. C., ed. *Canadian Annual Review*. Toronto.

International Monetary Fund. *Balance of Payments Manual*. Washington, 1948 and 1950.

Manitoba, The Government of the Province of. *Manitoba's Case — A submission presented to the Commission on Dominion Provincial Relations*. Part III, *The Effects of Federal Monetary Policy on Western Canadian Economy*, Winnipeg, 1937. This submission is the work of A. R. Upgren.

United States, Bureau of Foreign and Domestic Commerce. *Foreign Commerce and Navigation of the United States*. Washington, annually.

Upgren, A. R., and W. J. Waines. "The Mid Continent and the Peace" (numbers 1 and 2). A Report prepared for the Premier of the Province of Manitoba and the Governor of the State of Minnesota. University of Minnesota Press, Minneapolis, 1943–1944.

Index